MISSISSIPPI GOVERNMENT AND POLITICS

DALE KRANE & STEPHEN D. SHAFFER

Mississippi Government & Politics

MODERNIZERS VERSUS TRADITIONALISTS

UNIVERSITY OF NEBRASKA PRESS
LINCOLN & LONDON

The paper in this book
meets the minimum requirements of
American National Standard
for Information Sciences – Permanence of
Paper for Printed Library Materials,
ANSI Z39.48–1984.

Library of Congress
Cataloging-in-Publication Data
Krane, Dale.
Mississippi government and politics:
modernizers versus traditionalists /
by Dale Krane and Stephen D. Shaffer.
P.   cm.—(Politics and governments of
the American states)
Includes bibliographical references and index.
ISBN 0-8032-2715-9 (cl)
ISBN 0-8032-7758-X (pbk.: alk. paper)
1. Mississippi—Politics and government.
I. Shaffer, Stephen Daryl, 1953–   .
II. Title. III. Series.
JK4616.K73   1992
320.9762—dc20
91-24025
CIP

Other volumes in the Politics and Governments of the American States series:

Alabama Government and Politics
By James D. Thomas and William H. Stewart

Arkansas Politics and Government: Do the People Rule?
By Diane D. Blair

Nebraska Government and Politics
Edited by Robert D. Miewald

Oklahoma Politics and Policies: Governing the Sooner State
By David R. Morgan, Robert E. England, and George G. Humphreys

CONTENTS

TABLES, MAPS, AND FIGURES

JOHN KINCAID

Series Preface

The purpose of this series is to provide intelligent and interesting books on the politics and governments of the fifty American states, books that are of value not only to the student of government but also to general citizens who want greater insight into the past and present civic life of their own states and of other states in the federal union. The role of the states in governing America is among the least known of all the 83,217 governments in the United States. The national media focus attention on the federal government in Washington, D.C., and local media focus attention on local government. Meanwhile, except when there is a scandal or a proposed tax increase, the workings of state government remain something of a mystery to many citizens—out of sight, out of mind.

In many respects, however, the states have been, and continue to be, the most important governments in the American political system. They are the main building blocks and chief organizing governments of the whole system. The states are the constituent governments of the federal union, and it is through the states that citizens gain representation in the national government. The national government is one of limited, delegated powers; all other powers are possessed by the states and their citizens. At the same time, the states are the empowering governments for the nation's 83,166 local governments—counties, municipalities, townships, school districts, and special districts. As such, states provide for one of the most essential and ancient elements of freedom and democracy, the right of local self-government.

Although for many citizens the most visible aspects of state government are state universities, some of which are the most prestigious in the world, and state highway patrol officers, with their radar guns and handy ticket books, state governments provide for nearly all domestic public services.

Whether elements of those services are enacted or partly funded by the federal government and actually carried out by local governments, it is state government that has the ultimate responsibility for ensuring that Americans are well served by all their governments. In so doing, all the American states are more democratic, more prosperous, and better governed than most of the world's nation-states.

This is a particularly timely period in which to publish a series of books on the governments and politics of each of the fifty states. Once viewed as the "fallen arches" of the federal system, states today are increasingly seen as energetic, innovative, and fiscally responsible. Some states, of course, perform better than others, but that is to be expected in a federal system. Each state is unique in its own right. It is our hope that this series will shed light on the public life of each state and that, taken together, the books will contribute to a better, more informed understanding of the states themselves and of their often pivotal roles in the world's first and oldest continental-sized federal democracy.

DANIEL J. ELAZAR

Series Introduction

The more than continental stretch of the American domain is given form and character as a federal union of fifty different states whose institutions order the American landscape. The existence of these states made possible the emergence of a continental nation where liberty, not despotism, reigns and self-government is the first principle of order. The great American republic was born in its states, as its very name signifies. America's first founding was repeated on thirteen separate occasions over 125 years, from Virginia in 1607 to Georgia in 1732, each giving birth to a colony that became a self-governing commonwealth. Its revolution and second founding was made by those commonwealths, now states, acting in congress, and its constitution was written cooperatively and adopted separately. As the American tide rolled westward from the Atlantic coast, it absorbed new territories by organizing thirty-seven more states over the next 169 years.

Most of the American states are larger and better developed than most of the world's nations. Although Mississippi is a middle-sized state in every respect, its two and a half million people make it larger in population than forty-eight independent members of the United Nations, while its territory of 47,234 square miles is larger than sixty-nine independent countries.

The American states exist because each is a unique civil society within their common American culture. They were first given political form and then acquired their other characteristics. Each has its own constitution, its own political culture, its own relation to the federal union and to its section. These in turn have given each its own law and history; the longer that history, the more distinctive the state. Mississippi, for example, was carved out of the southern wilderness and formed into a rough-hewn slaveholding society, shaped by slavery and then by the Civil War and Reconstruction, which constituted the state's most prominent formative experience for a century and whose scars remain to this day. The state has been reshaped by the post–World War II civil rights struggle and what came to be called the Second Reconstruction of the 1960s.

Dale Krane rightly describes Mississippi's relationship with the federal government as one of "approach-avoidance"—seeking federal support for development from the time of its first settlement, yet resisting "encroachment" in matters affecting what for six generations was considered the Mississippi or southern way of life, namely slavery and racial segregation, always an extreme expression of southern departure from what became national norms. As Krane points out, the two seemingly contradictory approaches went hand in hand. I recall being in Mississippi in 1962 while Governor Ross Barnett was leading the resistance to desegregation, when two barges laden with chemicals sank in the Mississippi River. I recall Governor Barnett in his office using one phone to call the United States Army Corps of Engineers to rescue the citizens of the state's river towns from the toxic effects of the sunken cargo and on the other phone making dispositions to resist the United States Department of Justice, while thinking nothing of doing both.

Mississippi has benefited substantially from federal aid while still remaining at the very bottom of the heap in its poverty. Thus its dependence on Washington and the dependence of its citizens on federal programs are probably unmatched by any other state. Yet at the same time, its low position on the totem pole is fixed in the national mind, and the standard argument against increasing the role of the states in the American federal system and for enhancing the role of the federal government seems to rest perennially on the question, What about Mississippi?

Mississippi stands foursquare within the southern constitutional tradition, having moved from the simple document of its founding through the reforms of the Jacksonian era and the constitution of the Civil War era to its present document, adopted in 1890, which was designed to reflect the restoration of the power of the white establishment in that state after Reconstruction. That document has been modified in two ways, by the recurrent populism in the state and more recently by the civil rights revolution and Second Reconstruction. Still, in many respects Mississippi's constitution is very much in the broader Whiggish tradition of the states, what is often referred to as Jacksonian democracy in this volume and elsewhere.

Mississippi was settled as a southern frontier expanded westward in the late eighteenth and early nineteenth centuries. It was in the mainstream of the westward movement of various groups of southerners: white and black, English and Scotch-Irish, and the smaller ethnic groups as well. Moreover, it had a French tinge along its Gulf Coast from its first settlement before becoming part of the United States. Still, it emerged as one of the most culturally homogeneous of the American states. Like the rest of the Old Southwest, it attracted the rougher and in many respects poorer elements from the South, some of whom established successful plantations with all the external graciousness featured in the mythic antebellum South. More to the point, Mississippi had a much harsher slave system and much less concern for the kind of high cultural refinement that had become more widespread in the Southeast. Equally to the point, at the outbreak of the Civil War most of Mississippi was just emerging from the frontier conditions and was distinctly "backwoods."

Mississippi was a major battleground during the Civil War, one that featured the most destructive kind of fighting—cavalry raids and maneuvering over large stretches of territory—leaving massive destruction in its wake. The war and its consequences destroyed the frontier of development, perhaps more decisively in Mississippi than in any other state. As a result, over the next century, while the rest of the country moved on to the urban-industrial frontier, Mississippi was mired in trying to pull itself out of the effects of the war's destruction.

World War II brought some industrial activity, primarily shipbuilding along the Gulf Coast, but only after that war did the possibility of a new frontier open up for the state, and it was generally confined to the Gulf Coast. Today Mississippi's Gulf Coast is an integral part of the rurban-cybernetic frontier, while the rest of the state is still struggling to move on to the metropolitan frontier.

Not having any frontiers to speak of since the first, Mississippi has also been spared the side effects of the frontier with regard to population turnover, transience, and newness. With the exception of the Gulf Coast in recent years, population turnover in Mississippi has meant out-migration, principally of blacks seeking opportunity in the North. As a result, Mississippi's conservatism has become even more pronounced and the difficulties of change increased by the close and interlocking ties among its population, white and black.

Mississippi, at the very heart of the old solid South and the epitome of the Lower South in its demography, culture, and politics, is much more a product of its section than of the Union as a whole and has always been among the most active states in the sectional struggle between North and South. Today, with the race issue as a sectional one essentially behind the United States, the old North-South struggle manifests itself in new ways that also affect Mississippi.

For a century, what made Mississippi unique also made it among the most backward of American states by all the measures that Americans use to determine such things. Mississippi was indeed weighted down by its history, which prevented the two races that more or less equally (from a demographic point of view) shared the land from living and working together as equals to break out of the cycle of poverty and misery that had become the lot of most of its inhabitants, white and black. Mississippians of both races developed other means to gain satisfaction and even pursue happiness in place of economic progress.

For nearly a generation, however, since the Second Reconstruction, Mississippi has been undergoing a profound transformation, one that is repeatedly referred to in this book. The results of that transformation are already marked and are strongly manifested in Mississippi's politics and government. It seems fair to say that a new Mississippi is emerging. What it will retain of the old is one of the major subjects of contemporary Mississippi politics.

Preface

Many Americans have an outdated image of Mississippi. The Magnolia State has been stereotyped as inhabited by ignorant "rednecks" and ruled by a plantation elite. The state's fierce opposition to the civil rights movement of the 1950s and 1960s did little to dispel this negative image. A quarter of a century has passed, yet old stereotypes die hard. Many journalists outside Mississippi continue to portray the state as mired in backwardness and racism. Such national opinion leaders appear wedded to the picture of the state's culture and politics found in V. O. Key's landmark study of southern politics, published in 1949, and show less understanding of the many changes that have reshaped Mississippi and its political system. This book, while not ignoring the troubled history of the state, examines Mississippi's contemporary political situation in light of the new conditions that have emerged in the past twenty-five years. Economic, political, and social changes have swept Mississippi in recent decades. The old politics of exclusion has fallen by the wayside, to be replaced by a new politics of inclusion. Blacks, historically denied access to the ballot box and publicly reviled by racist demagogues, are today nominated to head major state agencies and are elected to important public office such as the United States Congress. Formerly a rural environment dependent on an agricultural economy, Mississippi has undergone increasing industrialization and urbanization, which are producing a more diversified economy and more varied life-styles. A tradition of neglected public services remains a problem, primarily because of the state's stubborn poverty. Yet, in the 1980s Mississippi played a leading role in the education reform movement, as residents committed the state to improving the quality of life for future generations.

We were encouraged by the series editors to go beyond mere facts and to organize the facts into an interpretation of Mississippi's politics that would convey its uniqueness to readers both inside and outside Mississippi. Reflecting the norms of our discipline, we were also expected to base our descriptions and analyses on evidence derived from the application of contemporary social science research. Finally, we were cautioned against merely writing a textbook. Although this volume can be used as a text in such classes as Mississippi government, state politics, and southern politics, it is also written to appeal to a more general audience.

To meet these challenging goals, we adopted a team approach. Despite the curiosity that exists about Mississippi, there has been very little analysis or study of the state's government and politics. Consequently we decided that only by bringing together a number of capable scholars would it be possible to generate the original information about the various components of Mississippi government and politics required by a project of this scale. All the contributors to this volume either live in Mississippi or have lived there during much of their professional lives, and all of them have published their own research on various aspects of the state's political system. Their creative and diligent work has produced a collection of information about Mississippi's political system and an analysis of those facts that exceeds the scope of any other existing study. Because of their contributions to this volume, we consider these colleagues "associate authors."

One danger inherent in a team approach is that team members may wander off on their own paths. Acting as editors, we used Elazar's cultural approach to the study of politics and government for two purposes. First, this cultural approach provided a common framework for organizing each chapter as well as the whole volume and tied the contributors together much the way a mountain-climbing team is connected by its ropes. We aggressively sought continuity of theme and writing style throughout the manuscript, and we rewrote entire chapters under the ultimate supervision of the associate authors. Our associates have been exceedingly gracious in working with us and in dealing with the numerous suggestions offered by us, the referees, and other readers. The common thread running through the chapters not only prevented each team member from "falling off the mountain" but, more important, allowed each contributor to help the others up the mountain by collegial advice and criticism.

Second, the political culture approach to Mississippi politics served as a vehicle for explaining the state's uniqueness and how that uniqueness fits into a more general understanding of state government and politics in America. The analyses embodied in this book go beyond the ordinary legal and organizational features of state government. We gain a clearer vision of a state's government and politics if we can see the connections between the critical features of the state's economy and history and understand how these factors shape the political culture of the state, which in turn is an important feature of the state's political system.

At the same time, we have worked hard to incorporate an emphasis on individuals—leaders and ordinary citizens—and to avoid the pitfall of analysis that focuses solely on societywide forces such as economic change. We have sought to explore the influence that economic and social forces have on public officials and on the state's citizens, and we have also explored the effects that government and politics "Mississippi style" have on the state, especially its recent development.

We would like to thank a number of persons and institutions at Mississippi State University (MSU) who made valuable contributions to this book. Doug Feig and graduate assistant Stacy Brown read the entire manuscript and offered helpful ideas that improved the final product. Tip Allen reviewed a number of chapters and imparted the wisdom of his four decades of professional experience in studying Mississippi's social and political system. Tom Handy doggedly refused to let heart surgery stop him from completing his chapter. The contributions of other MSU faculty are noted at the appropriate places. Other graduate students who ably assisted this project include Tom Davis and Denise Joy, who helped with the editorial work on most of the manuscript, and Jeong-sook Kim and Sheila Pickett Putnam, who had similar responsibilities for selected chapters. An outstanding undergraduate student, Charles J. Anderson, reviewed the history chapter as well as collected pertinent information about executive branch agencies. The capable secretarial assistance of Lisa Aplin and Cindy Henson is greatly appreciated. The staff members of the Mitchell Memorial Library, including Frances N. Coleman, associate director, were very generous with their time in helping us locate important data sources. We gratefully acknowledge funding support provided by the John C. Stennis Institute of Government and the MSU Social Science Research Center for various chapters or data sources used in this book.

Individuals not connected with Mississippi State University also made significant contributions to this volume. The leadership and encouragement of Daniel Elazar and his associates at the Center for the Study of Federalism, Temple University, not only launched this project but also helped keep it on course. Stanley Thames, University of North Texas, kindly shared his insights on Mississippi's political culture. Support by the Department of Public Administration and the College of Public Affairs and Community Service, University of Nebraska at Omaha, greatly aided the completion of this book. The referees chosen by the University of Nebraska Press were extremely thorough in their review of the manuscript, and the final product includes many of their valuable suggestions. John Kincaid, executive director of the Advisory Commission on Intergovernmental Relations, deserves special recognition for his dedication in making numerous insightful and detailed suggestions that improved each of the chapters. We also appreciate Joseph B. Parker's encouragement and his thoughtful comments about the manuscript. A special thank you goes to the many political figures and observers in Mississippi who graciously shared helpful information and on occasion thought-provoking interpretations about state politics. The access and perspective provided by these "insiders" helped the authors gather the pieces of information necessary to arrive at sound conclusions about the importance of particular events. Unless specifically noted, however, all conclusions and interpretations offered in this book are the responsibility of the authors of the individual chapters.

To meet the challenge given to us by the series editors, we have attempted to produce a rare blend of empirical analysis and critical interpretation. We have not limited ourselves to a mere recounting of facts but go on to interpret the evidence within the framework of Mississippi's political culture. Doing so allows us to analyze the state's political world from the viewpoint of Mississippians. We hope readers will find a gold mine of information that will permit them to reach conclusions about government and politics in Mississippi that might not have been obvious before.

We offer readers of this book the same advice we offer our students. Read with a critical mind, and remember that authors have their own personal values and professional orientations. Different people may view the same events or situations in very different ways and may offer very different interpretations of them. Suggestions regarding how the quality of life in the state may be enhanced through the political system are made throughout this book. It is expected, even encouraged, that readers will disagree with some of these interpretations and suggestions. Such disagreements are healthy in a democratic republic. We will be satisfied with our efforts if this book helps to stimulate further debate in Mississippi on how the political system can contribute to an improvement in the quality of life for all Mississippians.

MISSISSIPPI GOVERNMENT AND POLITICS

CHAPTER ONE

Culture and Politics in Mississippi: It's Not Just Black and White

Dale Krane and Stephen D. Shaffer

To understand Mississippi, you have to understand this. . . . The figures and charts and diagrams which point out Mississippi's economic position do not mean a damn thing to us. Most Mississippians will turn their backs on the facts and say, "Well, you don't see many people retiring from here and moving to New York City.". . . They say, if we have large-scale industry, we'll have crime and dope, and it will change our southern lifestyle, and it will defile our rivers and pollute our air, and it will bring in a lot of damn outsiders with all their strange ideas.

David Sansing, "State's History Helped Stop Growth," 1980

One thing about Mississippi, I would say this is the most change-oriented state in the nation. Folks in Mississippi are willing to try something new.

Jack Brizius, Pennsylvania education consultant, 1989.[1]

For starters, Real Mississippians never say "Mis-sis-sip-pi." They say "Mis-sipi."

Joe Rogers, "Real Missipians Stand When
Car Horn Plays 'Dixie,'" 1985

Historic changes announced by banner headlines appear with surprising frequency in Mississippi newspapers. Regional and even national attention focuses somewhat incredulously on the pace of change in this previously "closed society."[2] Since the Freedom Summer of 1964, the growing list of "firsts" (and "at long lasts") is impressive and includes:

—over 300,000 registered black citizens who now play a pivotal role in statewide elections

—movement of black leaders into the state's power structure

—emergence of a competitive Republican party

—successful challenges to the Old Guard dominance of state government

—substantial progress toward the professional administration of public programs and services

—the integration and comprehensive reform of public schools

Without a doubt, many of these changes have resulted from federal action brought about during the civil rights revolution in the South. There is also no doubt that the forces creating a "new Mississippi" reflect underlying trans-formations in the state's political, economic, and social structures that have been in progress for the last quarter century.

Yet the old ways persist. The list of obvious shortcomings remains too long and includes:

—the antiquated 1890 constitution, with its weak governorship and ex-cessively fragmented executive authority

—one of the nation's most regressive revenue structures

—inefficient county government

—incomplete compliance with the 1965 Voting Rights Act

—a judicial system in which 70 percent of the prisoners are black, while the state's population is only 36 percent black

—a state per capita income that is only two-thirds of the national average

—the dependence of approximately 35 percent of the state's population on some form of federal assistance

Some of these problems are not unique to Mississippi. Other southern states exhibit incomplete compliance with the Voting Rights Act, and blacks na-tionwide have been significantly overrepresented in America's prisons and on death row. Still, there remains the gnawing concern that an unusual num-ber of serious economic, racial, and political problems plague Mississippi. Some political observers trace these difficulties to the stubborn survival of an archaic and elitist orientation to state government and politics. Resistance to social change and defense of a semifeudal society are seen as inhibiting the full exercise of citizenship privileges. This contributes to regressive policies and sustains the highly visible deficiencies in Mississippi's quality of life.

The continuing political struggle between individuals seeking to maintain the status quo ante and those pushing for change is the principal theme of this study of Mississippi's government and politics. This hard-fought battle over the state's destiny raises many important questions that shape the analysis presented here. For example, Who are the main players in the public arena, and what are their bases of support? Can the average Mississippian influence the course of public affairs and, if so, how is this influence exercised? What are the institutions and processes that determine public decisions? What influence do the state's policies have on Mississippi's quality of life? What are the positive and negative features of the state's political order? And what reforms, if any, might remedy major inadequacies in state government?

STUDYING CULTURE AND POLITICS IN MISSISSIPPI

I believe that what happens in a small town in Mississippi with less of a population than three or four apartment complexes on the West side of Manhattan Island will be of enduring importance to America.[3]

Among the fifty states, Mississippi is one of the most critical in terms of understanding the government and politics of the United States. First, Mississippi exemplifies the essence of the American South, culturally and politically the most distinct region of the nation. Second, as the poorest state, Mississippi presents an especially difficult challenge to the nation's policies and programs for achieving economic growth. Third and most important, the American quest for individual equality and freedom has been put to its severest trial in Mississippi, and thus the character of race relations in the state serves as a continuing barometer of the nation's democracy.

One cannot be neutral about Mississippi. The state engenders a mixture of intense feelings and responses from natives and visitors alike. For some, the Magnolia State is "the beauty spot of creation," "the original Cotton Kingdom," and "a place that's produced the best damned writers in America." For others Mississippi is a land of "degradation, brutality, inferiority, exhausting poverty." Jason Berry explains that "Mississippi is a state of diametric oppositions; black and white, rich and poor, quarterbacks and sorrow, misery and beauty queens. Even the word 'Mississippi' evokes widely varied reactions from people who hear it."[4] It is these paradoxes that provoke the admiration and love, the fear and guilt that are aroused by no other state in America.

To capture Mississippi's special character and to illustrate how the government and politics of the state are shaped by its particular attributes requires more than a simple legal description of the basic institutions of governance. No one denies the importance of the constitutional dimensions of our governmental structures. It does make a difference if a state's legislature is malapportioned or its governor is restricted in authority over budget execution. But government and politics do not take place in a vacuum; instead, civic institutions exist within a larger cultural and economic context. Culture and economics are themselves, at least partially, the products of a community's geography and history. All of these factors act as "major determinants of policy and behavior insofar as they require, facilitate, constrain, and prohibit courses of action."[5] The interplay of these contextual factors with the structures of government shapes the specific roles of each structure—for example, the authority of the governor; defines the types of individuals who can hold particular positions—for example, a black on the state supreme court; and establishes the legitimacy of particular public policies and their enforcement—for example, the prohibition of alcohol.[6]

Despite the power and the spread of a nationwide popular culture, differences among the fifty states still survive—life in Mississippi is not the same as life in Massachusetts or in Montana. Intuitively, we know that the culture, economics, geography, and history of a state mold its government and create a system of politics different from that found in any other state. To understand the relation between the context within which politics is pursued and the type of government that emerges in a state, one must examine the state's political culture. Political culture is defined as "the particular pattern of orientation to political action in which each political system is embedded," which is "rooted in the cumulative historical experiences of particular groups of people."[7] Important aspects of a state's political culture that influence how the art of government is practiced are the expectations that citizens and politicians have of government and the types of people who become involved in politics and government. "To date, the most promising and comprehensive effort to map and classify American political culture is Daniel J. Elazar's scheme of moralistic, individualistic, and traditionalistic subcultures."[8]

Each of Elazar's three subcultures is grounded in contrasting conceptions of how the political arena is to be organized, how power is to be held and exercised, and how justice is to be achieved.[9] "These subcultures may be regarded as contemporary, modified manifestations of the ethnic, socioreligious, and socioeconomic differences which existed among residents of the three main sections of the original thirteen colonies."[10] The contrasting cultures of the New England, Middle Atlantic, and southern colonies produced differing systems of government and politics. The ideas and practices of public affairs in these three regions were eventually carried by various migrants to different parts of the United States. To examine the imprint of political culture on Mississippi politics, it is useful to describe briefly each of these three distinctive cultural contexts.

The *moralistic* political culture emerged out of the Puritan settlements of New England, with their emphasis on a commonwealth view of government and society. Politics, in the moralistic culture, is an important activity that should benefit the public good and be above private interests. Every citizen has a duty to participate without economic gain in the governance of the commonwealth. Nonpartisan, "amateur" politics is fostered as a means of increasing citizen participation and ensuring a more principled public debate. Government agencies should be organized to promote the efficient and effective delivery of public services and should be staffed with competent, politically neutral professional administrators. From New England, the moralistic political culture has spread across the northern tier of the Great Lakes states, across the wheat belt and the Rocky Mountain states, and into the upper northwestern states.

In the *individualistic* political culture, by contrast, citizens tend to view the political arena much like a marketplace, where "professional" politicians pursue profitable careers just as one would pursue a career in business. Individual political figures and political "corporations" (political parties) compete to provide services demanded by various groups of citizens. In return, political entrepreneurs receive various forms of compensation—for example, patronage and power. Citizens are perceived as clients who can be lured with public service products of reasonable quality and cost. Political leadership consists of negotiating bargains and deals that control the distribution of rewards to individuals and groups loyal to the leader or the corporation. Political rhetoric usually downplays issues and stresses the pragmatic policies "advertised" by the competing corporations. Government's principal purpose is to foster economic growth, primarily through the encouragement and manipulation of the marketplace. Bureaucracy is seen as a two-edged sword—as an unnecessary limit on political favors and as an organization necessary for delivering quality public products. This cultural orientation developed in the Middle Atlantic colonies, which had commercial economies, and then spread into the corn belt, across the central plains, and into portions of California.

The *traditionalistic* political culture emerged in the southern colonies, where efforts were made to recreate English manorial society, by relying first on indentured labor and later on slaves. Because it derives from an agrarian, precommercial mentality, the traditionalistic political culture is characterized by a hierarchical conception of civilization, with those at the top of the socioeconomic ladder maintaining a dominant role in public affairs. Real power is restricted to a small, self-perpetuating elite drawn from the established upper-class families. Political competition among the elites is characterized by personality contests and factional feuds that are constrained by a network of interpersonal relationships. The role of the government is to defend the status quo and to maintain traditional values. The mass of citizens (who are not slaves) are expected to defer to the decisions of the elites and to support the existing social structure. Because government has very few custodial responsibilities beyond ensuring a stable social order, large and costly government agencies are viewed as unnecessary and wasteful. From the southern seaboard, traditionalistic political culture has spread throughout most of the old Confederacy including Mississippi, across the Southwest, and into southern California.[11]

One can gain a better appreciation for political culture and its usefulness in the study of state politics by briefly examining variations in attitudes about political corruption. "By its very nature, corruption involves the perversion of public power for private purposes, and it is therefore an abuse of power."[12] Citizens of moralistic political cultures (e.g., Minnesota, Wisconsin) strongly condemn any abuse of public power. They demand "squeaky clean" government and insist on holding political figures accountable not only to the law, but also to high moral standards. By contrast, it is not unusual to find some corruption and graft in individualistic political cultures (e.g., Illinois, New York) because citizens tend to believe that politics, like business, sometimes involves bribes and kickbacks. "Wheeling and dealing" will be tolerated by the public so long as its costs do not become excessive, either as squandered funds or as poor services. Traditionalistic political cultures (e.g., Louisiana, Mississippi) exhibit high levels of political corruption because power is built out of patron-client relationships. Since government is viewed as a mere tool for the support of the upper classes, the private use of public funds and services is not perceived as a betrayal of the public trust; rather, it is held to be an appropriate action to maintain the traditional order. "Frequent and systematic corruption is, therefore, an integral part of traditionalistic politics."[13]

In applying the concepts of political culture to the study of state politics, one must be sensitive to the possibility that two or more political subcultures may exist in a state and that "the different subcultural regions of a state may become the basis for different parties, different strategies of action, different policies.''[14] Similarly, political conflicts within a state may be provoked by contextual changes in one part of the state that lead to new life-styles or new values.

We do not intend to focus solely on political culture, but it is necessary to explore the way political culture interacts with the other contextual factors (economics, geography, history) and with the structures of the political system. As we describe the basic features of Mississippi's political arena, our analysis will be guided by this sensitivity to the state's unique culture. Before moving ahead, we will briefly describe important features of Mississippi's geography, economics, and general culture. The next chapter will provide a review of Mississippi's political history and the emergence of the state's political subcultures.

THE UNIQUENESS OF MISSISSIPPI

> *Northerners, provincials that they are, regard the South as one large Mississippi. Southerners, with their eye for distinction, place Mississippi in a class by itself.[15]*

Not just "Yankees," but even fellow southerners view Mississippi—its citizens, its culture, and its politics—as unique in the South. This distinctiveness expresses itself in the diametric opposites noted by Jason Berry. Any exploration into the culture and politics of the Magnolia State must begin with this fundamental fact: Mississippi is a state of contradictions and extremes. Willie Morris, one of Mississippi's nationally recognized essayists, reveals these incongruities:

> *Mississippi, as God help us we all know, has often given itself to extremes, and through the years two of the greatest ones have been the desire, on the one hand, to dwell forever with all the myths and trimmings of a vanished culture which may never have truly existed in the first place, certainly not the way we wished it to, and the frantic compulsion, on the other, to reforge ourselves as an appendage of the capitalistic, go-getting, entrepreneurial North.[16]*

These extremes are visible everywhere in the state. For example, Mississippi is the home of the International Ballet Competition, the Delta Blues Festival, and the World Tobacco Spitting Championships. Headquarters for NASA's Space Technologies Laboratory, it is also a state where some families still live in wooden dogtrot shacks. Producer of Nobel and Pulitzer Prize winning authors, Mississippi also possesses one of the highest school dropout rates in the country.

These contradictions are only symptomatic of the state's enduring features. The unique and often remarkable behavior of the state's people is rooted deeply in the usual southern traits of "parochialism, fatalism, authoritarianism, ethnocentrism, and categorical resistance to innovation"[17] and shaped more specifically by the characteristics that "place Mississippi in a class by itself."

Geography

One element of Mississippi's uniqueness can be found in what Eudora Welty has called "the sense of place." Few places evoke such a combination of mystery and wonder as do the varied landscapes of the Magnolia State. William Faulkner and others have written about the influence of Mississippi's diverse landscapes—alluvial swamps and bayous, red clay highlands, vast pine forests, tabletop flat floodplains—on the life-styles of the people who settled the state. This relationship between the land and its people contributes directly to Mississippi's uniqueness.

The twentieth state admitted to the Union ranks thirty-second in size and thirty-first in population. Encompassing an area of 47,234 square miles, Mississippi is slightly smaller than Louisiana but slightly larger than Pennsylvania. Its mean length is 340 miles (about the same as Britain) and its mean width is 170 miles. Mississippi's total population in 1990 was 2,573,216, of which 35.6 percent was black. Of all county seats, usually the largest municipality in a county, 74 percent have a population of less than 10,000. Jackson, the state capital, is the only city with a population over 50,000 (map 1). Only three standard metropolitan statistical areas (SMSAS) exist wholly within the state.[18]

Mississippi is a very rural state. As late as 1980, only 47.3 percent of the state's population lived in urban areas, compared with a national average of 73.7 percent (only Vermont and West Virginia were more rural). Though Mississippi has only 7 percent less land area than its sister state of Alabama, its population is only 64 percent that of Alabama. In 1980, 36.4 percent of Alabama's population lived in nonmetropolitan areas, while 70.6 percent of Mississippi's citizens lived in nonmetropolitan areas.

But to see the state as it really is, one must understand its geographic diversity. Contrary to the national stereotype, Mississippi is not one gigantic

Map 1. Urban areas in Mississippi, 1990. (*Source*: 1990 U.S. census.)

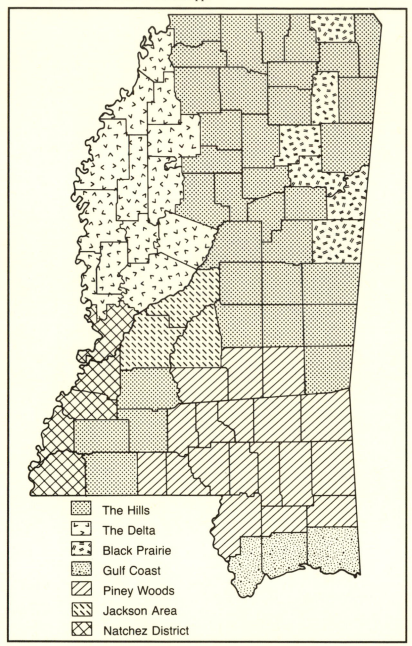

The Hills

The Delta

Black Prairie

Gulf Coast

Piney Woods

Jackson Area

Natchez District

Map 2. Geographic regions of Mississippi.
(Adapted from James W. Loewen and Charles Sallis, eds., *Mississippi: Conflict and Change* [New York: Pantheon, 1974], p. 16.)

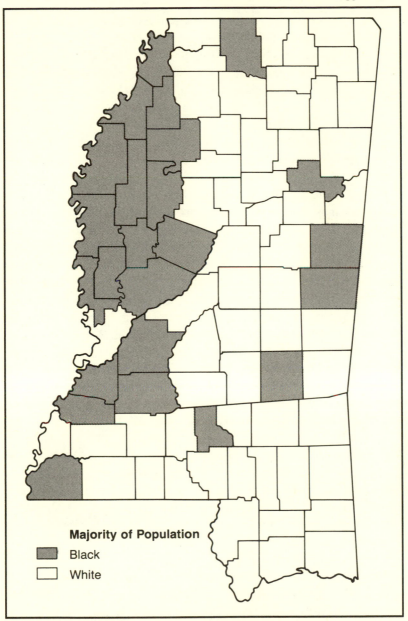

Majority of Population

▩ Black

☐ White

Map 3. Racial composition of Mississippi counties.
Dark areas denote counties in which blacks constitute
a majority of the population. Light areas are counties
in which whites are a majority. (*Source*: 1990 U.S. census.)

cotton plantation. Rather, the state contains at least six regions that exhibit their own economic, political, and social features (map 2). "The influence of geography on the historical development of Mississippi," writes John Ray Skates, "weighs heavy, fostering subtle, oftentimes turbulent differences."[19] Native Mississippians usually identify strongly with their region and with their hometown or rural community. This intense "sense of place" cuts across all class and race lines.

The most clearly defined region is the Delta, an almost perfectly flat alluvial plain lying in a half-moon-shaped expanse from the state's northwest corner to the Yazoo River. Bounded by the Mississippi River on the west and flanked by an irregular line of loess-loam hills on the east, the Delta contains some of the most fertile land in the nation. In a very real sense, the Delta is "artificial," because the original swamp and forest land was not drained and leveled until after the Civil War.[20] Protected by immense levees, the Delta gave rise to Mississippi's post–Civil War cotton aristocracy—the Delta planters. At the same time, the Delta "is the blackest belt of the South."[21] Its agricultural wealth was harvested by the labor of the region's black share-croppers and tenant farmers, whose number has always surpassed the white population. Today, thirteen of the state's twenty-four black majority population counties are found in the Delta; these counties have an average black population of 63.2 percent (map 3). The principal city in the Delta is Greenville (45,226), the largest municipality north of the state capital. In general, the socioeconomic pattern within Delta communities reflects the extreme inequalities of the region's plantation economy.

Just south of the Delta, running along the Mississippi River, is the state's first settled area. The Natchez District is composed of river lowlands and low hills that supported opulent cotton plantations before the Civil War. As in the Delta, a majority black population resides in three of the area's five counties. Two historic communities, Natchez (19,460) and Vicksburg (20,908), retain much of the French and Spanish Catholic heritage that links this area to New Orleans.

The dominant feature of Mississippi's landscape is a broken series of low hills separated by strips of prairie and flatwoods. In this geographic and cultural heartland of Mississippi one finds rich river bottom lands. Unfortunately, however, the Hills are predominantly red "gumbo" clay that supports only modest agricultural activities, such as cattle and poultry raising. The population of the counties in this extensive region range from about 8,000 to 38,000, with a typical county seat (the largest and often the only "urban" place in the county) of approximately 2,000 to 7,000 residents.

The largest of the Hills cities is Meridian (41,036), which grew because of its location on the rail lines from New Orleans to Birmingham. Because a plantation economy did not emerge in the Hills, blacks are less numerous than in the Delta and Natchez regions, usually constituting less than 35 percent of the counties' population. Generally, towns in the Hills do not exhibit the extremes in distribution of wealth found in Delta communities.

A countywide arc of highly fertile black soil enters east-central Mississippi and continues north by northwest to Tennessee. The Black Prairie, an extension of the South's black belt running across Georgia and Alabama, was the western part of the antebellum Cotton Kingdom. Large farms still operate in this area and yield a wealth that can be seen in some of the region's larger cities, such as Columbus (23,799) and Tupelo (30,685). A significant black population lives in the Prairie and composes a majority in two of the area's six counties.

Mississippi's southeastern and south-central sections consist of vast pine forests now owned largely by major paper manufacturers. Because the soil is so infertile, this Piney Woods region has been known historically as "de Po' Folks' Lan'."[22] Although much of the area is close to New Orleans, the towns of the Piney Woods region are among the state's poorest and most isolated localities. Like the Hills, the Piney Woods never developed a plantation economy; consequently the population is overwhelmingly white. Hattiesburg (41,882) serves as the urban center of the region.

Originally settled by the French and Spanish, the Gulf Coast is the state's most urban area besides the state's capital. A series of medium-sized cities form two SMSAS—Biloxi-Gulfport (combined population 197,125) and Pascagoula–Moss Point (combined population 115,243). These "strip" cities exhibit most of the features of similar beach communities along the Gulf of Mexico. Over 12 percent of the state's population lives in the three Coast counties.

Jackson (196,637), the state capital, is situated along the Pearl River where it turns southeast to flow toward the Gulf Coast. Somewhat to the south and west of the state's geographic center, Jackson's location in Hinds County puts it close to an area where the state's major regions converge. Jackson is the political, commercial, and cultural center of Mississippi. Smaller than Meridian for most of its history, Jackson and its neighboring suburbs have experienced rapid growth since World War II and now constitute the state's largest SMSA, with a population of 395,396. Typically, Jackson is described as a miniature version of Atlanta.

The state's other major population center consists of the bedroom communities near Memphis, Tennessee. About 30 percent of Mississippi's population now lives in the state's seven SMSA counties (DeSoto, Hancock, Harrison, Hinds, Jackson, Madison, and Rankin). About 40 percent of the population resides in the ten largest counties, while 60 percent lives in the state's remaining seventy-two counties. Approximately 55 percent of Mississippians reside on or south of a line formed by the cities of Meridian, Jackson, and Vicksburg.

These varied regions gave birth to distinctive subcultures because each region's geography imposed conditions that either enhanced or hindered the quality of life. For example, James Street, describing life in the red clay hills before World War II, wrote:

> There are no cities in "po' folks' lan'," and no plantations—only grubby little farms. The farmers are poor and the Negroes are poorer. . . . Many of the whites fall in that unfortunate classification of "trash." They live like Negroes, swarms of children and kinsmen in one tiny cabin where flies buzz all day and mosquitoes all night. . . . My hills are clay and my valleys are locked behind the forests. I dare you to come down here and try to live. I've got boll weevils to eat your cotton and wildcats to kill your sheep. . . . I can send malaria and pellagra for your children and hookworms crawl in my mud.[23]

Life in the red clay hills and the dense pine forests did not include the decorum and opulence of plantation society, nor did it embrace the cosmopolitanism of Natchez and the Gulf Coast. As the next chapter will recount, the poor white population of the Hills and the Piney Woods challenged with some success the political dominance of the plantation elites.

Until recently, Mississippi's regions have been relatively isolated from each other. Paved roads directly linking one county seat to neighboring county seats were completed only in the 1950s. Some adults have never traveled outside their home county! Large sections of Mississippi are cultural and economic satellites of Memphis and New Orleans. No commercial television station in the capital is able to beam news throughout the state. This isolation reinforces attachment to tradition and raises barriers to change.

Economics

The single most important and incontrovertible economic fact is that Mississippi is the poorest state in the Union. No other state finishes last or next to last on so many measures of progress. Mississippi's per capita income ($12,735 in 1990) is only 68.2 percent of the national average, ranking fiftieth in the nation. Twenty-four percent of the state's population, 18.7 percent of its families, and 30.4 percent of its children under eighteen live in poverty, more than in any other state. These depressed income levels are reinforced by the nation's highest illiteracy rate, the fourth highest unemployment rate, the lowest average hourly and weekly earnings for production employees, the slowest growth rate for service industries, and one of the nation's highest school dropout rates (33 percent).

As a consequence, Mississippians constitute the nation's largest percentage of food stamp recipients (18.6 percent of the population) and public aid recipients (11.1 percent). Approximately 35 percent of the state's residents depend on some form of federal assistance, and in thirty-two of the state's eighty-two counties, the principal source of income is federal transfer payments. As of 1981, sixty-six towns, or 23 percent of the state's incorporated areas, did not have sewer and water systems.[24] The number of physicians (per 1,000 population) ranks fiftieth, and the average life expectancy ranks forty-eighth. It comes as no surprise that the desperate conditions depicted in this litany of state rankings would prompt the governor in 1981 to warn that Mississippi was like "an emerging colonial nation."[25]

Despite the stubbornness of Mississippi's poverty, patches of progress and growth do exist. Mississippians live in one of the most crime-free states in the nation (forty-sixth in overall crime rate). From an environmental standpoint, the state's citizens enjoy a lush and verdant garden of fertile lands, abundant forests, and plentiful water. The state ranks among the top ten producers of cotton, rice, soybeans, and chickens. Oil and gas deposits are present, including one of the largest natural gas areas in the country. Mississippi consistently ranks as one of the top ten states in business climate, with its economy attracting a growing industrial sector. Mississippians now manufacture items such as aircraft components, apparel, building materials, chemicals, machinery, magazines, optical equipment, paper, and textiles. Mississippi-based facilities include the world's largest single-line production of titanium oxide, the world's largest producer of musical instrument amplification equipment, one of the nation's largest continuous-operation paper mills, and one of the most modern shipyards in the country.

To some extent, Mississippi's economic condition is tied to the more general growth patterns of the South. The post–World War II transformation of the Sunbelt has significantly reduced the differences between the South and other regions of the United States. Unfortunately, as the Southern Growth Policies Board observes, "the sunshine on the Sunbelt has proved to be a narrow beam of light, brightening futures along the Atlantic Seaboard and in the large cities, but skipping over many small towns and rural areas."[26] Mississippi, as the most rural of the southern states, has benefited the least from the region's boom.

Culture

Mississippi "is likely the most communal of all the fifty states."[27] Its scattered and often isolated farm communities exhibit an intimate village lifestyle of shared experiences and traditions. Personal and family heritage, as well as the history of the locality, is transmitted by elaborate storytelling that links one generation to the next and socializes the young into the customs and manners of their community. Because these towns and villages are so small, privacy is nonexistent outside the home. In communities where everyone knows everyone else (and everyone else's business), life functions much as in an extended family.

As is common in many nonmetropolitan areas, the class distribution in Mississippi communities is directly related to the town's political life. Middle- and upper-class status in Mississippi, as it does nationally, rests on the possession of some combination of education, income, position, and property. A town's aristocrats and would-be aristocrats are found among the ranks of the bankers, landowners, lawyers, merchants, ministers, physicians, and other "white-collar" professionals whose offices are on "Main Street" or the "courthouse square." As one moves away from Main Street, one enters the blue-collar or "redneck" world of auto repair garages, feed stores, garment factories, and lumber mills. Although the men and women who earn their livelihood in skilled and semiskilled manual occupations constitute a majority of the state's population, they or their representatives do not dominate local or state decision-making bodies. Rather, official authorities and unofficial leaders are drawn from the ranks of the elite. Not only do members of the upper stratum fill the positions of power, they also expect to control these positions. Furthermore, they expect individuals in the lower classes to defer to their decisions.

In addition to socioeconomic attributes, native Mississippians commonly make at least four other distinctions among individuals. First, they attach considerable importance to the judgment that one's behavior conforms to local norms. Despite the prevailing doctrine of "individualism," powerful pressures for social conformity exist within Mississippi communities. Persons who are not churchgoers or "good Christians," who are not law-abiding or responsible, who do not practice the special courtesies of southern hospitality, or who are not respectful of local rituals and symbols are labeled "trash" and are quickly excluded from the town's "decent folk" or "quality folk." (Note that poor but "quality" blacks will often be treated with more courtesy and respect than "trashy" whites with more income.)[28] "Decent folks" will explain to outsiders that much of the violence found in southern culture is caused by the "no account, trash."[29] Not to be considered "decent" is to be left outside the important informal "networks" that control and distribute advantages and benefits within the community. "Quality folks," for example, will be accorded legitimacy in discussions of community affairs.

Religious affiliations constitute another line of cleavage. Differences between Protestants and Catholics (who are few in number except on the Gulf Coast and along the Mississippi River) as well as between Protestant and non-Protestant "Christian" churches create a variety of status and social groupings. Socioeconomic status and church affiliation are closely associated; for example, lower-status persons are more numerous in the Fundamentalist and Pentecostal churches. One can even observe some individuals and families changing denominations as their fortunes change. Religious doctrines and values translate into policy preferences pursued in the public sector, as exemplified by wet-dry contests, battles over school curricula and opening stores on Sunday, and even support for or opposition to social services and the revenues to pay for "welfare." In communities where one's public identity is directly tied to one's denomination (e.g., church-league softball), the church becomes a powerful institution of social control and political action. Candidates for statewide office gain some advantage from the aid of their state Baptist or Methodist associations.

One's birthplace is another mark of distinction in Mississippi. Adults who were born and raised in their community belong to an exclusive group that seldom can be penetrated by outsiders, whether they be "Yankees" or native Mississippians "from some other town." Unlike Nebraska, where one is accepted as a Nebraskan after one lives in the state for "a winter and a summer," one must be born a Mississippian. Outsiders who are "decent folk" can become part of the larger town life, but they will find it difficult to enter into the intimate "friends and neighbors" networks built on age cohorts and old school ties. Local candidates easily capture important public office (e.g., city council or county chancery clerk) by virtue of having enough "kissin' cousins" or enough former football players they coached.

Many Mississippians live in unincorporated rural areas. This municipal-county division also affects Mississippi's culture. Middle- and upper-class life in many county seats resembles suburban life-styles throughout the Sunbelt. However, in the Hills and Piney Woods regions, life out in the county remains fixed in a preindustrial mode. The "Dogpatch" character of county life stems from the poverty of the land and enormous resistance to change. Because of their different life-styles and mind-sets, county residents and city dwellers often find themselves pitted against each other on many economic and political issues (e.g., the city may be wet, but the county dry).

All of these distinctions can be applied to Mississippi's black population. The principal difference, of course, is the much smaller number and proportion of white-collar blacks. Except for very small, all-white villages, every Mississippi community contains a black business and professional class. Even today "black business districts" retain their loyal clientele. In addition to this upper stratum, blacks who own income-producing farms or who hold steady, well-paying blue-collar and service jobs (e.g., as postal workers, bank tellers, factory workers, police, cashiers) constitute a black middle class. Their resources and life-style separate them from the black "underclass" of unskilled laborers who are intermittently employed or permanently unemployed. Black political leadership also comes from these upper- and middle-class families. These more affluent blacks have access to institutions and organizations that link them to white leadership (e.g., the local chamber of commerce or the Parent-Teacher Association).

It is important to emphasize the interrelation between blacks and whites in Mississippi localities. Jim Crow laws produced two separate worlds in Mississippi towns, and the black sections of town (e.g., "Froggy Bottom" in Philadelphia, "Catfish Row" in Vicksburg) usually lacked public facilities such as sidewalks, water and sewer systems, and streetlights.[30] Nevertheless, blacks and whites from the same city have been bound together by the shared experiences and traditions of their "place." Daily life in these hamlets has intertwined many blacks and whites into "friends and neighbors" networks that go beyond the workplace and carry over into civic affairs. Today whites will frequently include local black notables among the town's leadership.

Some attention to the social patterns of Mississippi culture is critical in understanding the state's politics. For example, who can raise what types of issues in the locality, who can voice legitimate concerns about the city budget or about the school superintendent, and who the local leadership will pay attention to are a function of a town's sociology. The informal "good ole boy" and "good ole girl" networks of these intimate places serve as the principal means for communicating opinions and mobilizing action (or inaction). Visible public authorities work closely with less "visible" but widely recognized "natural" leaders whose influence stems from their status as the head of a patron-client network within the town's informal organization. Competition among the leaders of the various networks occurs in a carefully controlled style of personality and popularity contests. Decisions are hammered out in private informal conversations among the patrons, and public dissent is not tolerated once a decision is announced. The local newspaper, for example, will be expected to justify and support the policy.

The litmus test for political influence is adherence to traditional beliefs, practices, and values. Outsiders are often deceived by the "small-bore name-calling, mud-slinging factional politicians" who sometimes turn Mississippi elections into contests of jokes and pranks.[31] Comic-opera posturing does not constitute real debate; its real purpose is to advertise one's name to voters, many of whom are illiterate. True dissent is repressed by the "ingrained folk resistance to change" and by the need to be accepted in small town society.[32] At city council or county board meetings, it is not unusual to see a citizen go through a lengthy apology as a preface to raising a point of view different from that held by the officials. Such hat-in-hand deference would shock those familiar with the outspoken style of New England town meetings.

Mississippi culture creates a political style that is best characterized as a "politics of place." Not just "place" in the geographic sense of one's hometown, but also "place" in the sense of one's socioeconomic standing as well as one's position in or out of the various informal "friends and neighbors" networks. Who a person is, what a person does, one's origins and family, and one's behavior or style (e.g., courteous or aggressive) go far to determine one's role in the political arena. Outsiders who question traditional customs and values will be politely but firmly "put in their place." Locals will politely inquire, for example, about a newcomer's church affiliation or family tree. These seemingly innocuous questions are more than the Magnolia State's famed hospitality; these pieces of information help locals "place" newcomers (from within Mississippi or from outside the state). Church affiliation, for example, offers the questioner a clue to whether the other person will be for or against liquor in an upcoming wet-dry election.

Certainly race influences the acceptance or rejection of a candidate or a citizen seeking redress of grievances. Some Mississippians still view the world in black and white, but for an increasing number, race is only one factor in sizing up another person's "place" in the community. One cannot escape the racial question in Mississippi politics, but one must avoid the trap that Mississippi politics is only about race-related issues.[33]

THE STRUGGLE BETWEEN TRADITION AND MODERNITY

Civic life is not divorced from other aspects of life in Mississippi. Quite the contrary, politics begins in the gatherings of men and women swapping stories and gossip on the church steps, in the hair salons and supermarkets, in the beer joints and quick-stops, at meetings of breakfast and luncheon clubs, and on the courthouse square. The facts, opinions, and judgments that emerge out of these small group meetings flow along the gravel back roads and paved city streets to the county seats, then to the state capital and to the United States Congress.

Mississippi politics are grounded in the grass roots of friendship networks that provide individuals with their identity and their sense of place in the community. As with all intimate arrangements, these networks exert powerful influences over a person's beliefs and behaviors. To go against the prevailing practices is to face censure and opprobrium for disagreeing with one's "friends and neighbors"; consequently a person or group urging change typically must be motivated by highly salient or intensely held beliefs or interests.

Because crusades to initiate change often meet strong and sometimes violent opposition, even from "decent folk," persons pushing new ideas or new practices must be vigorous in their efforts. If the struggle over change breaks the normally restrained manners of Mississippians, then the conflict can escalate into a highly personalized feud that can become dangerous. It is the fear of this action-reaction dynamic that underlies the endeavors of town leaders to avoid or, at the minimum, paper over conflicts. To allow a battle to get out of hand is to risk fragmentation of the small community. Stability is so strongly valued that many important and useful suggestions for innovation are stymied by the pressure to avoid rocking the boat.

However, persons who in good conscience believe in the need for new ways find that remaining silent means accepting a low standard of living or a high level of corruption, discrimination, and inefficiency. Such individuals will point out the fallacy of the old saying, "If it ain't broken, why try to fix it?'' For many the old ways are no longer ''good enough''; the old ways are ''broken,'' so these individuals become forces for change. This battle between status quo and innovation, between tradition and modernity, is an ever present axis of Mississippi's politics. In addition to illustrating the standard features of Mississippi government, the following chapters will explore the influences of Mississippi's intimate, localized culture on the workings of the state's political system.

CHAPTER TWO

The Origins and Evolution
of a Traditionalistic Society

Stephen D. Shaffer and Dale Krane

When a black Jacksonian looks about his home community, he sees a city where Negro citizens are refused admittance to the city auditorium and the coliseum; his wife and children refused service in a downtown store where they trade; students refused the use of the main library, parks, and other tax-supported recreational facilities. . . . He sees a city of over 150,000, of which 40 percent is Negro, in which there is not a single Negro policeman or policewoman, school crossing guard, or fireman.

Medgar Evers, NAACP state field secretary, 1963[1]

We deeply regret what happened here 25 years ago. We wish we could undo it. . . . We are profoundly sorry they are gone. Every decent person in Philadelphia and Neshoba County and Mississippi feels exactly that way.

Secretary of state and Philadelphia native Dick Molpus at a 1989 ceremony in Philadelphia honoring slain civil rights workers James Chaney, Andrew Goodman, and Michael Schwerner[2]

Mississippi's political culture has historically been a traditionalistic one, characterized by a hierarchic political and social system with established upper-class families motivated to preserve the status quo. A fundamental source of the state's traditionalistic political culture was the old plantation system, which was based on the subjugation of black slaves and the subsequent political dominance of Delta planters over poor white farmers.

THE ANTEBELLUM ERA

The original settlers of the state having a European heritage were of Anglo-Saxon ethnic background and had lived in other southern states, particularly Georgia, Tennessee, and the Carolinas.[3] Some settled in the Natchez region. The city of Natchez, on the Mississippi River, was the first major city in the state. The Natchez planters, with their ties to French culture in New Orleans, were aristocratic slave owners and intellectuals who had been educated in eastern colleges and abroad. They therefore employed private tutors and provided out-of-state educations for their children. Settlers in the eastern part of the state generally did not own slaves, and many were members of a lower socioeconomic class who found themselves farming less productive land. Before the Civil War, the Natchez planter class dominated state government and used state funds to promote their financial position. Mississippi's traditional reluctance to support public schools originated at this time, since these planters were unwilling to support public schools they did not use.[4]

The plantation system began in the river counties of the Natchez area and then spread into northern and central Mississippi, making Mississippi one of the major plantation states of the region. The 1830s were a boom period in cotton production, and by 1860 slaves constituted 55 percent of the state's population. Hence strong police measures were used to control the slave population. For example, it was illegal for slaves to learn to read and write, to use abusive language toward whites, to testify against whites in court, and to buy or sell items without permission from their masters. In 1831 a state law encouraged free blacks to leave the state, and in 1857 white masters were prohibited from freeing their slaves.

A historian of the antebellum era in Mississippi provides a nice summary of the state's traditionalistic political order: "State government rarely interfered in the lives of its citizens, concerning itself primarily with the problems and maintenance of the cotton economy. Keeping credit fluid, easing transportation difficulties, and regulating and protecting slavery were the accepted functions of the legislative and administrative branches of the state. . . . When the state became involved in the lives of Mississippians, however, it did so to uphold law and the existing social order rather than to effect social change. In 1848, for example, the state treasury paid out more to reimburse slaveholders for executed slaves than for a vaccination program, the school for the blind, and the Chickasaw Indian school combined."[5]

Unexpectedly, slavery had a negative long-term effect on the state's economic strength. This repressive social system retarded the development of a home market, thereby inhibiting industrialization and economic diversification and hindering the state's economic progress into the twentieth century. Using slaves rather than hiring free laborers discouraged white immigration, so the construction of transportation facilities, schools, and urban centers was hindered.[6] Manual labor was held in low esteem, and even white artisans and craftsmen received little compensation for their skills and products.[7]

Class differences among white Mississippians led to a competitive two-party system before the Civil War. The Federalists, who nationally constituted the more elitist and pro-business party, were popular among wealthy plantation families in Mississippi and among Natchez merchants and bankers. The 1817 state constitution, which included a tax payment requirement for voting and a property ownership requirement for holding office, was written largely by the Natchez elite. Most Mississippi planters were not yet financially established, so they supported the more egalitarian Democratic-Republicans Thomas Jefferson, James Madison, and Aaron Burr. The state as a whole was a fairly Democratic-Republican state.

As the Federalist party withered away across the nation, the Democratic-Republican party nationally became more aristocratic in its policies. Many Mississippians resented the eastern rule of the Virginia dynasty presidents and the undemocratic congressional "King Caucus" that nominated presidential candidates. When the popular war hero General Andrew Jackson sought the presidency, Mississippians flocked to his banner. The wave of Jacksonian democracy in the state led to the 1832 constitution, which abolished tax payment requirements for voting and property holding requirements for public office and provided for the popular election of all state officials "from governor to dogcatcher."[8] These Jacksonian changes created electoral rules that, in the future, would make it possible for lower-class whites to challenge the political dominance of the plantation owners.

The opposition Whig party, which contained remnants of Jackson's opponents, was favored by the same elements in Natchez as had supported the old Federalist party. Plantation wealth in northeast Mississippi began to rival that of Natchez. The state's first bank and first free school were established in Columbus, and by the 1850s the center of wealth had moved to the north central and northeast Hills area. As north Mississippi became more prosperous, planters in that area also joined the Whigs. Although the Jacksonian Democrats tended to dominate state elections, the presidential elections from 1836 to 1856 were fairly competitive, as they were nationally. In 1840 Mississippi even helped to elect the Whig general William Henry Harrison to the White House, because of dissatisfaction with hard economic times and the Democratic president Martin Van Buren.[9]

In the 1850s, however, the national Democratic party became more closely associated with the South's position on slavery, and the Whig party began to decline in the state. Many Whigs drifted into the short-lived American party whose "Know-Nothing" opposition to foreign immigrants, especially Catholics, appealed to nativist sentiments.[10] The Republican party's growth in northern states as the champion of abolition and free soil drove most Mississippians into the Democratic party and helped to inaugurate the one-party, Democratic tradition in Mississippi and other southern states.[11] Radical secessionists from Mississippi rejected the northern Democratic candidate, Stephen Douglas of Illinois, and walked out of the 1860 Democratic national convention. Ironically, mobilization of the state's voters in the 1860 election for John Breckenridge, a southern Democrat from Kentucky, helped guarantee Abraham Lincoln's election.[12]

RECONSTRUCTION AND REDEMPTION

Immediately after the Civil War, conservative whites, who held political power briefly, enacted the Black Code to maintain white supremacy. This code limited the civil liberties of blacks in many ways, such as by prohibiting them from leasing or renting land outside incorporated towns. The Black Code also required that black males sign labor contracts; those who failed to sign were subject to arrest as vagrants. An apprenticeship system required dependent blacks to be apprenticed to suitable whites, with first preference given to former owners. In one case the children of a self-sufficient black couple were apprenticed to former owners, who refused to release them; in another instance a judge decided that a black father had no legal authority over his nine-year-old daughter, who had been contracted against his will since she was deemed illegitimate. Many northern whites saw the Black Codes as an effort by southern whites to reenslave blacks. Subsequent Reconstruction governments repealed these measures.[13]

During congressionally imposed Reconstruction from 1870 to 1876, Republicans dominated Mississippi state government with the support of newly freed slaves. In the 1870 state legislature, which contained 107 members, 52 were white Republicans, 30 were black Republicans, and only 25 were white conservatives. After the 1873 elections, blacks held the important offices of lieutenant governor, secretary of state, education superintendent, and Speaker of the house. The only blacks in the United States Senate during the Reconstruction era were both from Mississippi—Blanche Bruce and Hiram Revels.[14]

The Republican Reconstruction government in Mississippi aggressively sought to improve government services and protect the rights of blacks. Railroads, bridges, and public facilities were rebuilt, levees were repaired, and hospitals and insane asylums were constructed. A state Civil Rights Act was passed in 1870 outlawing discrimination in public places and on public vehicles. For a brief period, state government transcended Mississippi's traditionalistic political culture, which called for limited government activity. The opposition press and some historians of the period charged that fraud and extravagance were widespread in the Reconstruction government, although subsequent "revisionist" historians have argued that these charges were exaggerated.

One of the most controversial Reconstruction measures was a public school law, opposed by many whites, that significantly increased student enrollment. Some whites resented having to pay property taxes to educate black children, whose parents often did not pay such taxes because they generally did not own land. Some whites opposed the "mingling of all classes," including the mingling of poor whites with rich whites. The fears of interracial mingling turned out to be unfounded, because segregated schools were maintained. During this period, for example, Alcorn University was established as the black counterpart to the white University of Mississippi. A final concern was that white Republican teachers would indoctrinate black children to support the Republican party. During Reconstruction the public school system became a major target of the Ku Klux Klan, which often intimidated teachers and destroyed school buildings.[15]

In 1875, as a reaction to their distaste for the Reconstruction government, conservative whites instituted the Mississippi Plan to ensure that the Democrats would carry that year's state elections. The Mississippi Plan included such tactics as intimidating blacks, stuffing the ballot box with Democratic votes, destroying Republican ballots, substituting Democratic for Republican tickets for illiterate blacks, and miscounting ballots. This plan permitted conservative Democrats to regain control of state government, whereupon they immediately impeached the black lieutenant governor Alexander Davis and forced the resignation of Republican governor Adelbert Ames.[16]

Conservative white Democrats solidified their hold on state government. In 1876 a complex election law was passed that permitted local election officials to require voters to know their section, township, and range, which was then applied primarily to blacks to disfranchise many of them. Given that blacks lived predominantly in the Delta and Natchez areas, the legislature included them in one shoestring congressional district that stretched from the Tennessee to the Louisiana border, so that at most blacks would control only one of the state's six districts.

After the poor Republican showing in 1876, many whites began to abandon the party, and by 1878 the party's leadership was controlled by blacks. Although the party remained a factor in local and sometimes state elections, the Republicans ceased to threaten Democratic supremacy in the state. Despite the disfranchisement of many blacks, the legislature apportioned its districts on the basis of white *and* black population, thereby permitting the conservative, aristocratic whites in the heavily black Delta region to dominate state government for the rest of the century.[17]

Having accused the Reconstruction government of excessive taxation and wasteful spending, the Redeemers pursued fiscal retrenchment. They cut property taxes, abolished many government jobs, and slashed funding for schools and public services, thereby reducing government spending from about $1,400,000 per year under the Republicans to $600,000 a decade later. Consequently, in the 1880s Governor Robert Lowry found the state woefully short of funds for operating schools, colleges, and other state agencies. Some public leaders began to argue that taxes were too low, while radical agrarian leaders accused the Redeemers of corruption and incompetence.[18]

The traditionalistic political culture had become so dominant in Mississippi that its vision of history even pervaded textbooks written by college professors. One prominent textbook cited the positive points about slavery: "In most cases public opinion and state law assured the slave of good treatment. . . . prevailing sentiment was inclined toward lenient treatment of slaves. . . . Usually the planter took a keen interest in his slaves, ministering to both their spiritual and their physical needs." This book decried the financial ruin caused by the Civil War by "the wiping out of a tremendous amount of property in slaves," each worth about $2,000.[19] The 1860 federal census had listed Mississippi as the fifth wealthiest state in the nation, but from 1870 on the state fell to the bottom.

Mississippi textbooks also attacked the Reconstruction legislature: "It did more to increase the state debt than to solve postwar problems. . . . Soon taxes began to skyrocket." One book summarizes Reconstruction as "Carpetbag and Negro rule" and describes conservative redemption in a section titled "The White Man Fights Back." The text continues, "After 1875, the old bitterness began to wane. Mississippi was back under the control of the white people, the Redeemers." With the departure of many carpetbaggers and Republicans, "it was Mississippi for the Mississippians from now on."[20]

SEGREGATION AND DISFRANCHISEMENT

In the closing years of the nineteenth century, racial segregation and white supremacy arose in Mississippi and other southern states. In 1888 racially segregated accommodations on railroads were required by the Mississippi legislature. By 1890 most cities had a dual cemetery policy, and parks, playgrounds, streetcars, waiting rooms, and elevators were racially segregated. Segregation in schools continued, and separation in churches intensified. As with poor whites, most blacks found themselves bound by the crop lien system to the oppressive yoke of sharecropping. White supremacy was ultimately enforced by lynching, in which local whites at times took the law into their own hands when dealing with blacks who had allegedly committed violent crimes against whites. Between the years 1882 and 1952, 534 blacks were lynched in Mississippi, more than in any other state.[21]

By 1890 many political leaders wanted a new constitution to replace the one written by the old Reconstruction government in 1869. Many white Mississippians, including the Populists, desired the "legal" disfranchisement of blacks for various reasons. Some felt that white Mississippians would never be free to divide on important economic and political issues as long as the presence of black voters encouraged white unity.

United States senator James Z. George, a former chief justice of the state supreme court and the most influential member of the 1890 constitutional convention's Committee on Suffrage and Elections, reflected the mood of most white Mississippians. On one occasion he was quoted as saying: "Our chief duty when we meet in Convention, is to devise such measures, consistent with the Constitution of the United States, as will enable us to maintain a home government, under the control of the white people of the State." Another time George argued that the black race was under the protection of whites: "Its incapacity must be guarded and its civil and political rights neither denied nor abridged, but white predominance must be secured in order that good government may be maintained."[22]

Convention delegate J. J. Chrisman urged disfranchisement as a "good government" move: "It is no secret that there has not been a fair count in Mississippi since 1875, that we have been preserving the ascendancy of the white people by revolutionary methods. In other words, we have been stuffing ballot boxes, committing perjury, and here and there in the state carrying the election by fraud and violence until the whole machinery for elections is about to rot down. No man can be in favor of perpetuating the election methods which have prevailed in Mississippi since 1875 who is not a moral idiot."[23]

The constitution of 1890 instituted stricter requirements for voting, such as a two-year state and one-year electoral district residency requirement, registration four months before the election, and a two-dollar poll tax payable two years before the election year. Voters would now be required to read any section of the state constitution or to be able to "understand" it when it was read to them or to give a "reasonable interpretation" of it. When some delegates expressed concern that this literacy and interpretation clause would disfranchise poor whites, others responded that it would be enforced only against blacks.[24]

The implementation of the 1890 constitution did indeed disfranchise some poor whites, but blacks were especially affected. Only 8,600 of 147,000 eligible blacks were registered in 1892. Among whites, 120,000 had been qualified to vote in 1890, but only 68,000 were registered in 1892. Whereas the poll tax helped disfranchise people of both races for financial reasons, especially during the difficult economic times of the 1890s, the literacy test was administered in an unequal manner to disfranchise primarily blacks.[25] The white elite in Mississippi had succeeded in limiting mass participation in politics. Indeed, as late as 1964 only 7 percent of blacks of voting age were registered to vote.

THE HILLS VERSUS THE DELTA

With the disfranchisement of most blacks, political divisions in the first half of the twentieth century in Mississippi often occurred over economic issues. Such cleavages often separated the more prosperous Mississippi Delta region from the poor Hills and Piney Woods areas.

Rich Delta planters like Senator LeRoy Percy often embodied the qualities felt desirable in aristocrats, such as honor, dignity, and fair dealing. Consequently the Delta often selected very able leaders who represented them effectively in the legislature. Politically, the Delta tended to be conservative on economic issues, opposing the New Deal welfare state as an infringement on states' rights and a destroyer of individual initiative. Although Delta whites supported segregation and disfranchisement, their paternalistic orientation led them to back improved health care and education for blacks, and their aristocratic characteristics led them to frown on campaigns based on racist demagoguery.[26]

In the late 1800s the Hills and the Piney Woods regions, dominated by poor whites, had become centers of agrarian discontent in which the Greenback, Grange, Alliance, and Populist movements grew. Shortly after the turn of the century, "neopopulist" candidates arose who adopted many of the old Populist themes. Neopopulist attacks on "predatory corporations," coupled with demands for reduction in interest rates and equalization of tax assessments, proved politically popular among poor white "peckerwoods" farmers.[27] New Deal–style programs such as social security and public assistance were applauded because they benefited lower-income whites. On the race issue, however, Hill whites often found racist rhetoric appealing, and they resented the allegedly better living conditions of black tenant farmers in the Delta compared with the lives of Hill whites. The Hills also tended to support Prohibition, while the Delta opposed it.[28]

Some early neopopulists, such as Governor James Vardaman, employed blatant and graphic racist rhetoric to attract the red clay Hill farmers. During the 1903 gubernatorial race, Vardaman, in a speech delivered in Columbus, was quoted as saying that the Declaration of Independence did not apply to "wild animals and niggers." On another occasion he accused the black of being "a lazy, lying, lustful animal which no amount of training can transform into a tolerable citizen." His nature, said Vardaman, was unlike the white man's, but "resembles the hog's." Regarding the black man's alleged lust for white women, he said, "We would be justified in slaughtering every Ethiop on the earth to preserve unsullied the honor of one Caucasian home. . . . We do not stop when we see a wolf to find if it will kill sheep before disposing of it, but assume that it will." Vardaman, who became known as the "Great White Chief," declared in reference to voting rights for blacks that there was "nothing in his individual character, nothing in his achievements of the past nor his promise of the future" that would entitle him "to stand, side by side with the white man at the ballot box."[29]

The animosity between these two regions was illustrated by the battle between Delta planter LeRoy Percy and Hill neopopulist James Vardaman for the United States Senate in 1910 and 1911. After the legislature selected Percy over Vardaman for the Senate seat in 1910, one of Vardaman's legislative supporters, Theodore "The Man" Bilbo, charged that he had been offered a bribe to vote for Percy. The legislature promptly denounced Bilbo after it was discovered that the bills he offered as evidence had been printed after the day he claimed he had accepted them as a bribe. Bilbo refused to resign from the legislature and proceeded to build a political career based on his alleged persecution by political opponents. In one campaign he received a scar from being hit over the head with a pistol butt by a political opponent whom he had described as "a cross between a hyena and a mongrel . . . begotten in a nigger graveyard at midnight, suckled by a sow, and educated by a fool."[30]

In a Democratic primary election in 1911, Vardaman was able to unseat Percy, and political power continued to shift away from the aristocratic Delta to the neopopulist Hills. The description of a campaign crowd in the Hills by Senator Percy's son illustrates the stylistic and class divisions that permeated Mississippi politics. "I looked over the ill-dressed, surly audience, unintelligent and slinking. . . . They were the sort of people that lynch Negroes, that mistake hoodlumism for wit, and cunning for intelligence, that attend revivals and fight and fornicate in the bushes afterward. They were undiluted Anglo-Saxons."[31]

Yet despite the racist demagoguery, neopopulists like Vardaman and Bilbo often pursued nonracist, progressive policies once in office. As governor, Vardaman significantly increased funding for education and teachers' salaries, indirectly helping blacks as well as whites. He created a state textbook commission and instituted competitive bidding. Vardaman also increased state regulation of insurance companies, railroads, banks, and utilities (which some believe may have unwittingly slowed the pace of economic development in Mississippi). He also ended convict leasing, improved conditions at the state prison, and fought for child-labor laws. Bilbo, as governor, established a state tuberculosis hospital, industrial schools, and a state commission for the blind, and he supported malaria control and the consolidation of rural schools.[32]

Therefore, despite the closed nature of Mississippi's traditionalistic society, in the first four decades of this century the state responded to some extent to the progressive movement that swept across the nation. With the "race issue" settled by Jim Crow laws, the fundamental economic cleavages within the white community resurfaced. The neopopulist movement arose with Vardaman's candidacy and was crystallized into a distinct voting bloc by Bilbo. It attracted large numbers of poor, uneducated "rednecks" who provided the votes to elect five neopopulist governors between 1903 and 1939.[33] The numerous progressive measures in the areas of education, health, labor, business, and agriculture that were adopted between 1908 and 1920 led some observers to conclude that this period was the most constructive in Mississippi history. One author concludes that the progressive movement was important in helping the state move forward by "battering down some of the bulwarks of conservatism in an agricultural state which had become static."[34] Although the success of Mississippi's neopopulists never quite reached the level found in Georgia, candidates representing the interests of the poor, "peckerwoods" populations in the Hills exercised more influence in state government than their counterparts in Alabama, Arkansas, Louisiana, or Texas.

THE STRUGGLE OVER MODERNIZATION

Throughout the twentieth century, Mississippi has had to struggle against its traditionalistic culture based on an agricultural economy to introduce a more industrialized base and progressive social change. That struggle continues today.

Some political observers feel that the constitution of 1890 has been a key impediment to economic development in Mississippi. They acknowledge that the constitution initially addressed the "populist" concerns of white eastern Hill farmers about business abuses, such as permanent business tax exemptions, city bonds to finance business construction that never took place, management abuse of railroad workers, and discriminatory utility rates. "The difficulty was that much specific, detailed language, which is in tone hostile to business, remained in the constitution after the problems of the 1880s were largely ended. Several recent students of the subject have concluded that the constitution's corporations article is at least outdated and, because of its anti-business timbre, may well have hampered the state's industrial development efforts."[35]

The system of higher education has occasionally been hurt by the forces of reaction. In 1930 Governor Bilbo, a great supporter of the "spoils system," gained control over the Board of Trustees of Higher Learning by appointing new members. He engineered the firing of 179 faculty and staff members who had opposed him politically, such as in his effort to consolidate the universities in the state into one location (the state capital, Jackson). Accrediting agencies suspended many of the universities until the succeeding governor, Mike Conner, reformed the board of trustees to provide staggered terms for members, which would make it impossible for one governor to gain control of the board. Higher education was also hurt by the Great Depression, which caused such a decrease in state funding that it was not until the 1946–47 fiscal year that state appropriations for higher education reached the level of 1930–31.[36]

From the initial speculative boom in the 1830s until the 1930s, Mississippi "was like one great cotton plantation."[37] The antebellum slave system and its successor, tenant farming, led to extreme income inequality. The state's only other economic resource—its immense pine forests—was decimated by outside lumber companies by the 1920s. Because of this dependence on one crop, Mississippi's economy "was like an underdeveloped Latin country."[38] In 1930 and 1931 cotton prices collapsed, and in 1932 mortgages were foreclosed on one in every ten farms. "On a single day in April 1932, one-fourth of the land area of Mississippi was auctioned for unpaid taxes."[39] Disaster finally provoked action to diversify agriculture and industrialize the economy.

To cope with plunging government revenues during the Great Depression, Governor Conner demonstrated great political courage in leading Mississippi to become the first state to institute a sales tax. At one point sales tax opponents, after a protest meeting of five thousand people, had even filled the corridor outside the governor's office. One protester had to be disarmed after pulling a pistol from his belt, pointing it at the governor's door, and yelling, "Stand back. I'm coming in." Since the state at that time was heavily dependent on the property tax, some proponents felt that the sales tax would be the most effective means to make blacks and poor whites pay taxes. The new sales tax broadened the tax base by requiring those who were not property owners to help pay the costs of government services.[40]

Hugh White, who became governor in 1936, instituted a major program to attract industry to Mississippi, which was called B A W I (Balance Agriculture with Industry). This program, viewed as "the keystone to 20th century industrial development efforts," helped attract outside capital, industry, and jobs to Mississippi with promises of locally financed factory construction and tax exemptions.[41] In the face of widespread public support for the B A W I program, section 183 of the state constitution, which prohibited such government aid to businesses, was essentially ignored. In the first five years, twelve plants were set up under B A W I-approved bonds, including Ingalls shipyard at Pascagoula, though most were garment plants. The wartime boom in manufacturing caused a de-emphasis on the B A W I program, but it was revived after the war. By 1958 the program had sponsored a total of 188 industrial projects, including 141 new industries and 47 plant expansions.[42] B A W I's success in luring manufacturing to the state also meant an influx of "Yankees," and some towns, such as Tupelo, even began to incorporate these "outsiders" into their leadership.

The B A W I effort may have reinforced the traditionalistic culture of the state by perpetuating the antiunion sentiment among political leaders. Many political leaders felt that businesses would be attracted to the state because of the cheap labor made possible by the weakness of labor unions. Labor leaders charged that antiunion sentiment was especially great in north Mississippi (north of Jackson, Vicksburg, and Meridian). Most firms attracted to Mississippi under the BAWI plan were apparel, textile, and furniture firms—low-wage industries that have long resisted unions. Mississippi's antiunion orientation was also reflected in the way state courts routinely granted injunctions against picketing and other union activities and in the passage of a 1954 right-to-work law. The political culture of the state has hindered the growth of labor unions. The focus on low-wage industries and the underfunding of education have limited Mississippi's ability to attract more high-technology industries that provide higher salaries.[43]

Tractors replaced mules in the 1920s, and mechanical cotton pickers replaced uneducated field hands in the late 1940s and 1950s. Although small numbers of blacks had left the state during World War I, approximately 300,000 blacks (and 100,000 whites) moved north to take jobs in the war industries during World War II. Many of the blacks who remained in Mississippi had few skills to survive in the state's emerging industrial sector. In the face of limited economic opportunities and of racial discrimination, the exodus of blacks to the North persisted until the 1970s. Blacks, who in 1900 had composed 58.5 percent of Mississippi's population, decreased to 49.2 percent of Mississippians in 1940 and 36.8 percent in 1970.[44]

Until the late 1960s the leadership of the city of Jackson preferred not to recruit outside industry because new factories might bring about unionization of the work force. Other Mississippi communities into the 1970s focused their economic development campaigns on business activities that would not employ large numbers of semiskilled or unskilled laborers. These smaller communities were afraid of two possibilities: the in-migration of outsiders and the movement of local blacks away from traditional occupations that kept them dependent on the local white establishment.[45]

A number of programs and agencies have helped to modernize the state. Free textbooks, increased funding for the aged, a state retirement system, a community hospital program, a quadrupling of the miles of paved highways, and the Jackson medical school were achieved by governors in the 1940s and 1950s. Mississippi established an impressive Research and Development Center in Jackson, which began to serve as a major force for change and economic development. The pace of progressive change has continued into the 1980s and even accelerated. Landmark programs like the Education Reform Act that significantly improved the public schools continue to transform the state's socioeconomic character.[46]

THE CIVIL RIGHTS STRUGGLE

The Civil Rights movement, which culminated in laws requiring desegregation and the enfranchisement of blacks, struck a major blow against Mississippi's traditionalistic political culture. With the United States Voting Rights Act of 1965, the political system opened up and black voter turnout soared. The increased power of blacks and other liberal groups encouraged the implementation of more progressive public policies. As blacks became heavily involved in the Democratic party, many conservative whites fled to the fledgling Republican party, stimulating two party competition in the state.

President Harry S. Truman's actions to secure basic civil rights for black Americans returned race to the forefront of Mississippi's politics. Governor Fielding Wright put the authority of state government behind the defense of white supremacy in his 1948 inaugural address when he declared, "Vital principles and eternal truths transcend party lines and the day is now at hand when determined action must be taken."[47] The explosion of racial animosity eclipsed the class-based battles between the Delta planters and the "rednecks" in the Hills and Piney Woods. Elections throughout the 1950s and 1960s became contests by candidates to establish themselves as the staunchest defenders of segregation.

In the 1954 *Brown v. Topeka Board of Education* decision, the United States Supreme Court declared segregated public schools to be inherently unequal and therefore unconstitutional. More than any previous step taken by the federal government, *Brown* stirred white supremacists into a frenzy. United States senator James Eastland accused the Court of "a monstrous crime. . . . The antisegregation decisions are dishonest decisions. . . . The judges who rendered them violated their oaths of office. They have disgraced the high office which they hold." He accused sociologists cited in the case of being "agitators who are part and parcel of the Communist conspiracy to destroy our country." In a more restrained vein, Governor Hugh White pledged resistance by "every legal means at our command."[48]

As segregation came under attack, Robert Patterson and thirteen other white businessmen in Indianola formed the first white Citizens' Council, which became a white-collar version of the Klan.[49] The N A A C P petition movement requesting school integration in five towns was destroyed after the names of signers were published and many of them lost their jobs, were refused credit, and sometimes were forced to leave town. A few white Mississippians resisted the Citizens' Councils, such as Hodding Carter, editor of the Greenville *Delta Democrat-Times*. (His son would serve as State Department spokesman under President Carter.) After writing an article titled "A

Wave of Terror Threatens the South," Carter was censured by the Mississippi House of Representatives on an 89–19 vote for "selling out the state for Yankee gold." Carter responded by writing: "I herewith resolve by a vote of 1 to 0 that there are 89 liars in the State Legislature. . . . those 89 character mobbers can go to hell collectively or singly and wait there until I back down."[50]

The Citizens' Councils, which spread from Mississippi to several other southern states, were "a counter-movement, a mobilization of individuals and groups who felt threatened by change."[51] Members of the councils believed that only mass action and total control could stop the subversion of Mississippi's traditional way of life. Local councils distributed segregationist literature, organized "Minute Men" to stage protests, published lists of blacks who engaged in any form of political activity, kept blacklists of professors sympathetic to integration, and orchestrated economic and social pressure aimed at driving black activists out of town and out of the state.[52] The Citizens' Councils gained access to the finances and police power of state government through their ties with the State Sovereignty Commission, an administrative agency charged with preserving segregation and equipped with investigators who could probe "subversive activities."[53] Working together, the Sovereignty Commission and the Citizens' Councils "created a climate of fear that has straight-jacketed the white community in a thought control enforced by financial sanctions, and has undone most of the improvements in race relations made over the last 30 years."[54]

In 1961 the hysteria turned into violent rage, as the Student Nonviolent Coordinating Committee (SNCC) began its voter registration drive in McComb. Beatings, bombings, and the murder of Herbert Lee in Amite County formed the white response to black demands for equal suffrage. Robert Moses, Dave Dennis, E. W. Steptoe, and Robert Zellner became legends among civil rights advocates for their determined stand in McComb. Similar events also took place in the Delta, where Fannie Lou Hamer, Lawrence Guyot, Aaron Henry, and Amzie Moore led voter education projects. Civil rights workers suffered physical attacks by "nightriders" and by state and local authorities. In some communities, white leadership stopped the distribution of federal government surplus food in an effort to pressure local blacks into resisting the appeals of "outside agitators."[55]

The hysteria reached a peak when a black former serviceman, James Meredith, attempted in 1962 to integrate the University of Mississippi (Ole Miss). Despite a court order requiring Meredith's admission, Governor Ross Barnett publicly pledged never "to surrender to the evil and illegal forces of tyranny." In mid-September Governor Barnett invoked the pre–Civil War doctrine of interposition as a means of blocking Meredith's entry into Ole Miss, and during the last two weeks of September, Mississippi officials successfully thwarted federal efforts to enroll him on four occasions.

Before one of the confrontations, Attorney General Robert Kennedy and Governor Barnett made an effort to effect a symbolic surrender in which federal marshals would level their guns at the governor and he would step aside. Such a "heroic" capitulation, it was hoped, would conciliate white public opinion in the state that overwhelmingly supported resistance. An argument soon developed between Barnett and Kennedy over whether the chief marshal or all of the marshals should draw their weapons. Eventually the plan was canceled out of fear that it might trigger a shoot-out at the university between federal and state authorities.[56]

By late September, with large numbers of federal forces moving into the state to secure Meredith's entry and the threat of major bloodshed increasing by the hour, Governor Barnett capitulated and permitted Meredith to be brought onto campus by federal marshals for enrollment. Other elements affecting Barnett's decision could have been his upcoming contempt trial in federal court for defying a court order requiring Meredith's admission and a threat by Robert Kennedy to make public their earlier negotiations.[57]

With Meredith's arrival at Ole Miss, a full-scale riot occurred, as white students and nonstudents threw rocks, bottles, and broken pipes at the marshals, fired guns, and overturned and burned cars and trucks. There were 160 federal marshals injured, 28 of them shot. Two bystanders, including a French journalist, were killed. President John F. Kennedy dispatched more than six thousand United States Army troops to help restore order. Peace and integration had finally come to Ole Miss.[58]

As black citizens continued to demand equal rights, white rage continued unabated. In 1963 the best-known black leader in Mississippi, state NAACP field secretary Medgar Evers, was ambushed and killed in his driveway in Jackson. Three civil rights workers, two of them white, disappeared in Neshoba County. Eventually their bodies were found buried under eighteen feet of clay. (A controversial movie released in 1988, *Mississippi Burning*, was based on this incident.) In summer 1964 "whites burned 37 black churches, bombed 30 homes, beat more than 80 civil rights workers, and made more than 1,000 arrests."[59] The Mississippi Ku Klux Klan promoted violence against blacks and fanned the flames of religious fanaticism and superpatriotism. Klan members argued that they were fighting communism and that the Red conspiracy included civil rights leaders, Jews, and the federal government.[60] National television broadcast pictures of the violence directed against blacks living in the South, and an aroused American public pushed Congress to enact the 1964 Civil Rights Act, outlawing racial discrimination in public accommodations, and the 1965 Voting Rights Act.

The violence did not deter Mississippi blacks from their quest for equal rights. A coalition of civil rights organizations in 1964 formed the Mississippi Freedom Democratic party and challenged the credentials of the all-white Mississippi "regular" Democratic delegation to the national party convention. A compromise devised by the national party was rejected by both sides. At that convention Fannie Lou Hamer raised the conscience of the nation by relating how she had been beaten by officials for trying to integrate a Winona bus station. By 1968 Freedom Democrats, more moderate blacks, liberal whites, and organized labor formed a "loyalist" coalition, loyal to the "national" Democratic party. The "loyalists" were successful in convincing the national Democratic conventions in 1968 and 1972 to seat them in place of the "regulars," because of widespread irregularities in the delegate selection process the regulars employed.[61]

Gradually, whites' attitudes began to change, and they started to accept the inevitability of integration. In 1963 the traditionally white land-grant institution, Mississippi State University, represented the Southeastern Conference in the NCAA basketball tournament despite the presence of integrated opposing teams.[62] Twenty-eight Methodist ministers spoke out against racial injustice, as did the First Baptist Church in Biloxi. Claude Ramsay, head of the state AFL-CIO, fought racial discrimination, and more and more newspapers argued for racial understanding.[63]

By 1965 the business community had become fearful that Mississippi's tarnished image would hinder economic development. An Ohio industrialist had refused to expand two Mississippi plants until the state "decides to become a part of the Union again." The Mississippi Economic Council urged compliance with federal law and support for public schools. Other business groups, including the Mississippi Manufacturers Association, endorsed this statement.[64] Paradoxically, the business community, which originally supported the Citizens' Councils and the Klan in their brutal defense of segregation, became the pivotal force in ending the violence. Economic realism, not moral outrage, convinced Mississippi's economic elites that the costs of segregation were too high. Once this realism was accepted, the violence against blacks stopped within a year.

MISSISSIPPI JOINS THE NEW SOUTH

Owing to the efforts of the federal government and the people of Mississippi, the state today possesses a substantially integrated society. The percentage of blacks attending integrated public schools is higher than in some northern states like New York and Illinois.[65] The percentage of eligible blacks registered to vote rose dramatically, from 7 percent in 1965 to 68 percent in 1970, and has remained significant. In 1976 Governor Cliff Finch was successful in unifying the loyalist and regular factions of the Democratic party and sending one delegation to the national convention. At the 1984 state Democratic convention, nearly half of the delegates were black. By 1987 twenty blacks sat in the state legislature, chairing important committees such as the House Education Committee, and a black represented Mississippi in the United States Congress (Mike Espy, representing the second "Delta" district). Change was even evident in the social arena, as blacks were selected for the titles of Miss Mississippi and Mrs. Mississippi.

An important source of progressive change in the state's political and social culture has been its youth. Symbolic of this generational change, in 1989 two black students, Steven Cooper and Kelvin Covington, were elected president and vice president of the student body at Mississippi State University, the largest university in the state, with a black enrollment of about 12 percent. They became the first blacks ever elected as student body leaders at one of Mississippi's traditionally white universities. In 1990 Kelvin Covington succeeded Cooper as the elected president of the student body.

Freed from racial violence, Mississippi joined the "New South." Through the 1970s, Mississippi rode the rising tide of the Sunbelt's "economic miracle." At mid-decade, average per capita income reached 86 percent of the southern average and 69 percent of the national average. By 1978 manufacturing jobs reached an all time high of 235,300, and the service sector was expanding rapidly.[66] Rural counties relying on agriculture experienced population out-migrations as Mississippians moved to the boom areas of Jackson, the Gulf Coast, the Tupelo-Columbus corridor, and the Memphis suburbs. Even the galloping inflation of the late 1970s did not dampen the boom.

After a decade of rapid economic improvements, the Sunbelt bubble burst, with serious consequences for Mississippi. The 1981–82 recession hit hard, and manufacturing jobs declined by over 15 percent.[67] The state's famous cheap labor could no longer save the economy as corporations moved factories overseas to take advantage of even cheaper labor. At the same time, federal cuts in real spending on welfare programs had a devastating impact on the state's poor, especially the working poor. Millions of federal dollars and the accompanying multiplier effect they generated disappeared.[68] With unemployment on the rise, state government revenues plummeted, throwing state government into a protracted budget crisis. Whereas the nation underwent sustained economic growth after the recession, Mississippi remained mired in economic stagnation throughout the 1980s. The combination of declining agricultural prices, falling energy prices, and the movement of many low-skill manufacturing jobs overseas slowed the state's economic recovery and demonstrated the need for a more diversified economy. State politics in the 1980s revolved around various proposals and strategies to end the fiscal crisis and to restart the state's economic engine. Without the likelihood of significant aid from Washington, state leaders were forced to look seriously at homegrown resources. Although a generational change occurred in political leadership in the postsegregation period, the battle lines over public policy remain strikingly familiar: traditionalists versus modernizers.

CHAPTER THREE

The Enduring Traditions of the State Constitutions

Tip H. Allen, Jr.

*Powerful political interests in the state have refused to allow the con-
stitution to be revised and modernized and their power thereby to be
threatened. Until there is sufficient force behind an effort for general
governmental reform, the state will have to continue in the posture of
fighting the evils of the 1880s and contributing to the evils of the
1980s.*

Eric C. Clark, state representative, 1986[1]

A constitution is a higher law that defines and limits the powers of government. The concept of constitutionalism is anchored in the theory of Aristo-
tle, who noted that "surely the ruler cannot dispense with general principles
that exist in law, for the rule of law is preferable to that of any individual."[2]
Since statehood, Mississippi has had four constitutions—the constitutions
of 1817, 1832, 1869, and 1890. The state's constitutional development illustrates how forces seeking to maintain the status quo have opposed those en-
deavoring to secure changes in the political system. This persistent struggle
between opposing political forces illustrates various aspects of the traditionalistic culture of Mississippi.

THE CONSTITUTION OF 1817: THE DOCUMENT OF STATEHOOD

In 1798 Congress created the Mississippi Territory, and it enlarged the area in
1804 to include most of the land comprising the present states of Alabama
and Mississippi. As the movement for statehood intensified, southern congressmen fought to divide the territory into two states to strengthen the re-

gion's power in the Senate. On March 1, 1817, President James Monroe signed the enabling act providing for the admission of the western section of the territory as the state of Mississippi and reorganizing the eastern part as the Alabama Territory.

Mississippi's first constitutional convention convened at the town of Washington in Adams County in early July 1817. Meeting in a brick Methodist church, the convention lasted six weeks. A majority of the forty-eight delegates were elected from the wealthy river counties south of Vicksburg, where the state's traditionalistic culture originated. The rest of the delegates represented the "Piney Woods" counties to the east. Reflecting the hierarchical structure of a traditionalistic political culture, most of the delegates were from the higher socioeconomic stratum. Even the poorer Piney Woods areas elected a number of men of property.[3]

The constitution framed in 1817 is a brief and uncomplicated document of eighteen pages.[4] It established a weak chief executive, reflecting the prevailing sentiment in the newly independent nation of suspicion toward a powerful executive. Mississippians still remembered their nation's bitter conflicts with the British king and colonial governors, as well as their own recent feuds with territorial governors. The governor was given little control over the administrative structure. All major state officials, except the popularly elected governor and lieutenant governor, were to be chosen by the legislature. Governors were saddled with two-year terms but could serve as many terms as the people desired.

Reflecting the constitutions of the federal government and most states, the legislature was bicameral (with two houses or chambers) and clearly the most powerful of the three branches of government. Known as the General Assembly, it selected members of the judicial branch in addition to the key administrative officials of the executive branch. Judges would serve until age sixty-five on condition they maintained good behavior. Sessions of the General Assembly were to be annual, with senators serving three year terms and representatives one-year terms.

Suffrage provisions in the constitution were fairly liberal for the period. All white males twenty-one or older who paid a state or county tax or had enrolled in the militia were eligible to vote. Although there were no property qualifications for voting, the governor and members of the General Assembly were required to meet certain property standards to hold office. Despite a religious test for officeholding, ministers of the gospel were prohibited from serving in public posts lest such service interfere with their pastoral duties.

The 1817 constitution was one of compromise between liberal and conservative elements, with the conservative forces in the wealthy western counties dominating, according to one scholar.[5] The convention made no provision for submitting the constitution to a popular vote.[6] Once in operation, it could be amended only by calling a constitutional convention. Such a convention required a two-thirds vote of the General Assembly and approval by a majority of voters in a public referendum. Congress approved the constitution, and Mississippi achieved statehood on December 10, 1817. An interesting footnote is that only six votes in the 1817 convention kept the new state from being named Washington rather than Mississippi.[7]

THE CONSTITUTION OF 1832:
IMPLEMENTING JACKSONIAN DEMOCRACY

Whereas the constitution of 1817 was basically a conservative document, the 1832 constitution was a product of the democratic theme in America that is often referred to as Jacksonian democracy, which emphasized greater popular participation in and control over the political process. It was established after a political struggle in which the traditionalistic leaders in the state sought to maintain their political power by opposing a new constitution.

Demand for constitutional reform during the late 1820s and early 1830s was generated by a strong public desire for a more direct involvement in government. At every session of the General Assembly between 1825 and 1830, lawmakers from the more recently settled areas of the state pushed for a convention referendum, but the older river counties, fearing a loss of power, were able to deny the two-thirds majority. In the 1830 session, many legislators from the river counties reversed themselves and supported an immediate public referendum. They feared that a convention would eventually be held and thought it was to their advantage to convene it before newly acquired Indian lands could be organized into counties. Many were concerned that the establishment of additional counties would produce an even more democratic convention. Mississippians overwhelmingly approved the convention referendum in the 1831 general election.

Forty-six delegates to the constitutional convention convened in Jackson in September 1832 in the small two-story state capitol on the corner of Capitol and President streets. After six weeks of work, they replaced the conservative constitution of 1817 with an eighteen page document permeated with Jacksonian ideas. For example, all constitutional officials formerly chosen by the legislature were now to be elected by the people. The property qualifications for holding office and the taxpaying or military service requirement for voting were eliminated. Reflecting the Jacksonian idea of rotation in office, the governor was limited to two terms of two years in any six-year period. In general, the chief executive remained weak under the new constitution.

A heated debate ensued over how judges should be selected. Delegates preferring the current appointment system were labeled "aristocrats." Those who favored electing some of them were called "half-hogs," and those who urged electing all judges were "whole hogs." Mississippi became the first state to provide for the popular election of all judges, and by 1861 all the states had followed its example.[8] Other significant changes in the 1832 constitution were provisions for legislative amendment of the document, establishing biennial legislative sessions, extending senators' terms to four years and representatives' terms to two, eliminating the office of lieutenant governor, and dropping the term General Assembly for the legislature.

The divisions at the 1832 convention were largely sectional, mirroring the patterns at the 1817 convention. The river counties and adjacent counties that constituted the base of the state's traditionalistic culture generally sought to preserve the status quo, while the more recently settled areas to the east and north worked for reform. This time, the delegates from the developing regions dominated the convention and framed a democratic constitution. But once again, a convention refused to submit its constitution to popular ratification.[9]

THE CONSTITUTION OF 1869: A LEGACY OF DEFEAT

Mississippi's constitution of 1869 was born of military defeat, while Mississippi was part of a military district under the supervision of General Edward Ord. General Ord called for a convention that would write a new constitution, guaranteeing the civil rights of freed blacks and meeting Congress's requirements for the state's restoration into the Union. Black participation in the process leading to the convention was very high, while white Democratic involvement was low owing to disfranchisement and discontent. Hence seventy-nine of the ninety-seven delegates elected to the convention were Republicans, and they constituted the core of the radical faction. Eighteen delegates were black, and so the meeting was labeled the "Black and Tan Convention." A former brigadier general of the Union army, Beroth B. Eggleston, was elected president, and he appointed members from the radical faction to chair the major committees. Compared with the six-week duration of the previous conventions, the 1868 gathering that assembled at the "old"

capitol in Jackson in January lasted 114 days and eventually framed a constitution of twenty-four pages.[10]

The sharpest controversy at the convention was not over enfranchising
blacks but over "proscriptive clauses" pertaining to former white voters and
officeholders. These clauses banned former Confederate military officers
and public officials from holding office and made it difficult for many former
white voters to register. The proposed constitution therefore constituted a
major threat to the state's traditionalistic and hierarchic political order, since
groups at the bottom of the social order, such as blacks, would be elevated
while groups at the top would lose political power. The controversial "proscriptive clauses" led to the constitution's defeat in a popular referendum, so
they were separated from the rest of the constitution. In a second referendum, the constitution was easily approved, but the "proscriptive clauses"
were defeated.[11] Supporters of the state's traditionalistic order had been dealt
a setback but not a fatal blow, and their persistent efforts to regain power
would culminate in the reestablishment of white conservative Democratic
party dominance at the conclusion of Reconstruction.

In addition to revisions of the franchise and political rights, the document
included other significant reforms. The governor's term was extended to
four years with no limitation on succession. He was also given the authority
to appoint judges with the consent of the senate, thus eliminating the elective
judiciary of the 1832 constitution. The office of lieutenant governor was
reestablished, and a chancery court was set up in each county. The framers
went back to the arrangement of the 1817 constitution and provided for annual sessions of the legislature. One innovation was the provision for a free
public school system, and the article on education provided the framework
for the public schools that has endured to the present. A poll tax was first introduced to Mississippi by the "Black and Tan Constitution." It was used to
support education and was not linked to the franchise.[12]

THE CONSTITUTION OF 1890: TODAY'S BASIC LAW

Shortly after conservative white Democrats regained control of state government in 1876, many Mississippians urged replacing the "Black and Tan
Constitution." A number of factors relating to the state's traditionalistic political culture played a role in the struggle for constitutional revision. Many
whites felt that the 1869 document was tainted because it had been framed in
a convention called by the federal military authorities and operating outside
the control of most white Mississippians. The poor Hill farmers thought that

a new constitution would enable them to unseat conservative Democratic leaders who had controlled state government since the end of Reconstruction. Agrarian groups also believed a new basic law would curb the power of corporations that hurt farming interests. The principal force behind constitutional revision, however, was the desire of whites to guarantee continued white Democratic control of Mississippi.

Efforts by legislators from majority white counties to call a constitutional convention failed in 1886 and 1888. Legislative opposition was centered in the more traditionalistic counties in the Delta and Natchez regions, which had black population majorities that were nevertheless largely under white political control. Convention opponents felt that the black vote was already being controlled by intimidation and fusion. Fusion was a practice whereby blacks would support continued white political control in return for black representation in a few local offices and sometimes one of the county's seats in the legislature. These conservative whites feared that legal disfranchisement of blacks would invite federal intervention into Mississippi politics. Conservatives had also grown accustomed to countering reform movements among Hill whites by raising the threat of the black vote becoming an independent political force. Such a threat typically led whites to unify behind continued conservative control of state government. Finally, conservatives feared that agrarian interests might radicalize an unlimited convention.

White counties in the legislature finally succeeded in calling a convention in 1890, as black counties became more supportive of constitutional reform. Black county support grew after the United States Senate passed the Lodge Force bill, which raised the threat of federal intervention in southern elections. Many conservative Democrats had also grown tired of electoral fraud used to control the black vote and preferred the "legal" disfranchisement of blacks. Meanwhile, white county support for a convention declined somewhat. Some Hill legislators feared that possible educational requirements in a new constitution would exclude many poor whites as well as blacks from voting.

Unlike the 1868 convention, Democrats dominated the 1890 convention, with 130 of the 134 delegates. The lone Republican was a black man, Isaiah Montgomery. He was a businessman and planter, founder of the all-black community of Mound Bayou. United States senator James Z. George, a progressive thinker known as "the Commoner" among his agrarian supporters, exerted the most influence over the new constitution.[13] Judge Solomon S. Calhoun, a former Confederate officer, was elected president of the convention, which assembled at the "old" capitol in Jackson on August 12, 1890.

Other notables included the president of Mississippi A&M College, Stephen D. Lee, and the chancellor of the University of Mississippi, Edward Mayes.

Unity among the delegates on the need to remove blacks from the political arena was reflected in the headline of the *Memphis Appeal* on August 26, 1890: "White Supremacy—The One Idea of the Convention." At that time Mississippi had a black population of 57.9 percent, with thirty-nine of its seventy-five counties containing black majorities. The convention passed an "understanding clause" whereby voters would be required "to be able to read any section of the Constitution of this State; or he shall be able to understand the same when read to him, or give a reasonable interpretation thereof." Opposition to the clause centered on many delegates from white counties who feared it would make illiterate whites ineligible to vote. Also, some delegates from black counties wanted to go further and require ownership of property. Middle-of-the-roaders from both groups of counties supported the understanding clause, believing that it would withstand legal challenges based on the Fourteenth and Fifteenth Amendments.[14] Subsequent statutes provided for the literacy requirement to be administered and evaluated by a county's circuit clerk. Isaiah Montgomery, the sole black delegate, acquiesced to the inevitable on the "understanding clause." He pointed out that the clause was "apparently one of unfriendliness" to his race but stated that he felt it would be in the interest of blacks and whites for illiterates to be eliminated from the electorate.[15]

Other restrictions on suffrage included longer residency requirements and the payment of a poll tax. To further reduce the possibility of black political power, the state was divided into three grand divisions for legislative apportionment, with equal representation in the house from each division. Two of these sections had majority white populations, while the Delta division had a heavy black majority. An electoral college system, designed to maintain political control by the white counties, was established for electing the governor and other constitutional officials. Though these franchise sections disfranchised most Mississippi blacks, as discussed in the previous chapter, the United States Supreme Court unanimously upheld them in 1898.[16] Commenting in 1973 on the franchise and apportionment sections of the 1890 constitution, former governor and United States Circuit Court of Appeals judge James P. Coleman observed that "modern evaluation of the work of the convention in this field must take into consideration the exceedingly difficult conditions prevailing for a quarter of a century before 1890."[17]

In other major actions the delegates continued the tradition of a weak governor and further diminished the strength of the office by making the governor ineligible for immediate reelection. A similar ban on succession was placed on the state auditor and treasurer. Jacksonian democracy persisted in the form of independent popular election of numerous executive officials, such as the lieutenant governor, secretary of state, attorney general, treasurer, and auditor. On the other hand, the governor gained the item veto over appropriation measures. Detailed legislative procedures and restrictions were included in the constitution, because of distrust of the legislature stemming from the Reconstruction period. The annual legislative sessions of the previous constitution were reduced to biennial meetings, with one being a regular session followed by a short session to deal only with appropriation and revenue matters. The terms of all elected state and county officials were set at four years. An appointive judiciary was retained because of a concern in black counties that elections might be influenced by the black vote. (However, constitutional amendments in 1912 and 1915 provided for an elective judiciary.) Other provisions on the judiciary were similar to those of the 1869 constitution.

Many provisions of the 1890 constitution are quite similar to those adopted by other states and the federal government. Article 3 provides citizens with a lengthy bill of rights guaranteeing political and civil liberties. Freedom of speech, the press, and religion, the right to assemble and petition the government, and the right to bear arms are guaranteed. Protected civil liberties include rights to a jury trial, a speedy and public trial, legal counsel, and subpoena to obtain witnesses. The practices of double jeopardy, unreasonable searches and seizures, cruel or unusual punishment, and imprisonment for debt are prohibited. Age and residency requirements for the offices of governor and state legislator are clearly specified in articles 4 and 5. Many constitutional powers of the branches are also fairly standard, such as the pardon power granted to the governor and the impeachment power given to the legislature. One constitutional barrier to increased public spending is the requirement that bills raising revenue receive an extraordinary three-fifths vote in each house of the legislature. As with any bill, a gubernatorial veto would require a two-thirds vote of each house to override the veto.

In response to agrarian demands, a number of restrictions were placed on the operation of corporations. One of the most significant was that their property would be taxed like that of individuals. Responding to a strong public outcry, the delegates prohibited the infamous system of leasing convict labor. Public education was promoted by the requirement that local funds be supplemented by the state general fund to provide an adequate education for all children. As in the 1832 and 1869 constitutions, constitutional amendments required a two-thirds vote of a quorum in both houses of the legislature and ratification by a majority of those voting in the election. Voters would have to vote on each amendment separately, so legislators could not combine amendments on different subjects into one referendum vote. No mention was made of a constitutional convention, but it was assumed the legislature possessed the power to call one.[18]

The convention completed its work by late October. The forty-eight-page constitution was nearly twice the length of the 1869 document. Majorities of both black and white county delegates opposed submitting the document to a public vote, fearing its rejection by voters. On November 1, 1890, the convention formally adopted Mississippi's present constitution by a vote of 108 to 8.[19] With 23,500 words, it is shorter than the constitutions of all adjacent states except Tennessee.

CRITICISMS OF THE 1890 DOCUMENT

During the past quarter of a century, significant economic and social change has swept Mississippi. Many people feel that a constitution framed for the environment of the 1890s cannot meet the demands of the late twentieth century. Studies in recent decades by civic and government groups as well as individuals from the political and academic realms have cited certain deficiencies in Mississippi's constitution. Despite 102 piecemeal amendments (as of 1990), many of the alleged weaknesses persist.[20]

Structure

Critics point out that Mississippi's organic law contains excessive detail, which at times places government in a straitjacket and necessitates frequent amendment to free policymakers to act. Some of the verbiage is simply an affirmation of powers the state already possesses through the division of powers under the federal system. Material in certain of the articles is uncoordinated, and some provisions do not relate to the article's main theme. Mississippi's constitution includes provisions on such functional matters as prisons, levees, education, and corporations. Constitutional experts recommend omitting such subjects, which are more appropriately regulated by laws. Finally, the document still contains material oriented toward nineteenth-century situations. The constitution prohibits atheists from holding office, outlaws any lottery, and prohibits a lengthy list of nineteenth-century railroad abuses.

The Executive

A major criticism of the constitution is that the executive branch suffers from too much diffusion of power and functions. The governor is a weak chief executive, largely because the constitution provides for the independent popular election of the heads of key executive departments. Because these officials receive their mandate from the people, they can work independently of each other and of the governor. The governor cannot require them to support or promote his programs. Although the constitution makes the governor "chief executive," much of the bureaucracy is beyond his control. By the 1980s the legislature had created approximately 135 agencies, most under the direction of a board or commission. Legislative supremacy and the diffusion of executive authority also relegates the governor to a limited role in the budgetary process. A constitutional requirement that appropriation bills must be separate and must deal with a single subject also interferes with the concept of a coordinated executive budget.

The Legislature

Many have charged that the 1890 document stipulates in too much detail the operating procedures of the legislature, which should be determined by the membership of the house and senate itself. Section 59 of the constitution, for example, required that bills be fully read on three different days in each house. Until this requirement was eliminated by a constitutional amendment in 1990, obstructionist legislators could invoke it to delay the legislature. The constitution still prohibits appropriation and revenue bills from being enacted in the last five days of the legislative session. Hence late passage of such bills requires the official extension of the session, even if all legislative work is completed. A recent staff report to the governor's Constitutional Study Commission argues that the large size of Mississippi's legislature could be a detriment to effective action. With 122 representatives and 52 senators, Mississippi has more legislators per capita than any other southern state. Large legislative bodies engage in excessive deliberation and usually require more committees, so their chairmen have greater opportunity to control the policy process. Big legislatures also rely on more detailed rules of procedure. Such detailed procedures work to the advantage of senior members and proponents of the status quo and disadvantage new members who are unfamiliar with the legislative maze.

The Judiciary

The Mississippi constitution establishes a dual system of circuit (law) and chancery (equity) courts that many judicial observers feel is outdated and unnecessary. Because the concepts of law and equity are merging, they could be administered by a single court system, as they are in many states. Many also feel that justice of the peace courts are products of the nineteenth century and should be replaced by a single court in each county to handle petty litigation. The constitution fails to provide any appellate court except for the supreme court, leading to nine overworked justices. Many judicial experts support the creation of an intermediate appellate court that would hear most cases, permitting the supreme court to limit itself to the most important appeals. Some would also prefer an appointive judiciary, to eliminate the partisanship that sometimes intrudes into judicial elections.

Local Government

Mississippi's counties are locked by the 1890 constitution into a framework that many feel is more suitable to an earlier era. Scattering power among a number of constitutionally designated officials tends to produce inefficiency and confusion in county government. For example, the constitution specifies that each county will be divided into five districts, each headed by an elected supervisor. Legally, the five-member Board of Supervisors makes policy for the entire county, but each supervisor has considerable authority over his or her own "beat." Although some local reform movements like the county unit system are currently under way, they encounter many problems. The constitution also fails to provide for merger or joint administration of local government units or services. Furthermore, significant home rule is not available to local governments.

Economic Development

Part of the antibusiness flavor of the constitution has been removed by recent amendment and interpretation. Yet some feel it still contains provisions that impair economic growth. A negative message is sent out to those wishing to incorporate by giving the legislature broad grounds on which to revoke a charter. Though seldom invoked, section 178 gives the legislature the "power to alter, amend, or repeal any charter of incorporation" whenever they deem it in the "public interest." The constitution also discourages innovative approaches by local governments to attract industry, because it restricts certain types of monetary or credit assistance to corporations. Finally, critics believe the governor's weak institutional position makes it difficult to provide strong leadership on economic development.

EFFORTS TO REVISE THE 1890 CONSTITUTION

There are a number of ways Mississippi's constitution could be significantly revised. The approach that permits the greatest amount of change is calling a constitutional convention to write an entirely new document, though delegates would have the option of retaining various features of the current constitution. Only one of the four conventions in Mississippi's history has permitted a popular vote on its constitution, but recent proposals for constitutional conventions have promised popular referenda. Another approach is for the legislature to submit a package of constitutional amendments to the voters for ratification. This approach would permit significant changes in the constitution without provoking fears over a massive rewriting of the entire document. It would, however, restrict the writing of constitutional changes to legislators, excluding other citizens who could serve in a convention. A more gradual approach to constitutional change is the less comprehensive avenue of piecemeal amendments proposed by the legislature and ratified by voters. Any of these approaches may be preceded by a constitutional commission, appointed by the governor or legislature, that studies the existing constitution and recommends changes.[21]

In the twentieth century there have been four significant attempts to call a convention to write a new constitution for Mississippi. Each effort was spearheaded by a governor after renewed public interest in constitutional change. Governor Theodore G. Bilbo tried to call a convention in 1916, but his proposal failed in both houses of the legislature. Seeking to implement some of the recommendations of a Brookings Institution study group, Governor Mike S. Conner sought a constitutional convention in his 1932 inaugural address. In 1934 the senate easily approved the call by a 43 to 5 vote only to have it defeated in the house by the narrow margin of 70 to 66. Elected in 1955, Governor James P. Coleman made a constitutional convention a major goal of his administration. His hopes were dashed in 1957 when a special session of the legislature rejected a public referendum on a convention. The house defeated the measure 78 to 61 after it had cleared the senate by a 27 to 19 margin.[22]

The most recent movement for constitutional revision began in the middle 1970s. It was sparked by the desire to move Mississippi forward in such areas as economic development and by the tight fiscal situation facing state government. Progressive Republican Gil Carmichael, in his unsuccessful campaigns for governor in 1975 and 1979 and lieutenant governor in 1983, strongly endorsed holding a constitutional convention. Several civic interest groups also produced short publications advocating a rewriting of the constitution. In 1985 Governor Bill Allain created the governor's Constitutional Study Commission and named 350 persons representing a broad cross section of citizens to sit on it. The commission's large size was designed to increase public support for a convention by soliciting ideas from as many different kinds of people as possible. Former Governor Coleman was named chairman of the commission.

The commission drafted a model for a new state constitution and urged the legislature to call a constitutional convention. One of the most significant proposals in the "model" constitution involved the executive branch, which would have been strengthened and made a manageable whole. Most of the state's numerous boards, commissions, and agencies would be grouped under fifteen departments. Except for four department heads who would continue to be elected by the people, the governor would appoint the department heads with the consent of the senate. He would also be given the sole authority for preparing an annual budget.[23] Special-interest groups were occasionally successful at influencing the commission. For example, the commission agreed to continue constitutional status for levee boards and reversed an earlier decision to strip the lieutenant governor of some of his powers in the senate. The group's deliberations received extensive coverage by the state's media.[24]

The winds of change sweeping over Mississippi gave hope to supporters of a new constitution. In 1986 the legislature finally permitted voters to decide whether to amend the constitution to permit the governor to immediately succeed himself. Voters ratified this amendment as well as a companion that permitted the state treasurer to succeed himself. Governor Allain urged the legislature to call a convention in his state of the state message in January 1987. At the start of the legislative session, house rebels were successful in limiting the powers of old guard Speaker C. B. "Buddie" Newman of Valley Park in the Delta region.[25] (Most of these house rules changes did not go into effect until the next legislative session, however.) Various progressive civic interest groups, especially Common Cause and Mississippi First, launched campaigns to urge the legislature to call a constitutional convention. The state AFL-CIO joined the convention movement, hoping to remove the right-to-work provision from the constitution. Opinion polls indicated that most Mississippi voters supported significant constitutional change.[26] Much of the state's press, including the Jackson *Clarion-Ledger,* urged calling a convention.

Bills calling for a convention provided for considerable public input, an important break with the state's traditionalistic culture that sought to limit public participation in politics. Voters were required to approve the holding of a convention and would then elect delegates from each house district. A new constitution would be submitted to popular ratification, with votes required on each article instead of on the document as a whole. Finally, under the Voting Rights Act any provision in a new constitution relating to voting or elections would require the approval of the United States Justice Department.

The Mississippi senate approved a convention referendum by an overwhelming 43 to 4 vote, but the measure died in the house. The House Constitution Committee voted 10 to 2 to kill the measure, and supporters filed a minority report that placed the bill at the back of the house calendar. Efforts to suspend the rules to take up the bill failed on votes of 55 to 60 and 59 to 58, because a two-thirds vote is needed to suspend house rules.[27] Interestingly enough, the house had been the roadblock in two previous important drives for a convention. The only consolation for backers of constitutional reform was that for the first time in the twentieth century, a majority of house members appeared to favor a convention.

Even with a constitutional study commission, the governor's strong backing, media support, campaigns by various interest groups, and favorable public opinion, the forces of modernization had lost a major contest in the legislature to those of the status quo. Three unrelated situations led to the death of a convention in the 1987 house. First, while not objecting to a constitutional convention in principle, the legislative Black Caucus opposed the specific bill providing for the election of all convention delegates. They feared that blacks would be underrepresented at the convention, and sought to amend the bill to permit the governor to appoint some delegates. Failing to amend the bill, eleven of fourteen black representatives and both black senators opposed it. Another concern of blacks was that special interests might control a convention.[28]

The lobbying campaigns of two strong interest groups—the Mississippi Manufacturers Association and the Farm Bureau Federation—also contributed to the convention's death in the house. These organizations were especially concerned that a convention might remove the right-to-work provision from the constitution or change property tax assessment ratios to disadvantage farmers or businessmen.[29] The Mississippi Economic Council, which had consistently supported constitutional revision, declined to take a position on the convention issue, deciding that the method of constitutional change should be left up to the legislature. Some observers felt that the house's delay in taking up the convention issue gave opposing interests a better opportunity to become organized.

Finally, the opposition of Speaker "Buddie" Newman and his lieutenants helped to doom a convention. Many political observers felt that house leaders opposed a convention because of their fear that it would write a constitution reducing their power and that of the legislature in general.[30] A similar situation had arisen in 1957, when Speaker Walter Sillers had opposed the convention movement spearheaded by Governor Coleman. Many supporters of a constitutional convention in 1987 had backed reform in the house rules to limit the Speaker's powers. Of those who voted to reduce the Speaker's power, 62 percent also supported the convention, while 70 percent of those who supported the Speaker registered a negative vote on calling a referendum.

The linkage between legislative reform and support for a convention was especially evident in the House Constitution Committee. All committee members had been appointed by Speaker Newman. Chaired by a Delta representative, Charles Capps, 70 percent of the committee's membership nevertheless came from outside the Delta section.[31] Nine of the eleven committee members who had sided with Newman in the rules fight opposed reporting out the convention measure. Opponents expressed concern that a convention would be dominated by special interests and would be too expensive. Many urged constitutional change through the amendment process.[32] The 1987 legislature did pass ten relatively minor amendments that were ratified by voters. They helped bring the state constitution into conformity with federal court decisions and removed some restrictions on corporations.

Proponents of a convention made their last major effort during the 1988 legislative session, and the election of reformist Speaker Tim Ford of Tupelo contributed to initial house passage of a convention referendum. Weeks passed as a conference committee ironed out differences between the house and senate versions of the referendum. Powerful interest groups such as the Manufacturers Association, the Farm Bureau, and the legislative Black Caucus lobbied vigorously to defeat the convention bill. The National Rifle Association also sought to preserve the status quo, fearing that a convention might eliminate the state constitution's protection of the right to bear arms. Meanwhile, public apathy was widespread, and few citizens made their views known to legislators. This type of government reorganization issue was too complex and unexciting for most average citizens. Hence the final version of the referendum bill, reported out of conference committee, died in the legislature.[33]

Despite the recurring defeat of major constitutional reform in the twentieth century, political leaders have responded to changes in their environment by amending the state constitution 102 times. The Progressive Era of public demands for direct popular selection of officials led to replacement of the appointive judiciary with an elective one in 1912 and 1915 amendments. A 1934 amendment establishing a board of trustees for institutions of higher learning prevented recurrences of gubernatorial interference in the operations of the state's public universities. The size of the supreme court was increased to nine justices in 1952, and a 1958 amendment clarified that amendments required a majority vote of those citizens voting for or against them. Business and conservative groups were successful in inserting a right-to-work provision into the constitution in 1960. County sheriffs and the state auditor were permitted to succeed themselves in 1962 and 1966. To cope with a growing workload, annual legislative sessions were established in 1968. When Mississippi officials resisted desegregation and opposed the enfranchisement of blacks, federal court decisions and statutes voided provisions of the state constitution that upheld white supremacy.

Constitutional change in the 1980s especially illustrates how the legislature has gradually responded to the forces of modernization that have swept the state. A 1982 amendment sought to promote professionalism and improve education by reorganizing the state board of education and making the superintendency appointive. Increased support for education was also reflected in a 1986 amendment that established a trust fund. Interest on income from the state oil and gas severance tax could be spent only on public elementary and secondary education and on vocational and technical training. Other amendments in 1986 protected the state employees retirement system by prohibiting the diversion of money to other purposes and provided for equitable classifications in the collection of property taxes. The same year, a longtime legislative foe of gubernatorial succession permitted a succession amendment to be reported out of his committee. He admitted that he was willing to try almost anything because of his exasperation with the slow pace of progress in Mississippi. Voters immediately ratified the gubernatorial succession amendment as well as another amendment permitting the treasurer to succeed himself.[34]

MISSISSIPPI CONSTITUTIONS IN RETROSPECT

Reflecting a traditionalistic culture, Mississippi politics from statehood to the present has tended to revolve around issues of class or race. These conflicts have been reflected in the traditions of the state's four constitutions. For example, the 1817 and 1832 constitutions were primarily oriented around matters of class. The 1817 document established an aristocratic tradition of government that was to be toppled by the tidal wave of Jacksonianism, which produced the more democratic constitution of 1832. Race was the major political concern at the time of the framing of the 1869 and 1890 constitutions. The main intent of the convention of 1868 was to ensure the political rights of the recently freed slaves and to insert proscriptive measures against former Confederates. On the other hand, traditionalists were quite successful at the 1890 convention. The principal goal of this white-dominated convention was to remove blacks from the state's political life. This tradition persisted until the federal government guaranteed the right of blacks to vote during the "Second Reconstruction" of the 1960s.[35]

The principal reason for writing the 1890 document has been nullified for over two decades. Yet some of the traditions that flowed into it from the Jacksonian constitution of 1832 are so entrenched that they stand as major barriers to the forces of modernization today. One barrier is the concept of a weak chief executive in administrative matters, which has caused a gravitation of power to the legislature. Another custom persisting since 1832 has been the popular election of constitutional officers and judges, although for an interim of four decades the latter were appointed.

It should be noted that every new constitution in Mississippi's history has been preceded by some major political development. The move for statehood led to the 1817 constitution. Widespread public support for Jacksonian democracy produced the constitution of 1832. The constitution of 1869 was a legacy of defeat in the Civil War. Finally, the strong desire to remove blacks from the political realm fostered the present constitution. In recent decades, the civil rights movement and the emphasis on modernization have been significant political developments in the state. However, federal court decisions regarding the racial content of the 1890 document, and the submission of piecemeal amendments aimed at modernization, have helped to prevent public mobilization behind the writing of a new constitution. The struggle between traditionalists supporting the status quo and modernizers seeking change continues.

CHAPTER FOUR

Public Opinion and Interest Groups

Stephen D. Shaffer

To some, Mississippi was synonymous with the KKK, *lynching, superstition, religious fundamentalism, back-looking, and past-loving.*
David Bodenhamer, 1979[1]

It looks to me like the winds of change have turned into a tornado.
Buddie Newman, Speaker of the Mississippi house, 1987[2]

For many years the conservative social and political views of the average white Mississippian, and the prevalence of status quo oriented interest groups, preserved a very traditionalistic political system. The historical weakness of political parties especially increased the importance of interest groups in the political process.[3] With the civil rights movement, television, and demographic changes such as generational change, rising educational levels, and increased numbers of migrants and professionals, the traditional political order found itself under attack. Many citizens acquired more progressive views, fueling the rise of interest groups dedicated to changing the status quo. Such progressive elements sought to increase citizens' involvement in the political system. Progressives also sought to improve the quality of life in Mississippi by supporting public education and other social programs.

PUBLIC OPINION IN A TRADITIONALISTIC SOCIETY

Economic disadvantage has significantly influenced Mississippi's social and political culture. In such a poor and rural state, in which people lack material possessions and cultural opportunities, social institutions like the family, church, and school have historically been very important. As one Mississippi native put it: "The church was undoubtedly the center of our lives—religious, educational, and social. . . . After church came the school. My high school was very small; only eight in the graduating class. . . . What I really had was a sensitive, conscientious tutor who was very much interested in my educational development. . . . Even before church and school was family. In addition to my brothers and sisters, of which there were five, I lived within walking distance of seven aunts and uncles with equally large families, and someone was always visiting one place or the other."[4]

In the small towns and villages that dominate Mississippi, citizens obtain information by swapping gossip and stories about local events. Newspapers in this intimate environment typically serve as bulletin boards by minimizing their reporting of national and international happenings and focusing instead on social affairs and sports. Small-town newspapers historically protected and promoted the values of Mississippi's traditionalistic society. As late as the 1960s the major statewide newspaper, the Jackson *Clarion-Ledger,* strove to preserve segregation. As the federal government sought to integrate Ole Miss in 1962, one *Clarion-Ledger* columnist wrote in reference to Attorney General Robert Kennedy: "Little Brother has evidently concluded that the South must be forced to abandon its customs and traditions in deference to 'world opinion'—especially that of Asiatic cow-worshippers and African semi-savages not far removed from cannibalism."[5] By the 1980s this traditionalistic orientation of the media had eroded, as television saturated the state, and the *Clarion-Ledger* became part of the Gannett national chain. Indeed, the newspaper won a Pulitzer Prize for its investigative reporting about the problems of the state's educational system. It aggressively pushed the 1982 Education Reform Act by labeling legislative opponents candidates for a "Hall of Shame."

The traditionalistic orientation of religion continues to play an important part in the lives of most Mississippians, often promoting conservative social and political orientations. In one survey, 56 percent of Mississippians having opinions approved of the Moral Majority, compared with only 38 percent of the national population.[6] Also, 86 percent of Mississippians supported requiring prayer readings in the public schools, and 68 percent wanted to require teaching of the biblical version of Creation.[7] Frequent churchgoers and "born-again" white Baptists are especially conservative. Those attending church every week are much more likely than infrequent attenders to abstain from alcoholic beverages, to oppose sexual equality, and to oppose any form of gambling.[8] White Baptists who feel they have been "born again" are much more supportive of the Moral Majority, creationism, and school prayer and much more opposed to school and neighborhood integration and abortion than are other whites.[9]

In addition to blacks, women traditionally were relegated to a subordinate social and political role. "The woman, tradition dictated, was to be set apart, protected and even exalted in words if not in deeds. . . . Women too, often look unsuccessfully for jobs, get fired if they find them, and find they are paid lower sums than a man receives for the same kind of work. . . . When certain church groups went from Mississippi to the International Women's Year convention in Houston, they publicized the state as one violently opposed to full citizenship rights for women and irresponsibly branded women feminists who supported the Equal Rights Amendment as lesbians."[10]

As late as 1984, 43 percent of Mississippians having opinions agreed with the statement: "Women should take care of running their homes and leave running the country up to men." Nationally, only 26 percent agreed with this statement.[11] Only 25 percent of Mississippians expressed opposition to a constitutional amendment banning all abortions except those necessary to save the life of the mother. Although 62 percent of Mississippians expressed support for the Equal Rights Amendment (ERA), the amendment died in legislative committee without a floor vote.[12] Even the views of many women in Mississippi reflect their conservative social environment, as shown by the Mississippi Federation of Business and Professional Women, which recently abandoned support for the ERA and abortion in the face of declining membership.

In many ways the most traditionalistic region in the state remains the Mississippi Delta. Even in the 1980s, many Delta communities are dominated by financially advantaged whites who are reluctant to change, while the great majority of blacks remain impoverished. Hence Delta society in some respects still resembles the antebellum era when a majority black population worked as slaves on plantations owned by rich whites. Although most Delta whites have accepted the contemporary norm of racial integration, a significant minority still resists it. In a 1988 survey of Delta whites, 30 percent preferred segregated schools, 37 percent endorsed segregated neighborhoods, and 37 percent objected to sending their children to majority black schools.[13]

Yet change is coming, even to the Delta. Living in one of the poorest areas in the nation, more and more Delta residents wish to solve the massive economic problems facing them instead of continuing to refight the Civil War. While satisfied overall with the quality of life in their communities, most residents hope for improvements in such basic things as salaries and living conditions. The younger generation especially yearns for change, and 72 percent of Delta residents under age thirty express a willingness to leave their community to find a better job, compared with 50 percent of all Delta residents. With national economic difficulties hurting farmers generally, economic recession has plagued white as well as black farmers in the Delta. Hence economic needs that are common to both races are increasingly salient to voters, replacing divisive racial matters. This political transformation is reflected in the landslide reelection in 1988 of a black congressman, Mike Espy, from the "Delta" district. Espy has worked hard to increase federal aid to the area and to encourage businesses to relocate there.

THE STRUGGLE OVER RACE RELATIONS

Historically, many white Mississippians have held racist and segregationist attitudes. Such attitudes were embodied in a response that a governor of the early 1900s, James Vardaman, made to a question about adequate educational opportunities for blacks: "Why squander money on his education when the only effect is to spoil a good field hand and make an insolent cook?"[14] Racist attitudes were so widespread that even as late as the 1960s one governor (Paul Johnson) was reported to say that the NAACP stood for "Niggers, Alligators, Apes, Coons, and Possums."[15] During the 1950s and 1960s, "race was the acute and overriding campaign issue, the pivot upon which most state elections turned." Most white Mississippians "unquestionably" opposed the *Brown v. Topeka Board of Education* decision and school integration.[16]

By the 1960s some Mississippi political and business leaders urged obedience to the law requiring a desegregated society, and the opinions of white citizens began to change. In a 1981 public opinion survey, 69 percent of white Mississippians supported and only 20 percent opposed school integration. These proportions were very similar to those of whites in other southern states, and only slightly more segregationist than those of whites nationwide (fig. 1). Even more illustrative of the change in racial attitudes that has swept the state, Mississippians were more supportive of neighborhood integration than whites in other southern states, and nearly as supportive as whites nationally.[17] Perhaps the high percentage of blacks in the state population, necessitating daily interaction between the races, promoted the increase in tolerance of whites.

Despite these changes, racial differences in the 1980s persist on many

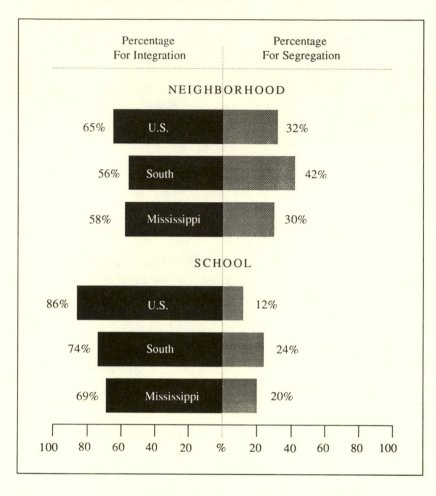

Figure 1. Racial attitudes of white Mississippians compared with those of other whites. Proportion of white Mississippians, white southerners, and white Americans nationally giving integrationist and segregationist responses on two major issues concerning general support for an integrated society—the right of blacks to live in white neighborhoods, and integrated versus segregated schools. Proportions giving integrationist responses are to the left of the centered vertical line, and proportions giving segregationist responses are to the right. Numbers fail to total 100 percent, since some people gave mixed responses or had no opinions. (*Sources*: National and regional results are from the 1980 General Social Survey, conducted by the National Opinion Research Center at the University of Chicago; Mississippi results are from a statewide survey conducted by the Social Science Research Center at Mississippi State University.)

political orientations. Blacks are more supportive of a progressive tax structure and spending on domestic welfare programs than are whites—understandable in view of their generally lower socioeconomic status. (Blacks
continue to earn less than half the income of whites.) Blacks are also significantly more cynical than whites about public officials in the state, feeling
that they treat white constituents better than their black constituents.[18] Such
racial differences are not unique to Mississippi; nationally, blacks are significantly more liberal than whites.[19] The greater existence of poverty and unemployment in Mississippi, as well as the legacy of racial discrimination and
repression, may intensify the problem.

THE EMERGENCE OF PROGRESSIVISM

By the early 1980s most Mississippians had become aware of the state's
problems and increasingly supported changes in the status quo. In a 1981
poll, most Mississippians urged state leaders to improve the educational system and attract industry in order to provide more and higher-paying jobs.
Specific educational improvements supported by the public included a mandatory school attendance law (supported by 91 percent of Mississippians),
state-supported public kindergartens (61 percent support and only 26 percent
opposition), and increased state and local government spending for public
education (70 percent). Such widespread support for educational improvements culminated in passage of the 1982 Education Reform Act, which incorporated these programs.[20] Public support also helped produce a major
teacher pay raise in 1988 to bring teachers' salaries closer to the Southeast
average and an equity-funding measure in 1989 that sought to guarantee a basic level of state support for all school districts.

Many Mississippians also came to believe that the governor's office was
too weak and should be strengthened.[21] A 1986 poll indicated that 75 percent
of Mississippians supported a constitutional amendment on gubernatorial
succession permitting a governor to serve two four-year terms in a row. In
November the same margin of voters ratified the proposed succession
amendment. The public vote was made possible after a longtime legislative
foe of gubernatorial succession, expressing dissatisfaction over the state's
slow economic progress, permitted it to be reported out of his committee for
a floor vote. In 1988 and 1989, however, only modest progress was made in
the area of government reorganization—a major goal of Governor Ray
Mabus—partly because of the legislature's reluctance to give the governor
more power. Less public support has greeted far-reaching proposals to per-

mit the governor to appoint the heads of executive departments that are now popularly elected. Mississippians continue to sympathize with Jacksonian democracy, preferring to directly elect many executive officials.

Mississippians advocating change have been unsuccessful in influencing the legislature in other areas as well. Legislative support for higher education has been uneven over the years. A 1986 poll showed that two-thirds of Mississippians preferred raising taxes instead of cutting spending for higher education, yet the legislature slashed spending for higher education and other state programs. Funding was restored in the next two years but then was essentially frozen. A likely explanation for uneven funding was that money was being diverted to increase funding for public elementary and secondary education. One method of funding public education—a lottery—has continually died in the legislature. Although 72 percent of Mississippians polled have supported a state lottery that earmarks income for education, religious organizations have continually opposed it on moral grounds. Some opponents also fear that a lottery would serve as a regressive tax, drawing a proportionately greater share of the income of poor citizens compared with wealthier persons.

Other changes in traditional state policies have also encountered resistance. Although 69 percent of Mississippians supported a law requiring the use of seat belts by front-seat passengers, the proposal continually died in committee as a perceived infringement on individual liberty.[22] The 1990 legislature finally passed a seat-belt law but provided no penalty for its violation. Progressive measures killed in recent legislative sessions include increased protection for tenants in their interaction with landlords, establishment of child-care facilities for state employees, and institution of a system of voter registration by mail to encourage turnout. In 1991 the legislature finally enacted landlord-tenant legislation as well as mail voter registration. An important break from the past was the state's settlement of a voting rights lawsuit in 1989 in a way that increased the number of black majority judicial districts. Attorney General Mike Moore also announced that the executive branch would no longer defend anti–civil rights lawsuits that were losing causes.

Mississippians increasingly look to government to provide solutions to problems so that the state can move ahead. In public opinion polls conducted throughout the 1980s, significant majorities of Mississippians urged state government to spend more money on improving public elementary, secondary, and higher education, attracting industry, building highways, and providing health care and other programs for the poor.[23] Opinion polls also demonstrated that citizens held state officials accountable for the perceived quality of life in the state. As fewer people in 1986 than in 1981 rated Mississippi an excellent place to live, public support for the legislature and the governor also declined.[24] Such increased public concern over political matters is a departure from the traditionalistic notion of elite domination and minimal public involvement in politics.[25]

GROUP DIFFERENCES IN POLITICAL ATTITUDES

Considerable change has occurred in Mississippians' political attitudes as rising progressivism and tolerance have replaced some traditionalistic orientations. Mississippi has shifted toward the rest of the nation in recent decades, with most residents accepting the modern welfare state and an integrated social order. It is instructive to examine how different Mississippians vary in their political views. Here I rely primarily on statewide public opinion polls conducted in 1981, 1986, and 1988, which contain pertinent information about the policy orientations of different groups of Mississippians.

One very important source of change is generational replacement. Younger white Mississippians are significantly more supportive of civil rights and liberties than are older Mississippians. Among younger Mississippians, 75 percent support women's rights, compared with only 37 percent of older residents (table 1). Among whites under age thirty, 80 percent support school integration and 65 percent support open housing. Among those over sixty, only 49 percent favor school integration and 34 percent support open housing. Young people are also more supportive of the Equal Rights Amendment, abortion, and gun control measures than are the elderly. Those under thirty are also more likely to express liberal views on various economic issues such as domestic welfare spending, health care, and labor union support. As time passes and elderly Mississippians are replaced by their offspring, the state should continue to become more tolerant and to reflect more closely the political orientations that have existed nationally.

Another important source of change is the political mobilization of black Mississippians. Black Mississippians are significantly more liberal than whites across a range of political issues. Economically, blacks are more supportive of labor unions, government-sponsored health insurance, public works, food stamps, and increased domestic spending and less supportive of a balanced budget. On civil liberty issues, blacks are more supportive of gun control and more opposed to the death penalty and to reinstating of the draft. On civil rights concerns, blacks are significantly more supportive than

Table 1: Policy Orientations of Mississippians

	Race		Party			Ideology		Age		Other Groups	
	White	Black	Dem.	Ind.	Rep.	Lib.	Con.	Under 30	Over 60	Under $10,000 Income	Over $20,000 Income
Economic Issues											
(1986) Pro labor unions	52	83	58	51	49	64	35	72	31	40	53
(1986) For health insurance	69	85	79	67	61	79	59	83	76	86	64
(1986) For public works	53	69	62	46	51	65	56	53	64	65	54
(1986) For food stamps	14	35	14	12	15	30	14	16	17	21	11
(1981) Against balanced budget	10	26	10	11	10	8	6	12	13	14	8
(1981) For more domestic spending	14	38	18	11	13	18	12	23	6	16	11
	White	Black	Dem.	Ind.	Rep.	Lib.	Con.	Under 30	Over 60	Male	Female
Civil liberties											
(1986) For women's rights	63	49	60	68	60	63	51	75	37	64	62
(1986) For gun registration	59	66	67	63	47	79	52	73	60	50	70
(1986) Against death penalty	14	53	19	17	4	16	14	15	16	9	19
(1981) Against draft	34	60	36	29	37	35	26	49	28	30	38
(1981) For ERA	56	80	68	52	46	79	41	66	42	60	52
(1981) Against school prayer	13	16	7	17	14	11	11	18	8	13	13
(1981) For abortion	27	25	18	32	34	24	22	37	12	27	27

	Race		Party			Ideology		Age		Other Groups	
	White	Black	Dem.	Ind.	Rep.	Lib.	Con.	Under 30	Over 60	Male / High-school dropout	Female / Some college
Civil rights											
(1981) For busing	21	63	19	20	23	28	15	25	20	—	—
(1981) For school integration	69	88	57	76	75	76	66	80	49	—	—
(1981) For open housing	60	NA	54	65	61	74	60	65	34	—	—
(1981) For Voting Rights Act	67	98	71	75	52	NA	63	53	65	—	—
Ideology identification											
(1986) % Liberal	16	23	17	17	12	—	—	20	10	21	14
(1986) % Conservative	43	34	34	40	53	—	—	30	60	38	48
(1981) % Liberal	12	33	19	12	5	—	—	9	3	19	12
(1981) % Conservative	46	22	34	46	64	—	—	34	63	44	48

Source: Statewide telephone polls conducted by the Social Science Research Center at Mississippi State University in October–November 1981 and February 1986.

Note: Table entries are the percentages of *white* Mississippians (except for column 2) taking the liberal position (on ideology the conservative position is also provided) on dichotomous issue items (except on domestic spending and ideology, where a middle-of-the-road category was also included). The liberal orientations of groups are underlined. The numbers in parentheses indicate the year of the survey when each item was asked. NA = not available.

whites of the Voting Rights Act, integrated schools in general, and busing to achieve racially balanced schools.

Clearly, the enfranchisement of blacks has added a more liberal group to the political environment, one that encourages public officials to pursue less conservative policies. Such racial divisions are hardly unique to Mississippi, since blacks across the nation are much more liberal than whites.[26] Racial differences over public policies in Mississippi today resemble racial divisions existing across the entire nation.

Political conflict outside the South since the 1930s has been fueled by economic divisions, as lower socioeconomic status groups have been more liberal on economic issues and more Democratic in partisanship than richer and more highly educated people.[27] Similar political cleavages exist in Mississippi today. Poor whites are somewhat more liberal on economic issues than are those with higher incomes. Whites in families making less than $10,000 a year are more supportive of health care, public works, food stamps, and domestic spending generally than are those in families making more than $20,000. High school dropouts are more likely to call themselves "liberals" than are those with some college education. By the 1980s even partisan orientations were finally being influenced by attitudes on economic issues. White Democrats were more supportive of labor unions, health insurance, public works, and domestic spending generally than were white Republicans. The old solid Democratic South tradition of a segregationist society and racial tensions continues to fade in Mississippi. Political cleavages based on economic issues are becoming more evident.

The election of Ronald Reagan saw the advent of gender differences on many political issues nationally, as women were somewhat more liberal than men on a diverse range of economic, social, race, and foreign affairs issues.[28] Gender differences are also evident in Mississippi, though they are somewhat narrower. Compared with men, women in Mississippi are more supportive of gun control and more opposed to the death penalty and the draft. Gender differences do not exist on economic or civil rights issues (these data are therefore omitted from the table). As more and more women in Mississippi enter the work force and become heads of households, facing low salaries and discrimination, Mississippi women may become more liberal on a greater range of issues, providing another impetus for change in state policies.

As Mississippi society becomes increasingly pluralistic with political attitudes differing between groups defined by age, race, sex, and socioeconomic status, the geographic regions of the state have become less distinctive. Political scientists in previous decades have referred to the state's deep-seated conservatism as the "Delta mind" and have discussed historical divisions between Delta and Hill residents.[29] Yet by the 1980s, except on the racial issues discussed earlier, attitude differences between whites from different regions of the state had become slight and differed in ideological direction from issue to issue.[30]

An example of the inconsistent ideological impact of region is provided by the 1988 poll comparing Delta residents with residents in the rest of the state. Although Delta residents expressed somewhat less liberal opinions than non-Delta residents on racial issues, Mississippians from the economically depressed and poverty-stricken Delta region were very willing to resort to an activist state government to promote economic development and assist socially disadvantaged citizens. Among Delta residents, 78 percent felt that state government should spend more on building highways (compared with 69 percent of non-Delta residents), 76 percent supported more spending on attracting industry (compared with 75 percent for the non-Delta population), 74 percent favored more college and health care spending (69 percent non-Delta), 65 percent favored more funding for antipoverty programs (57 percent non-Delta), and 59 percent favored more day-care spending (48 percent non-Delta).[31]

The winds of change are indeed sweeping across the state. The enfranchisement of blacks with the 1965 Voting Rights Act added a large and decidedly liberal group to the state voting electorate. Young people who grew up in a racially integrated society and attended school at a time when women were encouraged to pursue careers are much more supportive of the rights of blacks and women than are older generations. As racial tensions subsided, economic issues became more salient, and lower socioeconomic status groups and Democrats took more liberal positions on these issues. Even women, a politically weak group historically, began to acquire more distinct attitudes that favored resolving social problems without using force. As time passes and tradition continues to fade, these groups may play an increasingly important role in transforming the political landscape of Mississippi.

BUSINESS, PROFESSIONAL, AND FARM GROUPS

As in most states, business groups are among the most influential and active interest groups possessing considerable financial resources to influence the political process. One major textbook on the politics of the fifty states lists the Economic Council, the Farm Bureau, and the Manufacturers Association as the most powerful interest groups in Mississippi, along with public school teachers and associations of local officials like county supervisors.[32] Generally such business, professional, and farm groups have opposed change that was perceived as potentially harmful to their membership.

The Mississippi Manufacturers Association, established in 1951 with a contemporary membership of about 1,400 manufacturing firms, remains one of the most traditional and conservative groups. A foremost goal is to "reduce the size and cost of state government," and thus the association opposes increasing taxes to improve education. It also opposes a constitutional convention, because of the expense involved and a concern that an existing right-to-work clause might be eliminated from a new state constitution. The organization has supported the merging of school districts and consolidation of universities, tort reform (limiting business liability for "excessive" damage claims), and the 1987 highway bill (designed to make four-lane highways of one thousand miles of state roads by the year 2000). The association exerts influence over the legislature through weekly legislative bulletins sent to its members, a political action committee, and an active membership engaged in grass-roots lobbying.[33]

Another effective conservative group is the Mississippi Farm Bureau Federation. Founded in 1922 and representing 150,000 families by the late 1980s, the federation counters the declining power of agriculture in this century with effective lobbying efforts. The organization exists in each county, and members interview legislative candidates to determine their support for federation objectives. Weekly legislative newsletters are sent to constituents, who are urged to approach legislators. Members sit in the balcony and monitor the legislature, and a WATS line informs callers about the status of pertinent legislation. The federation has generally opposed tax increases, such as raising the 10 percent cap on property taxes to improve rural roads and bridges, as well as lowering the public vote margin needed to pass school bond issues from 60 percent to 50 percent. As already noted, the federation has also helped to kill a state constitutional convention.[34]

The Mississippi Economic Council (MEC), formed in 1948, is the most broadly based business association in the state. With a wide-ranging perspective on how economic development can be promoted, the MEC is viewed as one of the more progressive business groups in Mississippi. In recent years it has supported such measures as the 1982 Education Reform Act, improved funding of higher education, gubernatorial succession, and the unit system at the county level (so that expenditure decisions in counties would be made by professionally trained administrators). The MEC appoints committees to research state issues and polls its members regarding their attitudes on proposed policies. Members are informed about relevant subjects through a semimonthly newspaper and weekly legislative bulletins. The MEC informs the public about its views through a Speakers' Bureau (with two hundred volunteers) and weekly editorials sent to all state newspapers. MEC lobbyists also testify before legislative committees and meet regularly with legislators.[35]

Other business and professional groups have a narrower focus, concentrating on issues of concern to their more specialized membership. The Mississippi Bankers Association has successfully urged gradual deregulation of interest rates on major loans, and after years of dissension it achieved consensus among its membership for support of statewide and interstate banking (which became law in 1986).[36] The Retail Association of Mississippi has supported such issues as truth in advertising, bad checks legislation, outlawing transient merchants, tort reform, and antishoplifting measures.[37] Despite considerable business support for tort reform in 1986, the Mississippi Trial Lawyers Association contributed to its defeat by testifying against it in committee.[38] (In 1989 a less ambitious tort reform measure that merely decreased the time period for filing lawsuits rather than capping amounts for damages finally passed the legislature.) The Mississippi Medical Association has supported such measures as tort reform, mandatory seat-belt use, smoke-free areas in public buildings, and expanding state Medicaid to include pregnant mothers and young children.[39]

For years the Mississippi Association of Supervisors successfully opposed state mandating of the county unit system, and recently it unsuccessfully urged increased taxes for the needs of local government.[40] In 1988, despite public support for Governor Mabus's proposal to establish the unit system, county supervisors got the legislature to modify the proposal to require public referenda in each county on whether to establish the unit system for that particular county. Receiving 62 percent of the popular vote statewide, the unit system referendum passed in forty-seven of the eighty-two counties.

The Mid-Continent Oil and Gas Association's membership produces over 95 percent of the oil and gas in Mississippi. In 1982 this organization successfully killed an increase in the oil and gas severance tax, which was to fund the Education Reform Act. The association used effective lobbying techniques such as full-page newspaper advertisements charging that the tax increase would drive the industry out of the state. These ads also provided a toll-free telephone number for concerned readers to call the association.[41]

MORALITY-ORIENTED GROUPS

With the importance of religion and family in Mississippi's traditionalistic political culture, religiously oriented interests constitute an important part of the interest group environment even today. They often support conservative policies that are viewed as upholding traditional moral values.[42]

Right to Life is a single-issue group organized in the state in 1979 to oppose abortion. In the late 1980s the organization achieved passage of a state law requiring parental consent for abortions by minors, though a federal injunction requested by the ACLU temporarily nullified this law. It also helped kill state Medicaid funding for protein screening of pregnant women to detect possible birth defects, a practice that might encourage abortions. The organization testifies before legislative committees, publishes a bimonthly newsletter, and is particularly active in protesting outside abortion clinics. Especially effective tactics are telephone trees in which members across the state are urged to call or write their legislators on relevant bills.[43]

Individual churches and denominations often urge parishioners to approach legislators about moral issues. In the late 1980s the Christian Action Commission of the state Baptist convention coordinated lobbying efforts that helped defeat a proposed state lottery. Volunteers called Baptists around the state and urged them to make contact with their legislators. Southern Baptists have strongly supported state Sunday closing laws, which were recently repealed, while the Presbyterian denomination is heavily identified with the Right to Life cause. The lobbying of religious denominations may be especially important in influencing legislators who share that religion. In recent years, Baptist legislators have voted heavily against a lottery bill, while Presbyterian lawmakers strongly supported the parental consent for minors' abortion bill.[44] Religious groups have killed other gambling proposals in the legislature, except for a 1989 measure that permitted a cruise ship en route to international waters to begin gambling in territorial waters, and a 1990 measure legalizing riverboat gambling on the Mississippi River. They were enacted as economic development measures that would attract tourism.

LABOR ASSOCIATIONS

Chartered in Mississippi in 1957, by the late 1980s the state AFL-CIO had over 80,000 working-class members, though it has suffered declining membership because of rising imports. It often opposes the goals of the business organizations already discussed, such as tort reform and prohibiting collective bargaining in the public sector. In these two instances it has generally been on the winning side. It has been less successful in improving workers' compensation or actually unionizing the public sector. The association's major resource is people. Many labor union volunteers actively supported the election of Democratic congressmen Wayne Dowdy, Mike Espy, and Mike Parker by working in get-out-the-vote drives.[45]

An important political force was born with the unifying of separate black and white teachers' organizations in 1976 into the Mississippi Association of Educators (MAE). The MAE represents over half of the public school teachers in the state and distributes a monthly newspaper to members. It is very active in the electoral process, interviewing and endorsing candidates, funding them, and then using its large membership to staff phone banks and get out the vote on election day. In the 1980s, for example, it successfully supported the elections of congressmen Espy, Dowdy, and Parker (all Democrats) but was unsuccessful in promoting Dowdy to the United States Senate.

In the 1980s the MAE became increasingly involved in the politics of confrontation. In 1982 several thousand teachers demonstrated at the state capitol in support of the Education Reform Act. In 1985 17,000 teachers demonstrated at the capitol in support of starting to bring teacher salaries up to the regional average. Subsequently, the first teacher strike in the state's history (which was most noticeable in the more urbanized southern part of the state) resulted in a significant pay raise for teachers. Yet teachers' salaries in 1987 remained the lowest in the region, and the MAE was unsuccessful in urging the legislature to lower the 60 percent vote margin required for passage of school bond issues to a majority.[46] In 1988 the newly elected MAE-backed governor, Ray Mabus, proposed a state budget that sought to raise teachers' salaries to the Southeast average. A modified version of Mabus's proposal, providing a significant raise over two years, was enacted by the legislature. In 1990 further educational improvements fell victim to a funding dispute between the governor and the legislature, as Mabus sought to legalize a lottery and video poker and to increase fees for citizens using various government services, while many legislators preferred to raise taxes. Hence Mabus's education reform program BEST (Better Education for Success Tomorrow) went unfunded, and by 1991 teachers' salaries had fallen back toward the national cellar.

Rising educational levels and the in-migration of professionals have led in the past two decades to the emergence of various public interest organizations dedicated to changing the status quo. Their rise illustrates how Mississippi is evolving from a very traditionalistic state into a more modern, cosmopolitan state with a multitude of competing interest groups. A predecessor of these citizens' groups was the National Association for the Advancement of Colored People (NAACP), which has fought for basic human rights for blacks in Mississippi since the 1950s.

The NAACP was most active and successful in the 1950s and 1960s, promoting integration and voting rights for blacks. The pace of change was so great that Mississippi elected more blacks to public office than did any other state except Alabama (646 served in 1989). But complacency and declining membership started to plague the organization in 1970. In the 1980s the NAACP returned to its earlier tactics of economic boycotts and marches, leading the Indianola school board to hire a black superintendent and the Canton school board to appoint a black board member. It continued to resort frequently to the judicial system, successfully fighting for the establishment of a black majority congressional district in the Delta (which elected a black man—Mike Espy—in 1986).[47]

The American Civil Liberties Union was organized in Mississippi in 1969 to protect individuals' constitutional rights. With one of the smallest chapters in the nation, it relies heavily on lawyers who volunteer their time to file lawsuits against allegedly unconstitutional state actions. In the 1980s the ACLU was successful in court fights opposing prayer in the public schools, a law requiring minors to get parental consent for abortions, and the practice of using the lights in the Siller's state office building to form a cross at Christmas. The ACLU was also successful in 1980 in striking down a state law targeted against all foreign students, requiring them to pay the "full cost" of their higher education. (The law was passed in reaction to the Iranian hostage situation.)[48]

Another public interest group is Common Cause, formed in Mississippi in 1972 to promote government's accountability to the people. With a small membership and limited budget, it relies on newspaper editorials and a quarterly newsletter to promote its positions. It has successfully urged the establishment of an Ethics Commission, open records, open meetings, and a PAC (political action committee) reporting law, though it has been unsuccessful in getting the legislature to call a constitutional convention.[49]

The defeat of the Education Reform Act in the 1982 regular legislative session, after obstructionist maneuvers by legislative leaders, angered many professionals and progressives. Some formed an organization called Mississippi First to fight the Old Guard politicians and promote education. Their lobbying helped pass the act in a special legislative session later that year. Mississippi First then raised about $100,000 for the 1983 legislative elections, targeting fifty races and winning over half. The organization distributes a newsletter and raises money through direct-mail tactics. In 1987 it unsuccessfully fought for a constitutional convention and once again endorsed favored candidates in the legislative elections.[50]

The late 1980s saw the rise or increased activity of other progressive interest groups, making many political observers optimistic about Mississippi's future. In 1987 prominent business leaders formed the Council for Support of Public Higher Education in Mississippi, and in newspaper and television advertisements they urged the legislature to raise income taxes to increase funding for higher education (which had been cut the previous year). After losing in a close vote in an election year, the council broadened its mandate to include all levels of public education and backed Governor Mabus's successful effort to increase funding for public elementary, secondary, and higher education by $200 million. Anticipating the need to push for the governor's "Education Reform Act II," in 1989 the council merged with the newly formed Public School Forum of Mississippi, an organization of leading state businessmen, educators, and public officials modeled after the successful Public School Forum of North Carolina.[51] In 1987, Mississippi 2020 was formed by professionals in an effort to promote public awareness of the need to improve the quality of life in the state. The Mississippi Federation of Business and Professional Women (formed in 1921) has become more actively involved in the political process in recent years, supporting improvements in public programs such as elementary, secondary, and higher education.[52]

IMPLICATIONS

The pace of change in Mississippi has been great in recent years. Mississippi has been transformed from a relatively closed, rural, traditional, and conservative-dominated society into a more modern, cosmopolitan state with a multitude of competing interest groups. Although traditional institutions such as the family and religion remain strong, the increased number of young, well-educated residents has led to greater concern for promoting modernization. Economic concerns have become salient to many residents,

and improving education has become a popular issue. A well-educated population is seen as instrumental in attracting high-wage industries to the state.
Reflecting the public's support for modernization, an increasing number of
reform-oriented interest groups and political leaders have emerged in recent
years. They face traditionalistic interest groups and citizens, who remain a
force to be reckoned with. The great poverty of Mississippi also makes it difficult to fund many worthy, reform-oriented programs. It is therefore likely
that the struggle over the future direction of public policy in Mississippi will
be long and difficult.

CHAPTER FIVE

Party and Electoral Politics in Mississippi

Stephen D. Shaffer

Mississippi farmers put their faith in God, next year's crop, and the Democratic party.

F. John Wade, 1979[1]

Mississippi approaches a benchmark in its history, for the signs are present that past political traditions are crumbling. . . . Social change is gradually taking place in the state, as its population grows and diversifies, as urbanization increases, and as industrialization advances. . . . Republicanism in Mississippi is becoming tied to the type of socioeconomic cleavage which it represents nationally.

Raymond Tatalovich, 1976[2]

THE EVOLUTION OF PARTY AND ELECTORAL POLITICS

A Traditionalistic Political Order in Transition

For many decades the Democratic party served as the bulwark of Mississippi's traditionalistic culture. The cotton culture of the Delta was dependent on large numbers of black workers. This economic system produced a traditionalistic social and political order that promoted stability and resisted change. "Farmers had to cope with unpredictable weather and unpredictable cotton prices. But they could at least try to keep everything else stable."[3] Delta leaders sought to limit government spending and restrict popular participation in politics through a one-party system.[4] The state's rural and

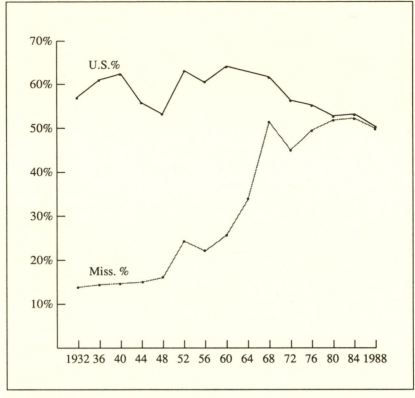

Figure 2. Voter turnout in presidential elections. (*Source*: U.S. Bureau of the Census, *Statistical Abstract of the United States, 1960, 1970, 1981, 1990* [Washington, D.C.: U.S. Department of Commerce, 1960, 1970, 1981, 1990].)

small-town geographic and social setting helped reinforce the traditional political order.

Historically, public participation in politics has been very limited (fig. 2).
As late as 1948 only 16 percent of the eligible adult population voted in the
presidential election. Turnout increased slightly in the 1950s as the civil
rights movement began and reached 34 percent in 1964 as the federal Justice
Department began to aggressively protect voting rights. The 1965 Voting
Rights Act, which outlawed literacy and constitutional interpretation tests
and authorized federal registrars to register blacks in areas of discrimination,
greatly expanded the Mississippi electorate. Turnout in the 1968 election
rose to 53 percent, only 8 percent below the national average. As politics became competitive in Mississippi and turnout declined nationally, turnout in
Mississippi in presidential elections in the 1980s fell only 1 percent below the

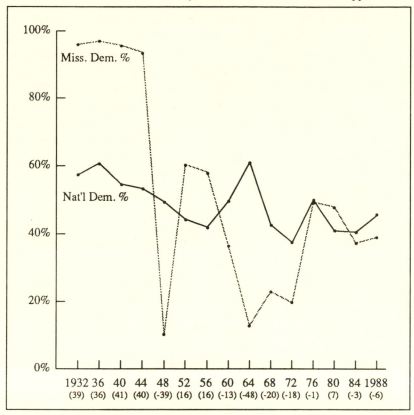

Figure 3. Presidential elections in Mississippi and the nation. Percentage of the total vote received by the Democratic presidential candidate in Mississippi (*broken line*) and the nation (*solid line*). Values in parentheses indicate the extent to which Mississippi was more Democratic than the nation (in percentage differences between the two lines). (*Sources*: U.S. Bureau of the Census, *Statistical Abstract of the United States, 1981, 1990* [Wash., D.C.: U.S. Department of Commerce, 1981, 1990]; Congressional Quarterly Inc., *Presidential Elections since 1789* [Wash., D.C.; 1975].)

national average. In view of the low socioeconomic status of the state's population, such heightened participation is especially impressive, since lower socioeconomic status groups have low turnout rates across the nation.[5]

The Democratic party, as the defender of white supremacy, was supported by the overwhelming majority of white Mississippians for nearly a century after the Civil War.[6] As late as 1944 Mississippi was one of the most Democratic states in the nation, casting 94 percent of its vote for presidential candidate Franklin D. Roosevelt (fig. 3). Indeed, the liberal orientation of

Roosevelt's New Deal program on economic issues may have reinforced the Democratic orientation of white Mississippians, who on average were significantly poorer than other Americans and therefore benefited from many New Deal programs. Those blacks who could vote generally supported the Republican party out of tradition as the party of emancipation from slavery. Until the 1950s, leading blacks such as lawyer Perry Howard led the small state "Black and Tan" Republican party. The Republican party's operations in the state were largely restricted to awarding federal patronage during Republican presidential administrations.[7]

Roosevelt's success in transforming the Democratic party from a subordinate party based in the South to a national party attracting lower socioeconomic status groups (such as blacks) spelled the beginning of the end of the one-party Democratic tradition in Mississippi. One of the first signals of the partisan realignment (changes in public support for the two major parties) occurred at the 1948 Democratic national convention, when the adoption of a strong civil rights plank supported by northern liberals and blacks led to a walkout of the Mississippi delegation and half of the Alabama delegation. A new third party, the "Dixiecrats," led by presidential nominee (and South Carolina governor) Strom Thurmond with Mississippi governor Fielding Wright as vice presidential candidate, carried the state in November, limiting Democrat Harry Truman to 10 percent of the vote. In the 1950s race was not a major issue in the presidential contests, but the popularity of war hero Dwight Eisenhower and his conservative orientation held the Democrats to much smaller victory margins than Roosevelt attained.

The Decade of Reaction—the 1960s

The election of John Kennedy as president in 1960 began a full-scale federal assault on racial segregation and voter disfranchisement in Mississippi and the rest of the South. Mississippi's support for the national Democratic party continued to decline, and the national party repeatedly failed to carry the state (fig. 3). Indeed, it even became socially acceptable for whites to vote Republican, and the Republican party made gains because of its conservative positions on economic and civil rights issues. Mississippi voted for an independent electoral slate pledged to Virginia senator Harry Byrd in 1960 and voted heavily for Republican Barry Goldwater in 1964, Independent George Wallace in 1968, and Republican Richard Nixon in 1972. In the 1964–72 elections, the conservative views of white Mississippians on many issues other than civil rights also played a role in minimizing their support for the more liberal Democratic presidential nominees.[8]

State politics was dominated by white resistance to integration, which infected the emerging Republican party as well as Democratic candidates and molded all the governors of this period. Governor Ross Barnett, elected in 1959, was reportedly the handpicked candidate of the white Citizens' Councils, and his campaign song declared, "Roll with Ross. / He's for segregation one hundred percent. / He's not a mod-rate like some other gent." In 1963 Republican Rubel Phillips pledged that he was a "staunch segregationist" and tried to tie his Democratic opponent to the unpopular Kennedy administration with the campaign slogan, "K.O. the Kennedys." But this issue was neutralized, since Democrat Paul Johnson was also a segregationist who had become known for a racist remark about the NAACP. Johnson was elected governor with 62 percent of the vote.[9]

In 1966 Republican Prentiss Walker, a chicken farmer elected to Congress on Goldwater's coattails in 1964, also attempted to tie a Democratic candidate—this time Senator James Eastland—to the Kennedy-Johnson administration. However, the conservative "Boll Weevil" Eastland was easily re-elected with 66 percent of the vote. (Boll Weevil is a term applied by the national press to conservative southern Democrats in Congress, who often vote with Republicans in opposition to the positions of most northern Democrats.) In 1967 Rubel Phillips ran for governor again, but this time as a racial moderate. After being reluctantly endorsed by the black-dominated Mississippi Freedom Democratic party, he immediately repudiated it as a "kiss of death type of endorsement." Democrat John Bell Williams, a segregationist who had been stripped of his congressional seniority for actively supporting Goldwater for president in 1964, was easily elected governor.

The Decade of Change—the 1970s

As desegregation progressed and blacks received the vote, the race issue became less salient in Mississippi politics, and more progressive candidates ran for office. As the forces of change in the form of television, the younger generation, rising educational levels, and in-migration of professionals swept the state, Mississippi politics began to resemble politics in other states. Voters became motivated by the same forces that existed throughout the nation, such as ideology, presidential coattails, and incumbency. Black power continued to grow as a political force, which inadvertently helped the growing Republican party by encouraging more conservative whites to support some Republican candidates.

In 1971 the continued organizational split between white and black Democrats led charismatic Charles Evers, black mayor of Fayette and brother of slain civil rights worker Medgar Evers, to run as an independent candidate for governor against Democrat William Waller. Waller won easily, and Evers received only 22 percent of the vote. (There was no Republican candidate.) Waller publicly proclaimed himself a "national" Democrat and became the first governor since Reconstruction to appoint blacks to public office.[10]

The year 1972 saw the election of two Republican congressmen, Thad Cochran and Trent Lott, representing the more urban fourth (the state capital, Jackson) and fifth (the Gulf Coast) congressional districts. Both Republicans were advantaged by factors that shape election outcomes across the nation, such as the retirement of a popular incumbent, a divisive primary in the other party, and presidential coattails. (President Nixon carried these districts with 76 percent and 87 percent of the vote, respectively.) Demonstrating the continued uniqueness of Mississippi, Republican Cochran was also helped by a split in the normally Democratic vote between a white Democratic candidate and a black independent. Reflecting the electoral advantages of congressional incumbency that exist nationally, both of these Republicans were reelected in subsequent years by substantial margins (68–100 percent), despite representing a traditionally Democratic state.

By 1975 Mississippi politics had become surprisingly progressive. Democratic gubernatorial candidate Cliff Finch successfully formed a black and working class white coalition by using "populist" rhetoric and a "workingman's" image. Finch's campaign symbol was a lunch pail with his name on it, and he devoted one day a week to working at different jobs like driving a bulldozer and pumping gas. Republican Gil Carmichael won a respectable 45 percent of the vote (Finch received 52 percent) after an issue-oriented campaign pushing progressive measures such as a new state constitution, the Equal Rights Amendment, handgun control legislation, and a compulsory school attendance law. As governor, Cliff Finch was successful in unifying the black and white factions of the Democratic party under cochairmen of both races.[11]

The 1978 retirement of Boll Weevil Eastland and the Democratic nomination of a white Democrat, Maurice Dantin, crystallized black disillusionment with the tradition that both of the state's United States senators were conservative white Democrats. The charismatic black leader Charles Evers entered the contest as an independent, brought in boxer Muhammed Ali to campaign for him, and toured the Delta to encourage black turnout. For the first time since Reconstruction, a Republican won a statewide election (Cochran was elected senator with 45 percent of the vote), as the normally

Democratic vote split between Dantin, who received 32 percent of the vote, and Evers, who received 23 percent. This prompted black leader Aaron Henry to remind Evers's followers that blacks had considerable influence within the Democratic party and would be hurt by the election of conservative Republicans.[12]

By 1979 the Democratic party was united once again, and Democrat William Winter defeated Republican Gil Carmichael with a whopping 61 percent of the vote. Winter had long been a racial moderate (which contributed to his defeat in the 1967 Democratic gubernatorial runoff primary). As governor he persuaded the legislature to enact the landmark 1982 Education Reform Act.

Convergence with the Nation—the 1980s

An increasingly competitive political environment characterized the 1980s. Republicans carried Mississippi in all three presidential elections, because of the liberalism of Democratic presidential candidates and the popularity of Ronald Reagan and George Bush. Yet the partisan gap between Mississippi and the nation was far narrower than in the 1960s, illustrating the declining salience of the race issue among whites as well as increased activism by more liberal voting groups such as blacks (fig. 3). The rising strength of the Republicans forced the Democratic party to reinvigorate its diverse, biracial coalition. Although Republicans carried the presidential races and two Senate contests, Democrats were victorious in other prominent elections. The forces of dealignment transformed the political landscape as voters moved away from blindly voting for one party and focused more on the qualities of the candidates.

By 1981 the partisan identifications of Mississippians had shifted from heavily Democratic to a much more balanced state: 48 percent of Mississippians labeled themselves Democrats, compared with 18 percent Republican and 34 percent Independent.[13] Historically one of the most Democratic states in the nation, Mississippi was now only modestly more Democratic and less Republican than the nation as a whole. Reflecting the national pattern, Mississippi temporarily became more Democratic in 1982 during an economic recession occurring under a Republican administration, but then it became more Republican in 1984 and 1986 as the overall economy recovered and President Reagan's popularity increased. By 1986 white Mississippians were evenly split between the two parties. Yet the state overall remained somewhat more Democratic than the nation as a whole, primarily because of the large numbers of blacks and lower-income whites in the state. By 1990,

45 percent of Mississippians called themselves Democrats, while 27 percent were Republicans and 28 percent were Independents.[14]

Elections in the second and fourth congressional districts illustrate the importance of the black vote and the fragile nature of the Democratic coalition. A special election was held in 1981 for the fourth congressional district seat—a seat previously held by Republican Jon Hinson, who had resigned after being charged with attempted oral sodomy involving an employee of the Library of Congress in a Capitol Hill restroom. In this Democratic success story Wayne Dowdy, the white Democratic mayor of McComb, defeated Republican Liles Williams by a narrow 1 percent of the vote. After Dowdy pledged to vote for an extension of the Voting Rights Act, black leaders rallied to his cause. He was also successful at winning much of the lower-income white vote, as his opponent ran ads attacking labor unions. Dowdy defeated Williams again in 1982 with 53 percent of the vote after stressing his strong support for social security, an issue that cut across racial lines, and his appointment of a black administrative assistant. He effectively used his incumbency to gain re-election by larger margins.

Racial divisions were more evident in the second congressional "Delta" district, which had been redrawn in 1982 to include a 54 percent black population majority. In this contest for an open seat, veteran black state legislator Robert Clark won the Democratic nomination and faced former circuit judge and Democrat-turned-Republican Webb Franklin. Ideology was a major factor in this contest. Franklin had compiled a conservative, law-and-order record as judge, and Clark attacked the effects of Reaganomics in this low income district. The Franklin campaign was also accused of trying to make race an issue by having as an initial slogan "The One for Us" and by including Robert Clark's picture in his campaign brochures. Franklin's campaign also ran a television commercial showing a Confederate monument in his hometown with the candidate saying, "You know, there's something about Mississippi that outsiders will never, ever understand. The way we feel about our family and God, and the traditions that we have."[15] On election day black turnout was lower than expected, perhaps because in the campaign Clark had stressed his acceptability to whites. (He served as chairman of the state House Education Committee.) Many also viewed his campaign organization as inept. Franklin won 51 percent of the two-party vote and went on to defeat Clark a second time by the same margin in 1984, despite court-ordered redistricting that increased the black majority of the district to 58 percent.

The 1983 gubernatorial contest illustrated the power of a unified, biracial

Democratic coalition. Democrat Bill Allain ran a populist campaign stressing his image as a fighter who as attorney general had opposed utility company price hikes. The Republican challenger was a little-known, wealthy,
conservative Clarksdale planter, Leon Bramlett. As the campaign progressed and Allain continued to hold a substantial lead, a group of Bramlett's
wealthy supporters charged that the divorced Allain was a homosexual.
They produced signed statements from three male prostitutes who claimed
they had had intercourse with him.[16] Allain denied the charges and went on
to win the election with 55 percent of the vote to 39 percent for Bramlett.
Two days after the election at the state NAACP convention, Allain thanked
blacks for supporting him. Two months later the three transvestites retracted
their stories. The bizarre episode initially hurt the Allain administration, as
well as raising doubts in the minds of many people.

   The 1986 elections further demonstrated the strength of the majority
Democratic party when economic issues are salient and the party remains
united. As in the 1982 and 1984 election campaigns, Democratic party officials like Senator Stennis, Governor Allain, and the state party chairman
campaigned for the black Democratic nominee for the second congressional
district. Democrat Mike Espy blamed Republican Franklin's support of Reagan administration policies for the poor economic conditions in the black
majority and rural district. Enough whites stayed home or supported Espy to
elect him (with 52 percent of the vote) as the first black congressman from
Mississippi since Reconstruction.

   The decade of the 1980s ended in a demonstration of the extent to which
forces that motivate voters in Mississippi are the same as those motivating
voters throughout the nation. Incumbency and its themes of constituency
service are very powerful, and presidential coattails may also play some
role. In 1988, Congressmen Sonny Montgomery (third district) and Jamie
Whitten (first district) breezed to reelection victories over token opposition
with 89 percent and 78 percent of the vote, respectively. Even Congressman
Mike Espy easily won reelection with 65 percent of the vote, despite being a
liberal black in a racially divided district. Espy united the Democratic party
by stressing his incumbency, his service to the district, and popular economic issues. Mississippi gained a second Republican senator as House Minority Whip Trent Lott won 54 percent of the Senate vote to defeat Wayne
Dowdy. Despite a very conservative voting record, Lott used his funding advantage to wage a nonideological television campaign that stressed his service to the state. He may have also been helped by President Reagan's statewide popularity and Bush's landslide victory in Mississippi. Yet presidential

politics failed to influence any House contest, as voters supported attractive candidates regardless of party. By 1989 Democrats controlled all five United States House seats, including Lott's old district. Freshman Democrats in the fourth and fifth districts had been elected as moderates, independent of the national party.

The Democratic party also remains dominant in state and local offices, though Republicans have made some gains in the wake of the Reagan presidency and the Bush-Lott victories in 1988. After the 1987 state elections, Republican representation in the legislature increased from three to seven state senators and from five to nine representatives. In 1989 and 1990, over seventy state and local Democratic officials reportedly switched to the Republican party. By 1990 Republican representation in the legislature had reached a historical high of nine senators and seventeen house members. Yet these gains still left the minority Republican party with only 17 percent of the membership of the upper chamber and 14 percent of the lower chamber.

One reason for continued Democratic dominance in state and local politics is the inclusiveness of Mississippi's Democratic party, reflecting a history of one-party domination. Democrats constitute a broad coalition in the state, including such ideologically diverse persons as conservatives Sonny Meredith and Sonny Montgomery and liberals Mike Espy, Hodding Carter, Jr., and Aaron Henry. Hence serious candidates are able to run as Democrats regardless of their political philosophy, and victorious Democratic officials naturally reflect the ideological orientations of their districts, which vary from one part of the state to another. Many serious candidates prefer to run as Democrats rather than as Republicans, because they are well aware of the historical Democratic advantage reflected even today in the public's partisan identifications. This Democratic partisan advantage is especially important in less visible state and local elections, because many voters lack interest in these races and knowledge about the candidates or issues and therefore merely vote consistent with their partisan identifications.[17] As Mississippi Republicans further consolidate their gains at the federal level and in party identification, it is likely that they will continue to make greater inroads in state and local elections.

PARTISAN AND ELECTORAL DIFFERENCES AMONG VOTING GROUPS

Socioeconomic Classes and Other Social Groups

For many years after the Civil War, Mississippians remembered the Republican party as the party that had waged the "Yankee" war effort against them and instituted military occupation and Reconstruction of the South. The overwhelming majority of white Mississippians—rich or poor, from high school dropouts to college graduates—proudly wore the Democratic party label. Hence, traditionally there were no significant partisan differences between voting groups in Mississippi. Indeed, some Mississippians were so intensely partisan that they were referred to as "yellow dog" Democrats— they allegedly would vote for anyone who was running as a Democrat, even a yellow dog! The one group most likely to be Republican—blacks—was largely disfranchised.

As the national Democratic party began to promote civil rights and protect labor unions during the New Deal era, many Mississippians came to fear that the party was moving away from them and becoming too liberal.[18] The party's support for civil rights during the Kennedy and Johnson administrations, and its nomination of northern liberals like Hubert Humphrey, George McGovern, Walter Mondale, and Michael Dukakis for president, solidified people's perceptions that the national Democratic party had become substantially more "liberal" than the Republican party. By the 1980s white Mississippians who thought of themselves as "conservatives" had moved away from the Democratic party and were more likely to call themselves Republicans than Democrats (table 2). Self-identified liberals largely retained the Democratic label, as did many middle-of-the-road residents.[19]

Ronald Reagan deserves special recognition as a boon to the state Republican party. His great personal popularity appeared to increase support for the Republicans among a number of social groups. Mississippians rating his job performance as excellent or good were more likely to call themselves Republicans than Democrats, while those rating him only fair or poor were heavily Democratic. Furthermore, among those rating Reagan highly, Republican strength increased during the 1980s, suggesting that popular approval of the Republican president's performance led to an increase in the number of Mississippians calling themselves Republicans.

As Mississippians increasingly viewed the Republicans as the conservative party and the national Democrats as the liberal party (more concerned about poor people and minorities), Republicans made gains among more socially advantaged Mississippians.[20] Throughout most of the 1980s, white Mississippians with higher incomes and college educations were more likely to call themselves Republicans than Democrats. The Democratic party was much stronger among lower income residents and high-school dropouts. While these groups are less likely to vote on election day than the more socially advantaged, the large number of disadvantaged citizens is an important foundation of the state Democratic party. Whites falling between these

Table 2: Correlates of Party Identification among White Mississippians

	Democratic Identification						Republican Identification					
	1981	1982	1984	1986	1988	1990	1981	1982	1984	1986	1988	1990
Family income												
Under $10,000	53	56	49	48	49	54	14	11	22	22	17	19
$10–20,000	46	43	40	28	46	31	25	24	22	32	24	40
Over $20,000	26	34	23	28	22	27	30	24	26	39	38	42
Education												
High-school dropout	53	59	47	37	47	53	17	11	20	25	24	21
High-school graduate	43	42	29	35	38	34	20	18	20	34	33	30
Some college	21	28	29	26	23	22	34	32	29	41	32	48
Ideology												
Liberal	55	46	33	32	40	26	11	20	12	28	23	39
Moderate	41	49	33	34	40	39	21	12	23	28	23	26
Conservative	27	31	26	23	25	21	37	33	30	43	40	56
President's Performance												
Excellent-good	28	27	26	23	24	27	32	30	29	41	40	42
Fair-poor	59	59	52	56	57	45	8	12	9	18	11	24
Age												
Under 30	32	30	26	24	34	21	25	34	31	40	37	56
31–60	41	44	32	31	26	29	23	16	19	36	33	36
61–98	49	59	51	50	56	46	21	14	18	20	16	25

	Democratic Identification						Republican Identification					
	1981	1982	1984	1986	1988	1990	1981	1982	1984	1986	1988	1990
Residence in Mississippi												
0–15 years	23	33	24	21	24	28	25	24	27	36	46	40
Over 15 years	43	46	38	36	36	33	23	19	22	33	27	36
Sex												
Male	37	38	29	28	36	26	23	21	19	37	27	42
Female	43	50	41	39	33	37	23	19	27	30	33	33
Race												
White	40	44	34	33	37	32	23	20	23	34	32	37
Black	75	78	67	76	76	74	7	7	7	8	6	6

Sources: Robert H. Swansbrough and David M. Brodsky, *The South's New Politics: Realignment and Dealignment* (Columbia: University of South Carolina Press, 1988); Stephen D. Shaffer, "Changing Party Politics in Mississippi," in *The South's New Politics: Realignment and Dealignment*, ed. David M. Brodsky (Columbia: University of South Carolina Press, 1988), table 13.4; and state-wide opinion polls conducted by the Social Science Research Center at Mississippi State University.

Note: Table entries indicate the percentages of white Mississippians of various demographic groups who psychologically identify with the Democratic and Republican parties. Entries do not total 100% because of Independents, who are excluded from the table. *N* sizes are omitted from the table to save space; they normally exceed 100 and always exceed 34. The last row provides the partisanship of blacks.

groups—the middle-income whites and high-school graduates—have become fairly evenly divided between the two parties.

Another important source of Democratic party strength is among blacks, who constitute about 30 percent of the state's adult population. Blacks began to move toward the Democratic party in the 1930s, as Roosevelt's New Deal economic programs helped lower-income citizens of both races. In the wake of the Republican nomination of Barry Goldwater for president in 1964—the only senator outside the South who voted against the 1964 Civil Rights Act—and of conservative Ronald Reagan in the 1980s, Mississippi blacks have become heavily Democratic. In the 1980s about 74 percent of blacks considered themselves Democrats and only 7 percent were Republicans. While some speculate that as blacks become more educated and attain higher incomes, many will become Republicans, such socioeconomic status (SES) divisions have not yet emerged. Indeed, higher SES blacks in Mississippi are even more Democratic than are lower SES blacks, perhaps reflecting a greater knowledge of partisan politics and of the Democratic party's liberal orientation that promotes civil rights programs.[21]

Many have observed that demographics are on the side of the Republican party in the South. Unlike the elderly, young people have no personal experience with the Great Depression and how Roosevelt's Democratic party gave hope to millions of poverty-stricken Americans.[22] Instead, the young have grown up in a more affluent society, and many fear an active federal government that may tax their hard-earned incomes to help people they feel should be doing more to help themselves. Beginning in 1982, white Mississippians under thirty became more likely to call themselves Republicans than Democrats, a development especially evident by 1990 (table 2). Another important battleground for the partisan future of Mississippi has become the middle-aged, where Republicans gained a slight advantage over Democrats beginning in 1986. On the other hand, Democrats retain a significant advantage among whites over sixty. Mississippi blacks are heavily Democratic regardless of age, although older blacks are even more heavily Democratic than younger blacks.[23]

It has also been suspected that migrants from other states are more Republican than natives and have helped to bring the kind of competitive two-party politics to Mississippi that exists in most other areas of the nation. Opinion polling data provide some support for this argument, since whites who have lived in Mississippi less than fifteen years are somewhat more likely to be Republican than Democratic, while longtime residents are generally more likely to be Democratic than Republican.[24] On the other hand, there are no significant differences among blacks with different lengths of residency in the state.

The election of Ronald Reagan as president caused a "gender gap" to emerge outside Mississippi, as women moved more toward the liberal Democratic party and men toward the Republican party.[25] The gender gap has begun to appear in Mississippi as well, although it has usually been modest. In every year except 1988, women have been significantly more likely to call themselves Democrats than have men. On the other hand, both sexes were equally likely to label themselves Republicans, and until recently Republicans have generally been outnumbered by Democrats among both men and women. As Mississippi continues to modernize, perhaps women will someday become more politically distinct and mobilized. A growing battle between the sexes would be a fascinating development in a state long known for its success in Miss America contests, and it would signal another important transformation in the state's traditionalistic culture.

Some political scientists have speculated that Independents may serve as a halfway house between the Democratic and Republican parties, as conservative Democrats disillusioned with the liberal orientation of the national party may first begin to call themselves Independents and later convert to the Republican party. It is interesting that some groups that are especially likely to be Republican—such as the more educated and richer, the young, white, and male—are also particularly likely to be Independents, suggesting continued Republican gains among these groups in future years (calculated from table 2). Yet Independents are fairly evenly distributed among all ideological groups, underscoring the popularity of the Independent label in the state.

By the 1980s, not only were social groups in Mississippi divided with respect to their psychological attachment to political parties, but they also supported different parties in the voting booth. Liberals and lower SES groups were much more likely to vote Democratic in presidential and United States Senate elections, while conservatives and higher SES groups were more likely to vote Republican (table 3). In the 1988 presidential campaign, for example, Democrat Michael Dukakis was favored by 83 percent of blacks, 72 percent of the under $10,000 income group, 64 percent of self-identified liberals, and 63 percent of high-school dropouts. Republican George Bush was supported by 80 percent of self-identified conservatives, 79 percent of whites, 73 percent of those making over $20,000 a year, and 70 percent of those with some college education. The gender gap was also evident. Mondale and Dukakis were favored by 46 percent and 43 percent of women, respectively, but only 32 percent and 35 percent of men. All five Democratic

Table 3: Political Differences among Demographic Groups

| | Presidential Vote | | Senate Vote | | |
	1984	1988	1982	1984	1988
Ideology					
Liberal	60	64	76	53	75
Moderate	42	58	67	41	44
Conservative	22	20	63	36	31
Party identification					
Democrat	66	78	85	65	74
Independent	21	17	60	32	26
Republican	14	4	35	20	16
Years lived in Mississippi					
15 or less	24	33	58	36	38
Over 15	42	39	71	45	45
Race					
White	20	21	64	31	28
Black	85	83	80	74	85
Age					
18–30	39	42	71	45	55
31–60	37	36	67	42	39
61–98	41	50	69	43	44
Education					
High-school dropout	52	63	78	56	55
High-school graduate	38	32	74	36	52
Some college	28	30	58	41	29
Income					
Under $10,000	66	72	75	65	61
$10–20,000	40	50	63	39	59
Over $20,000	20	27	65	27	31
Sex					
Male	32	35	65	39	45
Female	46	43	71	47	42
Congressional district					
1	37	38	66	51	51
2	47	49	71	43	47
3	32	41	61	54	40
4	52	31	68	36	49
5	24	34	75	33	30

Source: Statewide opinion polls conducted by the Social Science Research Center at Mississippi State University.

Note: Table entries are the percentage of likely voters who expressed the intention to vote for the Democratic candidates in each year.

presidential and Senate candidates were somewhat stronger among longtime residents of the state, while Republicans were more favored by relative new-comers.

Majorities of self-identified Democrats and Republicans consistently supported the candidates of their parties, while Independents favored the victorious candidate in each case. Being nonaligned with a party, Independents presumably were more influenced by the characteristics of the candidates, such as their personal attributes, issue positions, and incumbency. That Independents favored the Republican candidate in four of these five elections, and by very significant margins in the presidential races, suggests that many self-proclaimed Independents may have underlying Republican sympathies. Such Republican sympathies may be especially noticeable among the large numbers of Independents who have a higher socioeconomic status. On the other hand, these particular elections were contested by popular, well-known, and attractive Republicans and may therefore not be typical of many elections in the state, especially state and local elections. In any event, the future should see Independents continuing to play a pivotal role in the electoral process.

The 1982 Senate contest illustrates how a popular incumbent, especially a Boll Weevil Democrat, can narrow voting differences among social groups. Many voters approved of Senator John Stennis's service to the state, but some were torn between his Democratic partisanship and his relatively conservative voting record. Stennis was supported by 76 percent of self-identified liberals, presumably because he was a Democrat facing a conservative Republican associated with Ronald Reagan (table 3). Yet Stennis's voting record led 63 percent of self-identified conservatives to support him as well. His Democratic partisanship helped attract 80 percent of the black vote, while his record of performance also garnered 64 percent of the white vote.

A major component of the state's traditionalistic political culture—a monolithic one-party system that preserved white supremacy—has clearly disappeared. It is being replaced by a competitive two-party system that is very similar to the national party system in terms of party support among various social groups. The Democratic party in Mississippi is strongest among more liberal and socially disadvantaged groups, such as the poor, high school dropouts, and blacks. The state Republican party's support is based in more conservative and higher SES groups. Despite this transformation of the political party system, Mississippi's traditionalistic history is reflected in the sizable Democratic party advantage among the elderly and longtime residents of the state. Although the Republican party has made impressive gains in recent years, it is unlikely that the political pendulum will swing in the opposite direction to make the Republican party the new majority party in the foreseeable future. The state's large numbers of blacks and disadvantaged whites have a natural home in the Democratic party. A more likely future for Mississippi is one of increasingly intense partisan competition.[26]

Geographic Divisions

Political conflict between the Delta and Hills regions in the first half of the twentieth century was made famous by V. O. Key in *Southern Politics*. Delta whites (led by rich planters) tended to be conservative on economic issues such as the New Deal because of support for individual initiative and states' rights, while Hill whites (often poor farmers) were neopopulists who supported New Deal programs that benefited lower-income whites. From the 1920s until the 1960s, Democratic gubernatorial primaries were contested by conservative candidates who tended to be strongest in the Delta and neopopulists who were strongest in the Hills.[27] The emergence of socioeconomic cleavages between the modern Democratic and Republican parties has supplanted these traditional regional differences within the state.

The geographic implications of Democratic electoral support among lower SES groups such as minorities and Republican support among higher SES groups are quite clear. In presidential elections, black majority counties provide the only solid base of support for liberal Democratic candidates. As Reagan in 1984 and Bush in 1988 swept the state with 62 percent and 60 percent of the vote, all of the counties that Mondale and Dukakis carried (except for one in each election) had black population majorities (map 4). Most counties with black majorities are in the Delta region (see map 3), so the rise of black political power has caused the Delta counties to make a 180-degree turnabout toward liberalism.

A more successful strategy for national Democrats in Mississippi is suggested by the case of Jimmy Carter, a moderate liberal from a southern state, who narrowly carried Mississippi in 1976 with 51 percent of the vote and then narrowly lost it with 49 percent in 1980. Carter was able to expand beyond his party's black counties base by including majority white counties in the rural and tradition-bound northeast (map 5). These figures suggest that national Democratic tickets that are relatively moderate and oriented toward the concerns of the South have the greatest potential to carry the state, while more liberal Democratic tickets lead to Republican presidential victories.

The insulation of state elections from national politics (by being held in

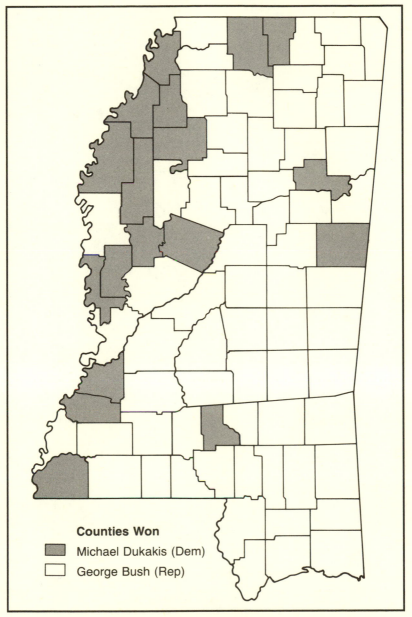

Map 4. The 1988 presidential election.
Dark areas denote counties won by Democrat Michael Dukakis.
Light areas denote those won by Republican George Bush.
(*Source*: Dick Molpus, *Mississippi Official and Statistical Register,
1988–1992* [Jackson: Mississippi Secretary of State, 1989].)

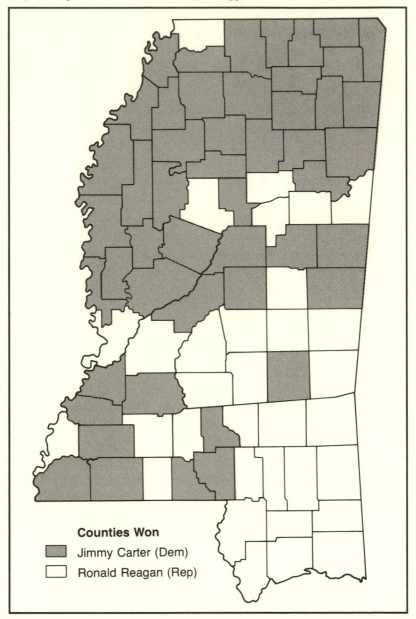

Map 5. The 1980 presidential election.
Dark areas denote counties won by Democrat Jimmy Carter.
Light areas denote those won by Republican Ronald Reagan.
(*Source*: Dick Molpus, *Mississippi Official and Statistical Register,
1980–1984* [Jackson: Mississippi Secretary of State, 1981].)

odd-numbered years) enhances the ability of Democratic gubernatorial candidates to project more moderate images and to construct more broad-based and victorious coalitions, compared with their party's presidential hopefuls. In recent gubernatorial general elections (except in 1987), Republican support among better-educated, higher-income, and more professional occupational groupings has given them a geographic base in the more urban counties of the state. In receiving 45 percent of the popular vote in 1975, Republican Gil Carmichael carried the counties of Hinds and Rankin (containing the city of Jackson and its suburbs), the Gulf Coast counties of Harrison and Jackson (with cities such as Gulfport, Biloxi, and Pascagoula), Lee (growing city of Tupelo), Lafayette (Oxford, home of the University of Mississippi—"Ole Miss"), Oktibbeha (Starkville, home of Mississippi State University), Lowndes (Columbus), Warren (Vicksburg), Lauderdale (Meridian), Jones (Laurel), Forrest (Hattiesburg), Adams (Natchez), as well as the counties of Washington, LeFlore, and Marion (map 6). Against the popular Democrat William Winter, Carmichael in 1979 received only 39 percent of the vote, carrying only three of these counties (Rankin, Harrison, and Jackson). In Republican Bramlett's losing bid in 1983 that also garnered 39 percent of the vote, Bramlett carried seven of the same counties that Carmichael had carried in 1975, as well as neighboring Lamar County.

THE MODERN ERA OF DEALIGNMENT

In recent decades, the nation has undergone a process known as "dealignment," as more and more voters are calling themselves "Independents" rather than Democrats or Republicans and are voting for the "candidate" rather than the party. Congressional candidates throughout the nation are routinely minimizing their partisan labels and stressing the nondivisive issue of their service to all their constituents.[28] To a large extent Mississippi politics mirrors this national development as well, as three senate elections of the 1980s and the 1987 gubernatorial elections demonstrate.[29]

The 1982, 1984, and 1988 Senate Elections

In 1982 Democratic senator John Stennis faced a serious electoral challenge for the first time since he was elected in 1947. The challenger was Haley Barbour, a veteran of state Republican politics for nearly a decade, who was able to spend more money than the incumbent. (Barbour spent $1,107,378, compared with $907,717 for Stennis.) Policy issues were not important in the

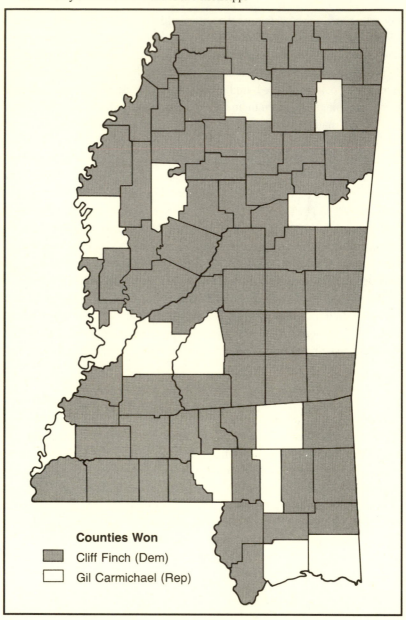

Map 6. The 1975 gubernatorial general election.
Light areas denote counties won by Republican Gil Carmichael.
Dark areas denote those won by Democrat Cliff Finch.
(*Source*: Dick Molpus, *Mississippi Official and Statistical Register,*
1976–1980 [Jackson: Mississippi Secretary of State, 1977].)

campaign, since both candidates were relatively conservative and were Reagan supporters. The thirty-four-year-old challenger's campaign slogan was, "A Senator for the 80s" (unspoken continuation: "rather than a senator in his eighties"), which drew attention to Stennis's major vulnerability—his age of eighty-one.

In fall 1981 Stennis initially relied on the old politics of visiting each county's courthouse, but he quickly shifted to a more modern campaign style. He hired a professional campaign consultant, who ran television advertisements that very effectively blunted the age issue. The ads showed Stennis working long hours in Washington, bounding up steps, and climbing a scaffold to inspect a shipyard. (The camera shows a quiet Washington, D.C., at dawn. The voice says: "It is dawn in the nation's capital. The nation sleeps." Camera shifts to show Stennis working behind his desk at his office. Raised voice: "But one senator is already on the job—John Stennis of Mississippi.") Stennis also stressed his seniority and his work for the state, such as delivering on federal funding for the Tennessee-Tombigbee waterway.[30]

A major problem that Barbour faced was low name recognition, since he had not previously run for political office, and veteran Stennis was clearly the better-known candidate. When asked why they intended to vote as they did, 78 percent of the comments in a poll referred to Stennis, and only 22 percent referred to Barbour.[31] Attributes of the candidates were clearly more important to voters than their partisan affiliation: 42 percent mentioned Stennis's favorable personal attributes or accomplishments, such as his experience, seniority, and job performance, and only 12 percent felt he was too old for the job. To a lesser degree Stennis also benefited by being a Democrat in a Democratic state—17 percent of voters mentioned his party as a reason for voting for him. Reflecting the issueless campaign, fewer than 10 percent of voters mentioned policy issues as reasons for their votes. Stennis easily won reelection with 64 percent of the vote.

In 1984 Republican Senator Thad Cochran ran for reelection without a black Independent in the race to help him by splitting the normally Democratic vote. Despite a conservative voting record, he had a moderate image because of his support for domestic programs important to the low-income state, such as food stamps, rural housing, and aid to "developing institutions" (black colleges). Cochran was challenged by popular former governor William Winter, who was hailed as the architect of the 1982 Education Reform Act. However, some political observers felt that Winter hurt himself and created an image of indecisiveness when in December 1983 he first accepted and then rejected the chancellorship of Ole Miss and then took more than six weeks to enter the contest.[32] Outspending the challenger by $2,791,749 to $738,739, Cochran stressed popular themes such as his seniority and constituency service. One advertisement depicted an elderly lady who had not received her social security check. "And she looked to Thad, and Thad delivered," said the announcer.

Once again incumbency was the key factor in the election, but the name visibility aspect of incumbency was not the problem for Winter, since he had been a prominent former governor. The incumbent senator had an extremely popular image, with 96 percent of the comments about him favorable. (Winter was also popular, but at a lower level; 81 percent of the comments about him were favorable.) Once again candidate attributes completely overshadowed partisan or issue considerations: 67 percent of the comments about the candidates referred to their personal or performance attributes, while 12 percent referred to policy issues and 10 percent referred to partisan considerations. Voters thought both candidates had done (or would do) a good job as senator, but Cochran's seniority, experience, and work for the state gave him the advantage over Winter. Coffee-shop talk about the indecisiveness issue did not appear to be important, since fewer than 1 percent of respondents mentioned indecisiveness or the Ole Miss episode as a reason for voting against Winter.[33] Cochran won reelection with an impressive 61 percent of the vote.

In 1988 conservative Republican Trent Lott received 54 percent of the vote to defeat moderate Democrat Wayne Dowdy and gain the Senate seat vacated by Stennis. A key strategic decision was Lott's use of effective television advertisements produced by the Robert Goodman agency in Washington to counter anticipated attacks on his conservative house voting record.[34] These visually appealing ads portrayed Lott as a defender of social security, student loans, highway funding, the environment, and other programs for which he had previously voted to reduce funding. Paid for with a campaign war chest estimated at a record $3.2 million to Dowdy's $2.1 million, Lott's ads dominated the airwaves.[35] Lott also stressed themes relied on by incumbents, such as his influence in Washington as House minority whip and his service to his constituents. Newspaper pictures showed him meeting with other prominent political leaders such as Senate minority leader and presidential candidate Robert Dole. On a stop in northeast Mississippi, Lott pledged improved highways and more jobs. On the Gulf Coast Lott claimed credit for the $8 million Fort Bayou Bridge in Ocean Springs, and in Hattiesburg his spokesman claimed that Lott had secured federal funding for flood control projects in Laurel and Hattiesburg.[36]

As in the two previous Senate elections, voters appeared to be most influenced by the overall images of the candidates' personal qualities and their performance in office rather than by partisan or ideological concerns. In one poll, voters generally perceived that Lott had done a "good job," that he had helped Mississippi, and that he was influential, able, experienced, and qualified, and some just said they liked him without being specific. Contrary to the views of some political observers who interpret election outcomes in ideological terms, partisanship and ideology appeared to have little influence over the election outcome. Although some voters mentioned Lott's conservative philosophy as a reason for supporting him, an equal number mentioned Dowdy's support for domestic programs such as welfare and education as reasons for voting Democratic. Partisan considerations also canceled out, as Dowdy's advantage in being a Democrat was countered by voter affection for Reagan and approval of his party's performance while controlling the White House. Mississippi voters continue to dealign and to behave independently of the two parties, voting for the candidates instead of the parties.[37]

The 1987 Gubernatorial Election

The 1987 gubernatorial race also illustrates how candidates have become more independent of the traditional party organizations and how many voters base their decisions on the characteristics of the candidates rather than their partisan ties. The Democratic nominee was Ray Mabus, thirty-nine-year-old Harvard Law School graduate. As state auditor, Mabus had received much publicity for his numerous investigations into illegal practices of county and local officials, such as some politically powerful county supervisors. Mabus was also strongly committed to improving education, having been an architect of the 1982 Education Reform Act while a member of Governor Winter's staff. The Republican nominee was a progressive Tupelo businessman, Jack Reed. Chairman of the state board of education, Reed had actively supported the 1982 Education Reform Act, as well as serving as a member of the Council for Support of Public Higher Education. In the 1960s his had been one of the lonely voices counseling racial tolerance and moderation.

The general election campaign reflected bipartisan agreement on the progressive goals of improving education, attracting industry, and reforming government, as well as some differences on how to achieve these goals. For example, while both candidates supported raising public school teachers' pay to the Southeast average, Mabus pledged to accomplish this in one year, while Reed suggested a longer time frame, such as four or five years. Stylistic differences between the candidates were interesting. Reflecting the growing public distrust of politicians that has swept the nation, Reed's television and newspaper ads stressed that he was "not a professional politician" but a successful businessman and civic leader. Mabus's television ads talked about his fight against government corruption as auditor and about his promise of a new day dawning in Mississippi with his progressive public policies, so that under his administration "Mississippi will never be last again."

Borrowing from Carter's successful nonideological approach in the early primaries of 1976, when he promised a government "that is as good, and honest, and decent, and truthful, and fair, and competent, and idealistic, and compassionate, and as filled with love as are the American people,"[38] Mabus promised "a government that is as honest and hard-working as the people of this state."[39] Reed's campaign ran a television advertisement that showed a farmer standing next to a horse and saying (paraphrased): "When Mabus promises to raise teachers' salaries to the Southeast average without increasing my taxes, he doesn't credit me with the horse-sense that ole Nell here has. Why I deal with that kind of thing every day." Then the farmer picked up a shovel and began to clean up horse manure. This advertisement was very similar to one that aired in another state in 1980 with the same scene and antitax theme.[40] By the 1980s Mississippi political campaigns were employing media consultants and pollsters with nationwide experience and relying on some of the same themes and approaches used in other areas of the country. (Mabus employed Doak, Shrum, and Associates of Washington, D.C., while Reed hired Ailes Communications of New York City.)[41]

Spending a record $2.9 million (shattering the $2.3 million mark set by Sturdivant earlier in the year) and exceeding Reed's $1.8 million, Mabus nevertheless won with a modest 53 percent of the vote. Despite an independent and progressive image, Reed was seriously hurt by receiving little support from blacks, who associated anyone on the Republican ticket with conservative Reagan policies unpopular in the black community. He was unable to carry any majority black county. Reed also lost some urban counties such as Hinds and the Gulf Coast to Mabus. Mabus's impressive educational background and progressive image attracted significant support from higher SES voters who normally vote Republican, thereby helping him carry more urban and Republican counties.[42] Reed did make inroads into some traditionally Democratic rural counties. Mabus's crusade as auditor against corruption and inefficiency at the county level hurt him among county supervisors, who are especially influential in rural areas. Perhaps the national Republican party's association with the conservative position on social issues like abortion and school prayer and Reed's stress on the importance of the family also helped the Republican carry more conservative rural areas that normally vote Democratic out of tradition.

This election illustrates how gubernatorial as well as Senate campaigns can become personalist and heavily influenced by the characteristics of the candidates involved. It also shows how the political context can shape voting patterns. The absence of ideologically distinct candidates can lead to a politics of quicksand as traditional political patterns are rearranged in response to a changing political environment.

STATE PARTY LEADERS

The State Party Organizations

Some political scientists have pointed out that despite the growing number of citizens who call themselves Independents and who vote for the "candidate" instead of the party, many state party organizations are fairly strong and active, especially in the Republican party. In the South the aggressiveness of Republican party organizations and improved Republican electoral fortunes have forced Democratic organizations to become more active.[43] The Mississippi state party organizations conform to this regional pattern fairly well. The Republican party is the better organized, more active, and better financed, and the Democrats have become more active in recent years in response to this growing Republican challenge.

Both political parties have executive committees and chairs in all eighty-two counties of the state, though they vary in how active they are. Democratic county committees are especially active in state election years in order to certify Democratic candidates. Republican county committees are most active in urban areas and least active in rural areas, reflecting the party's electoral strengths and weaknesses.[44] Reflecting their party philosophy of states' rights, Republicans permit their county organizations the autonomy to adopt their own platforms.[45]

Each party has an established state headquarters with a fluctuating number of staff members. In nonelection years, both parties retain such key positions as chairman, executive director, political director, and administrative assistants. Staffing reaches a peak during election years with the addition of field directors and manned phone banks for get-out-the-vote drives. The parties are able to attract as staff members talented, college-educated people who are motivated by an interest in politics, a need to gain experience, and a desire to meet people. Because of low salaries, staff turnover is very high, and most staff members leave after only one or two years. In the wake of Republican presidential and Senate victories in 1988, some Democratic state and local officials switched to the Republican party. State auditor Pete Johnson's switch in 1989 gave the Republicans their first statewide elected position since Reconstruction. Democrats responded by upgrading the position of executive director and hiring a Massachusetts native with experience in the Mondale-Ferraro campaign who pledged to modernize the state party.[46]

Both parties have respectable financial resources with diverse funding sources, although the Republicans have a decided edge with an average annual budget in the late 1980s of $500,000, compared with about $200,000 for the Democrats. The Republican financial structure includes: the United Republican Fund, consisting of about 1,300 people who pledge $10 to $15 each month, which is the lifeblood of the party because it provides a steady income; a telemarketing operation involving ten employees who make phone calls each weeknight to Republicans and those living in Republican areas (generating on average $150,000 a year); a direct-mail approach that employs an outside firm; fund-raising dinners each year boasting prominent speakers such as presidential hopefuls; and the Capital Foundation, consisting of about one hundred major donors who contribute at least $500 a year, which makes contributions to candidates and funds capital purchases for the state party (such as a recently acquired computer).

The state Democratic party also raises funds through direct mail, phone calls, a bank draft program, and fund-raising dinners. County Democratic organizations periodically hold "Beans and Greens" dinners and rallies with prominent state figures such as the governor and state party chairman as speakers. The funds raised are divided equally between the state party and county party. Each year a prominent national Democrat speaks at the Jefferson-Jackson Day dinner to raise funds and attract new members. The Democrats also have a master file of people who have in some way demonstrated recent support for the Democratic party or its candidates. Funds solicited from this group help to finance special projects (such as a new state party headquarters).

The state parties are actively involved in helping to elect their candidates by making modest financial donations and conducting substantial get-out-the-vote drives. The state Democrats sometimes contract with political consultants to assist their candidates, while the Republicans frequently offer candidate training schools. Both state parties have access to polls conducted by their candidates, and the state Republican party sometimes conducts its own polls. Both parties are also active in platform writing, adopting platforms at the state party conventions held in presidential election years. Republican state party chairmen have been active in recruiting community leaders to run as Republican candidates, while some members of the Democratic state executive committee have engaged in similar candidate recruitment. Neither party makes preprimary endorsements of candidates, but they do encourage party members to meet with and consider all of the party's hopefuls.

Recent party platforms illustrate how the parties agree on the need to reform state and local government, attract industry, and improve education but disagree on many economic and civil liberty issues. In the late 1980s both parties supported reforming the constitution of 1890; strengthening the governor's office by letting the governor run for reelection; more efficiently managing government through adopting the county unit system for centralized highway building and repair and consolidating city and county services; reforming the judicial system through uniform sentencing guidelines and restitution to victims; raising teachers' pay to the Southeast average; and making many highways four lanes to help attract industry. Differing ideological emphases arose on civil liberties issues. Democrats stressed their support for affirmative action and sex equality legislation. Republicans stressed support for school prayer, revoking bond for repeat offenders and drug addicts, and requiring prisoners to work and get job training. On economic issues, Democrats supported national health insurance and hospital cost containment legislation, while Republicans want to require able-bodied welfare recipients to work and to limit liability judgments against businesses (tort reform issue). On labor-management issues, Democrats proclaim their support for collective bargaining, while Republicans reiterate their support for right-to-work laws and opposition to public employee strikes.

The State Party Conventions

Recent decades have seen tremendous political change reshaping the nature of the state's political parties, as blacks have gained considerable influence within the state Democratic party. At the 1984 Democratic state party convention, for example, 48 percent of the delegates were black, accurately reflecting the 47 percent of Democratic party identifiers in the state population who were black. Blacks have made fewer gains within the Republican party, largely because of the dearth of black support for the Republican party. For instance, only 7 percent of the delegates at the 1984 Republican state party convention were black, reflecting the mere 12 percent of Republican party identifiers in the state population who were black.

State and national studies of party activists and officials have found them to be more ideologically polarized than the public as a whole, and modern-day Mississippi conforms to that pattern. For example, 75 percent of delegates to the 1984 state Republican party convention labeled themselves "conservative" and only 1 percent liberal, while 53 percent of the delegates to the state Democratic convention called themselves "liberal" and only 9 percent conservative.[47] Across a range of diverse issues, Democratic delegates consistently supported the more liberal position than did Republican delegates, and more often than not majorities of each party were found taking the opposite point of view on a given issue (fig. 4: letters above line). The public generally holds more moderate views. Majorities of Democratic and Republican identifiers, for example, decline to identify themselves as liberals or conservatives. Hence, on all issues examined except one the ideological distance between party activists is greater than that between partisans in the general population (fig. 4: letters below line signify the population).

When one considers the diversity of a state population, which includes blacks who are generally liberal and whites whose ideological orientations depend on their socioeconomic status, age, and sex, it is understandable that the Republican party is not automatically advantaged electorally by issues. The ideological polarization of party leaders should not impede the development of a competitive two-party system in the state, but it does suggest that neither party is likely to become dominant because of its ideological issue orientations.

CONTINUITY AND CHANGE IN MISSISSIPPI POLITICS

Continuity and change are evident in the role of the state's political culture in shaping partisan competition. In the 1950s and 1960s, when state political leaders opposed racial desegregation, the traditionalistic culture completely structured political competition as candidates of both parties resisted integration. In the 1980s traditional values were still evident, especially in national elections. Candidates closely associated with the liberal philosophy of the national Democratic party were viewed by opinion leaders as being outside of the limits of acceptability and had little chance of winning in state

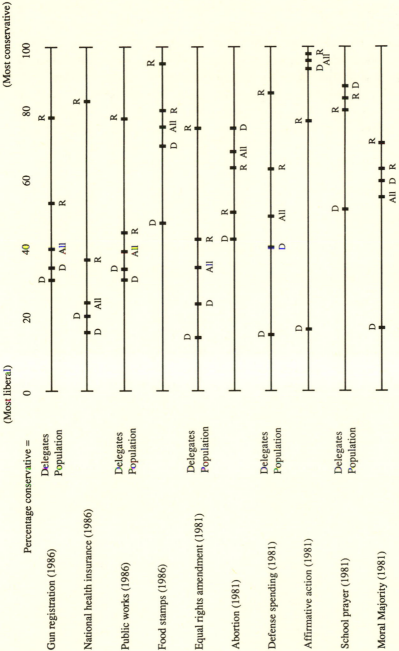

Figure 4. Policy differences between partisan elites and masses. The points on the line reflect the percentages of groups taking the conservative position on each issue. Letters above the line represent delegates; letters below the line represent average citizens classified by self-identifications. D = Democrats; R = Republicans; "All" includes citizens of all parties, including Independents. The public surveys were conducted in the years in parentheses; the delegate surveys were derived from statewide telephone polls conducted by the Social Science Research Center, Miss. State Univ.; delegate surveys were conducted by the author at the Democratic and Republican state party conventions.)

wide elections. "Liberals" were sometimes elected in smaller geographic units, but some began to moderate their views as they became part of the political establishment. On the other hand, widespread public support for political and educational reforms at the state level reflects a transformation of Mississippi's political culture in a more progressive direction. More and more candidates who are progressive on state issues are being elected to office. Their claims that their policies would benefit all citizens and be good for business strike a responsive chord among contemporary Mississippians.

CHAPTER SIX

The State Legislature:
Representatives of the People
or the Powerful?

Douglas G. Feig

As we enter the fourth quarter of the twentieth century, the Missis-
sippi legislature remains something of an anachronism. . . . The
legislature has strenuously guarded its legislative prerogatives and
extends its influence into the executive branch in numerous ways.
The legislature has been slow to adjust to the changing political re-
alities within the state.

John Quincy Adams, 1976.[1]

Many political observers have criticized the legislature for being an archaic
body that is too slow to respond to the changing needs of citizens. Such criticisms are especially important in a state where the legislature is so powerful
and where it has extended some of its influence into the executive branch.
The issue of executive versus legislative power recurs in Mississippi politics
and has played a role in unsuccessful efforts to call a convention to rewrite
the 1890 constitution. Yet legislative predominance is more the result of constitutional provisions that weaken the governor than of provisions that grant
inordinate power to the legislature. In fact, in some respects the 1890 constitution places more constraints on the Mississippi legislature than is typical of
state constitutions. Constitutional critics go so far as to claim that the legislature is straitjacketed by the stringent provisions of the constitution.

Given what is known about legislatures in general, the consequences for
Mississippi of its tradition of "government by legislature" appear to be several. First, government-induced change should proceed at a very slow pace.
Legislative bodies are poorly designed to initiate change; they are largely re-
active institutions.[2] Second, politics should be personality oriented rather

than policy oriented.[3] Legislatures are disjointed institutions; developing coherent, integrated programs is not their strong point. Instead, legislatures feature personal-style politics. Activity within the institution is explained largely by the personal influence wielded by strategically placed legislators; the "programs" that emerge are a hodgepodge of proposals favored by those individuals. Closely related to this second likely consequence of legislative governance is a third: legislative decision making should be significantly influenced by local or regional political forces.[4] Legislators are elected from relatively small single-member districts; a state legislature is essentially a collection of local officeholders. Thus politics in a state dominated by its legislature should be relatively parochial.

It is not surprising that many social and political leaders in a state with a traditionalistic political culture prefer legislative domination of the political system. Leaders of the executive branch are better able to provide energetic leadership in an effort to rapidly change the status quo and threaten entrenched interests. Legislative politics, on the other hand, is so parochial and personalist that change occurs very slowly.[5] The style of politics in a "government by legislature" is more compatible with the expectations of a citizenry rooted in a traditionalistic political culture.

THE MEMBERSHIP

The constitution provides for a large state legislature—122 members of the house of representatives and 52 members of the senate. Per capita, Mississippi has one of the largest state legislatures in the country. Critics claim that large legislatures depend more on detailed procedures and committee chairmen, advantaging senior members and proponents of the status quo. Some have fought for a constitutional convention in an effort to reduce the size of the legislature. Both representatives and senators serve four-year terms; elections are held in "off-off" years (i.e., 1979, 1983, 1987, etc.).[6] Since 1970 the legislature has held annual sessions. The length of the session immediately following an election is 125 days, and the remaining three sessions run 90 days each. Changing to annual sessions was one of the ways Mississippi participated in a major organizational shake-up that was common to many legislatures in the aftermath of the Supreme Court's reapportionment decisions.[7]

The Mississippi legislature is currently apportioned entirely into single-member districts. Until a federal court order in the 1970s, the legislature employed a mixed system that relied primarily on single-member districts, augmented by multimember districts in the more populous areas of the state. Currently legislators are elected in a general election employing the plurality rule, which follows a party primary employing the majority rule. If no would-be party nominee receives a majority of the vote in the primary, a run-off primary is held in which only the top two candidates' names appear. Since the general election is usually dominated by candidates of the Democratic party, the crucial election becomes the primary. Thus, in most cases the de facto election rule is the majority election rule.[8]

Districting

In the years since blacks emerged as an effective political force, the drawing of legislative district boundaries often provoked controversy. In the aftermath of *Reynolds v. Sims,* the state's legislative redistricting plan was declared unconstitutional on the grounds of racial gerrymandering.[9] Districting that followed the 1970 census also encountered problems involving race. Blacks feared that use of multimember districts in populous areas with sizable black populations, such as Hinds County, might hinder the election of blacks. The multimember district feature of this plan was declared unconstitutional, and a court-modified plan, which divided the multimember districts into sets of single-member districts, was quickly put into place for the 1975 elections.[10] Still another plan, which secured Justice Department approval under section 5 of the 1965 Voting Rights Act, was used for the 1979 elections. Those elections featured the election of significant numbers of blacks to the legislature (especially to the house) for the first time since Reconstruction. By contrast, the districting that followed the 1980 census encountered relatively little objection. Table 4 illustrates the increased number of black legislators in recent years.

Electoral Competition

Historically, since the 1890s, elections to the Mississippi legislature have not been very competitive.[11] Although competition has increased over the past two decades, it remains relatively low (table 4). In no election since World War II have more than half of either chamber's members faced an opponent in the general election. The Republican party has started to field a credible slate of candidates for legislative seats. Its efforts paid off especially well in 1979, when nearly half of all legislative districts featured competitive general elections. Since then the picture has returned to normal, with only about

Table 4: Characteristics of Mississippi State Legislators

Characteristic	Year Elected											
	1951		1959		1967		1975		1983		1987	
	House	Senate	House	Senate	House	Senate	House	Senate	House	Senate	House	Senate
Age												
Under 35	30	27	35	27	32	18	33	12	27	17	14	8
Over 55	27	33	22	22	24	14	17	19	12	17	18	23
Born in state	91	88	83	86	87	84	87	96	84	94	84	85
Occupation												
Farmer	32	28	37	21	26	18	20	14	13	8	10	10
Business	13	13	12	21	20	14	8	24	43	52	39	42
Lawyer	31	43	23	42	30	57	37	41	26	21	25	23
Professional	12	8	8	6	7	4	19	18	11	13	16	12
Religion												
Catholic	4	4	3	4	6	2	7	4	7	12	7	10
Methodist	34	29	27	39	33	33	24	34	24	29	29	12
Baptist	44	33	48	37	40	43	41	46	48	40	46	56
Presbyterian	11	19	10	2	9	8	15	10	11	10	8	12

Year Elected

Characteristic	1951 House	1951 Senate	1959 House	1959 Senate	1967 House	1967 Senate	1975 House	1975 Senate	1983 House	1983 Senate	1987 House	1987 Senate
Freshmen	56	67	65	67	41	47	42	29	30	25	29	23
Black	0	0	0	0	1	0	4	0	14	4	16	4
Women	2	0	3	0	2	4	1	0	2	0	6	6
Competition												
In primary	NA	NA	NA	NA	NA	NA	84	77	57	65	62	54
In general	NA	NA	NA	NA	NA	NA	31	27	34	31	33	31

Source: Dick Molpus, *Mississippi Official and Statistical Register* (Jackson: Mississippi Secretary of State, various years).

Note: Table entries are percentages of state house and senate members falling into each category. Data are for every other legislative session elected in the years listed at the top. NA = not available.

one-third of the districts having more than a single candidate on the general election ballot.

The primaries have featured more competition, however. Over the past twenty years, from one-half to five-sixths of legislative seats have been contested in the first primary. The great majority of these contests were settled without the need for a second, runoff primary; hence, even in the primaries, electoral competition is not particularly severe. Legislators who are interested in reelection are usually reelected. Despite the modest increase in competition since World War II, freshmen legislators have come to make up a smaller portion of the membership in both chambers (table 4). The emergence of the nonfreshman, returning legislator may signal a drift in the direction of professional, "career" legislators rather than "citizen" legislators. Such a trend has been observed in a number of other states.[12]

Composition

Several trends are reshaping the makeup of the Mississippi legislature. First, there has been a continuous and marked decline in the number of farmers serving in both houses (table 4). Although Mississippi is a rural state, this decline mirrors the decline of the agricultural sector in the state and throughout the nation. Coinciding with the decline of farmers has been a pronounced increase in the number of businessmen serving. Many of these businessmen identify themselves as "businessman-farmers" of various sorts; their appearance calls attention to the difficulty many have in making an adequate living solely as farmers. Here they are classified as businessmen unless it is clear that their business activity is secondary to their farming.

Consistent with other national trends is the gradual decline in the number of attorneys in the legislature. Today, only about 25 percent of the legislators are attorneys.[13] The number of other professionals serving has fluctuated, but the long-term trend has been a slight increase in their numbers. Many of these professionals are educators employed in public elementary, secondary, and higher education. The Mississippi Supreme Court recently ruled that legislators who work for state universities or public schools are guilty of violating the conflict-of-interest provision of the Mississippi constitution.[14] If they are precluded from serving in the legislature while holding such jobs, the number of professionals may begin to decrease.

Although the establishment of the runoff primary preceded the reentry of blacks into the electorate by many years, some argue that it has had the effect of making the election of blacks to legislative office less likely. Only a handful of blacks serve in the Mississippi legislature, even though about 36 percent of the state's population is black. All black legislators have been elected from districts having sizable black majorities.[15] Before 1967 no blacks served in either house. The increase in their numbers is largely because of the federal Voting Rights Act of 1965, which greatly increased the number of black voters. It also reflects the discontinuance of multimember legislative districts in the state's more heavily populated areas.

Compensation

Mississippi legislators are compensated in a variety of ways. First, each receives $10,000 per legislative session. In addition, each may claim a per diem (per day) allowance of $76 during the legislative session, although the legislator must actually be present to claim the per diem. Legislators also earn a salary of $800 for each whole month of the year that the legislature is not in session. Finally, during the legislative session, members are compensated at the rate of 20¢ a mile for one trip a week from Jackson to the legislator's district. Thus, all together, Mississippi legislators receive about $20,000 to $25,000 a year in compensation and reimbursement of expenses.

ORGANIZATION

Standing Committees

Like other legislative bodies, both chambers of the Mississippi legislature have systems of standing committees that play a major role in the passage of legislation. The committee system of the Mississippi legislature is remarkable for its size and diversity, partly reflecting the large number of legislators specified by the state constitution. The senate and house each have a system of twenty-eight committees.[16] There are an additional six joint committees, for a total of sixty-two standing committees in the entire legislature—roughly one committee for every three legislators! This is far more than the typical state legislature.[17] Only two state senates have more committees than the Mississippi senate, and only seven state houses have more than the Mississippi house.[18] In fact, the Mississippi legislature has more standing committees than does the United States Congress, a body with more than three times as many members. Furthermore, like Congress, many of the legislature's committees make use of subcommittees. One consequence of the large number of committees is that each legislator serves on several. Most house members serve on four to six committees, while senators serve on six to nine.

Legislative Staff

The more committees a legislator serves on, the more difficult it is to do an effective job as a committee member. In some legislatures this problem is mitigated by providing staff to help the legislators. Such is not the case in Mississippi. Across the nation, legislators benefit from access to two sorts of staff: personal staff, who work for particular legislators, and committee staff assigned to a particular standing committee, who serve the members of that committee on committee-related matters. Although legislators serving in about half of our state legislative bodies have personal staffs, Mississippi legislators do not.[19] In addition, Mississippi committee staffs are not routinely available to assist members. In the Mississippi house and senate, only some of the standing committees have professional, as distinct from clerical, staffs. By contrast, in over two-thirds of the remaining states, all standing committees have professional staffs.[20] Committee clerical staffs are available to assist committee members with correspondence, however.

In a guide to state legislative staffing patterns, Simon identified eleven types of legislative staff organizational forms.[21] She characterized Mississippi's pattern as "separate house-senate staff." Six other states were placed in the same category. In most such states, Simon found that the staff was small and consisted of generalists. Typically, legislatures in such states had a tradition of strong legislative leadership and one-party government; quite commonly, the lieutenant governor was a major political actor. Thus it is not at all surprising that the Mississippi legislature does not make use of a sizable professional, permanent staff: its staffing system is typical of states with similar leadership and party systems. But regardless of the factors that have given rise to this limited separate house-senate staff system, the result is that in Mississippi, if the work of the standing committees is to be accomplished it must be done by the legislators. And with their numerous committee assignments, they lack the time to consistently do a truly effective job.

Constituency Service

In general, Mississippi legislators are not well equipped to engage in extensive constituency service or casework. They have no personal staffs, and the only committee staff they can rely on are clerical personnel. Furthermore, though members of the Mississippi senate have a limited franking privilege, house members have none. Nevertheless, most legislators assist their constituents as far as they are able. They do so primarily by serving as referral agents, directing constituents to the appropriate state agency to service their requests for assistance or information. On occasion legislators will themselves assist a constituent in need of help. But given the shortness of the legislative session, the large number of committee assignments most legislators hold, and the paucity of legislative staff, constituency service plays a much smaller role in the life of the Mississippi legislator than is the case with congressmen in Washington. The job of the Mississippi legislator is primarily writing laws rather than running errands for constituents.

The Importance of Committees

The importance of legislative committees derives from their role in the passage of legislation: all proposed legislation must be reviewed, and recommended, by one of the committees before it can be scheduled for a vote in either chamber of the legislature.[22] Hence committees function much like specialized "little legislatures," and the legislature works by a process that Woodrow Wilson once called "an odd device of disintegration."[23] Bills that meet with an inhospitable reception in committee are likely to be "killed" (for an example, see "Bouncing the Bad Check Bill" below), and bills reported out favorably by a committee have very bright prospects of eventual passage.

An additional hurdle that bills may face in Mississippi is the prospect of being "double referred" (referred to two committees rather than one). Such bills must be reported out of both committees before they can be put on the calendar for a floor vote. Such double referring of bills is common. Although this tactic is sometimes employed to make a bill's passage less likely, it is primarily used to ensure that all interested legislators are consulted before a bill is put to a vote on the floor. Thus the standing committees in the Mississippi legislature play a vital role in the passage of new legislation.

Committee Appointments

Generally, representatives are appointed to committee posts by the Speaker of the house, while senators (except those serving on the Rules Committee) are appointed by the lieutenant governor, who serves as that body's presiding officer. Powerful Speakers are something of a tradition in the house. It is a generally accepted practice for them to use their appointment power to reward legislative allies and punish opponents. There has historically been no practice similar to the seniority rule (found in the Congress) governing committee appointments and chairmanships. In fact, unhappiness over former Speaker "Buddie" Newman's use of this appointment power was one of the factors leading to the 1987 "revolt against the Speaker" discussed below.

Although the lieutenant governor has long had the same committee appointment power in the senate that the Speaker exercises in the house, until recently it was not used to advance his legislative objectives. This has changed significantly in recent years under the direction of Lieutenant Governor Brad Dye. Dye's objectives in using his appointment power do not appear to differ greatly from those of former Speaker Newman, but he has exercised the appointment power more adroitly and with greater attention to the views of senate members.[24] In the final analysis, however, senate committee appointments may be used by a lieutenant governor to advance his own legislative goals with the expectation that at some point friends will be rewarded and opponents punished.

In 1988 the retirement of Speaker Buddie Newman led to the election as Speaker of a leader of the 1987 revolt, Tim Ford of Tupelo. On one hand, Ford is viewed as more progressive than Newman, and the house has generally operated in a more democratic fashion under his speakership. On the other hand, Ford has been criticized for backing an unsuccessful effort to reverse some of the 1987 house reforms, as well as for allegedly retaliating against political opponents. On the senate side, although Dye has been supportive of many educational improvements, he has been accused by journalists of hindering various government reform proposals. Dye's sympathy for the philosophy of "If it's working all right, don't fix it" is perfectly compatible with the state's traditionalistic culture.

Committee Chairmen

In the Mississippi legislature, committee chairmen exercise great power. The chairmen schedule committee meetings, appoint members to subcommittees, and refer bills to subcommittees. In addition, chairmen preside over committee meetings; hence bills they oppose can be killed by the simple device of not putting them on the committee agenda. Although a majority of committee members have the authority to overrule a chairman on these matters, they rarely exercise this authority. Opposing a chairman can put a committee member in great jeopardy. Even after a bill is reported out of a committee favorably, the chairman may still kill it. When it is called up for debate on the floor, the committee chairman can merely fail to call the bill, which effectively places the bill at the "heel" (bottom) of the calendar, where it may languish until time expires at the end of the legislative session.

In many respects, the power exercised by committee chairmen in the Mississippi legislature resembles that exercised by their counterparts in Congress (especially during the days of the strong chairman, which existed before the democratization of Congress in the early 1970s). But there is one very important difference: in the Mississippi legislature, committee chairmen are appointed by the Speaker and lieutenant governor. There is no established tradition of letting the most senior committee member of the majority party serve as chairman, as in Washington. Both the Speaker and the lieutenant governor use this appointment power to ensure that these important committee posts are occupied by allies rather than opponents. Thus, whereas in Congress it has been traditional to conceive of the committee chairmen and the elected chamber leadership as competing centers of power, in the Mississippi legislature these two groups are more like members of the same leadership "team." Interestingly enough, with regard to this issue, Congress appears to be changing a bit in the direction of the "team" concept.[25]

House and Senate Leadership

Probably the greatest difference between the Mississippi legislature and the United States Congress is the absence of sets of party leaders in the legislature. No discussion of Congress would be complete without a survey of the House Democratic leadership, the House Republican leadership, and the analogous Senate leadership groups. Many state legislative bodies also have fairly elaborate sets of legislative leaders.[26] But there are no party groups, either Republican or Democratic, in either house of the Mississippi legislature. Reflecting the state's traditionalistic culture and its history of one-party domination, both legislative chambers are overwhelmingly Democratic. Hence neither party in the legislature has reason to organize. The house and senate have their institutional leaders, but they are not chosen by political party caucuses.

The house leadership consists of the Speaker, elected by the entire house, and the newly created office of house Speaker pro tempore, also elected. The senate has no strong leadership elected by its members. The presiding officer and leader of the senate is the lieutenant governor, who is popularly elected from a statewide constituency. The senate pro tempore is elected by the senate, but this is not a powerful position. The lieutenant governor and his senate allies together form a leadership group, but none of them is elected by the senate. Thus neither chamber has an elaborate leadership system. Again, Mississippi's pattern is atypical. Of the ninety-nine state legislative bodies in the United States, only eight have as few as two legislative leaders.[27]

Powers of the Leadership

The Speaker and the lieutenant governor exercise a great deal of power. They traditionally have appointed all committee members, chairmen, and vice chairmen in their respective chambers. (The "revolt of 1987" has limited this power, however.) Neither leader's appointment power has historically been constrained by a seniority system, so reelected members may be reassigned to different committees than they previously served on. Both leaders may use their appointment power to advance their legislative objectives.

The Speaker and the lieutenant governor also preside over floor debate. Although both chambers have rules committees with important powers (which vary somewhat from chamber to chamber), they are not as important as the House Rules Committee in Washington used to be. These committees influence the scheduling of bills for floor debate, but they do not set the terms for such debate. Nor do they have the power to kill bills. In Mississippi the Speaker sits on the House Rules Committee, ex officio. The membership of the Senate Rules Committee is elected by the senate. It is chaired by the lieutentant governor, an innovation that Dye negotiated on assuming the statewide office back in 1979. The scheduling of legislation and the terms of floor debate can therefore be significantly influenced by the Speaker and the lieutenant governor.

In conclusion, if the Speaker and lieutenant governor exercise their powers with discretion and some respect for the opinions of their legislative colleagues, they are both in a position to have an important say in what happens in their chambers. There is no opposition party to thwart their wills; there is no contending center of power lodged in the standing committees to frustrate them; they need only contend with each other and with groups and persons outside the legislature. Thus, in the Mississippi legislature a good deal of power is in the hands of two men. At least it used to be.

The House Revolt of 1987

Discontent over the power of the Speaker of the house had been building since the early 1970s.[28] Unsuccessful revolts against the house rules, which granted the Speaker so much power, occurred in the 1970s and early 1980s. They were led by persons outside the Speaker's leadership group but failed to attract a majority of members, much less the 60 percent margin required to change house rules. Rebellious legislators opposing the Speaker were often punished with relatively inconsequential committee assignments. An example was Cecil Simmons, who was the fifth most senior member of the house. After participating in the 1984 revolt, Simmons was not reappointed to two powerful committees he had served on, Appropriations and Judiciary A. Nor was he reappointed to the Committee on Public Health, in which he had a special interest (his wife is a medical doctor). Simmons's new committees met so seldom that he occupied his time by enrolling in the Mississippi College School of Law (from which he graduated in 1989). Legislators who were loyal to the Speaker in the rules fight were rewarded.

Early in the 1987 legislative session, house members revolted against Speaker C. B. "Buddie" Newman and reduced the power of the speakership, while leaving Newman in the post (within months he opted not to seek reelection). The rebel program changing the house rules passed on a 75 to 45 vote, and included the following items. The Speaker was limited to two four-year terms. His power over committee appointments was restricted; house members would rank their committee preferences and be guaranteed membership on three of their top seven choices. In addition, the twelve most senior members residing in each congressional district were guaranteed positions on the powerful committees of Ways and Means or Appropriations (six members on each of the two committees).

The house Speaker lost the power of appointing the membership of the Rules and Management committees. The Rules Committee was changed radically. In addition to the Speaker and two others, it would consist of two members from each of the state's five congressional districts. These ten members would be elected by the representatives residing in those districts. The Management Committee is important to members because it allocates office space and staff. Management Committee members would now be elected by congressional district caucuses.

The position of Speaker pro tempore was reinstituted and given considerable power: the pro tempore would preside whenever the Speaker chose not to do so; he would chair the Management Committee; and he would serve on the Rules Committee. Cecil Simmons, a prominent leader of the revolt against the Speaker, was promptly elected by representatives as Speaker pro tempore. His election marked a great personal triumph for a political career that had so recently experienced defeat and near oblivion. Another rules change precluded anyone from serving as chair or vice chair of two or more committees. Thus, overall, the Speaker's control over committee assignments was greatly curtailed, he was limited to two terms, and another leadership position was created and given significant powers.

In some ways the Mississippi house reforms resemble a combination of two United States House revolts of the twentieth century: the revolt against Speaker Joe Cannon in the early years of the century, and the collection of committee reforms of the 1970s directed at the entrenched privilege of the more senior House members, commonly referred to as "the democratization of the House." Like the revolt against Speaker Cannon, the Mississippi revolt greatly reduced the powers of the Speaker by limiting his powers over committee appointments and by creating countervailing centers of power. (In Washington, the powerful House Rules Committee dates from this period.) In both revolts, the seniority principle was instituted to settle some of the committee assignment decisions previously made by the Speaker.

On a smaller scale, the Mississippi revolt resembles the more recent "democratization of the House" by limiting the number of committee leadership positions that a prominent legislator can hold. In a sense, the congressional revolt against Speaker Cannon eventually resulted in the need for the "democratization of the House." Speaker Cannon's control over committee assignments and chairmanships was largely replaced by a reliance on the seniority rule. Fifty years later, a perceived overreliance and abuse of the seniority rule produced "the democratization of the United States House." Only time will tell if history will repeat itself, this time in Mississippi.

THE REST OF THE STORY

Descriptions of legislative elections, committees, and leadership systems—no matter how accurate and detailed—fail to adequately convey the flavor of legislative life. To accomplish this, let us turn to stories of actual legislative histories, which cover the range of legislative action. Since legislators are human beings, their attitudes and motivations are often similar to those of the citizens who elected them. In addition, much of their behavior is shaped to suit the desires and expectations of significant nonlegislators. So in a sense these case studies are stories not only about the Mississippi legislature, but also about Mississippi politics in general. Readers should realize, however, that such stories provide only part of the picture of what the Mississippi legislature is "really" like.

Bouncing the Bad Check Bill

Mississippi retailers have long been concerned about "bad checks." In recent years, over $9 million a year has been lost because of bad checks. The bad checks of interest to these retailers were not those written by average citizens inadvertently overdrawing their accounts. Rather, the concern was with con artists who move into a small city, set up a checking account with a sizable deposit, and establish rapport with local merchants by making a series of modest purchases by check. Then on a single day they make a series of major purchases at numerous outlets—all paid for by checks on a now exhausted account—and leave town with the merchandise. Under Mississippi law, all that a victimized merchant could do to cover the loss was to hire an attorney and attempt to bring a civil suit, if the con artist could be found. For a large merchant experiencing sizable losses, this might well be a viable option. But for a smaller merchant, even successful legal action would be fruitless, since the attorney's fees would exceed the value of the merchandise lost by any one merchant. Thus, in a good many cases no legal action would even be attempted. Of course the district attorney could bring criminal charges against the con artist, but even if successful, that would not help the merchant recover the loss.

Then in 1985 the Retail Association of Mississippi learned about a new Alabama law that appeared to be successfully dealing with bad check con artists. Under the Alabama law, a victimized merchant would report the swindle to the local district attorney. The district attorney was empowered to notify the offender that if restitution was made within thirty days (or if arrangements for it were made) and a fee was paid to the district attorney's office, no criminal prosecution would follow.

Since the Alabama law seemed to be working, the Retail Association arranged for a similar proposal to be introduced into the Mississippi House of Representatives before the 1986 legislative session. It passed the house with almost no opposition and was sent to the senate, where it was forwarded to the Judiciary Committee. The Judiciary Committee chairman, an attorney, assigned the proposal to Subcommittee B, known around the state capitol as "killer bee" for its reputation as a final resting place for stillborn legislative proposals. The bill got a hearing before the full Judiciary Committee late in the session, but time was short and the chairman suggested the proposal be reviewed by a special study committee for consideration at the next legislative session.

Disappointed, the Retail Association made new plans for the 1987 session. This time the proposal was introduced in both houses so that each would have plenty of time to examine it. The chairman of Senate Judiciary Subcommittee B, also an attorney, indicated that he would wait for the house to consider the proposal first so that his subcommittee could deal with the house bill. However, he assured the bill's sponsors that their proposal would get a full hearing and be brought to a vote before the full Judiciary Committee.

Meanwhile the house acted quickly, and the "bad check bill" was among the first bills that it passed. Its bill was forwarded to the senate and eventually to Subcommittee B, where it just sat. When it became clear that nothing was going to be done, the members of the Retail Association went to work on their legislators and got some action. A full Judiciary Committee hearing was held on the proposal late in the session. As the committee chairman carefully read through the text of the entire bill, the number of committee members in attendance dwindled until a quorum was no longer present. The chairman took note and adjourned the hearing without taking a vote on the bill.

Thus Mississippi law remained unchanged, and about $9 million a year continued to be lost by Mississippi merchants to bad check con artists. The reason for this state of affairs seemed simple: current Mississippi law benefited attorneys, since it required angry merchants to proceed individually against the con artists by retaining their own attorneys. The bill's opponents said the proposal was unconstitutional: it involved using the criminal justice process to collect civil debt. Inasmuch as some—but not all—of these same legislators show little interest in other civil liberties issues, the sincerity of their concern in this case is suspect. Since attorneys chaired both the Senate Judiciary Committee and Subcommittee B and dominated the membership of the committee, it appeared that the prospects were dim for changes sought by the Retail Association.

Undaunted, after the end of the 1987 session the retailers began actively "educating" their legislators and local notables, and they held high hopes for the next legislative session. In addition, the committee chairman did not seek reelection, the subcommittee chairman received a surprisingly strong challenge to his renomination, and a third major senate opponent of the proposal died. In the 1988 session of the legislature, the bad check bill finally became law.

Despite eventual passage, the history of the bad check bill illustrates the importance of legislators holding key committee positions. Success in the Mississippi legislature may hinge less on the quality of one's proposal than on having the support of the right people. Hence the programs that carry the legislature's stamp of approval may be nothing more than a combination of proposals favored by key legislators.

The Whole Milk Bill, or Has Mississippi Been Milking the Cow for More Than She's Worth?

Until 1986, Mississippi was one of only three states that required milk to have a minimum of 3.5 percent butterfat content before it could carry the label "whole milk." The United States Department of Agriculture recommended a minimum of 3.25 percent, and the remaining forty-seven states agreed. This Mississippi law imposed costs on processors of dairy products serving Mississippi and neighboring states. They either had to maintain two completely separate lines of whole milk products and keep their distribution separate or else just sell the higher-cost 3.5 percent milk everywhere. Barber Milk of Tupelo opted to do the latter, even though it made their whole milk less competitive in Alabama and Tennessee, where they had to compete with whole milk whose butterfat content was only 3.25 percent. Heritage Farms Dairy (Kroger) in Murfreesburo, Tennessee opted to produce a special whole milk product in containers labeled 3.5 percent for its Mississippi retail outlets.

The Mississippi Dairy Products Association offered a simple solution: Mississippi should bring its law into conformity with the USDA standard. A proposal to that effect was introduced in the 1984 legislative session, but it failed to get out of committee in either house. History repeated itself in 1985. One problem was that some dairy products processors in south Mississippi were lukewarm about the proposal. One of the other two states making use of the 3.5 percent standard was Louisiana. Thus, if Mississippi changed to the 3.25 percent standard, these south Mississippi dairy processors would find themselves in the same situation the north Mississippi dairy processors were in with the 3.5 percent standard. There was talk of waiting a year and trying to coordinate a change with Louisiana.

Because of the division between the two groups of dairy products processors, the Mississippi Farm Bureau Federation was unable to take a firm position in favor of the change. Furthermore, the proposal was opposed by many Mississippi dairy farmers, who saw it as threatening their income, since the amount dairy farmers are paid for their milk is based in part on its butterfat content. In reality, the Dairy Products Association proposal would have had no effect on farm income, since any butterfat not used in milk could be marketed as other dairy products such as butter and cheese. But with so many farmers in financial trouble, they were not about to take any chances over this issue. Also, the legislative proposal's official statement of purpose did not help matters; it identified the legislation's purpose as to "redefine the milk fat content of milk."[29]

In 1986 the Dairy Products Association had a slightly modified version of its earlier proposal introduced in the legislature. Its purpose now read as follows: "To define milk sold at retail according to the Food and Drug Administration's Code of Federal Regulations, Title 21, Section 131.110."[30] In addition, after its initial irresolution, the Farm Bureau came down firmly in favor of the change to the 3.25 percent standard. Modifying the proposed legislation, having the support of the Farm Bureau, and working hard to "educate" the appropriate legislators paid off. The legislation passed rather easily later in the 1986 session.

The story of the "whole milk bill" shows the importance of local political forces in Mississippi's legislature, as legislators respond to constituent pressure. With legislators locally elected from single-member districts, this "constituent pressure" is divided into a mishmash of conflicting political pressures emanating from a multitude of local legislative districts. Such conflicting pressures slow the pace of legislation and delay changes in the status quo.

Widening the Roads That Lead to Economic Salvation

Many Mississippians are concerned about their state's "distinction" of finishing near the bottom on so many indexes of economic well-being. They seek to promote economic development in order to improve the state's standing on economic indicators and provide citizens with a better quality of life. Proposals to improve Mississippi's economic infrastructure and especially its transportation system have been debated for decades.

In the early 1970s, the "corridor" plan was devised, whereby four-lane, limited-access highways would be built to link all major Mississippi cities. In addition to the interstate highways currently in existence, this plan called for such roads to link Tupelo to both Memphis, Tennessee, and Birmingham, Alabama; Corinth to Tupelo to Columbus-Starkville; Columbus-Starkville to both Jackson and Meridian; Columbus to Winona to Greenville; and Vicksburg to Greenville. It was an ambitious proposal, but it was underfunded and as a result ended up being a "widening and overlay" program instead.

In the mid-1980s, an organization of businessmen in support of improved highways emerged. It was named A H E A D—Advocating Highways for Economic Advancement. A H E A D played a role in developing an ambitious proposal to improve the state's highways, which was brought before the 1986 legislative session. Although there was strong support for the program, especially in the senate, it never passed because of differences over funding. The house favored funding the program on a pay-as-you-go basis (with tax money), while the senate favored the use of bond money.

After defeat in the 1986 legislative session, the chairman and vice chairman of the House Transportation Committee vowed to have a proposal that could win house support ready for the 1987 session. While preparing their proposal, they kept in close contact with the leaders of A H E A D. The resulting proposal called for a thousand-mile, $1.5 billion, ten-year program funded by a 5¢ a gallon increase in the gasoline tax. The stretches of roadway to be upgraded were identified in the legislation. Though not greatly different from those identified in the earlier "corridor" plan, this time a case was made for these particular roads on the basis of traffic count.

The proposal encountered controversy early in the session. Governor Bill Allain, threatening to veto any bill calling for a tax increase, countered with his own scaled-down version, to be financed solely by bond money. The governor's modest proposal met with a cold reception in the legislature and never had a serious chance of passage. Instead, a period of protracted negotiations took place primarily over the issue of financing—taxes versus bonds. Given the cost of the proposed program and the fact that a tax increase was called for, a great deal of public attention was focused on these negotiations.

An additional complication involved legislators from the Gulf Coast. The Coast already had an adequate system of four-lane highways, and since Coast counties were already paying a special "sea wall tax" on gasoline, Coast legislators were almost unanimously opposed to a major highway program. The support of some of these legislators was essential, because a veto by the governor was expected. Legislative leaders warned Coast legislators to show more concern for the welfare of the entire state or their region's pet projects would encounter opposition in future sessions. In the meantime, A H E A D was flexing its muscles: one A H E A D luncheon attracted 1,200 people.

The final bill reflected the importance of negotiation and compromise in the legislative process. The highway program would be funded from five sources: increases in both the gasoline tax and license fees; earmarking of future state and federal highway funds; and some surplus bond-generated funds. The plan was stretched to fourteen years, partly to allow sufficient funds to be generated without higher tax increases. The highway bill now had such widespread support in the legislature that it was passed over the governor's veto. Inasmuch as 1987 was an election year and the highway bill included tax increases, its relatively easy passage surprised many people. The story of its success sheds a different light on Mississippi politics than do the other case studies. It shows that quick and decisive action on a large scale is possible, even within a political system dominated by the legislative branch.

AN ASSESSMENT

The behavior of the Mississippi legislature, exhibited in these case studies, is largely consistent with the expectations set forth at the beginning of this chapter. The legislature tends to move slowly, its actions tend to be disjointed and its "policies" incoherent, and local political forces often play a decisive role in influencing legislators' votes. The bad check and whole milk stories illustrate what often happens to seemingly rational legislative initiatives: delay, obstruction, and frustration. Yet both bills eventually were passed. The highway bill tells a different story, as does the history of the Education Reform Act to be discussed in chapter 10. In these instances well-organized groups, spearheaded by ambitious "political entrepreneurs" and working with sympathetic legislators, were able to push through major pieces of legislation involving tax increases within twelve months of upcoming general elections.

The highway and education reform bills were of the "omnibus" variety involving numerous titles and subsections—the type of bill one might expect to be picked apart in a legislative body. Both included substantial tax increases: not boosts in relatively painless "sin" taxes, but increases in the types of taxes that people notice, sales and gasoline taxes and license fees. Both were passed within a year of the next general election, and though there was some concern about voting for a tax increase in an election year, support for these bills played almost no role in hindering the reelection of any legislator. Mississippians appeared to be moving away from a traditionalistic history that sought to limit government spending on domestic programs. Most voters seemed willing to pay higher taxes to improve education and the state's highway system, hoping that such programs would attract more industry offering higher-paying jobs.

The epigraph to this chapter offers a caricature of the Mississippi legislature as it exists today. Legislative bodies are rarely agents of reform, and the Mississippi legislature is no exception. Seldom do legislative bodies, including Mississippi's, get ahead of the voting public and provide leadership on the major issues of the day. But the Mississippi legislature is not "something of an anachronism." It reflects the political culture of the state and has historically defended the traditionalistic political and social order.

Yet the winds of change were blowing across Mississippi in the late 1980s, reshaping the institution of the legislature itself. House members revolted against the powerful Speaker in 1987 and elected a "rebel" as Speaker early in the 1988 session. In addition, newly elected governor Ray Mabus successfully lobbied the legislature on behalf of progressive proposals, such as major educational funding increases and political reforms like the unit system. Mississippi will likely continue to undergo some political change and adjustment. The legislature, however, will play a major role in determining the pace and nature of that change.

CHAPTER SEVEN

The "Weak" Governor

Thomas H. Handy

The governor is given the chief executive power and a mandate to faithfully enforce the laws. However, that obligation does not carry with it a corresponding grant of power.

William N. Ethridge, Jr.,[1]

Political observers have historically viewed Mississippi's governor as significantly weaker than the legislature. When rating the formal powers of all fifty governors, political scientists have consistently placed Mississippi in the weakest category.[2] Not only does the governor face an independent and powerful legislature, but much of his own branch of government is also independent of his supervision.[3] The heads of eight executive departments and the lieutenant governor are directly elected by voters, and numerous boards and commissions administer public policies independent of any real managing authority by the governor (fig. 5). Yet even in the area of gubernatorial authority, change is coming to Mississippi. In the 1980s the governor's formal power was strengthened by a constitutional amendment permitting him to serve two consecutive terms and by a law that gave him complete authority over the proposal of an executive budget.

Increasing the formal power of a governor has implications for the state's culture as well as its political system. And while formal powers are important in that regard, equally important are the informal powers a governor possesses. Much as Franklin Roosevelt was able to reshape the American political system and institute a modern welfare state, so might an astute governor of Mississippi promote modern programs that effect changes in its political system and culture. As the most visible state official, for example, the

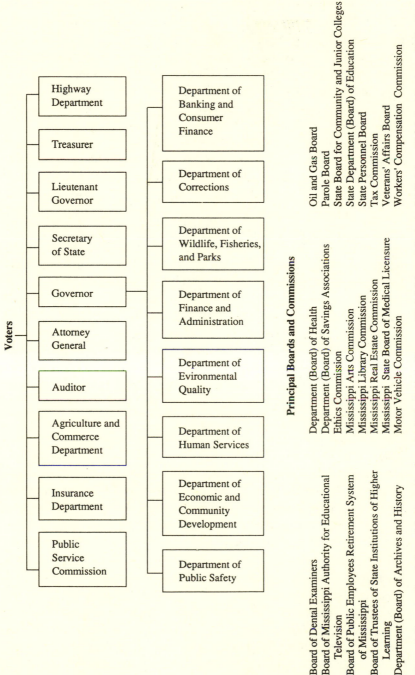

Voters

Highway Department	Department of Banking and Consumer Finance
Treasurer	Department of Corrections
Lieutenant Governor	Department of Wildlife, Fisheries, and Parks
Secretary of State	
Governor	Department of Finance and Administration
Attorney General	Department of Evironmental Quality
Auditor	
Agriculture and Commerce Department	Department of Human Services
Insurance Department	Department of Economic and Community Development
Public Service Commission	Department of Public Safety

Principal Boards and Commissions

Board of Dental Examiners
Board of Mississippi Authority for Educational Television
Board of Public Employees Retirement System of Mississippi
Board of Trustees of State Institutions of Higher Learning
Department (Board) of Archives and History

Department (Board) of Health
Department (Board) of Savings Associations
Ethics Commission
Mississippi Arts Commission
Mississippi Library Commission
Mississippi Real Estate Commission
Mississippi State Board of Medical Licensure
Motor Vehicle Commission

Oil and Gas Board
Parole Board
State Board for Community and Junior Colleges
State Department (Board) of Education
State Personnel Board
Tax Commission
Veterans' Affairs Board
Workers' Compensation Commission

Figure 5. Organizational chart of the executive branch of Mississippi. (*Sources:* Dick Molpus, *Mississippi Official and Statistical Register, 1988–1992* [Jackson: Mississippi Secretary of State, 1989]; Mississippi Executive Reorganization Act of 1989.)

governor has the opportunity to mobilize public opinion behind progressive programs. This opportunity has been greatly enhanced in recent years by the public's growing perception that there are shortcomings in the state's governing system and by its increasing resentment of the state's last or near last ranking on so many ratings of social and economic conditions in the fifty states. By the mid-1970s, as one scholar observed, "for the first time in more than a century, Mississippians seem[ed] more interested in economic progress than in race."[4]

The governor has several roles to fill. And though they are not all of equal importance in effecting changes in the state's political system and culture, each plays a part in portraying the position the governor occupies in the state's government. As chief executive, the governor oversees the implementation of many public programs, proposes an executive budget, and appoints to office people who share his political values. His power is especially great during crises that threaten the public order and well-being. As ceremonial head of state, he represents Mississippi when dealing with political and business leaders outside the state. By proposing and pushing his legislative program, a governor also has the potential to become the "chief legislator." His visibility, statewide constituency, and potential for mobilizing public opinion give him the opportunity to embody the public will. Finally, as a two-party system emerges in state government, the governor may blossom as a partisan leader championing a party platform.

CHIEF EXECUTIVE

The Mississippi constitution specifies that "the chief executive power of this state shall be vested in a Governor." This power encompasses such standard executive authority as being the commander-in-chief of the state's armed forces (the militia) and granting pardons and reprieves. It also encompasses some power to supervise the executive branch. But though it imposes the obligation that "the governor shall see that the laws are faithfully executed," the constitution gives him very limited power to fulfill that obligation. It grants only the power to "require information in writing from the officers in the executive departments of the state on any subject relating to the duties of their respective offices," order an audit of any executive office, and fill judicial and executive vacancies. Meanwhile, it fragments the power to supervise the executive branch by requiring the popular election of the lieutenant governor and the heads of four executive departments and by permitting the statutory creation of four more executive departments with popularly elected heads and some 135 independent boards and commissions.

The independently elected executive positions have lately served as training grounds for future governors. For example, before becoming governor, Ray Mabus served as auditor and Bill Allain as attorney general. Occupants of such independently elected statewide positions have sometimes been preoccupied with promoting their own political future rather than supporting the governor's programs. Their independence is strengthened by the absence of any constitutional limit on the number of times they may run for reelection. And these independent executives may impede gubernatorial policies for philosophical reasons as well. In the Mabus administration, the lieutenant governor was viewed as skeptical of the governor's ambitious executive reorganization proposal (discussed later), as well as establishment of a lottery to pay for educational improvements. Such weak support for the governor by the lieutenant governor is especially critical because of the latter's position as leader of the state senate.

On the other hand, popularly elected state executives may decide to act as part of the governor's "team," if they agree with the governor's program or believe he is supported by voters. In the Mabus administration, Secretary of State Dick Molpus, Attorney General Mike Moore, and Governor Mabus shared a reform-minded, change-oriented agenda.[5] When the legislature in 1990 killed Mabus's lottery proposal for funding educational improvements, Moore closed down bingo parlors operating in the state as being illegal lotteries until a supreme court decision to the contrary. The move increased public pressure for a lottery, as some senior citizens and military veterans who played bingo joined the ranks of lottery supporters.

The 135 boards and commissions in the executive branch vary greatly in their importance and are not completely independent of the governor's supervisory influence. Five agencies spend over two-thirds of the general fund budget, leaving 130 or so to spend less than one-third of it.[6] More than half of the state's agencies have fewer than seventy employees, and a third have fewer than twenty. The governor makes over five hundred appointments, almost all to positions on commissions or boards that oversee state agencies. These appointments provide the governor and members of his staff with contacts for information, suggestions, and requests. The influence these appointments provide is illustrated by Governor Winter's actions after being apprised of an agency head's misconduct. He immediately phoned the appointed chairman of the commission that oversaw the agency, reviewed the matter with him, inquired if anyone was available to immediately take over the agency, and suggested an emergency meeting of the commission. Within twelve hours the commission had met, removed the agency head for cause, and replaced him with another person from the agency.[7]

The governor appoints a majority of members of approximately seventy-four boards, commissions, and authorities. Indeed, except for the state elected officials and a dozen boards or commissions on which state and local elected officials serve as ex officio members, there are only eleven minor agencies to which the governor makes no appointments. He appoints the heads of a dozen agencies, including such important ones as the Tax Commission, the Bureau of Narcotics, the Probation and Parole Board, and the Game and Fish Commission. He is also chairman of seventeen boards or commissions that are of minor importance, such as the Memorial Stadium Commission, the Library Board, and the Hospital Commission, though at their meetings the governor is usually represented by a member of his staff.

The principal contacts between the governor and the agencies are the members of the governor's staff.[8] Many staff members have government experience and have developed a network of agency contacts. Less experienced staff members initially rely on the contacts of the more experienced members and then begin developing their own networks. Gubernatorial staff members often make requests, obtain information for the governor, or impart his suggestions. In most instances, an experienced observer attested, the relationship between the governor's staff and state agencies is cooperative rather than conflictual.[9] Yet governors, staff members, and agency leaders sometimes disagree over issues such as what direction public programs should take, what the funding priorities are, or who has authority for program development. In 1990 the state superintendent of public education expressed displeasure that Governor Mabus's Education Reform Act II had been drafted by the governor's staff without input from the Board of Education. The same year, the commissioner of higher education expressed concern over gubernatorial and legislative emphasis on increased funding for elementary and secondary education rather than on all levels of education.

The constitutional power of the governor to seize the account books of an agency and have them audited can be used to promote his political agenda. In 1986 Governor Allain urged the creation of a department of transportation headed by a gubernatorial appointee. It would have included the Highway Department, headed by three popularly elected commissioners. He also opposed any tax increase in a year of financial difficulty for the state and urged diverting some uncommitted money from the Highway Department into the state's general fund. Becoming frustrated with the Highway Department's "evasive" response to his questions regarding how many of its funds were unencumbered (uncommitted), Allain seized the department and its books by executive order. The attorney general upheld the seizure and audit of the account books but ruled that the governor had no authority to seize and operate the department. After the audit, $23 million was found to be unencumbered, and the legislature ultimately diverted most of it to the general fund. Opposition by Highway Department personnel and supporters nevertheless led to a legislative defeat of the proposal for a department of transportation.

The governor's organizational authority has increased in recent decades. A 1968 law gave the governor the sole power to contract with the federal government for federal grants. Governor John Bell Williams promptly appointed a director of the newly created Office of Federal-State Programs. By 1990 the office had grown to approximately three hundred employees, who administer grants making up more than a quarter of the state's budget. In 1984 an executive office of the governor was created, which gave the governor direct authority over the Medicaid program and the General Services Bureau. The latter controlled state buildings (office spaces), grounds, surplus property, and the capitol facilities. The act also set up a Fiscal Management Board consisting of the governor and two gubernatorial appointees. Its director, appointed by the governor, was responsible for purchasing, insurance programs, fiscal management, and the executive budget.

The administrative reorganization act of 1989 established five new departments, whose heads are appointed by the governor with the consent of the senate. They include the Departments of Finance and Administration; Economic and Community Development; Human Services; Wildlife, Fisheries, and Parks; and Environmental Quality. This act did not greatly increase the governor's managerial powers; most of the programs administered by the new departments were already controlled by the governor. For instance, the newly created Department of Finance and Administration included the Office of Federal-State Programs, General Services Bureau, and Fiscal Management Board. Governor Mabus was unable to obtain legislative approval of his proposal for a more sweeping reorganization of the executive branch into twelve departments headed by gubernatorial appointees.

In addition to some authority to make appointments in the executive branch, Mississippi's governor can make appointments to fill judicial vacancies. Because of the power of incumbency whereby appointed judges generally are repeatedly elected, the governor acquires some potential for shaping the general direction of public policy. In the 1980s, Governors Winter and Allain broke with the state's traditionalistic culture by appointing a woman, a black, and a liberal to the Mississippi Supreme Court. These appointees then went on to win reelection in their own right.

Despite changes in recent decades that caused a 1983 study to put him thirty-third in appointive power,[10] Mississippi's governor remains weaker in organizational and appointment powers than governors in most states. Forces that have limited the governor's ability to manage the executive branch are common in some degree to the experience of all states. They include the heritage of Jacksonian democracy, the principle of neutral competency, a history of governors who assumed a passive role as managers of the executive branch, and legislative leaders who aggressively sought authority over executive matters at a critical time.

Jacksonian Democracy

The principles of Jacksonian democracy have exerted considerable influence over the Mississippi executive branch. The principle that public officials should have short terms was reflected in a constitutional provision prohibiting governors from seeking immediate reelection after serving one term. A succession amendment adopted in 1986 eliminated this prohibition.[11] That public officials should be held directly responsible to the people through popular elections is an even more enduring principle. As of the late 1980s Mississippi remained one of only four states (joined by Louisiana, North Carolina, and North Dakota) that elected more than eight state officials in addition to the governor. In addition to five popularly elected constitutional officials, state law provides for popular election of highway commissioners, public service commissioners, the insurance commissioner, and the commissioner of agriculture and commerce.

Recent years have seen some change in the number of statewide elected officials. The elective position of land commissioner was abolished in 1976, and most of its responsibilities were transferred to the secretary of state's office. In 1984 the elective position of state superintendent of education became appointive, selected by the appointed nine-member Board of Education. In recent years, scandals involving elected highway commissioners and public service commissioners fueled anew some debate over whether those positions should also be made appointive.

Neutral Competency

As more and more services and functions were added to American state governments after the Civil War, machine politics arose as an instrument for coordinating administrative efforts in the face of the Jacksonian democratic principle of independently elected executives. Because corruption increased in state and local political machines, the progressive movement (arising around the turn of the century) strove for "neutral competence"—"an attempt to separate politics from administration."[12] "As demands for more government services grew during the twentieth century, the new services were increasingly provided by government institutions politically independent of governors, legislatures, mayors and city councils,"[13] so that "by 1990 many states had 100 or more boards and agencies."[14] This form of administering state programs became known as commission government.

Increased state services that gave rise to commission government came later to Mississippi than to most states.[15] Whereas the political struggles in northern and midwestern states brought more and more government services between the Civil War and the end of the century, the struggles in Mississippi during that time were over different issues. Those struggles brought, first, the 1875 electoral overthrow of the Reconstruction government by a coalition of whites under the Democratic party's conservative business leaders, then the elimination of meaningful black political participation by the new 1890 constitution adopted under the leadership of the same coalition, and finally the first statute in the country (in 1902) to provide for primary elections.[16] Only then, in the ensuing elections of 1903, was the conservative Democrats' control of government broken by the farmer-populist Democrats.[17] A flood of progressive legislation ensued in the next two decades, creating dozens of new agencies, and Mississippi acquired the commission type of government that some states had been experiencing for thirty years or so.

In the 1920s and 1930s growing urbanization and the Great Depression caused pressures for improved state services and economy in state government. By 1937 nineteen state governments had had varying degrees of success in consolidating state agencies into larger units for managerial efficiency, and by 1952 twenty-eight states had become involved in that process.[18] Mississippi was among the twenty states retaining a large number of separate agencies during that time, having a separate one for virtually every program. And when it finally approached reorganization in the 1970s and 1980s, it did so piecemeal.

The "Passive" Governor

Mississippi governors typically have not sought substantial managerial powers. Governors either agreed with the principle of neutral competency or acquiesced in legislative establishment of new agencies based on that principle. A powerful weapon that provides governors some leverage over legislation is the veto power. And yet throughout the first eight decades of the twentieth century, no Mississippi governor resorted to the veto power to kill a proposed agency simply because it had been established outside his managerial control.

Mississippi governors even resisted the establishment of an executive budget, an essential tool for managerial control of the bureaucracy. In 1918 the legislature mandated that the governor present it with an executive budget in each legislative session.[19] But governors in the 1920s merely viewed proposing a budget as an additional chore that they had neither the time nor the inclination to perform. They ignored the intent of the law and merely forwarded to the legislature the proposals they received from the agencies. In 1932 the legislature renewed its effort to obtain an executive budget by creating a budget commission with the governor as chairman and the tax commissioner, who had ready access to revenue data and a staff, as deputy chairman. And in 1936 it further sought that objective by giving the budget commission a secretary, appointed and dismissed by the governor, and its own staff chosen by the secretary but dismissed only with the approval of the governor. In 1954, two scholars observed, "Carefully drafted and prepared, the budget has suffered in the legislature because no one administrator claims responsibility for it. Transmitted to the legislature by the governor as the work of the secretary of the Budget Commission, the budget is credited by the secretary to statisticians of the commission."[20]

Governors of Mississippi have been reluctant to resort to constitutional conventions as a means of expanding their managerial control over the bureaucracy. A Brookings Institution study led to proposals in late 1931 that would have greatly increased the managerial power of the governor by reorganizing state government into fifteen departments. At the time, Governor "Mike" Conner and the legislature were preoccupied with the severe financial crisis of the Great Depression. Thus the governor backed the reorganization plan as a way to save money by reducing administrative costs instead of applauding the increased managerial power it would give him. Meanwhile reorganization opponents, including the Highway Department and the lieutenant governor, argued that reorganization could mean a loss of jobs during the depths of the depression. They repeated a remark that Governor Conner had made opposing a suggestion that the state might soon need a new office building. Conner had observed that after the anticipated reorganization had taken place, there would be plenty of room in the existing facilities for the state employees who remained. The proposal for a constitutional convention that would initiate amendments to reorganize state government died in the legislature.

In the 1950s Governor J. P. Coleman also fought unsuccessfully for a constitutional convention. He supported gubernatorial succession, which would have increased the governor's power ranking. But other goals for a new constitution, such as the separation of tax collector and sheriff and the elimination of constitutional provisions that had become obsolete, were irrelevant to increasing the governor's power. Furthermore, Coleman did not advocate any overhaul of the executive structure of government that would have transferred any state agency to the governor's control.

An Aggressive Legislature Moves into Management

Legislative involvement in the executive function of administering programs began in 1944, when conditions of World War II produced a cooperative spirit between the executive and legislative branches. Governor Thomas Bailey sought to attract industry by revitalizing the B A W I program (Balance Agriculture with Industry), which was reinstituted under an Agriculture and Industrial Board of twenty-four members. The board included two senators and two representatives to better coordinate the efforts of the executive and legislative branches in recruiting industry.

In 1952, Speaker of the House Walter Sillers returned from the national convention of the Democratic party convinced that the state should begin preparations to defend its racial segregation policies from coming moves by the national government to promote civil rights. State leaders became enraged over the 1954 *Brown* decision of the United States Supreme Court, which ordered the desegregation of public schools. Meanwhile, the governor's office was occupied by seventy-four-year-old Hugh White, who was preoccupied with taking trips in an effort to attract industry. It was at that point that "Walter Sillers and a good many of his legislative associates decided that the legislative branch ought to exert more influence over the policies of state government."[21] The first step, taken in 1955, was to gain legislative control over the budget commission. While the governor was retained as its chairman, the other members became two senators and two representatives appointed by the lieutenant governor and the Speaker, respectively. In 1968, two years after Sillers's death, the commission was increased to eleven members by adding the lieutenant governor and two more senators, and the Speaker and two more representatives.

By the technique of board membership, the legislature's role in administrative matters was later extended into office space allocation, purchasing, personnel management, health care, public employees retirement, economic development, and several other administrative areas. By December 1983, thirty-seven senators and representatives sat on the boards or commissions of ten executive agencies. Attorney General Bill Allain filed a lawsuit charging that having legislators serve on executive boards and commissions was an unconstitutional breach of the separation of powers ordained by the constitution. In *Alexander v. State By and Through Allain,* the state supreme court agreed with the attorney general and ordered legislators off executive boards and commissions.

A reorganization removing legislators from executive bodies took effect July 1, 1984. Yet the legislature refused to completely abandon the administrative field. The reorganization bill provided that a senator and a representative could be appointed as observers to meet with the Data Processing Authority and with the Mississippi Council on Aging. Two "observers" from each house were also appointed to meet with the Mississippi Health Care Commission, the Board of Trustees of the Public Employees' Retirement System, the Mississippi Board of Economic Development, and the State Personnel Board. Such observers had no vote during the proceedings of these bodies, but they were allowed to participate in their discussions. Initially these legislative "observers" were almost as influential as they had been as members of the governing bodies.

The 1984 reorganization gave the governor sole authority over proposing an executive budget. Yet it also created a Legislative Budget Office, which functions under the supervision of a joint committee of the legislature. In the first few years after reorganization, the budget produced by this legislative agency was more closely followed by the legislature than was the governor's proposed budget. Even in the late 1980s, the remnants of the Sillers-led intrusion into executive affairs were still noticeable.

PRESERVER OF GOVERNMENT

Mississippi's constitution places the governor in the position of being the guarantor of government. It makes him responsible for seeing that any condition that prevents government from operating, in whole or in part, is removed. This power is not peculiar to Mississippi, and its influence over public policy is essentially confined to the area of law and order. However, public perception of gubernatorial failure to adequately cope with a crisis facing the state can doom a governor's administration.[22] Examples of crises

producing gubernatorial leadership have included hurricanes that periodically strike the coast of Mississippi, as well as racial incidents in the
1960s such as the riot over the integration of the University of Mississippi. In
addition to civil unrest and natural disasters, disruptions to public order may
be produced by threats to public health occasioned by epidemics or chemical
spills.

Whenever ordinary civil authority cannot maintain public order, the governor must take charge and restore civil authority as soon as possible. He
may issue a proclamation stating the emergency, announce the general actions undertaken, and declare limited or complete martial law. To cope with
an emergency, the governor can command existing municipal and county
police forces, the state police, units of the national guard, or citizens pressed
into militia duty. He can also press carpenters, doctors, electricians, or engineers into public service if their professional skills are necessary for repair-
ing damage or helping the injured (such as after a hurricane). If necessary, he
can even commandeer private property, materials, and equipment. The governor's actions are constrained by the availability of funds to pay for the
goods and services used and by the threat that judicial review will deem his
actions excessive for the earliest practical restoration of normal conditions.

A small-scale disruption in the regular order in civil affairs exists when
vacancies occur in the elected positions of government. Those occurring in
the legislative branch are filled by a special election, for which the governor
issues a call and sets the date. In most cases of vacancies in the executive and
judicial branches, the governor has the power to restore the normal operation
of government by making temporary appointments. Temporary judicial appointments made during a legislative recess expire at the end of the next session of the senate unless the senate confirms a nominee before then.

Mississippi's governor has one emergency power that is unique among
the states. Because of allegations over the mishandling of public money during Reconstruction, various provisions were included in the 1890 constitution to combat embezzlement of public funds. The governor has the power
and duty to suspend any state or county tax collector or treasurer who is alleged to be defaulting; appoint a temporary replacement; investigate the
questioned account; and, depending on the result of the investigation, either
restore the suspended person to office or see that appropriate criminal
charges are brought.[23]

HEAD OF STATE

As ceremonial head of state, the governor represents Mississippi when dealing with such external entities as the federal government or out-of-state business executives. From the days when Governor Henry Whitfield (1924–28) rallied support for legislation to create the "new image" of a pro-business climate and, especially after Governor Hugh White succeeded in his initial administration (1932–36), to establish the nation's first state effort to attract industry through a subsidy program,[24] Mississippians have expected their head of state to actively encourage national and, later, foreign industry to move to the state. In fulfilling that expectation, governors have gone to the Far East, South America, Europe, and several national locations with information and proposals. Governor Mabus, for example, extolled the virtues of the state to business leaders in New York City and flew to Japan and Europe seeking investments in the state.

Another dimension to this aspect of the governor's head-of-state role began developing when an intensification of the civil rights struggle in the 1950s and 1960s magnified the state's negative image. In the hope of maintaining some influx of industry, investment, and tourist trade on the one hand, and staving off or reducing federal reprisals on the other, governors were forced to take part in combating that image. In the vital image-making realm of national television, Governor Coleman appeared twice on "Meet the Press" and once on "Face the Nation" in such efforts. Since then, every governor has played a part in those efforts by being on national television and national radio and by giving interviews to national press figures. Generally speaking, the intensity of the negative image has decreased considerably in recent years, but there have been high-intensity flare-ups from time to time. In 1989 Governor Mabus was actively engaged in combating such a flare-up brought about by the film production *Mississippi Burning*.

As noted earlier, the governor, as head of state, is the only person authorized by state law to enter into grant-in-aid contracts with the federal government. During the Johnson and Nixon presidencies from 1964 to 1974, total spending on federal grant-in-aid programs increased dramatically. The number of federal grant programs and amount of expenditures increased from 51 programs spending $9.8 billion across the nation in 1964 to 550 spending $52 billion in 1973.[25] The governor appoints the executives who are entrusted with administering the federal-state granting programs. While federal grants include guidelines, they usually permit some flexibility in using funds and personnel in determining how federal objectives will be met. Governors can also use state funds or staff members attached with the Office of Federal-State Programs to research and promote gubernatorial programs. Governor Allain depended on the office to research a proposal for creating a department of transportation that would combine several agencies of state government. Governor Winter used funds to hold a series of public forums throughout the state that proved to be instrumental in the passage of the 1982 Education Reform Act.

One consequence of this flood of federal programs and money has been extensive reorganization in state governments across the country. "A major wave of state government reform took place between the mid-1960s and the mid-1970s,"[26] and the administrative reforms that continued into the 1980s granted most governors "far more management powers than they had ever had in the past."[27] As a consequence, those governors were transformed from "good-time Charlies" to more capable and professional managers.[28] Such changes came more slowly to rural states like Mississippi. The increases in administrative authority given the office in recent years are but small steps toward making the governor a real administrative manager.

CHIEF LEGISLATOR

Because the president's office is the clearinghouse for all budgetary and legislative requests from federal agencies, the president is sometimes called the "chief legislator." Since state agencies in Mississippi can appeal directly to the legislature in both of these matters, it would be a misnomer to apply that title to the governor. Yet Mississippi's chief executive has strengths that the president lacks. The most important of these involves the governor's power to call special sessions of the legislature and to employ the item veto.

Mississippi is one of only twenty states that grant the governor the sole power to call the legislature into special session.[29] The president has the same power, but it ends at that point, whereas the governor, except in cases of impeachment, has the sole authority to set the agenda of the special session. Amplifying that difference is the fact that Congress's annual sessions have no constitutional limitation on their length, whereas the legislature is limited to a 125-day session following the election of state offices and a 90-day session in the other years.

Governor Winter's summoning of a special session in December 1982 to consider his educational reform program provides a classic illustration of how this gubernatorial power can be used to achieve policy goals. Legislators found themselves working in the atmosphere of a "goldfish bowl."

Teachers and pro-education interest groups pressured lawmakers, and the media aggressively reported on each stage of the legislative process. Legislators expressed concern that other needy state employees would be ignored if they approved the governor's request to raise just the teachers' salaries. Winter promised that if progress was made on education reform, he would extend the call to include pay raises for other state employees. The result was a landmark Education Reform Act, a tax increase, and pay raises for teachers and other state employees.[30]

A second important tool that the governor can use to influence the legislature is the veto power. Instead of being forced to veto an entire appropriations bill, the governor, unlike the president, is able to veto only those items he disapproves of. And in regard to all vetoes, Mississippi is one of twenty-four states that make it most difficult for the legislature to override a governor's veto. Not only is a two-thirds vote required instead of a simple majority, but the constitution specifies two-thirds of the entire membership of each chamber, not merely of those present and voting.[31] In conflicts with the legislature, governors are able to remind legislators of their veto power by observing that "a governor is worth two-thirds minus one of the legislature."[32] In meetings over legislation, leaders of both branches of government are well aware of the power of the veto. Even a governor's expression of doubt or mild reservation about a provision of a bill, a knowledgeable observer stated, can cause legislators to modify it to avoid a possible veto.[33]

The Allain and Mabus administrations illustrate the diverse ways the veto power may be wielded. In 1987 Allain threatened to veto an income tax increase that would have helped fund higher education and other financially strapped agencies. The day before a house vote, he sent a letter to lawmakers claiming that federal income tax reform and improved economic conditions would generate more revenues than previously expected.[34] He reportedly met with some legislators individually and threatened to campaign against them if they voted to raise taxes.[35] The tax bill died in the house, after narrowly failing to gain the 60 percent approval needed for tax measures. On the other hand, widespread interest group and legislative support for the 1987 highway bill produced a successful override of Allain's veto. Allain's veto of a substantial teachers' pay raise in 1985 (funded by a tax increase) was also overridden after angry teachers staged their first strike in Mississippi history. During the Mabus administration, the legislature rejected the governor's recommendation to close the state's obsolete charity hospitals. Mabus had argued that because of federal matching funds, diverting the money saved by the closings to the Medicaid program would significantly increase funding for medical services for needy Mississippians. He proceeded to veto the appropriations for charity hospitals. The governor's veto was upheld, and his legislative goal accomplished.

A less tangible resource of governors is their interpersonal skills—their ability to persuade legislators to support their programs. Personal talks with legislators give a governor the opportunity to use his interpersonal skills. Some governors institutionalize meetings with key legislators. Governor Winter met weekly with the lieutenant governor and the Speaker of the house. Even when they were unable to resolve their differences over legislative issues, each benefited by gaining a better understanding of the positions of the others.[36] Governors are assisted by their legislative liaisons, who lobby legislators on behalf of the chief executive's program. Usually one or two gubernatorial staff members serve as legislative liaisons, but sometimes the number rises to half a dozen.

PUBLIC LEADER

The election of Andrew Jackson as president in 1828 gave rise to a new role for the nation's chief executive—that of a popular leader who embodied the hopes and dreams of average Americans. Presidents and governors often point out that they are most knowledgeable about and concerned with the needs of the entire nation or state, thanks to their national or statewide constituency. Legislators, on the other hand, have more parochial interests because they are elected from geographically confined, single-member districts. Chief executives seek popular support by claiming that they identify and empathize with average citizens and share their concerns and attitudes. As presidential candidates of the 1840s claimed that they had been born in modest log cabins (like their constituents), so too do contemporary governors of Mississippi stress the interests they have in common with citizens. Governor Cliff Finch campaigned for the office by carrying a lunch pail with his name on it and by working at a different blue-collar job each week. Governor Allain cultivated a "populist" image as a fighter for average citizens. He fought against higher taxes, and as attorney general he had taken on the utility companies.

One important asset of governors is their tremendous visibility to citizens, compared with other state officials. Virtually everyone knows who the governor of Mississippi is and can offer an opinion about his performance in office. In contrast, individual legislators are far less visible and receive much less coverage in the media. In a 1989 poll, only 22 percent of Mississippians

Table 5: Public Popularity of Mississippi Governors

	Winter		Allain		Mabus	
	1981	1982	1984	1986	1988	1990
Ideology						
Liberal	56%	70%	60%	43%	56%	50%
Moderate	60	54	43	51	52	47
Conservative	59	48	34	39	60	43
Party identification						
Democrat	55	61	53	42	64	49
Independent	59	49	34	41	56	45
Republican	65	49	39	48	62	44
Years lived in state						
15 or less	59	60	43	37	62	49
More than 15	59	55	44	44	60	47
Race						
White	60	52	39	42	58	44
Black	53	65	54	44	65	52
Age						
18–30	53	56	43	44	65	52
31–60	61	55	37	40	58	42
61–98	61	57	52	46	61	48

	Winter		Allain		Mabus	
	1981	1982	1984	1986	1988	1990
Education						
High-school dropout	52	57	47	43	59	35
High-school graduate	52	52	43	42	57	51
Some college	69	59	41	43	67	51
Income						
Under $10,000	62	61	47	47	54	49
$10–20,000	54	51	40	43	60	40
Over $20,000	63	54	41	41	63	50
Sex						
Men	57	52	42	41	56	38
Women	60	59	46	44	65	54
Congressional district						
1	58	62	42	44	56	43
2	62	58	44	43	58	43
3	61	50	41	54	64	49
4	56	54	49	43	68	48
5	56	55	44	32	59	53

Source: Date are from statewide opinion polls conducted by the Social Science Research Center at Mississippi State University.

Note: Table entries are the percentages of Mississippians approving of the governor's job performance (rating it as excellent or good).

could correctly recall the name of their state representative, and only 15 percent could name their state senator.[37] Furthermore, Americans are often cynical about legislative institutions, since they associate them with unpopular actions such as tax increases or obstructionist tactics.[38] The visibility of the governor, his role as "public leader," and public distrust of the legislature provide an opportunity for governors to mobilize citizens behind their legislative proposals.

Mississippi governors in the 1980s have occasionally been successful in attracting public support for their policies. Governor Winter held public forums across the state to mobilize public support behind his education reform program. Public pressure, supportive interest groups, and crusading newspapers were instrumental in convincing the legislature to enact the 1982 Education Reform Act. Governor Allain was repeatedly quoted in the press as promising to veto any tax increase, and he was usually successful in minimizing the rising tax bite. American presidents tend to be successful at persuading Congress to enact their legislative program during their "honeymoon period." In their first few months in office, governors have a similar opportunity to translate popular support into legislative results. In his "honeymoon period," Governor Mabus proposed an executive budget that dramatically increased funding for all levels of education, and the legislature hiked education spending by approximately $200 million.

The political war over a proposed state lottery in 1990 illustrates how the public can threaten electoral sanctions against legislators. Mabus backed a lottery as a way of helping to pay for Education Reform II without raising taxes. He publicly stressed a simple theme—that the legislature should simply let the people decide whether the state should have a lottery by letting the public vote on whether to remove the constitutional ban on a lottery. After the state senate killed the lottery proposal, Mabus claimed that the senate had "told the people of Mississippi to 'shut up, your right to vote does not matter.'" Citizen supporters of a lottery flooded the capitol switchboard with protests. Some compared the legislature to political institutions in the Soviet Union and Nazi Germany and claimed that Eastern Europe had become more "democratic" than the Mississippi legislature. One senator promptly announced his intention to retire. Another summed up the public response: "Governor Mabus did a heckuva job pounding it home to let the people vote on it. Some good people in the Senate will lose their jobs because of it."[39]

The public often responds to a governor's image and programs. Winter was elected governor in 1979 as an economically conservative, business-oriented candidate. Although popular among all social groups, he was especially popular in 1981 among Republicans and people with college educations (table 5). By 1982 Winter was aggressively promoting progressive programs such as public kindergartens and other education reforms. Compared with the previous year, he gained support among liberals, blacks, and self-identified Democrats and lost some support among conservatives and Republicans. Allain, elected governor in 1983 with a "populist" image, was significantly more popular in 1984 among liberals, Democrats, and blacks than among other Mississippians. His strenuous opposition to any tax increase led to significant cuts in state programs and services. By 1986 he had gained some public support among Republicans and conservatives and had lost support among liberals, blacks, and Democrats. Elected governor in 1987 as a reform-minded, pro-education candidate, in 1988 Mabus was popular among all social groups. He was especially popular among young, well-educated, and higher-income citizens, who presumably were especially receptive to his message about the need to improve education in order to attract industry. His midterm slump in all social and political categories may be attributed to shortcomings in his interpersonal skills and a perceived arrogance in efforts to achieve the reforms desired.

A major problem for governors relying on public opinion to push their legislative programs is that citizens are often uninformed about political issues and fail to express their views to legislators. On the great majority of issues, the "folks back home" whom legislators hear from are not average citizens but people directly affected by legislative proposals. Interest group lobbyists are especially aggressive in following legislation and keeping in touch with legislators. Legislators realize that, on some issues, support for what polls indicate most citizens want will be unnoticed and unrewarded. Rejection of a powerful interest group's position, however, can result in defeat at the polls.

PARTY LEADER

A competitive two-party system arose nationally in the 1790s, and Thomas Jefferson was elected president in 1800 as a Democratic-Republican. As the most visible public official in America, Jefferson came to be viewed by congressmen and Americans generally as the leader of his political party. The role of party leader has given presidents additional influence when dealing with other political leaders. Presidents can appeal to party loyalty when seeking congressional support for their legislative initiatives. Even if a president's party fails to control Congress, the nation's chief executive can usually rely on congressmen from his party to uphold his vetoes of bills he disagrees with.

Mississippi governors are also viewed as the leaders of their party, but this role provides them far less political leverage over legislators than that enjoyed by governors in strong two-party states. In the absence of partisan organization and party-line votes in the legislature, multi-factionalism reigns within the Democratic party, and Democratic legislators feel no partisan pressure to support their party's governor. As the Republican party gains strength and becomes a greater threat to Democratic candidates in state elections, the role of party leader could give Mississippi governors more leverage over the legislature. Legislators presumably would realize that if they failed to support popular party programs the governor advocated, they would be jeopardizing their party's position as well as their own.

AN ASSESSMENT

Mississippi's governor remains less powerful than the state legislature. The large number of independent boards and commissions and independently elected executive officials limits his ability to effectively manage the executive branch. It is easy for agency heads to "go native" and reflect the views of their co-workers and clients rather than those of the chief executive. The problem of agency heads going native exists even in political systems where chief executives choose their own department heads and have the power to fire them unilaterally, as in the federal government. In states like Mississippi, department heads can act with even greater freedom when informing legislators of their disagreements with the governor's policies or budget. And efforts to permit Mississippi governors to form a cabinet by selecting their own department heads encounter opposition from many citizens sympathetic to the ideals of Jacksonian democracy. Mississippians define "democracy" as letting voters directly elect key executive officials.

The office of governor in Mississippi has nevertheless become more influential in recent decades, as governors have sought to meet increasing public demands for leadership in pursuing modernization and industrialization. Developments in the 1980s, such as gubernatorial succession and acquisition of sole authority over proposing an executive budget, strengthened the governor. These two features alone, if in existence in 1981, would have led Thad Beyle to rank the formal powers of Mississippi's governor as "moderate" instead of "weak." Instead of being forty-eighth in the nation in formal gubernatorial power, Mississippi then would have been tied with five other states for thirty-sixth.[40]

In the final analysis, however, less formal attributes such as the political skills of a governor are at least as important as legal powers in determining whether an administration will be viewed as a success or a disappointment. Governors must develop those skills and become activists in seeking political allies and public support if they are to become the focal point for translating public opinion into public policy. And having done so, they must challenge traditional legislative supremacy over public policy. Skill in framing the program over which that supremacy is challenged will make a difference in its success or failure. It must be understandable, attractive, and a true reflection of the public's will. Then, even in a traditionalistic political culture like Mississippi's, aroused public opinion can carry the day.

CHAPTER EIGHT

The Antiquated Judicial System

Diane E. Wall

*The state's court system is traditional in nature and large scale re-
form has not taken place. Mississippi is one of two states maintaining a separate chancery court system; still operates an extensive justice of the peace network; and although the need for one seems
present, the state continues to operate without an intermediate court
of appeals.*

Ronald G. Marquardt, 1976[1]

Over a decade later, this quotation continues to paint an accurate portrait of
Mississippi's outdated judicial system. Mississippi has been ranked fiftieth
on an index of legal professionalism.[2] In an effort to improve the situation, in
1977 the legislature authorized creation of a judicial council for a three-year
period to collect and organize information from the components of the justice system. But the council died in 1980 after the legislature refused to extend its authorization. "Bring us into the twentieth century!" exclaimed
Larry Houchins, executive director of the Mississippi State Bar Association,
as he discussed problems, such as the processing of information, in Mississippi's judicial system.[3] In agreement with Houchins's appraisal, retired
chief justice Neville Patterson concluded that "justice is denied when justice
is delayed."[4] He urged funding a judicial council and unifying the court system as ways of resolving many of the problems plaguing Mississippi's antiquated judiciary.

Mississippi's traditional judicial system may be largely attributed to the
constitution of 1890 and the state's dominant traditionalistic political culture.[5] The state constitution influences the organization, jurisdiction, and

administration of courts; the qualifications and selection of judicial personnel; and the meaning of the law itself (especially article 6). Chapter 3 aptly indicated that the 1890 constitution, as amended, established and now perpetuates forms and structures from a bygone era. Mississippi's traditionalistic political culture further preserves those structures and procedures, such as the distinction between law and equity (the principle of equity provides justice when the law cannot). Also, the inherent nature of the court system makes it typically the last government entity to embrace change.[6] Mississippi has resisted moving away from an outdated judicial system because "we have a bunch of political bailiwicks in the judiciary, therefore a reluctance for change."[7] But change is coming, faster than some anticipated, and not soon enough for many "court watchers."[8]

JUDICIAL SYSTEM

Criminal and civil conflicts are brought to state courts by executive branch prosecutors and private lawyers; cases are processed by judges along with, in some instances, juries; and the resulting decisions may administer the law, resolve conflicts, and/or make public policy.[9] Judges, lawyers, legal staff, elected officials, support agencies, professional legal organizations, advocacy groups, and law schools are the major components of the judicial system. Mississippi's judicial system resolves conflicts, determines justice, and shapes the course of public and private actions.

THE COURTS' STRUCTURE, JURISDICTION, AND SELECTION

The organization and jurisdiction of Mississippi state courts are displayed in figure 6. Courts of limited jurisdiction (having limited authority over cases) include the justice court, municipal court, county court, family court, and youth court. The general jurisdiction court of law is the circuit court. Issues of equity (disputes the rule of law cannot resolve) are restricted to a separate chancery court system. In most states equity cases—issues concerning family matters and land disputes—are processed in a general jurisdiction law court. The only statewide appellate court in Mississippi is the supreme court. At the top of the court hierarchy, this court has jurisdiction over all legal matters on appeal.

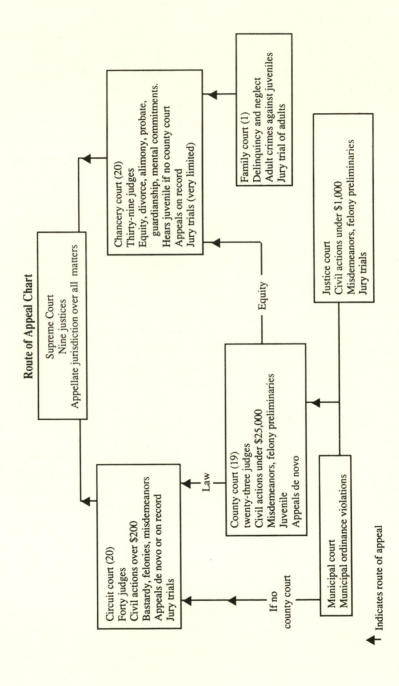

Figure 6. Mississippi state court structure. (*Source: Mississippi Judiciary Directory and Court Calendar* [Jackson: Mississippi Secretary of State, 1989], p. 2.)

Justice Court

At the roots of the judicial system is the justice court (formerly justice of the peace). Each beat in a county may have a justice court judge, who does not have to possess a law degree. As of 1989, only 5 of the 189 justice court judges were lawyers.[10] Along with this court's name change in 1975, the legislature mandated a minimum educational qualification of a high-school degree. Justice court judges are elected for four-year terms and are paid a salary rather than compensated by fees. This court has jurisdiction over civil cases involving values under $1,000 and misdemeanors in the area of criminal law. Justice courts also have a committing role for persons charged with serious crimes under criminal law. Therefore these judges can issue search warrants, set bail, and hold preliminary hearings to ascertain if there is sufficient evidence to hold a trial in a higher court. If desired, individuals may have their cases heard anew in the county court (if one exists in their locale) or in circuit court. Jury trials in justice court are permissible by statute but are rarely used.

Municipal Court

The municipal court is comparable to the justice court in each county. As an exception to Mississippi's elective judiciary, municipal judges are appointed for four-year terms by the governing authority, which also determines their salary. In cities under 10,000 population the mayor may serve as the judge (without additional pay), and a law degree is not required. For cities over 10,000 the judge must be an attorney, and these cities may have as many as three judges. A municipal judge hears cases involving violations of city ordinances and other minor offenses. Additionally, this judge serves as a committing official, having the same role as the justice court judge. Appeals from this court are heard as new trials in the county court (if one exists) or in the circuit court.

County Court

The county court does not exist in all eighty-two counties. By law larger counties may have this type of court. The largest counties, such as Harrison and Hinds, have more than one county court judge. As of 1990, there were nineteen county courts with a total of twenty-three judges. Why are there so few courts? Some court watchers believe there is a sufficient workload to justify such courts in every county, but financing them is a problem. They point out that counties must fund county courts, and some counties are too poor to afford to operate them. So why are there any? Court watchers believe that lawyers prefer to avoid justice court. The legal qualifications for county court judges are more demanding than for justice court judges. A person elected to the four-year term of county court judge must meet the same requirements as a circuit and chancery judge, being at least twenty-six years old and a qualified elector who has five years experience as an attorney-at-law. Salary is based on the county's classification and population size.

The civil law jurisdiction of this court is limited to cases involving $25,000 or less. Criminal law jurisdiction includes both misdemeanors (punishable by less than one year in jail) and felonies (punishable by one year or more in prison). To help reduce the workload of the circuit courts, civil and criminal cases (except capital punishment cases) may be transferred to the lower county court. In civil cases both sides must consent to a transfer. These judges also have jurisdiction over juveniles, because youth court is an adjunct of the county court. Only Clay County operates a separate youth court. Twelve-person juries are available to adult defendants in county court, and an appeal goes to the circuit or chancery court, depending on the nature of the case.

Youth and Family Courts

The last two limited jurisdiction courts are youth court and family court. Mississippi has adopted the nationwide approach that children under age eighteen should be treated differently before the law than are adults. Therefore youth courts were established as an adjunct of county courts, or as a division of the chancery court if no county court exists. The proceedings are civil rather than criminal, and the public is excluded (the philosophy is to protect rather than prosecute). No child under thirteen years old can be prosecuted in a criminal case. For felony charges against a child thirteen years old or older, the case can be certified (sent) to circuit court. If the charge is punishable by death or a life sentence, the circuit court has exclusive jurisdiction. The newest and increasing caseload for youth court involves truancy, because the Educational Reform Act of 1982 reestablished compulsory attendance in Mississippi. School attendance officers report to county, family, or youth court. Youth court decisions may be appealed to the Mississippi Supreme Court.

The only family court is in Harrison County, although Hinds County assigns one of its three judges exclusively to juvenile matters. A family court judge is elected for a four-year term and must have the same legal qualifications as Mississippi's other trial judges, although this court is considered in-

ferior to the circuit and chancery courts. Included in this jurisdiction are juvenile delinquency, child neglect, and adult crimes against juveniles. Adults
may have a jury trial, and appeals go to chancery court.

Circuit Court

The circuit court is the general trial court for major criminal and civil cases.
There are twenty circuit court districts, each serving an average of four counties.[11] The districts may encompass as many as seven counties or may be restricted to one highly populous county that generates a substantial caseload.
The legislature is entrusted with drawing the boundaries of the circuit (and
chancery) court districts. The number of judges within a district varies from
one to four, the total number statewide being forty. The legal qualifications
for election to a four-year term of office are being at least twenty-six years
old and a qualified elector who has five years' experience as an attorney-at-
law. Circuit court sessions are held in each county in rotation.

Jurisdiction includes civil cases involving values of over $200 and se-
rious criminal cases. Twelve-person juries are available to defendants in
criminal cases, with a unanimous vote required for conviction. Decisions in
civil cases require agreement among only nine of the twelve jurors. Cases
first tried in justice court, municipal court, and county court may be retried
in circuit court. Appeals proceed to the state supreme court.

Chancery Court

Equity issues are processed in the Mississippi Chancery Court. This division
of law and equity derives from the origins of our court system in early English history. At that time, disputes that could not be resolved by the rules of
law were taken to the King's Chancellor to be decided using principles of
fairness. This evolved into the English Court of Chancery. Twenty chancery
courts with thirty-nine judges (chancellors) are spread across the state in a
different array than are the circuit court districts. Each district has from one
to four judges, depending on caseload. Judges are elected for four-year terms
and must have the same legal qualifications as circuit court judges. The jurisdiction is complex, but it basically includes disputes involving equity, di-
vorce, alimony, questions of mental competence, matters involving minors,
and processing of estates. The right to a jury trial is limited, and appeals are
directed to the supreme court.

Supreme Court

Mississippi is one of twelve states that has only one general jurisdiction appellate court (authority over cases of record on appeal).[12] The Mississippi Supreme Court originally consisted of three justices. It reached its current size of nine justices in 1952. The modern practice is for three justices to be elected from each of three geographical districts on a partisan ballot for staggered eight-year terms. Legal qualifications for office are being at least thirty years old, a citizen of the state for five years, and a practicing attorney for five years. When vacancies occur in the positions of chief justice and presiding justice, they are filled based on seniority on the court. A majority of the court's caseload is civil in nature rather than criminal, although the percentage of criminal cases is increasing. As of 1988, 45 percent of all issues settled on their merits (630) were criminal cases.[13]

Since 1975, the court has sat in panels comprising three justices to render final decisions. The electoral district of the justice plays no role in determining which panels he or she is assigned to.[14] Each panel is responsible for six cases a week and is chaired by either the chief justice or one of the court's two presiding justices. A unanimous decision by one of these panels is considered a decision by the whole court. One of the panel members writes the opinion of the court, and only the name of that justice is readily available to the general public. During the process of writing the court's opinion, justices not on the panel have the right to object to the decision, which would send the case to the whole court for consideration (en banc). This panel procedure was devised to alleviate the burdensome caseload facing the supreme court. However, petitions for rehearing, constitutional questions, and matters pertaining to death penalty cases are required to be heard by the entire court. Figure 7 illustrates the court's increasing workload.

In 1975 one sitting justice, Henry Rogers, strongly objected to three-judge panels as a denial of due process.[15] He asserted that there were not enough judges participating to provide the necessary range of backgrounds to reach a sound decision. Recent research analyzing Mississippi Supreme Court decision making confirms that there is wide voting variation among the nine justices.[16] Former chief justice Neville Patterson explains that there just is no more effective way to handle the increasing number of cases brought to the court—some frivolous and others deadly serious, such as the very time consuming death penalty cases.[17]

The state supreme court is generally not an activist body. Therefore it has issued few major decisions that have dramatically affected public policy in

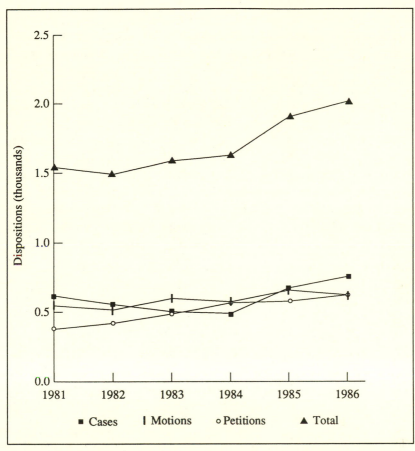

Figure 7. Mississippi Supreme Court caseload. (*Source*: *Mississippi Supreme Court Annual Report, 1986* [Jackson: Mississippi Supreme Court, 1986], table 2.)

Mississippi. A landmark case in 1975, *Newell v. State,* has the potential to drastically alter the court's relationship with the other two branches because the supreme court justices asserted their right to make the rules of the supreme court.[18] For example, several legislators were upset with the court's 1989 decision that their rules of criminal procedure were to be applied in a child abuse case, rather than the statute enacted by the legislature.[19] The court's most recent landmark decision was in 1983 in *Alexander v. State of Mississippi By and Through Allain,* when the court agreed with Attorney General Allain that having legislators serve on executive branch boards and commissions violated the separation of powers ordained in the state constitution; it ordered legislators removed from such bodies.[20] However, the court has refrained from applying the separation of powers principle to the lieutenant governor, who exercises a significant legislative leadership role under senate rules.[21]

Throughout the 1980s the court was ideologically split; its justices were somewhat evenly distributed from liberal to conservative when voting to decide cases involving economic issues and the rights of those accused of crimes. Lenore Prather, the only woman justice, generally occupied the ideological middle of the court.[22] Perhaps the broad spread of the ideological positions on the court discourages it from taking a more activist role in shaping policy. In addition, the absence of an intermediate appeals court hinders the ability of a state supreme court to play a more visible and prominent policy-making role, since it finds itself preoccupied with a routine and heavy caseload.[23]

PERSONNEL

Mississippi has about 220 state judgeships that require a law degree. These positions are filled from a pool of 4,750 lawyers. Very few judges are female, and even fewer are black. Supreme Court Justice Lenore Prather became the first female chancery court judge when she was appointed in 1971 (seventeen years after the state's first woman judge, Zelma Price, who served as a county judge). She also became the first woman on the supreme court when she was sworn into office in 1982. By early 1989 supreme court justice Reuben Anderson, circuit court judges Fred Banks and Lillie Blackmon-Sanders, and chancery court judge Isaac Byrd were the only state judges who were black, along with some nonlawyer justice court judges. All four were initially appointed by governors to fill vacancies. Only 13 percent of lawyers in Mississippi are female and 5 percent are black, compared with 53 percent of the state's population that is female and 36 percent that is black.[24] Yet a slightly higher percentage of lawyers in Mississippi are black than the national average.[25] Also, there are far more black lawyers in the state today than in the late 1960s, the early days of Justice Anderson's law practice, when "there were only five other black lawyers practicing in the whole State."[26]

Legal staff for the judicial posts is virtually nonexistent. Circuit and chancery court judges must do their own legal research as they travel around their circuit. However, supreme court justices recently benefited from an increase in the number of their law clerks to two per justice. Also, creation of the office of court administrator has spread from the supreme court all the way down to the county court. The administrator helps the judge by doing such nonjudicial tasks as maintaining statistical reports, coordinating duties of the court clerks, providing general administrative support, and acting as liaison with the general public and lawyers.[27]

SUPPORT AGENCIES AND OTHER MAJOR COMPONENTS

Three support agencies have been created since 1970. The newest is the Mississippi Commission on Judicial Performance, created by a constitutional amendment in 1979 and set up to investigate misconduct and disability among judges. This is similar to the role of the state bar in supervising lawyers' behavior. The commission is composed of seven judicial members selected by various judicial associations, two nonlawyer members appointed by the governor, and one attorney chosen by the state bar. The commission makes recommendations to the supreme court for its action. In its first decade in existence, the commission processed over 1,200 complaints against judges from all courts; it has recommended rehabilitation as well as punishment. The commission also serves an educational role by making recommendations for the continuing education of judges.[28]

Another support agency, the Judicial Council, was not reauthorized by the legislature in 1980. It served to collect, analyze, and disseminate statistics on the functioning of all state courts. The Judicial Council is further discussed in the section on resource issues. The third support agency is the Judicial College, housed in the University of Mississippi Law Center. In 1976 the college began providing in-career training for attorneys and judges.

Other legal education opportunities in Mississippi include one public law school, the University of Mississippi School of Law, established in 1854; an accredited private school, the Mississippi College School of Law, established in the mid-1970s; and other programs approved by the Mississippi Commission on Continuing Legal Education.[29] Until 1985, anyone wishing to practice law in Mississippi, except for University of Mississippi School of Law graduates, was required to pass a bar examination. Several groups effectively challenged this policy so that today all graduates of law schools must take the bar exam. Currently, lawyers in the state must complete twelve hours of continuing education each year, but training requirements for the judgeships vary.[30]

Only one of the legal organizations in Mississippi was created by the legislature—the Mississippi State Bar Association. Founded in 1906, membership in the Mississippi State Bar Association was made mandatory for all resident practicing attorneys in 1932.[31] The bar association officers select an executive director and staff to aid the board of commissioners in formulating rules of conduct, processing complaints about professional conduct, providing advisory opinions, recommending legislation regarding the courts and law, and providing educational and social activities.[32] County bar associations are also active.

Numerous nationally affiliated legal professional organizations for judges, trial lawyers, defense lawyers, and prosecutors are active in Mississippi. A predominately black bar association, the Magnolia Bar Association, was established in 1955.[33] The Mississippi Women Lawyers Association was created in 1976. Other categories of legal personnel in Mississippi also have nationally linked associations, such as the Mississippi Association of Legal Assistants and the Mississippi Association of Legal Secretaries.

Major issues confronting the judicial system reflect the drastic need for Mississippi to modernize its system. Problems include reorganization, resources, the selection process, and ethics. None of these are exclusively problems of Mississippi's judicial branch, but owing to the judiciary's unique nature, they are exacerbated in Mississippi's antiquated judicial system.

THE ISSUE OF STRUCTURAL REORGANIZATION

Abolishing Justice Courts

In the past, the justice court system has been severely criticized on several counts. Two relatively recent modifications may have saved the justice court. The change from fee-based compensation to a set salary alleviated the situation in which one justice court judge earned more in one year than the governor or the chief justice of the supreme court.[34] This change was forced by a 1981 federal court decision that held that the fee system violated due process of law.[35] Also, "forum shopping," in which defendants strategically selected which justice court judge would decide their cases, has now been reduced.

Additional recent changes are that the number of justice court judges in a county has been limited to five; justices now have permanent offices provided by the county; and a justice court clerk position was created, with case assignments rotated among the judges. These changes have reduced the political clout that justice court judges can exercise within the state, and coupled with the increased educational qualifications of these judges, they make this court draw less attention than it once did. Complaints about justice court judges as a percentage of all complaints filed with the Mississippi Judicial Performance Commission dropped from 71 percent during 1980–85 to 55 percent for 1986.[36] Complaints dropped another 4 percent in 1987 but then increased by 6 percent in 1988.[37] Justice Anderson believes this court is improving. He points out that there are no practicing lawyers at all in Issaquena County and only three in Sharkey County. Justice court, in which a lawyer need not be present, "serves a purpose—some [litigants] could not afford any other way."[38]

Merger of Law and Equity Courts

Judicial reorganization involving the merger of law and equity courts has long been debated, but not all jurists agree about the wisdom of merger. Justice Prather likes the specialization produced by the law versus equity distinction. She pointed to her chancellory background as being extremely helpful to her supreme court case opinion that changed a major rule regarding children.[39] Chief Justice Roy Noble Lee agrees that "the division suits Mississippi—it's a way of life."[40] Justice Patterson has been ambivalent, however. As a former chancellor in Lawrence County for sixteen years, he described how lawyers had to drive long distances to get to the proper court, while the other kind of court was close at hand. For that reason, Patterson supported a merger. But he expressed concern that merger would be a political bombshell that could prevent a unified court system. "You see, most counties have two clerks paid on fee basis—circuit and chancery."[41]

Court Redistricting

The process of redistricting, when the state legislature redraws the boundaries of court districts, is often controversial. Changing circuit and chancery court districts can affect the workload of the judges and the livelihood of circuit and chancery court clerks (who operate on a fee system). It can also enhance or threaten the judges' political power (reelection chances). In addition, redistricting proposals may minimize or enhance black political representation. In the 1980s the redistricting of circuit and chancery courts in Mississippi provoked an intense quarrel over their composition and organization.

Black leaders pointed out that even in 1987 none of the chancellors were black and only one black served as circuit judge, so blacks constituted only 1 percent of all seventy-nine judges. A black state senator, Henry Kirksey, initiated a lawsuit, *Kirksey v. Allain* (which became *Martin v. Mabus* before it finally was resolved). This case alleged that the defendants failed to obtain United States Justice Department clearance before making changes in the circuit and chancery court districts, ignored the "one-person, one-vote" principle, drew new district lines that diluted black voting strength, and used multimember districts which dilute black voting strength in some districts. In 1986 a three-judge federal panel halted the election of thirty-three Mississippi trial judges (fifteen circuit, fifteen chancery, and three county court posts), because the Voting Rights Act of 1965 applied to judicial elections and the laws altering those posts had never received federal approval.[42] Columnist Sid Salter criticized the legislature for failing over a three-year period to devise an adequate redistricting plan, forcing the federal government to take action: "The lawmakers sat on their baronial hands and ignored reality."[43]

In 1988 Judge Barbour ordered that single-member sub-districts replace the violative at-large, multimember districts.[44] On December 29, 1988, Attorney General Mike Moore settled *Martin v. Mabus* out of court, agreeing that at least in the Delta districts, voters could elect judges in single-member sub-districts making up each judicial district. Moore then made a historic announcement that his office would no longer defend until the bitter end the state's position on lawsuits brought against it by civil rights groups, if the state appeared to be fighting a losing cause.[45]

Elections for all circuit and chancery seats across Mississippi were held in 1989. After the first primary, Carroll Rhodes, lead counsel for the plaintiffs, observed: "Changes are occurring in how our judges are being elected, but more changes are needed before we have a truly represented judiciary—one chosen from all segments of our population. Interestingly, the immediate result [of the court case] will probably be more women than blacks elected. Hopefully, we will get beyond the day of race counting in voting patterns, but not yet. The judiciary is slow to accept changes."[46]

In the 1989 general election, the number of blacks winning circuit and chancery judgeships increased from one in the previous statewide election of 1982 to four; 5 percent of judges were now black. The redistricting litigation proved more successful in increasing the number of black candidates; 11 percent of the primary candidates and 8 percent of the general election candidates were black in 1989, compared with only 2 percent in the preceding statewide general election.[47] Key barriers to greater black representation in the judiciary still must be overcome. As late as 1989 only 5 percent of Mississippi lawyers were black, providing a small pool from which judicial candidates could be drawn. Also, judicial incumbents, who are overwhelmingly white, are routinely reelected.

Intermediate Appellate Court

Unlike thirty-eight other states and the United States judiciary, Mississippi lacks an intermediate appellate court. Two plans have been suggested by persons desiring such a court. One is an intermediate appellate court that would provide the final appeal for all criminal cases. Former chief justice Patterson has not favored this option for many reasons, including a clouding of who (chief justice of supreme court or intermediate appellate court) would be at the top of the court hierarchy. Also, he argued that death penalty cases would have to be heard by the Mississippi Supreme Court anyway. Besides, to Patterson, "one of the pleasures of the supreme court job was diversity (variety) of kinds of cases."[48] Therefore Patterson has supported the second plan—an intermediate court that would make "the supreme court a *writ* court" (one that decides which cases it will accept in order to settle major issues of law).[49] Justice Prather agrees but doubts there is enough legislative commitment to fund that change.[50] As chief justice, Walker encouraged streamlining and other innovations to put off adding that court, thereby saving money.[51] Chief Justice Lee wants a study first, perhaps by the National Center for State Courts, to find out what kind of court would suit Mississippi.[52] The legislature established a special study committee on this issue to report back to the 1990 legislative session. Marquardt concludes that "the lack of an intermediate court has been so devastating to the system that the quality of the court's work has been seriously impaired."[53]

THE ISSUE OF RESOURCES

Lack of judicial resources is the overwhelming problem. Major concerns are staffing, salaries, caseloads, information processing, and agency support. At the core of the problem is the old-fashioned judicial norm that the judiciary does not politically assert its funding needs, such as by lobbying the legislature at budget time.[54] However, by the mid-1980s supreme court clerk Susan Gordon had begun to assert the needs of the supreme court—with very positive results.[55] One result of lobbying the legislature was that the supreme court and other major state courts began to implement a statewide tracking system for court cases using computers and, especially, compatible computer programs. Also, many large problems began to be resolved with small sums of money. Money can be obtained, according to Gordon, when legislators are informed of needs and occasionally brought over to the Carroll Gartin Justice Building to see things for themselves.

Staffing

Some court watchers find it ironic that whereas state judges are paid thousands of dollars, they do not have secretaries or law clerks and often are housed in buildings that are falling down. As a result, it can be very difficult to make contact with one of the judges who travels the circuit's counties. The executive director of the Mississippi State Bar Association suggests as a solution that the legislature create a separate budget for the judiciary.[56] There is only one line in the budget for the state judiciary, excluding the supreme court. Currently the judicial system receives 1 percent of the general budget. Carl Baar concludes that the judicial "situation in Mississippi and Missouri is not unexpected. In states with limited and itemized, rather than mixed or general state judicial funding, budget making tends to focus on achieving mathematical accuracy rather than assigning program priorities."[57]

Salaries

In regard to salaries, Mississippi supreme court justices in 1984 were ranked first in a nationwide comparison, which was adjusted for per capita state income.[58] However, Justice Patterson related one comment by a community leader who said that after finding out that the chief justice is paid only $60,000, his respect for the office had declined because as a businessman he made more money than the person who decides life and death matters.[59] Perusal of a Jackson Clarion-Ledger article featuring state salaries clearly indicates that something is faulty.[60] Fee-paid circuit and chancery court clerks in many instances make more money each year than the state's top judges.[61] A position paper to the Mississippi legislature recently observed that judicial salaries had fallen behind increases in the Consumer Price Index.[62] Judges make less on the average than most attorneys appearing before them. Also, Wall's study of Mississippi Supreme Court elections uncovered an instance in which an incumbent and challenger ended up spending almost the equivalent of one year's pay in their campaign—highly unusual for a judicial campaign in Mississippi.[63]

Caseload

Most court watchers agree that the growing caseload is even more serious than are pay inequities. Justice Prather indicated that the supreme court justices were well aware that there were two hundred more cases filed last year than the year before.[64] "There are too many lawsuits (frivolous ones); also too few justices, that is, there is no intermediate appellate court to screen out cases."[65] Justice Patterson believed the court was at a dangerous point because justice is delayed and overburden leads to mistakes. Justices feel pressured not to give a case the time it deserves. Appellate justices "need time between cases to change gears."[66]

The nature of the caseload also contributes to overburden. Capital punishment cases in Mississippi, such as Edward Earl Johnson's conviction for killing a Walnut Grove town marshal, can take as long as eight years to resolve. Since a person's life is at stake in these cases, the whole court hears the case, and the justices devote extraordinary deliberation to the issues brought before them. On May 20, 1987—the day of Johnson's execution—several individuals experienced the draining impact that capital convictions have on the judiciary. The supreme court clerk had been up late, and one of the justices was on call throughout that night in case there was any last-minute development. Also, court personnel knew that the day after Johnson's execution would bring yet another capital punishment case on initial appeal. The impact of the Johnson disposition cannot be viewed as unique. Forty-eight people awaited execution in Mississippi at that time.[67] According to Justice Anderson, "they never go away"—he was processing the Pruett death penalty appeals after Johnson's execution (Anderson already had heard motions on fifteen different issues in that case).[68]

Loss of time and drainage of personal energy are evident to anyone who has been close to the total processing of even one capital punishment case. Furthermore, the drain on the judiciary is not solely on the supreme court. The retrial of Pruett included a three-day jury selection process that included individually questioning 188 of the 221 potential jurors regarding pretrial publicity and their personal opinions on the death penalty.[69] Chief Justice Roy N. Lee gave an illustration of the typical cost to local government for a capital case. In Scott County a twenty-eight-year-old man killed two women. This death penalty case required a change in venue (a trial at a location different from the one where the crimes occurred) to the coast. Lee stated that the circuit clerk recorded the cost as $30,000 for the first trial. After the defendant's successful appeal to the supreme court, a second trial was required—costing another $30,000. The county in which the trial would have normally been held has to pay the bill, which includes transport and lodging for the whole court at the new location.[70]

Unknown to the casual observer, however, utilities cases also take enormous amounts of court time and energy. When Patterson first reached the supreme court, he heard a utilities case on appeal consisting of eighty-two volumes of court record and had only one law clerk for assistance. He said it took him about two months just to read the record! His opinion for the court was sixteen pages long.[71] The number of cases filed and processed therefore does not tell the whole story of court overload.

Information Processing

Closely linked to the caseload problem is the courts' inability to process information efficiently. Until the late 1980s, most of the state's courts still kept paper records. As a response to the "paper glut," the supreme court clerk's office in the late 1980s originated a master index system so that information about cases, from the moment they are filed to their final disposition, can readily be retrieved. Because data are not computerized, most legal research is done manually.[72] Lack of computer access results in an inefficient use of personnel time and, at times, an inability to know the current status of a legal issue as it moves through the judicial hierarchy. Also, unlike some states, court transcripts are usually not put on microfilm, let alone videotaped during the trial. There are signs that some of these innovations are in Mississippi's future. For example, the Statewide Computerization System Committee is pursuing the goal of obtaining software so that the judiciary can tie in with the state's mainframe computer, and in late 1987 Jackson County courts began videotaping cases experimentally. However, a profession based on tradition and procedure can be slow to change. In many instances change occurs in Mississippi when the burden just becomes too great.

Support Agency

There also is a need for a judicial center. The short-lived sixteen-member Judicial Council was funded by the United States Law Enforcement Assistance Administration program about ten years ago.[73] For three years this unit collected and analyzed data on courts across the state, data that are not currently available. Justice Patterson has supported a "unified court system" in which the principal officer of the courts (the chief justice of the supreme court) can allocate judicial resources (circuit court judges) according to the changing needs identified by a Judicial Council. He found that it was very difficult to move a circuit court judge temporarily to another district to help out on the caseload because the automatic assumption was that the judge needing help had been loafing on the job. Without the Judicial Council, Patterson said, no hard facts can be generated on judicial workloads.[74]

If a resource like the Judicial Council is so sorely needed, why was it not renewed? Perhaps no one has the answer. Patterson, who was chairman of the Judicial Council, pointed out that the council made several controversial recommendations before it died, such as to abolish the justice of the peace system and change the chancery and circuit court fee system. These recommendations made the Mississippi Judicial Council politically volatile. Patterson concluded, "the Council recommended getting rid of the justice of the peace system—the J.P.'s had more political clout!"[75] Former Lowndes County justice court judge Charles J. Younger points out that many citizens like the justice court because it responds to the "little man." And the fee system may encourage judges to be efficient. "Having a different viewpoint on the time put into the job, a justice court judge will open up on Saturday—even come in at night."[76]

Summarizing the factors involved in the death of the council, its former staff attorney, Luther T. Brantley III, points to three major aspects. He said, "What brought the issue to a head was the Council's position on the justice court. Also, several circuit and chancery court clerks were opposed to the Council because it required them to submit caseload information without reimbursement. (These clerks earn their livelihood from the traditional fee system.) Additionally, there were some personal dynamics going on, too."[77]

THE ISSUE OF THE SELECTION PROCESS

Almost three-fourths of our states elect some of their judges. For most of this century Mississippi has elected major judicial offices using a partisan ballot. Until very recently that election really occurred in the Democratic primary, because of Mississippi's one-party system. Some observers have labeled Mississippi's judicial selection system an appointive one in reality, because incumbents initially appointed to fill vacancies appear to be consistently returned to office until their retirement. In an interview, Justice Prather jokingly referred to the well-known maxim that "a judge is a lawyer who knew the governor."[78] Only recently have a few supreme court justices been forced into general election contests. Also, the race most frequently containing more than one candidate in the primary is that for the justice court, which is basically a part-time job.

It is doubtful that Mississippi's traditional method of selecting judges will change anytime soon. True two-party competition will eventually spread to the judiciary, but only after it becomes firmly entrenched in the other branches of government. Many scholars urge adoption of the merit selection system. In that system the governor appoints judges from a list of qualified candidates developed by a judicial selection committee. However, most Mississippi trial judges polled in a 1974 survey favored the current selection process.[79]

A recent study investigated the prevalent image of Mississippi as essentially having an appointive system.[80] Incumbent supreme court justices are not returned to office without devoting resources to winning. The contested primaries between the years 1932 and 1985 overwhelmingly contained an incumbent; hence competitive races were not restricted to filling vacant seats. One-fourth of the ballot appearances by incumbents during that period were contested, and almost 20 percent of contested races saw the incumbent supreme court justice defeated. Also, the average cost of a campaign during that period increased fivefold. The study concluded that the power of incumbency reigns, but the tremendous campaign effort and expenditures reinforce the notion that Mississippi's Democratic primaries do matter.[81]

Not too long ago some Mississippians urged the legislature to adopt nonpartisan judicial elections. However, former chief justice Patterson believed that this suggestion did not get through the legislature because many thought it would disrupt a civil rights lawsuit pending at that time.[82] Chief Justice Lee endorses the elective process. He "talked to judges from all over the U.S. and supports retention elections—running on the record. This makes the judge feel answerable to the people, but not just on an individual case."[83] The three most recent governors have used a nomination committee to process applicants for judicial vacancies, which is similar to a merit selection system. Although not adopted by statute, this plan appears to be popular with the bar. Under this executive branch modification, the first woman and first black were appointed to the supreme court.[84]

THE ISSUE OF ETHICS

Ethics rules are imposed on judges by canons as professional self-policing by bar associations, such as the American Bar Association, or sometimes are set out in state statutes. Judicial ethics cover situations involving judges' activities relating to financial and business dealings, political parties, interest groups, elections, and other kinds of political participation. They must remove themselves from cases in which they have any business or personal (such as family) interest. Canons also limit the ways judges may be politically active. Research is inadequate to substantiate the public's assumption that judicial ethics restrict judges more effectively, compared with other political actors who are not controlled by codes.[85]

In 1979 Mississippi adopted a constitutional amendment creating the Commission on Judicial Performance.[86] Rule 6 of the commission's code specifies grounds for discipline and retirement.[87] This rule cites the grounds contained in the Mississippi constitution of 1890, the Code of Judicial Conduct of the Mississippi Conference of Judges, the Mississippi Justice Court Officers Association's code, and the Mississippi Supreme Court code of professional responsibility. When the commission cannot resolve the complaint and believes it has merit, a formal complaint is referred to the supreme court for a judgment. In 1988 the commission disposed of 152 complaints: 141 were final dispositions (123 of these were dismissals), and the other 11 complaints were combined into 7 formal complaints referred to the supreme court. Sixteen complaints before the commission were informally resolved by a letter of agreement or memorandum of understanding with the judge.[88]

The commission's recommendations to the legislature reflect ethical problem areas in the state. Past recommendations that have been legislatively enacted focus on the justice court—establishing records uniformity, eliminating judge shopping, and additional mandatory education—and the training of constables.[89] The commission's recommendations in 1986 demonstrate continued concern about case processing and administrative authority within the justice court of each county and the need for training and continuing education requirement for all judges, because education of justice court judges reduced complaints against them.[90] As an indicator of the state's progress, in 1988 the commission recommended that justice courts should have administrative authority over constables, and that constables should have four to eight hours of training in the area of civil process (owing to a great increase in complaints about constables).[91]

Mississippi does not seem to have the pervasive judicial ethics problems of its neighboring state, Louisiana. In line with other political patterns in Louisiana, Glick and Vines highlight that state's permissiveness toward judicial participation in off-the-bench activities.[92] Mississippi is not immune to scandal; however, the most famous case in Mississippi is not that of a state judge, but instead the perjury conviction of United States district judge Walter Nixon, Jr. Nixon, the second federal judge in the United States ever to be convicted while sitting on the bench, was impeached by the United States House of Representatives in 1989 and removed from office after conviction by the Senate.

A major ethics issue, which will escalate as the state tackles its drinking-while-driving problem, is the widespread practice of fixing driving under the influence (DUI) tickets by justice court judges. Justice court ticket fixing is only the tip of the iceberg—it includes higher courts. According to Luther Brantley III, director of the Mississippi Commission on Judicial Performance, in some counties the percentage of ticket fixing is as high as 25 percent.[93] Two examples illustrate this problem. In May 1985 a former Lowndes County justice court judge pleaded guilty to two counts of a twenty-five-count federal grand jury indictment against him for accepting $4,400 to drop DUI charges. Two years later a Grenada County justice court judge resigned and pleaded guilty to two counts of mail fraud for fixing DUI tickets for cash payments and favors to friends.[94] The federal charges against the former judge included accepting about $2,000 in ten ticket cases from May 1985 to February 1987. The defense most often used by ticket fixers is "everybody fixes tickets. . . . It's a fairly well established custom."[95] So well established that even after those federal convictions, the Commission on Judicial Performance had to recommend that a justice court judge be removed from office because from 1985 to January 1988 he failed "to report 28 DUI convictions and 552 routine traffic convictions . . . to the Mississippi Department of Public Safety."[96] As noted earlier, Mississippi often waits for the federal courts to activate change.

ASSESSMENT

In 1973 Mississippi had the lowest ranking (score) of the fifty states on an index of legal professionalism. This index comprises American Bar Association standards on five factors: selection system, court structure, judicial administrator and staff, office tenure, and salary.[97] By 1989 Mississippi was still at the bottom in legal professionalism, but its absolute score had increased somewhat because of improved administration: a position of supreme court counsel and administrator had been created, and some counties had hired a court administrator.

As the 1980s ended, a major problem throughout the judicial system continued to be a lack of essential resources. Insufficient resources partly reflect the financially strapped condition of Mississippi government in general—a government that oversees the poorest state in the nation. Judges of the main trial courts cannot be reached efficiently because secretaries are not provided when they ride circuit. One of the newer county court judges does not even have a live telephone during grand jury sessions. The phone is switched off during the whole session because the judge's office is in the grand jury room. At the supreme court level, insufficient resources result in undesirable workloads. For example, the unrelenting trail of capital punishment cases overburdens this system beyond comprehension—holding captive lawyers, circuit court judges, and the supreme court's justices, administrator, clerk, and staff. The morale of supreme court justices is summed up in Justice Anderson's reflections on the day when he would no longer be on the court and "then could see the kids on a regular basis."[98]

People connected with the judicial system, as well as legislators, bear some responsibility for Mississippi's antiquated judicial system. Justices of the peace resisted replacement of the fee system with salaries. Many circuit and chancery court clerks continue to fight to preserve the fee system, which maximizes their incomes. Some circuit and chancery court judges, concerned about their political futures, were apprehensive of redistricting. Indeed, the nature of the judiciary itself—reflected in the importance of precedent—seems to work against change. The legislature also exhibits a bias against change. A majority of legislators sitting on the judiciary committees are lawyers. People in the judicial system who oppose change are often active in making their views known to legislators. The failure of constitutional revision efforts in the legislature impedes improvements in the judicial system. Many enlightened justices and court watchers continue to fight for judicial reforms, however. Reforms in the rules of the state house of representatives could eventually lead to legislation that might help the judiciary leap into at least the twentieth century. Yet Lucedale Circuit Court Judge Darwin Maples aptly sums up the Mississippi experience: "Our reforms have always been a piecemeal thing. One thing you learn in all this is that reform efforts aren't for the short-winded. Lawyers and judges are slow to change."[99]

CHAPTER NINE

Mississippi's Taxing and Spending: Have Things Really Changed?

Edward J. Clynch

Such a philosophy, therefore, would admit that only the legislature is the proper governmental instrument to allocate the State's money among departments. As a consequence, it is believed that the budget agency ought to be an agent of the state legislature. . . . Such a policy, of course, does not support progressive governmental practices. . . . It simply seeks to perpetuate the status quo so as to avoid increased taxes.

Donald S. Vaughn, 1956[1]

Most public policies in Mississippi emerge from an ongoing tug of war between change agents pulling Mississippi into the mainstream of American life and status quo forces that resist a restructuring of the traditional order. Budget procedures and taxing and spending decisions affect every sector of society and hold center stage in this struggle. Rules of the budget game control which actors participate in allocating state resources. Revenue decisions determine who pays for government activities and how much. Expenditure decisions set priorities among the services that government provides its citizens.

In Mississippi, to a large extent, budget allocation practices and taxing and spending decisions determine whether the values of traditionalists or modernists prevail. Ironically, these competing groups do not really disagree about the consequences of more taxing and spending or of a gubernatorially dominated budget process. Supporters of the status quo view increasing services, raising taxes, and enhancing executive power over spending decisions—at the expense of the legislature—as threats to the traditional order. Change advocates agree. They believe that a strong governor could successfully improve government services so critical to social advancement, even if additional taxes proved necessary. Moving Mississippi into the American mainstream requires services that allow all citizens to function in a modern society. Every segment of the population, including the state's 36 percent black citizenry, needs "modern conveniences" including adequate health care, meaningful public education, and good highways.

Economic conditions, in many ways, shape this struggle for control of Mississippi's destiny. Sustained economic growth often provides adequate public resources to increase services without raising taxes. Sluggish economic conditions coupled with popular demands for more services force public officials to cut existing programs or raise taxes. The need to move resources from one place to another often energizes efforts to change the budget-making process. Altering the budget rules, however, enhances the power of some players at the expense of others, and the losers resist. The government's claiming a bigger share of private wealth by raising taxes and government fees seldom appeals to individuals or businesses. Clearly, public officials prefer to say yes to increased services without restructuring government or imposing more taxes.

In the 1960s and 1970s Mississippi's economy experienced robust expansion. Zooming out of the 1973–75 recession, it performed better than the national economy during the late 1970s. The gross state product (in 1982 dollars) increased by 18.8 percent between 1976 and 1980, compared with a 12.7 percent climb in the gross national product (GNP).[2] The state's per capita income moved from 54 percent of the national average in 1960 to 71 percent in 1979. Mississippi entered the 1980s with the nation's lowest per capita income, yet only South Carolina, with an 18 percent gain, increased its percentage of the national average at a rate greater than Mississippi's 17 percent.[3]

In the early 1980s Mississippi fell into a recession, and its economic growth came to a halt as the country's growth surged after the 1982 recession. World conditions, including declines in agricultural prices, falling energy prices, and the offshore movement of low-skilled manufacturing jobs, buffeted the state's economy. Mississippi's 1985 per capita income slipped to 67 percent of the national average.[4] In 1982 dollars the state's gross product between 1980 and 1985 grew only 2.6 percent, while the nation's GNP increased by 12.5 percent.[5] By the mid-1980s Mississippi's economy continued to trail national indicators. The state's 1988 per capita income remained at 67 percent of the national average.[6] The state's gross product grew 8.7 percent from 1985 through 1988, compared with a 10.1 percent growth in the GNP.[7]

Economic difficulties in the 1980s limited the growth in Mississippi's government resources and exacerbated major conflicts between the forces of change and supporters of the status quo. As Mississippi moves into the 1990s, many aspects of the traditional political order persist. Nevertheless, during the 1980s change agents enhanced the governor's role in budget making and produced greater funding for programs, such as public education, beneficial to lower socioeconomic status groups.

ALLOCATING RESOURCES: HAS THE BUDGET-MAKING PROCESS CHANGED?

Supporters of Mississippi's traditional order have relied on legislative leaders to prevent unwanted change. Governors come and go, but key legislators are the rocks of stability and continuity. Until the 1983 "separation of powers decision," Mississippi state government operated as a de facto quasi-parliamentary system with state agencies responsible to the legislature.[8] Legislators appointed by the presiding officers of the two chambers—the Speaker of the house and the lieutenant governor (president of the senate)—served on many boards and commissions. Agency directors (selected by the boards and commissions) and nonlegislative members of those boards frequently took their cues from these legislative board members.

Despite occasional changes in the budget process before 1983, the legislature maintained control of spending decisions. Legislative leaders received agency spending requests and stage-managed approval of the budget. Furthermore, legislative leaders often approved changes in budgets after agencies had begun to spend their money.

Mississippi governors gained the authority to submit an executive budget to the legislature in 1918, but they were initially reluctant to use this power as a management tool. Governors never revised departmental requests and did not provide the legislature with a revenue estimate. The job of balancing income and spending remained with the legislature.[9] In 1932 the financial crisis facing Mississippi, coupled with a critical report on Mississippi government issued by the Brookings Institution, led to creation of a Budget Commission. Although the law designated the governor as chairman, it also made a trusted member of the permanent legislatively appointed bureaucracy, chairman of the State Tax Commission Alfred Holt Stone, the Budget Commission's assistant director. For the next twenty years the commission's assistant director consulted with agency heads and proposed a budget that normally recommended a reduction or no change in agency spending. Governors simply endorsed the assistant director's budget. The legislature then restored money or added additional resources without any gubernatorial recommendation.

In 1955 budget making became even more legislatively dominated with the creation of a five-member (later eleven-member) Commission on Budget and Accounting. Legislative leaders dominated the commission's membership, and the governor was relegated to the position of nonvoting chairman.[10] The Budget Commission hired a director, who served at its pleasure to supervise the operations of the professional staff. The state constitution limited governors to a single four-year term, whereas the lieutenant governor and other legislative leaders could serve an unlimited number of terms. Hence experienced legislative leaders were usually more knowledgeable about budgetary matters than were governors. Governors found themselves unable to overcome their weak formal authority over the budget. The legislative leaders, who controlled the Budget Commission, made the major decisions during the budget preparation, legislative approval, and budget implementation stages.[11]

Mississippi government edged toward a more executive-centered system with the "separation of powers" state Supreme Court decision in November 1983. This decision removed legislators from boards and commissions having executive responsibilities, such as implementation of the budget. The legislature could continue to be involved in policy-making—budget preparation and approval—but not in budget execution or implementation. The legislature preserved as much of its authority as possible by enacting senate bill 3050 in May 1984, which established a legislative budget making process. A Joint Legislative Budget Committee (JLBC), consisting of the same legislative leaders that made up the outlawed Budget Commission, would propose a legislative budget. The committee's staff arm would consist of a legislative budget office having a director and six analysts.

The governor's authority was enhanced by creation of a Fiscal Management Board (FMB), consisting of the governor and two of his appointees, which would oversee state government spending. The governor was authorized to hire an FMB director and six analysts. He also gained a veto power over FMB actions, since his concurrence was necessary in any FMB decision. In July 1984 Governor Allain gave the Fiscal Management Board the responsibility of preparing the executive budget and designated the FMB director as the state's budget officer.[12] In 1989 the legislature abolished the Fiscal Management Board and created the Department of Finance and Administration, whose executive director serves at the will of the governor. In a formal sense, the legislature recognized the governor's right to submit a budget unencumbered by other actors. Consequently Mississippi's budget-making process has come to resemble the pattern found in Texas, where the legislature receives two budget proposals, one from the governor and one from the leaders of the legislature.[13]

Has Control of Budget Decisions Really Shifted to the Governor?

While the new budget process gives the governor more influence than before by permitting him to develop an executive budget proposal, the legislative leadership still retains considerable clout. In most cases the JLBC budget is the basis for legislative action by serving as the legislature's "working document." In effect, the legislative leadership writes the legislative budget, which is then submitted to the full legislature. During consideration of the budget many legislators, lacking knowledge concerning the intricacies of a very complex document, take their cues from their leaders. The legislative leadership also oversees conference reports, presented at the end of the session, thereby controlling adjustments to the JLBC document. In short, Mississippi remains a long way from an executive-centered system.

The first governor operating under the new budget-making process, Bill Allain, showed little interest in establishing spending priorities. This was ironic, since Allain, as attorney general, had brought the separation-of-powers lawsuit that toppled legislative budget hegemony. The FMB staff would propose funding ongoing programs and then develop a plan for spending any remaining funds based on Allain's public statements. They took the plan to Allain and told him, "Governor, we believe these are your priorities." He generally accepted them with little comment.[14] Governor Allain's passivity may have reflected his awareness that only limited new money existed and his belief that, in any event, the legislature would disregard his budget.

One key area in which Allain was successful was diverting special fund money to help financially strapped agencies. During the financial crisis of 1986, he advocated shifting $22 million in earmarked highway special funds to the general fund to help pay for other programs. The legislature moved $10 million to the general fund during its 1986 session and moved an additional $12 million (that had been frozen the previous year) to the general fund in 1987. Since July 1986, state law subjects most state-generated special fund money to budget recisions (cutbacks during the fiscal year) in the same manner as general fund appropriations. The money cut from special funds moves to the general fund, reducing the size of cuts required in general fund agency budgets.

The initial period of Governor Ray Mabus's administration suggested that he might be more successful in increasing executive influence over budget making. In December 1987, for example, the JLBC proposed a standstill budget for the fiscal year beginning July 1, 1988. Newly elected Governor Mabus used the legislative budget as a starting point and suggested minor cuts of $8 million from the $1.6 billion total. He then seized the initiative with proposals to raise elementary and secondary teachers' salaries to the southeastern average and to significantly increase support for higher education. He envisioned obtaining the $200 million needed to pay for his education package from money saved by his selective cuts, by denying state employees a pay raise, and from additional state revenue not anticipated by the JLBC when it wrote its budget. The legislature essentially enacted the governor's far-reaching proposal to improve education, although many state employees received raises as well. In 1989 the legislature kept its commitment to public school teachers by funding the second year of a teachers' pay raise. Mabus was less successful in subsequent years, as the legislature rejected his efforts to legalize a lottery and video poker and to raise fees for citizens using various government services. Hence, Mabus's education reform program known as BEST (Better Education for Success Tomorrow) went unfunded, and spending on higher education was cut in the recession year of 1991. During the 1991 legislative session, Mabus successfully opposed efforts to increase the general sales tax. The lack of new revenue resulted in reduced funding for higher education and other programs.

Governors may also use the formal powers granted them by the constitution to influence the budget. In 1989 Mabus closed the state's three charity hospitals, which were increasingly viewed as substandard and obsolete, by vetoing their appropriations. Despite a lobbying campaign by hospital employees and supporters, the legislature was unable to override his veto. Since state Medicaid spending is matched four to one by the federal government, the reallocation of the $7 million previously spent on the charity hospitals to the state Medicaid program also captured an additional $28 million from the federal government. Mississippi planned to add 90,000 persons to the Medicaid rolls over the next two years. Mabus also used his constitutional power to call a special session in 1989 after the legislature, reflecting a philosophical reluctance to issue bonds to pay for long-term state needs (conservatives preferred to pay cash), rejected his capital improvements bond package. After public attention became focused on the legislature's alleged "failure" to "complete its work," lawmakers enacted a $78.5 million package in bonds to finance improvements in schools, prisons, and office buildings. It represented the first installment of a projected five-year capital budget request.

When revenue collected fails to equal projections, usually during economic recessions, governors gain additional policy control over spending patterns. The governor is mandated by law to keep revenue in line with expenditures. During the 1980s budgets were cut four times after spending already had started. Although the state maintains a "rainy day fund," it provides little relief for budget shortfalls since its balance is only about 1 percent of the general fund budget.[15]

The state's chief executive may make cuts in general fund budgets in varying amounts, but no budget can be reduced by more than 5 percent. Once the governor cuts *all* general fund agencies by 5 percent, any additional reductions must be uniform and across the board. Governor Allain used this recision power in 1986 to promote the policy goal of protecting public education from budget cuts. His first recision in November 1985 had trimmed $47 million by cutting most agencies by 4.32 percent. The second budget recision in January 1986 trimmed agency budgets to the 5 percent cap but exempted several programs in elementary and secondary public education. If a third recision had taken place during the fiscal year, elementary and secondary education would have suffered additional cuts, because state law requires cuts of 5 percent in all agencies before any further reductions can be made.

Governor Allain's actions also gave some leeway to agencies with more than one budget, which influenced spending patterns. Although he cut each agency's overall appropriation by the same percentage, the governor permitted agencies with multiple budgets to cut them unevenly. For instance, in November 1985 the Institutions of Higher Learning was ordered to trim its nineteen budgets by 4.32 percent ($12.4 million). The "College Board" proceeded to cut universities by only 2.91 percent and made up the difference by reducing the budgets of other units by larger amounts. The board chopped 6.42 percent from the Cooperative Extension Service and 7.6 percent from the Medical Center. Other state agencies with multiple budgets, like the State Board of Health, also trimmed budgets by variable amounts.[16]

MISSISSIPPI'S TAX AND FEE SYSTEM: A TWO DECADE ASSESSMENT

Tax systems vary along several dimensions, including diversification, capacity, effort, and burden. A diversified tax system includes a range of taxes that generate revenue in different economic circumstances. For instance economic downturns may affect revenues from general sales differently than they affect receipts from severance or motor vehicle taxes.

Tax capacity refers to the ability of the tax system to generate revenues. Broad-based taxes such as general sales and individual income taxes produce more revenue than selective sales taxes. At the same time, the wealth of a state's taxpayers affects the amount of revenue generated by the tax system. For instance, a 5 percent general sales tax with no exemptions will generate more revenue in high income states than in low-income states.

Tax effort concerns the extent to which a taxing entity takes advantage of its tax capacity. The tax effort may vary in two jurisdictions having similar economic capabilities if one government uses higher tax rates. For instance, if citizens of two states collectively generate the same amount of total personal income, state A, which taxes individual incomes at 6 percent, will generate more income than state B, which taxes individual incomes at 4 percent.

Tax systems also vary in terms of the tax burden placed on taxpayers. The notion of burden includes the proportion of private wealth or income that is claimed by policymakers to pay for public programs. Traditionalists who view the government's role as limited to preserving the status quo strive to minimize government spending on social programs, thereby limiting the tax bite on citizens. Tax burden also refers to the percentage of income paid in taxes and fees by persons at various income levels. Progressive tax systems generally rely on graduated income taxes and require that people who earn more pay a higher percentage of their income in taxes than residents with lower incomes. For instance, the federal government requires that individuals in the upper income bracket pay 33 percent of their taxable income in taxes, while those in the middle and lower income tax brackets pay lower percentages of their earnings. On the other hand, regressive tax systems tend to rely on consumer taxes, such as the broad-based general sales tax, which require everyone to pay the same rate regardless of income. Such consumer taxes place a greater burden on low income groups, who must use a higher percentage of their wages to purchase taxed necessities than do people with higher income. More affluent individuals typically use a larger percentage of their earnings for savings, home mortgages, and other items not covered by consumer taxes.[17]

Table 6: State Revenue Sources in Mississippi

	Fiscal Year			
	1964	1976	1984	1988
Consumer taxes/fees				
General sales tax	37.2%	41.9%	41.3%	40.4%
Selected sales taxes				
Insurance	3.0	2.2	2.6	3.2
Tobacco/beer/liquor	9.6	5.7	3.3	4.7
Gasoline tax	22.7	12.7	5.4	10.8
Total consumer taxes	72.5	62.5	52.6	59.1
Income taxes[a]				
Individual income	8.8	10.4	12.1	14.4
Corporate income/franchise	2.1	4.5	7.9	6.7
Total income taxes	10.9	14.9	20.0	21.1
Other revenue sources				
Severance tax	5.2	2.3	4.8	2.1
Motor vehicle (excluding gas tax)	2.9	1.9	1.9	2.5
Inheritance tax	0.5	0.4	0.4	0.6
Ad valorem	2.2	1.1	0.0[b]	0.0
Nuclear power	0.0	0.0	0.0	2.0
Other taxes	0.9	0.5	0.2	0.2
Non-tax revenue[c]	4.9	16.4	20.1	12.4
Total State-Generated Revenue (millions of dollars)	$236.5	$1,015.1	$2,128.8	$2,468.9

Sources: Annual State Financial Report for Fiscal Years ending June 30, 1964 and 1976, Mississippi State Auditor; Fiscal Management Board 1988 Comprehensive Annual Financial Report for fiscal years ending June 30, 1984 and 1988.

Note: Table entries are percentages of total state revenue provided by each source.

[a]For fiscal year 1964 the "individual income tax" figure includes both individual and corporate income. Before 1976 a separate figure for individual and corporate income was not reported. Fiscal year 1976 is included in the table because it is the first year that Mississippi separated corporate income from individual income taxes and recorded it with the business franchise tax.

[b]Less than 0.1%.

[c]Includes fees, fines, permits, interest on investments, and charges for department services.

Let us now turn to an assessment of Mississippi's tax system along the yardsticks of diversification, capacity, effort, and burden. As part of this assessment, I compare Mississippi with southeastern and national patterns. In the 1980s a fierce struggle emerged between traditionalists and modernizers, as the latter fought to improve education and other public services in Mississippi. The display of tax data from the past two decades allows us to determine whether this conflict has altered the nature of the state's tax system. In addition, using data from across time permits us to assess whether Mississippi's tax system is moving closer to regional and national tax patterns.

Who Pays in Mississippi and How Much?

The increased modernization and industrialization of Mississippi during the 1960s and 1970s produced a significant increase in state revenue and some revenue diversification. Consumer taxes have continued to provide the major source of revenue, yet they steadily declined as a percentage of total revenue (from 72.5 percent in 1964 to 52.6 percent in 1984) as Mississippi moved toward a more diversified tax system. During the period of economic stress in the 1980s, this downward spiral appeared to bottom out and even reverse itself, as consumer taxes grew to 59.1 percent of state revenues (table 6).

Among consumer taxes, Mississippi's general sales tax has consistently been the largest single generator of revenue, providing about 40 percent of state revenue. Meanwhile, selective sales taxes generated a progressively smaller share of state revenue, declining from 35.3 percent of total revenue in 1964 to 11.3 percent in 1984. However, a five cents a gallon increase in the gasoline tax and higher tax rates on alcoholic beverages expanded the selective sales tax share of state revenue to 18.7 percent in 1988.

Between 1964 and 1984 the state's move toward a more diversified tax structure was reflected in the increased percentage of state revenue generated by business and personal income taxes, which grew from 10.9 to 20.0 percent. The state's budget has become more dependent on individual income taxes, which rose steadily from 8.8 percent of all revenue in 1964 to 14.4 percent in 1988. Revenue from corporate taxes (and franchises) rose from 4.5 percent of the budget in 1976 to 7.9 percent in 1984 but then declined to 6.7 percent by 1988.[18] All remaining taxes and revenue sources, such as the severance and inheritance taxes, have fluctuated in importance, providing about 20 percent of total revenue.

Political developments, such as the conservative tax-cutting mood that swept across the nation in the late 1970s and the need to fund the Education

Table 7: State Tax Burden for Different Income Levels in Mississippi

Gross Income (family of four) ($)	Estimated Taxes Paid					
	General Sales[a] ($)	Sales as Percentage of Gross Income	Individual Income[b] ($)	Individual as Percentage of Gross Income	Total ($)	Total as Percentage of Gross Income
			1970			
3,500	124	3.5	0	0.0	124	3.5
6,500	181	2.8	0	0.0	181	2.8
9,500	230	2.4	75	0.9	305	3.2
12,500	272	2.2	170	1.3	442	3.5
15,500	311	2.0	290	1.9	601	3.9
18,500	347	1.9	410	2.2	757	4.1
25,500	433	1.7	690	2.7	1,123	4.4
30,500	479	1.6	890	2.9	1,369	4.5
45,500	542	1.2	1,490	3.3	2,032	4.5
95,500	738	0.8	3,490	3.6	4,228	4.4

Estimated Taxes Paid

Gross Income (family of four) ($)	General Sales[c] ($)	Sales as Percentage of Gross Income	Individual Income[d] ($)	Individual as Percentage of Gross Income	Total ($)	Total as Percentage of Gross Income
			1985			
3,500	94	2.7	0	0.0	94	2.7
6,500	185	2.8	0	0.0	185	2.8
9,500	264	2.8	0	0.0	264	2.8
12,500	330	2.6	0	0.0	330	2.6
15,500	360	2.3	0	0.0	360	2.3
18,500	415	2.3	78	0.4	493	2.7
25,500	490	1.9	334	1.3	824	3.2
30,500	558	1.8	580	1.9	1,138	3.7
45,500	674	1.5	1,330	2.9	2,004	4.4
95,500	1,026	1.1	3,830	4.0	4,858	5.1

Sources: F. Glenn Abney, "Taxes and the Philosophy of Mississippi Government," *Public Administration Survey* 18, no. 6 (July 1971), table 2, p. 5. The 1970 estimates for $25,000 and $30,500 income levels and all 1985 estimates were computed by the author.

[a]Estimates taken from 1970 federal income tax form 1040, United States Internal Revenue Service.

[b]Estimates of individual income taxes after subtracting exemption of $6,000 and standard deduction of $1,000.

[c]Estimates taken from 1985 federal income tax form 1040, United States Internal Revenue Service.

[d]Estimates of individual income taxes after subtracting exemption of $12,500 and standard deduction of $3,400.

Reform Act, altered Mississippi's tax burden. The 1979 tax cut made progressive changes by granting more generous personal income tax exemptions and larger standard deductions; the threshold below which families of four paid no taxes rose from $7,000 to $15,900. In addition, the sales tax on residential utility service, water, and prescription drugs was eliminated.[19] In 1982 the tax rate on income exceeding $10,000 increased from 4 to 5 percent. Other recent changes have been in a regressive direction, as the general sales tax rate rose from 5 to 5.5 percent in 1982 and from 5.5 to 6 percent in 1983.

Overall, these tax changes have reduced the tax burden for most Mississippians, as well as provided a more progressive tax system (table 7). At every income level (except two), Mississippi families paid a smaller share of their income in general sales and individual income taxes in 1985 than in 1970.[20] Although the percentage of personal income claimed by the general sales tax rose (in current dollars) for every income level except the lowest, the share of personal income claimed by the income tax fell for every income group except the highest. The slightly greater progressivity of these combined taxes in 1985 was apparently due to the more generous income tax standard deductions and exemptions (which helped lower- and middle-income groups), and the income tax rate increase (which especially burdened high-income Mississippians). Yet the state sales tax remains regressive, since it covers many necessities and services used by taxpayers across income levels, such as food and auto repairs; in 1985 it still consumed 2.7 percent of the income of the poorest Mississippians, compared with only 1.1 percent of the income of the wealthiest citizens.

Who Pays and How Much: Mississippi Compared with Other States

Mississippi's tax system has diversified during the past two decades, yet the state's revenue distribution still differs from regional and national patterns. Compared with the Southeast and the nation, Mississippi remains more dependent on the sales tax and less reliant on individual and corporate income taxes (table 8). Mississippi also depends more on federal aid as a source of revenue. In 1988 federal assistance accounted for 31.5 percent of Mississippi's total revenue, compared with 23.8 percent for the southeastern states and 22.6 percent for the entire nation.

Mississippi has often been criticized for the low quality and limited nature of many of its public services, compared with those provided by other states. Some attribute poorly funded public services to a conservative desire to keep taxes too low. However, another important explanation for inade-

Table 8: Sources of State Government General Revenue, 1988

Tax Sources	United States	Southeast	Mississippi
Federal aid to state	22.6%	23.8%	31.5%
Local aid to state	1.5	0.7	0.6
Property tax	1.1	0.8	0.5
General sales tax	19.5	22.6	25.7
Individual income tax	18.0	14.4	9.0
Corporate income tax	4.9	4.1	2.5
Other taxes	15.8	18.0	16.6
User fees	7.7	8.6	8.6
Miscellaneous revenue	8.9	7.0	5.0
Total revenue	100.0%	100.0%	100.0%

Source: Computed from data presented in Advisory Commission on Intergovernmental Relations (ACIR), *Significant Features of Fiscal Federalism,* vol. 2 (Washington, D.C.: ACIR, August 1990), table 68.

Note: Table entries are the percentage of state government general revenue received by each tax source.

quate government services is the state's extreme poverty. Mississippi's tax capacity clearly lags behind that of other states. Over the past two decades, based on the representative tax system of the Advisory Commission on Intergovernmental Relations, the state's tax capacity remained behind those of both the nation and the Southeast (table 9). In 1988 Mississippi's tax capacity was only 65 percent of the national average; the tax capacity of the Southeast as a whole was 84.4 percent of the national average.

Over the past two decades Mississippi has taken advantage of its limited tax capacity at a rate similar to that in other states. Its tax effort has been only slightly less than the national average, being 98 percent of the national average in 1967, 97 percent in 1979, and 94 percent in 1988. Mississippi's tax effort exceeds that of the Southeast, which has ranged from 87 percent to 90 percent of the national average (table 9). However, the state's poverty and lack of tax capacity mean that an average tax effort will not produce the same amount of revenue generated by other states making a similar effort. To some extent, the high level of federal assistance reaching Mississippi compensates for this situation.

In terms of "who pays" for public goods and services, comparing Mississippi to the Southeast and the nation reveals some interesting facts. One recent study measuring tax burdens in the mid-1970s evaluated each

Table 9: Tax System Capacity and Effort

	1967	1979	1988
Tax System Capacity			
United States	100.0	100.0	100.0
Southeast	79.2	84.8	84.4
Mississippi	64.0	70.0	65.0
Tax System Effort			
United States	100.0	100.0	100.0
Southeast	90.4	87.2	88.5
Mississippi	98.0	97.0	94.0

Sources: Advisory Commission on Intergovernmental Relations (ACIR), *Significant Features of Fiscal Federalism*, vol. 2 (Washington, D.C.: ACIR, August 1990), tables 105–6.

Note: Table entries are the Mississippi state tax system and regional average scores for tax capacity and effort as a percentage of the national average. Tax capacity is the amount of revenue each state would raise if it applied a national average set of tax rates to twenty-six commonly used taxes; the national average tax capacity score is set at 100, and the state and regional scores reflect their per capita tax capacity divided by the per capita average for all states. Tax effort is the ratio of a state's actual tax collections to its tax capacity; the national average is set at 100, and the state and regional scores reflect their tax efforts divided by the average for all states.

state and serves as the basis of this analysis.[21] Mississippi's tax system, like the tax systems in most states, forces the less affluent to pay proportionally more in taxes than the affluent. Nevertheless, Mississippi's state tax system and state and local taxes combined were more regressive than either the national or the southeastern average (table 10). Such a regressive tax structure, which places a greater burden on the economically disadvantaged, is consistent with Mississippi's traditional political culture, where more financially advantaged interests have tended to exercise significant influence over public policy.

Mississippi depends more on its sales tax and less on its individual and corporate income taxes than other states do (table 8). The general sales tax serves as a major contributor to Mississippi's greater than average regressivity. Only one state (Arkansas) uses a general sales tax that is as re-

Table 10: Tax Progressivity versus Regressivity

	General Sales Tax	Individual Income Tax	Total State Taxes	Total State and Local Taxes
U.S. average index of tax progressivity	−.11	.17	−.04	−.07
Southeast average index of tax progressivity	−.15	.21	−.08	−.08
Mississippi average index of tax progressivity	−.18	.43	−.09	−.10

Source: Computed from Donald Phares, "State and Local Tax Burdens across Fifty States," *Growth and Change*, 16, no. 2 (April 1985): 39, table 7.

Note: Table entries are for fiscal year 1975–76. Positive values signify a progressive tax effect and negative values a regressive tax. The closer the values are to 1 and −1, the greater the progressivity and regressivity.

gressive. Mississippi's individual income tax is very progressive, but given the size of its contribution to the state's total revenue stream, its total impact does not offset the regressive general sales tax. The state's individual income tax progressivity exceeds the national and southeastern averages by a wide margin, with only one state (Connecticut) using a more progressive individual income tax.[22]

Explanations for Mississippi's Revenue Structure

One important explanation for the nature of Mississippi's revenue system over the past three decades has been the desire of state leaders to keep taxes low. Officials believe that low taxes promote economic development by attracting industry and keeping it in the state. As an illustration, a 1982 report by the Mississippi Economic Council (MEC), the state's "chamber of commerce," claims: "A key factor is the improvement and maintenance of a favorable business climate, and an essential part of this climate has been the state's tax structure and its tax rates."[23] Former governor Bill Allain also adhered to this low-tax philosophy. In his 1986 state of the state address, Allain pledged: "I do not propose, and I will veto, any tax increase in the state of

Mississippi. I think it would be counterproductive. I do not believe the people could stand for that.''[24] To ensure that his position was clear to everyone, at a press conference two weeks later Governor Allain displayed a stone tablet containing the chiseled words ''Veto tax bill'' and ''No special session.''[25]

Concern over high corporate income taxes functions as a major barrier to increasing individual income tax rates, especially of the highest bracket. Since the same rate structure applies to both businesses and individuals (with most business income being taxed at the highest level), business opposition to increases makes it difficult to raise rates on individuals. Since 1960 state income tax rates have bounced up and down, with three cuts and two increases. Overall, these changes resulted in lower tax rates, with today's top 5 percent bracket less than the 1960s' top 6 percent bracket.[26]

Mississippi was also affected by the taxpayer revolt that swept the country in the wake of California's Proposition 13.[27] The Mississippi legislature sought to provide relief to individuals who are the ''producers'' in the state, so it raised the standard deduction and the level of personal exemptions of the individual income tax. Hence nontaxable income for a family with four personal exemptions increased from $7,000 to $15,900, and the percentage of four-member families exempt from paying income taxes increased from 22.4 to 39.8 percent. While middle-income persons benefited from the tax cut, the change also removed less affluent citizens from the tax rolls. The percentage of black four member families exempt from income taxes rose from 46.7 to 66.2 percent, while the proportion of white families exempt grew from 13.8 to 29.9 percent.[28]

Racial and income divisions in Mississippi are also barriers to reforming the tax structure to create a more progressive system. Reflecting the state's traditionalistic society, higher-income whites leading the state have been successful at ensuring that all citizens pay ''a fair share'' of taxes. As previously noted, the generous income tax cut of 1979 removed a large number of both black and white residents from the individual income tax rolls. This progressive step, however, was offset by increases in the sales tax rate, which rose from 3 percent in 1955 to 6 percent in the 1980s.[29] Bill Minor, a longtime respected observer of Mississippi government and politics, concludes: ''There is a certain amount of unspoken racism in the theory of heaping more taxes on consumers rather than putting more on property owners or corporations. All blacks have to buy food, but not many of them own property or businesses.''[30]

An Assessment of Mississippi's Revenue Structure

Mississippi's current tax and fee system has been shaped by national economic, social, and political conditions to more closely approach regional and national patterns than it did two decades ago. However, Mississippi's revenue mix still differs from national and regional norms in noticeable ways. The state's movement toward a more progressive tax structure puts it nearer to tax systems in other states, but Mississippi continues to place a higher priority on regressive taxes paid by individuals. Corporate income taxes have increased, and the share of state tax revenue generated by this source is closer to regional and national norms than a decade ago. Nevertheless, Mississippi's dependence on revenue from the corporate income tax still lags behind the southeastern and national averages in order to protect the state's "business climate." In conclusion, state political leaders still favor resolving the question of "how much" by limiting the tax bite as much as possible, and they favor resolving the question of "who pays" by ensuring that all income groups pay a "fair share."

SPENDING THE MONEY

In Mississippi, reformers advocate altering expenditure priorities to help the have-nots and ultimately redistribute political, economic, and social power. Traditionalists recognize that the spending initiatives of reformers will redistribute power in society, so they vigorously support existing allocation patterns. Table 11 examines spending for major functional categories over the past three decades. The general fund consists of taxes raised by state government, while the special fund contains federal dollars that Mississippi spends at the state level as well as fees charged by agencies. Elementary and secondary education, higher education, and public health (which includes Medicaid) are major programs that each exceeded 15 percent of the budget. Moderate expenditures include public works (which includes highways and other state construction projects), local assistance, and social welfare, each generally surpassing 5 percent of the budget. These programs in 1988 accounted for 77.8 percent of general fund expenditures and 80.3 percent of combined general and special fund spending.[31]

Table II: Mississippi General and Special Fund Expenditures in Recent Decades

	1964			1974		
	General Fund	Special Fund	Total	General Fund	Special Fund	Total
Highest expenditures						
Elementary/secondary education	48.3%	3.1%	18.5%	43.3%	11.8%	22.6%
Higher education	10.9	11.5	11.3	16.9	12.8	14.2
Public Health	1.4	0.7	0.9	1.5	1.1	1.2
Moderate expenditures						
Public works	1.8	41.2	27.8	4.6	31.3	22.2
Local assistance	8.5	10.5	9.8	6.2	10.1	8.7
Social Welfare	8.3	17.1	14.1	6.3	17.4	13.6
Minor expenditures						
Executive branch	0.6	0.0ᵃ	0.2	0.7	0.0ᵃ	0.2
Hospitals	6.3	0.2	2.3	5.5	0.5	2.2
Corrections	1.2	0.0	0.4	1.8	0.3	0.8
Debt service	4.2	4.3	4.3	2.0	4.5	3.6
Legislative branch	0.7	0.0	0.2	0.6	0.0	0.2
Agriculture, commerce, economic development	3.0	1.0	1.7	4.3	0.5	1.8
Public protection	0.6	1.6	1.3	2.0	2.8	2.5
All other categories	4.2	8.8	7.2	4.3	6.9	6.2
Total funds (millions of dollars)	$158.1	$307.9	$466.0	$499.2	$961.3	$1,460.5

	1984			1988		
	General Fund	Special Fund	Total	General Fund	Special Fund	Total
Highest expenditures						
Elementary/secondary education	40.9%	7.9%	19.6%	46.7%	11.3%	26.9%
Higher education	19.2	17.4	18.0	17.2	22.7	20.3
Public Health	8.2	17.6	14.3	7.2	22.3	15.6
Moderate expenditures						
Public works	1.1	21.3	14.1	0.2	17.9	10.1
Local assistance	4.2	9.3	7.5	4.0	0.1	1.8
Social Welfare	2.5	6.5	5.1	2.5	8.0	5.6
Minor expenditures						
Executive branch	0.9	4.0	2.9	0.6	7.1	4.2
Hospitals	5.2	2.1	3.2	4.6	3.1	3.8
Corrections	3.4	0.2	1.3	4.1	0.2	1.9
Debt service	0.7	4.2	3.0	0.8	1.4	1.1
Legislative branch	0.5	0.0	0.2	0.6	0.0	0.3
Agriculture, commerce, economic development	4.1	0.4	1.7	3.4	0.3	1.7
Public protection	3.0	0.9	1.6	2.5	1.6	2.0
All other categories	6.1	8.2	7.5	5.6	4.0	4.7
Total funds (millions of dollars)	$1,336.3	$2,416.5	$3,752.8	$1,620.8	$2,063.8	$3,684.6

aLess than 0.02%.

Sources: See table 6.

Note: Table entries are percentages, which total 100% in each column.

Education Programs

Mississippi had great difficulty making progress in public elementary and secondary education between 1964 and 1984. As the federal government pursued the desegregation of schools, white support for the public schools declined. General fund support for elementary and secondary education declined steadily from 48.3 percent of the budget in 1964 to 40.9 percent in 1984. Only the increase in federal funds (in the special funds category) kept the share of the state's total spending on public education relatively unchanged. Yet between 1974 and 1984, education's share of special funds as well as general funds declined. These difficulties for public education helped stimulate political activism among teachers and civic groups, leading to the education reform movement of the 1980s.

Between 1984 and 1988, general fund spending for elementary and secondary education increased dramatically, and education's share of the general fund expanded from 40.9 percent to 46.7 percent. By 1988 the piece of general fund pie served to integrated public elementary and secondary education finally rivaled the slice given to segregated education in 1964. Special fund resources dedicated to elementary and secondary education also increased—from 7.9 percent of all special funds in 1984 to 11.3 percent in 1988; education special funds increased by $42.4 million, a 22.3 percent rise. The net result was that elementary and secondary education's share of combined general and special fund spending rose substantially from 19.6 percent of the budget to 26.9 percent.

The higher priority given to spending on public education is due to the 1982 Education Reform Act and subsequent improvements. Allocating state resources to public kindergartens, a $3,400 teachers' pay raise, and teachers' assistants for grades one, two, and three signaled a major victory for reformers. In fact, Mississippi put these changes into place despite the need to reduce budgets for other programs because of declining state revenues. The new programs significantly increased educational opportunities for poor children, many of whom are black. Because some middle- and upper-class parents continue to send their children to private kindergartens and academies for grades one to twelve, support for public education is less than unanimous. Consequently, Mississippi's elementary and secondary schools are still underfunded in many localities, but the reformers have turned the corner in recent years.

Meanwhile, higher education in Mississippi was being treated as a more favored child up until 1984. Higher education's share of the general fund increased steadily, from 10.9 percent in 1964 to 19.2 percent in 1984, paralleling enrollment growth. Junior colleges and universities also gained a greater share of special funds; higher education received 17.4 percent of all special funds in 1984, compared with 11.5 percent in 1964. Higher education's share of the total budget rose steadily from 11.3 percent in 1964 to 18 percent in 1984.

A closer examination of general fund spending suggests that there may be a connection between spending for elementary and secondary schools and for higher education. General fund spending for public education at all levels between 1964 and 1984 hovered around 60 percent (59.2 in 1964, 60.2 in 1974 and 60.1 in 1984), but this aggregate stability concealed shifting support patterns for different educational levels. Over this twenty-year period, general fund support for elementary and secondary education dropped while support for higher education increased. Meanwhile, elementary and secondary education was significantly helped by federal funds, which grew from $9 million in 1964 to $162 million in 1984. These conflicting trends suggest that state (general fund) resources were shifted to higher education when federal money for elementary and secondary education became available.

The two-decade pattern of substituting elementary and secondary special funds for general fund resources and shifting freed-up general funds to higher education reversed during 1984–88. The share of the general fund allocated to higher education dropped from 19.2 to 17.2 percent, while its share of special funds grew from 17.4 to 22.7 percent. In effect, general fund money was moved from higher education to the elementary and secondary level, and junior colleges and universities replaced the lost revenue with student fee increases. Postsecondary students in the poor state of Mississippi pay among the highest tuition rates in the Southeast. General fund support for all levels of education rose from 60.1 percent in 1984 to 63.9 percent in 1988. The education share of general and special funds combined jumped from 37.6 percent to 47.2 percent. Clearly, Mississippi's spending priorities shifted in favor of education, although higher education users must pay more than before.

Noneducation Programs

In the past few decades, public health has also become a higher priority. Public health rose from 1.4 percent of the general fund in 1964 to 8.2 percent in 1984, as the state increased its contribution to the federal Medicaid program. Public health's share of special funds also rose dramatically—from less than 1 percent in 1964 to 17.6 percent in 1984—as the federal government matched state contributions to Medicaid. Between 1984 and 1988 both general and special fund support for health increased only marginally. Cuts in federal programs and accompanying reductions in state matching accounted for this leveling. Clearly, Medicaid illustrates how a federal program's matching requirement can significantly shape state spending.

Social welfare, by contrast, significantly declined between 1964 and 1984 as a proportion of the state budget, despite a tripling in dollar expenditures. Consuming 8.3 percent of general fund spending and 14.1 percent of overall spending in 1964, by 1984 welfare spending had dropped to only 2.5 and 5.1 percent, respectively. Both general and special fund support for welfare remained static after 1984. Social welfare's funding woes are quite evident when compared with the increased support provided to public health. General non-Medicaid health spending grew tenfold between 1964 and 1984, increasing from $2 million to $20 million. Clearly, Mississippi public officials place greater emphasis on public health programs than on social welfare endeavors, reflecting the average citizen's more negative attitude toward welfare spending in general.[32]

Public works—resources used for highways and public buildings—has suffered the biggest decline in terms of share of spending, despite increased dollar expenditures. In 1964 public works constituted 27.8 percent of total expenditures and outdistanced its nearest rival, elementary and secondary education, by almost 10 percent. Over the next twenty years, public works spending (in current dollars) increased about five times in terms of the general fund and rose about four times in terms of total spending. Although its share of the general fund budget did not change, its proportion of total state spending decreased from 27.8 percent in 1964 to 14.1 percent in 1984. Public works funding fell further after 1984, composing only 10.1 percent of total spending in 1988. Constituents notice spending for public works, particularly highways, but this function's share of total spending now ranks fourth, behind elementary and secondary education, higher education, and public health.

Though a small percentage of the budget, corrections has experienced a steady rise in importance. General fund spending for prisons and related purposes rose from a 1.2 percent share of the budget in 1964 to 4.1 percent share in 1988. In fact, between 1984 and 1988 general fund dollars spent on corrections rose from $44.9 million to $66.4 million; this 48 percent funding increase surpassed that of any other category (though elementary and secondary funds increased far more in actual dollars). Mississippi, like many states, found itself under a federal court order to improve its correctional facilities. In addition to improving the penitentiary at Parchman, the state was required

Table 12: 1988 per Capita State and Local Government General Expenditures

	Higher Education	Elementary and Secondary Education	Highways	Health and Hospitals	Public Welfare
United States	$255	$690	$226	$252	$352
Southeast	224	589	217	277	229
Mississippi	242	556	198	359	241

Source: Advisory Commission on Intergovernmental Relations (ACIR), *Significant Features of Fiscal Federalism*, vol. 2 (Washington, D.C.: ACIR, August 1990), table 87.

to build additional prisons or to keep the inmate population constant. Mississippi constructed several new facilities, including a new prison near Jackson. In 1986 the legislature bit the bullet and provided money to operate the prison, even though it cut back other state services to fund educational reform items.

No precise measures exist to determine whether Mississippi's state spending offsets the state's relatively regressive tax system. Increased spending for elementary and secondary education helps the lower socioeconomic strata more than upper-income groups. Expanded health care, particularly Medicaid spending, produces the same result. On the other hand, spending for higher education benefits middle- and upper-income groups and provides less advantage for persons at the bottom of the economic ladder. Only 38 percent of students starting the ninth grade eventually graduate from high school and attend college.[33]

Mississippi's Spending Compared with That of Other States

To compare Mississippi's spending priorities in the 1980s with those of other states, let us focus on five important functions of state and local governments: higher education, elementary and secondary education, highways, health care and hospitals, and welfare. One measure of spending priority is per person expenditures on a program. Such calculations show the level of "state and local" support (expenditures) per citizen. Comparisons between states are based on state and local spending combined, since states vary in the mix of state and local support for various functions, particularly elementary and secondary education.

Mississippi has historically made higher education a top priority. Per person expenditures in 1988 in Mississippi were $242, greater than the southeastern average of $224, and only slightly less than the national average of $255 (table 12). On the other hand, elementary and secondary education received a lower priority. Mississippi in 1988 spent only $556 per person on elementary and secondary education, significantly less than the southeastern average of $589 and the national average of $690. In view of the historic neglect of such important programs, it is understandable that Mississippi would show preference for elementary and secondary education and increase its share of general fund expenditures between 1984 and 1988.

Spending priorities on noneducation programs also vary, depending on the nature of the program. The increased priority of public health programs over the past decades is clearly reflected in per capita spending. In 1988 Mississippi spent $359 per person on health care and hospitals, considerably more than the southeastern per capita average of $277 and the national average of $252. At the same time, the state's decreased emphasis on public welfare is reflected in its lower per capita standing relative to most states. Although Mississippi's $241 per capita exceeds the southeastern figure of $229, the state lags significantly behind the national average per capita expenditure of $352. Compared with these two programs, highways seem to occupy a middle position in terms of priority. Per person spending for highways in Mississippi is only slightly lower than the southeastern and national spending patterns.

ASSESSING BUDGETARY POLITICS IN MISSISSIPPI

The struggle in Mississippi between reformers wishing to change the status quo and supporters of the traditional order has shaped taxing and spending decisions over the past three decades. Mississippi's tax and fee system has moved closer to national and regional norms than it was in the 1960s. In recent years the state's tax system has become more progressive in its impact on individuals, but it still depends more on regressive sales taxes and less on individual and corporate income taxes than do those of other states. The idea that everyone should pay a "fair share" still dominates tax and fee policies.

Reformers have begun to carry the day in Mississippi. Governors now propose their own executive budgets, and Governor Mabus has used the executive budget to focus legislative attention on his priority of improving public education. The legislature nevertheless retains considerable influence by proposing its own budget and enacting all appropriations measures. Especially noteworthy is that reformers were successful in providing new money for education during a period of tight revenues in the mid-1980s. To fund public kindergartens and other educational enhancements, reductions were made in other programs. Yet Mississippi's traditionalistic history is still very noticeable in taxing and spending patterns. The state's current situation is best captured by the title of a recent report on southern development published by the Southern Growth Polices Board: "Halfway Home and a Long Way to Go."

CHAPTER TEN

The Struggle over Public Policy in a Traditionalistic State

Dale Krane

Do you know that there are two types of conservatives in Missis-sippi? The first type of conservative is against any kind of change, in any form, at any time. The second type is not against change, they just don't want to change right now!

Traditional political joke in Mississippi

The goods and services produced and delivered by public agencies are the primary points of contact between citizens and their government. Citizens judge the quality of government and the performance of public officials by the attributes of the programs and policies provided (or not provided). The treatment one's child receives from public school teachers, the number of potholes on one's street, the regular collection of garbage, and the speed of response by the police powerfully shape a citizen's perception of government. In a very real sense, government for the individual citizen is what government does for and to that citizen.

It should first be pointed out that the term *public policy* refers to what governments choose to do *and* what they choose not to do. If a state government chooses not to provide publicly funded abortions, that choice is just as much the state's policy as if the choice were to fund abortions. Second, a policy choice implies the pursuit of a goal, as policymakers seek to attain some desired state of affairs (e.g., lower costs for businesses or more access to education). Third, if the policy choice requires action (e.g., the expenditure of funds), then the policy also involves a plan of action or a pattern of activity believed to be capable of attaining the desired goal (e.g., nutritional programs for pregnant low-income women reduce the number of babies born with impaired mental capacity, thus lowering the number of individuals who cannot care for themselves). However, the policy selected may not always achieve the desired outcome.

Public policies are the principal tools by which the public's representatives fulfill the public's preferences about the future quality of life in the state. For example, the "Balance Agriculture with Industry" (B A W I) program of the 1930s evolved out of the necessity to broaden Mississippi's economic base. At that time the economic conditions were so desperate that the state's leadership sought out any industry, even low-wage ones, that would move to Mississippi. To lure manufacturing plants, state officials not only touted the willingness of Mississippians to work for very low wages, they also created antiunion laws and agreed to underwrite new plants with property tax exemptions and state subsidies for industrial park development. Fifty years later, today's policies for economic growth still include attracting manufacturing plants, but state officials and citizens prefer to entice high-wage, nonpolluting industrial operations.

Public policies simultaneously provide benefits for an individual, group, or region and impose costs on other individuals, groups, or regions. Concentrating highways in one or two areas of a state deprives other areas of adequate transportation. A classic definition of politics says that "politics is who gets what, when, where, and how."[1] That is, policies emerge from bargaining over the distribution of the benefits and costs of government action. To a very large extent, the attributes of a state's policies reflect the political alignments within the state, which in turn are a product of the state's economic and social characteristics as well as its political culture. In Mississippi, public policies often emerge out of a struggle between groups pressing to modernize the state and those seeking to maintain the status quo.

A PROFILE OF MISSISSIPPI'S PUBLIC POLICY

About 166,000 state and local employees work to bring public services to the state's citizens.[2] Almost 70 percent of all civil servants in Mississippi work for local units of government, and the single largest group is, of course, public school personnel.[3] Compared with other states, Mississippi ranks twenty-eighth in employees per 10,000 population and ranks eighth in local government employees. Georgia, Louisiana, and South Carolina have proportionately larger public work forces, while Mississippi's civil service is proportionately larger than those of Alabama, Arkansas, North Carolina, and Tennessee. On the other hand, Mississippi's public employees receive the lowest average annual wage in the nation (FY 1989 = $17,365, or $1,447 gross per month).[4]

Agencies and Programs

State government employees perform a variety of important jobs. For example, employees of the Department of Agriculture and Commerce are entrusted with inspecting agricultural products, promoting their sale domestically and internationally, and developing alternative crops. They also help farmers with financial problems to renegotiate their loans through a mediation service. The department is headed by a commissioner who is elected from a statewide constituency. Mississippians have tended to value stability in this position, since only five commissioners have been elected since the agency's creation in 1906. Agriculture in Mississippi has been undergoing the same transformation as in other states, as farming has become a big business concentrated into fewer hands. The number of farms in the state declined from 260,000 in 1945 to only 34,000 in 1987; meanwhile, the average size of a farm rose from 74 acres to 315 acres.[5]

The current commissioner of agriculture and commerce, Jim Buck Ross, is especially known for establishing the Mississippi Agriculture and Forestry Museum in Jackson, a tourist attraction that is one of the finest agricultural museums in the nation. Ross is a traditional southern gentleman, and his humorous exchange in 1984 with visiting vice presidential candidate Geraldine Ferraro drew national attention. When discussing the state's new blueberry crop, Ross asked Ferraro if she could bake blueberry muffins. She retorted, "I sure can. Can you?" Jim Buck Ross responded, "Down here in Mississippi the men don't cook."[6]

The state Highway Department supervises the construction and maintenance of all highways and highway bridges, rest areas, and welcome centers, and the state aid (farm-to-market) road program. The department's chief executive officer is appointed by and reports to the state Highway Commission, an independent board composed of three members who are elected separately from multicounty districts. The commission acts as a policy-making body and controls the allocation of funds among the three districts. For example, of the $172.4 million appropriated for fiscal year 1985, the commission spent $62.7 million (36.4 percent) in the central district, $62.2 million (36.1 percent) in the southern district, and $47.5 million (27.5 percent) in the northern district.[7]

More than 10,000 of the state's 71,000 miles of roads and streets are the direct responsibility of the Highway Department. In addition, the department cooperates with county governments to administer the over 23,000 miles of state aid roads. The department works together with the Highway Safety Patrol to lower the number of fatal motor vehicle accidents in Mississippi, which is the fourth highest in the nation. One cause of these accidents is the poor quality of the state's highways, such as the large number of two-lane roads in this hilly and rural state. Of Mississippi's interstate mileage, 29 percent merits a poor "serviceability" rating—only one state has a higher percentage of interstate miles in need of repair.[8]

The Insurance Department licenses and regulates the practices of all insurance companies, burial associations, fraternal societies, and mobile-home manufacturers and dealers. It also administers the state fire code. The department is headed by a commissioner of insurance, who is elected state-wide by the voters. With a managerial staff of six professionals and limited authority over divisive issues, the department's decisions tend to be noncontroversial. In 1977, for example, the insurance commissioner was renominated and reelected without opposition.[9]

The Public Service Commission is entrusted with regulating all for-hire transportation, communication, electric, gas, water, and sewer utilities in the state. It must approve requests for changes in rates for these services, ensuring that the requested rates are just and reasonable. It also ensures that rate schedules are adhered to, that services rendered are reasonably adequate, and that facilities constructed or acquired are necessary for the convenience of the public. The Public Service Commission is an independent board composed of three members who are elected separately from the same multicounty districts as the highway commissioners. Recently commissioners have come under fire for holding secret business meetings with representatives of the utilities they regulate, leading to legislative efforts to ban the practice.[10]

The Workers' Compensation Commission is a three-member independent board that administers Mississippi's workers' compensation law, which provides benefits to workers injured on the job (or victims of occupational diseases). The commission also serves a judicial function in resolving disputed claims. Historically, business interest groups have been effective at limiting the benefits provided to workers under this law. Business groups argued that improved benefits would increase the cost of doing business in Mississippi and discourage industry from moving to the state. Few Mississippi workers were members of unions, weakening the political power of trade union lobbyists who sought to increase workers' compensation benefits. Mississippi was one of the last two states to even pass a workers' compensation law guaranteeing any payments to injured workers.

A study by a national commission in 1977 indicated that Mississippi had complied with only eight of nineteen "essential" recommendations to ensure that the workers' compensation system provided adequate coverage and benefits. Mississippi was ranked forty-seventh in the nation in terms of compliance and maximum weekly benefits provided, a low rating that persists even today.[11] The maximum weekly benefit for temporary total disability ($212.58 in 1990) is now set at two-thirds of the average weekly wage in the state. Exempt from the workers' compensation program are businesses employing fewer than five employees and nonprofit fraternal, charitable, cultural, and religious organizations.[12]

The Department of Education oversees the operation of the state's 887 elementary and secondary schools, which are organized into 152 districts. In 1990 approximately 500,000 students, almost 20 percent of the state's total population, were enrolled in public schools. Over 26,000 teachers taught these students, for a pupil-teacher ratio of 19.1 to 1 (1986 U.S. average, 17.6; Mississippi rank, forty-first). Public school enrollment at the state level is evenly divided by race (55 percent black and 45 percent white), and approximately 93 percent of all schoolchildren attend public schools.[13]

Expenditures per full-time student total $3,151 (1989–90 rank, forty-ninth) versus the United States average of $4,890. As late as 1986 Mississippi teachers ranked forty-ninth in the nation in salary, with an average annual salary of only $18,443 compared with the national average of $25,313. In constant dollars, the 1985–86 compensation for teachers was 2 percent *less* than the average salary in 1969–70. Pay raises in the late 1980s elevated the state to forty-third in the nation in 1989–90 with an average annual teacher salary of $24,364, compared with the national average of $31,166. Subsequent pay freezes because of tight state budgets sent Mississippi's ranking in teacher salaries back toward the national cellar (forty-eighth in the nation in 1990–91). The per pupil appropriations for textbooks in 1986 was $7.83 (rank, fiftieth), significantly lower than Alabama ($20), Louisiana ($22), and South Carolina ($21.32).[14] The 1988 dropout rate equaled 33.1 percent (rank, fortieth), and only 54.8 percent of the state's population twenty-five years or older had completed four years of high school (1985 rank, forty-eighth). For the 60 percent of Mississippi high-school graduates who took the American College Test (ACT) college entrance exam in 1989, the average score was 15.9, in contrast to the national average of 18.6, resulting in a last-place ranking among the twenty-eight states that rely on the ACT.[15]

Mississippi's system of higher education encompasses eight state universities, a state medical school, a research and development center, and a Gulf Coast research laboratory, all under the jurisdiction of a constitutionally separate Board of Institutions of Higher Learning ("the College Board").[16] The three largest, "comprehensive" universities are the University of Mississippi, Mississippi State University, and the University of Southern Mississippi. Three universities are historically black institutions of higher learning (Alcorn State University, Jackson State University, and Mississippi Valley State University), and another institution is one of the nation's two publicly supported universities for women (Mississippi University for Women). The eighth public university, Delta State University, is in Cleveland and serves the northwest area of the state. Total system enrollment in 1989 was 52,543, and enrollments at individual campuses varied from 1,691 at Mississippi Valley State University to 13,141 at Mississippi State University. The 1989 state appropriations for the eight institutions equaled $3,994 per full-time student (12 percent below the southeast average), so the average student paid $1,790 in tuition (21 percent above the regional average) to partially compensate for this funding shortfall. Mississippi faculty salaries ranked twelfth of the fifteen southern and border states at $35,008 in 1989 but then fell toward the regional cellar after a budget freeze the next year. As late as 1980, only 12.3 percent of the state population aged twenty-five years or older had completed four years of college (rank, forty-sixth).[17]

Mississippi also supports a network of fifteen junior colleges that operate thirty-four educational centers. Originally vocational-technical education was their primary mission, but the state's junior colleges expanded their services to provide professional and semiprofessional training, courses for academic transfer to senior universities, start-up assistance to business and industry, and community-oriented adult education, seminars, and workshops. Each junior college functions under its own local board of trustees composed of representatives from the counties it serves. Total public junior college enrollment almost equals the total system enrollment of the senior universities. Although the smallest junior college has an enrollment just under 1,000, the largest junior college surpasses in enrollment (about 8,000) the student body of five of the eight universities.[18] State appropriations account for 57 percent of junior college funds, and local government contributions make up 16 percent of their funds.

Employees of the State Board of Health are responsible for programs that prevent tuberculosis and sexually transmitted diseases, assist family planning, provide maternal and child health care, offer home health services, license child care centers, protect the quality of drinking water and food, and work to control radiation.[19] A critical effort of the department involves lowering the state's infant mortality rate (1988: 12.8 per 1,000 live births). Although the rate has declined over the past decade, Mississippi still has the second highest rate in the nation. This problem is especially acute in the black community, where infant mortality (16.8 in 1988) is nearly double the rate for whites (9.2). The black infant mortality rate in Mississippi exceeds the rate in places such as Costa Rica, Cuba, Czechoslovakia, and Hong Kong. Paradoxically, thirty-two states have higher black infant mortality rates, while fourteen states have higher white infant mortality rates.[20] The scarcity of physicians in several counties contributes to this tragic situation; for example, as late as 1987 fourteen of the state's eighty-two counties had fewer than five active physicians. Over half of the state's physicians are concentrated in just five counties.

Protection of the disadvantaged and provision for the needy fall to the care of the Department of Human Services (formerly the Department of Public Welfare). The social "safety net" cast by the department has to be wide, because Mississippi has the largest percentage of public aid recipients in the fifty states (1988, 11.1 percent of the state's population). By contrast, the Department of Human Services, while bearing the highest caseload in the nation, has operated with the lowest administrative cost in the nation.[21] Aid to Families with Dependent Children (AFDC), food stamps, Medicaid, and Supplemental Security Income (SSI) are four of the most important forms of welfare assistance. Mississippi manages all four programs within the context of national government finance and regulation, which permit state governments substantial discretion in the administration and financing of these programs. In effect, states may vary their degree of "generosity" in regard to policy choices such as the size of the AFDC and SSI payments above the national minimum or the number of optional medical services offered to those eligible for Medicaid. States may also put more money into one program than another. As noted in the previous chapter, a very serious problem facing welfare programs in Mississippi today is the precipitous decline in state funding for social welfare.

Thirty percent of Mississippi's children live below the poverty level (1985, 30.4 percent; rank, fifieth). Children are the principal beneficiaries of AFDC funds, and they become eligible because the father fails to provide adequate support (usually because of absence) and the mother cannot support the children by herself. The 1987 AFDC payment to a three-person family (one parent and two children) was $120 per month (rank, forty-nineth), or an average of $38.44 per month to each of 122,393 children and 48,481 adults.[22]

On a common measure of the "adequacy" of AFDC payments, Mississippi's 1987 payment level provides only one-tenth of the state median income.[23]

The food stamp program supplements recipients' income so they can obtain a nutritionally adequate diet. Unlike the USDA commodity surplus program that distributed surplus food, the food stamp program uses vouchers that are legal tender for food. In 1988 487,000 Mississippians received the equivalent of $305 million in food stamps, or about $626 per person. One important dimension of food stamp policy is that in states with lower AFDC grant levels, recipients are allowed a "bonus value" of more food stamps. The effect of this extra bonus raises the "adequacy" of welfare aid—Mississippi's "adequacy" rank jumps from last to about thirty-eighth.[24]

Medicaid assists needy persons by paying doctor and hospital bills. States control who is eligible beyond the national minimum. Mississippi awards Medicaid payments to AFDC and SSI recipients as well as to other categorically needy persons; for example, children in poverty from intact families and pregnant women (with income up to 185 percent of the poverty level) receive Medicaid. In 1988 Medicaid paid medical bills estimated at a total of $414 million, or $1,131 per recipient, for 366,000 Mississippians. The 1989 decision to close the state's charity hospitals and significantly expand the Medicaid program should increase the number of needy citizens eligible to receive Medicaid payments.

Supplemental Security Income provides a guaranteed minimum income for any citizen who is aged, blind, or disabled. In 1985 SSI assistance went to 110,900 Mississippians. The average monthly payment to the 50,900 aged beneficiaries was $133 (rank, twenty-fifth) in comparison with the national average of $164, and the average monthly payment to 58,200 disabled beneficiaries was $226 (rank, thirty-second) in comparison with the national average of $261.

DETERMINANTS OF PUBLIC POLICY

Conflicts over "who gets what" generate demands for public action. Whether the motive is altruism or greed, justice or profit, issues arise that force public officials to make choices in terms of who benefits and who pays. Discovering why particular issues emerge in a state and how the policies that result from the issue conflict differ from similar policies in other states enhances one's understanding of public policy. Four classes of factors explain policy differences among the fifty states.

Societal Context

First, the societal context sets constraints on what is feasible public policy. Both the range of public services and the amount of resources that can be devoted to a given policy or program are limited by Mississippi's poverty. Although the state's spending effort on public schools, for example, ranks in the top one-fifth, it remains next to last in per pupil expenditure; obviously, the state's dead last rank on per capita income severely reduces the amount of money it can devote to any one program.

Similarly, rurality imposes another type of constraint on feasible policy in Mississippi. Because the state's population is scattered thinly throughout a relatively large geographic expanse, the cost of public policy is increased by the need to ensure that even isolated villages receive basic public services. Compare Mississippi with Minnesota, a state where about half the population lives in the Minneapolis–St. Paul metropolitan area. In Mississippi it is difficult to take advantage of economies of scale commonly relied on in other states to lower administrative costs. Rurality also makes a virtue out of self-reliance, and a distant government is more often held to be the cause of one's troubles than the solution to one's problems.

Second, the societal context in Mississippi structures the nature of political competition. Race and class have historically influenced the types of problems addressed by government and how they are resolved. Efforts to defend class or race privileges restrict the acceptable alternatives for achieving a particular policy goal and may even lead to violence. A major battle over the 1982 Education Reform Act, discussed later, arose over how it should be funded. Some sought to increase the regressive burden of the sales tax, while others desired to spread the cost of education reform across more affluent sectors of the economy. Those depending on oil and gas for their livelihood defended their personal interests by opposing Governor Winter's proposed increase of the severance tax.

Third, societal context has shaped the state's political institutions. The renewal of planter political strength at the end of post–Civil War Reconstruction led to a state constitution that created a weak governorship and a fragmented state government. Rurality has contributed to the persistence of the justice court judges as a system of informal neighborhood law enforcement. It has also formed the power base for the previously unassailable county supervisors; but notice that as the urban population has grown, the county supervisors' clout has diminished.

Fourth, the state's economic and social conditions determine the type and behavior of political leaders. Widespread poverty eliminates most Mississippians from contesting for public office, thus leaving a highly skewed pool of candidates drawn from the most affluent and literate segments of the population. A large rural population produces a cadre of leaders whose values are at odds with the growing urban and suburban populations of the state's capital and the Gulf Coast. This divergence leads to the formation of "conservative caucuses" within the legislature that oppose cosmopolitan and urban life-style policy initiatives.

Another clear illustration of the impact of societal conditions on political leadership can be seen in the post–World War II challenge of commercial and industrial leaders to control of the state by agrarian based elites. As more and more capital and labor became employed in the modern sectors of the state's economy, over time business leaders reduced the power of the old planter class. One has only to observe the steady growth of political influence exercised by business organizations such as the Mississippi Economic Council and the concomitant decline of the Farm Bureau.

Political Culture

Transformations in the state's traditionalistic political culture, driven not just by economic change but also by demographic and social change, affect Mississippi politics by altering the values and preferences of the participants in the political arena. For example, most larger cities and county seats now serve as home to a group of professionals (e.g., accountants, architects, physicians, real estate agents) whose income and life-styles do not depend on traditional agricultural pursuits. More Yuppie than plantation owner and certainly not redneck, this professional class is committed to progress, which they define as making their community more attractive to new business and industry. The tightfisted, penny-pinching, low tax approach to government justified on the basis of creating a "good business climate" is directly challenged by the newer professionals, who emphasize the use of public policy to enhance the quality of life (e.g., better schools, more parks, fine arts events) as the best strategy for attracting new business and keeping the younger generation from leaving home.

Managers of local factories and stores (e.g., Wal-Mart) that belong to national corporations as well as the owners of local franchise outlets (e.g., McDonald's) also belong to the "new business" leadership. The wages paid (including pension and health benefits) by McDonald's or Wal-Mart upset the old leadership's control over local labor.[25] These new wage rates, coupled with federally enforced antidiscrimination laws, brought new money into the black community and contributed to the growing number of blacks who hold "white-collar" jobs. This nationally based service industry employment broke the economic leash of tenant farming and manual labor that had constrained blacks' participation in the political arena. These new wages have also improved economic conditions among whites who used to depend on unskilled or semiskilled jobs.

This clash of "cultures" in the state's small towns is projected onto state politics. Demands to end corruption in highway construction and county government, battles over public school quality, and reform of the court system all reflect the economic and life-style changes occurring throughout the state. The emergence of a viable Republican party at the statewide level is in part a function of these cultural changes. Similarly, changes in the state's political culture dramatically altered the types of candidates who can successfully compete for statewide public office.

Institutions of Government and Politics

Variation in the characteristics of government institutions has long been identified as a significant determinant of policy differences among political jurisdictions. For example, states with strong governors benefit from a rational and coordinated approach to policy development and program management. Because the strong governor can hold state agency administrators accountable for their performance, the citizens in turn can hold the governor accountable for the conduct of the executive branch. Mississippi's fragmented state government, itself a by-product of the state's political culture and history, contributes to the political and policy differences from other states. Perhaps only Texas has historically had as weak a governor and as strong a Speaker as Mississippi. Groups and organizations backing gubernatorial candidates often discover that electoral victory does not yield policy results. Quite the contrary, the groups connected to entrenched and powerful legislators or to the lieutenant governor dominate the policy process.[26]

Variation in political party institutions also explains policy variations among the states. States where a high and keen level of two-party competition exists regularly produce innovative solutions to public problems. Just as competition in the marketplace fosters product diversity, so too in the political arena. Healthy competition between the party in power and the "loyal opposition" breeds a more open and accountable government. Despite the gains of the Republican party, Mississippi continues as a largely one-party state at the state and local level. The price for this lack of competition is the state's low ranking on policy innovation. When compared with other states and the year when a new public program (e.g., automobile registration, compulsory school attendance, fair housing, merit system, nurses' licensing, zoning) was adopted, Mississippi ranks fifieth.[27] Part of the explanation for this "shrinking violet" approach to public policy is the poverty of Mississippi, which limits funding available for programs, as well as the state's political culture, which resists any change. However, the lack of two-party competition in the state also reinforces this slowness to adopt new policies.

Political Leadership

Ultimately, the nature of public policy in a state rests on the shoulders of the state's leaders. In a footnote to his chapter on Mississippi politics, V. O. Key observed: "Poverty or no, on some matters Mississippi could have moved more rapidly. In 1948, for example, its legislature adopted a workmen's compensation act, the forty-eighth state to adopt such legislation. Even at this late date a policy considered elsewhere to be only the most elementary justice aroused extended and bitter debate."[28] As Key forcefully illustrates, the constraints imposed by the larger societal context, the state's political culture, and the attributes of its governing and political institutions do not exonerate public officials from responsibility for the quality of life in the state. What distinguishes a statesman is the skillful use of bargaining and compromise to forge a majority coalition out of warring parties. The ability to lead by building consensus behind a needed program or by blending diverse views into a creative policy, even at the risk of political costs, becomes an act of leadership. Therefore the composition and behavior of a state's political elite is a critical determinant of that state's politics and policies.

The leadership core in Mississippi has been undergoing considerable change in recent years. The adoption of merit-based civil service for state administrative personnel in the 1970s resulted in professionally trained public managers' moving into important policy-making positions. Twenty-five years after the passage of the 1965 Voting Rights Act, one now finds blacks serving in the state legislature, heading executive branch agencies, and sitting on the state supreme court. State elections in 1987 dramatically altered the composition of the state executive branch by replacing a core of political leaders whose careers reached back into the era of segregation with a new generation of "baby boomers."[29] State auditor Ray Mabus was elected governor despite opposition from powerful county supervisors. Supervisors had opposed the auditor's crackdown on their provision of free services to private individuals (e.g., grading and graveling a farmer's driveway or digging a burial plot on the family farm) in return for electoral support.

"SUCCESS" AND "FAILURE" IN THE MISSISSIPPI POLICY PROCESS

Public policies never exist in a vacuum. Typically, demands for public action begin when an economic or social problem begets conflict over its resolution (e.g., who cleans up and who pays to clean up a polluted stream). Because the problem often involves intensely held competing viewpoints, "the issue is joined" as different individuals, groups, or organizations (private and public) express their varying opinions about the appropriate government response to the problem. The following two case studies illustrate this struggle to use public resources to achieve a particular vision of the state's future. Furthermore, the case studies reveal important clues about the determinants of public policy in Mississippi and how these causal factors affect policy outcomes. An example of a policy "success" and an example of a policy "failure" provide the necessary contrast to aid in drawing some observations about the general process of policy formulation in Mississippi.

The 1982 Education Reform Act

For most of the post–World War II period, public education in Mississippi remained trapped in the basic structures established by the "equalization" or "minimum foundation" program in 1953.[30] Although the state allocated funds equally to students of all races, local school boards, which could choose to supplement the state allocation with their own resources, often spent more local tax dollars on white students. As late as 1980–81, for example, the 1953 system permitted a $1,204 per pupil difference between two school districts only thirty-five miles apart on opposite sides of the state capital.[31] Despite the state-mandated "minimum foundation" curriculum that was to be taught in all public schools, the 1953 system also allowed school districts to vary widely in the character and quality of their course offerings and facilities.

Through the 1960s, public education suffered severe body blows as a result of the massive resistance to integration. The old compulsory attendance law was abolished early in the decade, and once the federal courts overturned the "freedom of choice" doctrine, the number of pupils attending private schools more than doubled between 1968 and 1971. Legislative action during the 1970s concentrated on efforts to keep teachers' salaries from falling too far below the levels in other southern states. Occasionally calls for administrative and curricular reforms (e.g., school consolidation, public kindergartens, compulsory attendance) would provoke a legislative battle, but these proposals were defeated by Old Guard legislators opposed to "unnecessary frills" and "socialistic" or "communistic" trends in public education.

William Winter made public school reform his main campaign pledge when he gained the governorship in the 1979 election. Winter worked to build a coalition of Mississippians who were increasingly distressed about the quality of the state's public education. For example, corporate executives from other states who were being courted to bring their operations to Mississippi bluntly told the state's economic leadership that companies would not locate in Mississippi because of the school system's poor reputation.[32] By 1980 Mississippi was the only state without publicly funded kindergartens. Efforts by the governor to secure reforms in the 1980 and 1981 legislative sessions failed to dent the Old Guard intransigence.

Governor Winter changed strategies in 1981 and initiated a statewide series of speeches to mobilize public support for a comprehensive reform package. Not only did the plan contain previously proposed administrative and curricular changes, it also recommended new funding mechanisms, including raising the oil and gas severance tax for the first time since 1944.[33] Even in the face of strongly worded appeals by the governor that "Mississippi has been fiftieth long enough" and that "it's boat-rocking time in Mississippi," the bill died in the house on a "deadline" day for floor consideration of bills reported out of committee. Old Guard Speaker of the house C. B. "Buddie" Newman was widely viewed as playing a major role in its defeat, as he adjourned the house and proceeded to walk off the podium on the "deadline" day. Newman ignored a dozen representatives who stood up to request immediate consideration of the education bill. He was accused of violating house rules requiring that when a dozen members stand, a vote should be held on whether to adjourn.

Through the summer and fall, several events occurred that reopened the fight for reform. First, the governor launched another statewide round of speeches combined with public rallies to bring visibility to his reform package. Second, ABC's "20/20" show gave national coverage to the condition of Mississippi's schools and in the process laid much of the blame on the deliberate inaction of the Old Guard in the state legislature, especially Speaker Newman. Third, intense debate reignited over the governor's tax plan, including a saturation media campaign by the oil and gas industries opposing any increase in the severance tax. Legislative study committees from the two chambers released competing plans for school improvements.

The 1982 legislative session had passed one item that allowed the reformers to keep the crusade for education alive—a proposed constitutional amendment to establish a lay board of education that would select the state school superintendent. A scandal over the misuse of sample copies of textbooks had entrapped the elected superintendent and heightened the statewide perception that school policy had failed. The referendum on the lay board quickly became a public opinion test case on reform, and Governor Winter capitalized on the momentum generated by its passage by calling a special session of the legislature. Winter unveiled a forty-six-point comprehensive plan that, if passed, would have resulted in a total overhaul of Mississippi's public schools and a complete break with the 1953 "equalization" system.[34]

Leaders of both chambers answered the governor's call by publicly questioning the need for and cost of a special session. Not only was there division over the various options in each chamber but more important, the majority viewpoints in the two chambers diametrically opposed each other.[35] For example, the House Education Committee supported public kindergartens, while the Senate Education Committee preferred a reading assistance program for the first three grades. Each chamber targeted different taxes as the source of new money to pay for the reforms.[36] The special session operated in a "fishbowl atmosphere" of intense media coverage. Proponents (e.g., Mississippi Association of Educators, NAACP, Chamber of Commerce, Business and Professional Women, League of Women Voters) and opponents (e.g., petrochemical industry, oil exploration companies, private school association, some fundamentalist religious bodies) of reform mounted demonstrations on the grounds of the state capitol.

In this highly charged situation the fate of education reform depended on the outcome of complicated legislative maneuvers. During the first week of the session, the key struggle took place in the house over kindergartens. Opponents of reform believed that if kindergartens died in the house, the chamber more disposed to support them, the whole reform movement would be undercut. A crucial compromise to restrict the Education Committee and the Ways and Means Committee to their traditional jurisdictions ended a bitter intercommittee feud. Second, the governor altered his stand on the severance tax.[37] Following these two compromises, the house overwhelmingly passed the reforms.

Pressure for action shifted to the senate, where the Finance Committee pushed through a bill to delete kindergartens from the house bill and to substitute a 1 percent increase in the sales tax for the house's multisource revenue approach. Kindergartens survived on a 26 to 25 vote, but the price was a three year delay in implementation. For two days the conference committee was frozen in the double bind of kindergartens and taxes. The senate conferees insisted on the sales tax as the only politically feasible source of revenue. They also insisted on a three-year delay in the implementation of kindergartens. The house delegation held firm to an immediate start for kindergartens and to the belief that a sales tax hike would hurt poor people. During the closed-door lobbying by the governor and various interest groups, a movement surfaced to stop any reforms because of a provision to consolidate school districts (from 154 to 82; that is, one per county). This gambit fanned fears of further integration in areas where municipal schools were predominately white in pupil composition and rural county schools were predominately black.

Sunday, December 19, produced an agreement to delay mandatory public kindergartens until 1986 (a four-year delay to allow some school districts to build enough classrooms) and to fund the reforms with one-half of 1 percent increase in the sales tax, the addition of a new 5 percent bracket for taxable personal income above $10,000, and no increase in the oil and gas severance tax. Representative Simpson, the governor's floor leader, stated, "It's (the final bill) probably worst as far as taxation and the best as far as education." Black legislators were in a predicament over their distaste for a sales tax hike and their desire to upgrade public education. On Monday, December 20, the reform compromise passed both chambers. Representative Tommy Walman observed at the end of the special session, "It's all been worth it. This is the most significant thing to happen in education since 1953."

The 1986 Plan to Reorganize the Highway Department

Highways are "big stakes" politics in state government. In rural states like Mississippi, farm income and small-town economic growth depend on a well maintained system of roads that connects farms to markets and also links the state's diverse regions. Not only is the public's "interest" significant, but highways also mean big bucks to construction companies, land developers and owners, businesses and stores, and even whole communities and their elected representatives. Mississippi, like some states, vests responsibility for highways in a multimember board. Usually these boards are "chosen by the governor, but with prescriptions neutralizing partisanship and perhaps guaranteeing occupational and regional representation."[38] Echoing the state's Jacksonian traditions, Mississippi's three-member Highway Commission is the only elected board in the fifty states. This separate election insulates the commission from direct gubernatorial influence. In addition, independent election also thrusts each commissioner into election campaigns that heighten the temptation to exchange favorable decisions for contributions from persons with a stake in highway construction and location.

Adding to the commission's historic independence is the state gasoline tax, which yields a pool of money designated, or "earmarked," for highways. Until 1986 the commission could freely spend funds that had been appropriated by the legislature, and it was immune from general budget cuts because its "special fund" came from federal dollars, fees, and state tax diversions. Even during severe budgetary retrenchment in other agencies and programs, highway spending continued. Furthermore, the commission controlled the pace at which funds were encumbered for specific projects; this meant it could build a substantial reserve of uncommitted money while other agencies went begging. Most states and the federal government earmark gasoline taxes and other user fees for highways, arguing that those who benefit from the service should pay for it. Efforts to divert gasoline taxes to other programs generate concern that the quality of a state's highways will decline. Yet Mississippi appears to place a greater priority on highways than on education and social welfare programs, leading to some political support for diverting unspent highway money to other programs in financially difficult times.[39]

Efforts to reorganize the Highway Commission have been rare. On the other hand, criticism of the commission's policies has been frequent, at least since Governor John Bell Williams in 1968 labeled highways the "weakest link in Mississippi's transportation system."[40] Over the next two decades, the Highway Commission suffered from repeated criticism by the legislature, by governors, and by the business community. Even the Federal Highway Administration critically observed that per motor vehicle Mississippi's highway costs are considerably above the national average.[41]

In 1986 Governor Bill Allain, as part of his response to the state's five-year budget crisis, launched a two-pronged attack to liberate the unencumbered reserve of highway funds for use in other policy areas and to reorganize the commission under a unified department of transportation. The governor's plan met stiff opposition in the legislature, especially in the senate.

Since previous public and private reports urged the consolidation of the state's transportation programs (which are scattered among thirty-seven boards and commissions and seven agencies), Governor Allain argued that his proposal was "nothing new." However, his demand to move unencumbered funds from the Highway Department's "special fund" to the state's "general fund" in order to cover budgetary shortfalls was an arrow aimed at the heart of the commission's independence and power.[42] The governor justified his action as a remedy for the prolonged budget crisis that imposed multiple budget cuts on most state agencies. Allied with the legislature's "no tax" faction, Allain believed the growing pressure from advocates of "no more cuts" in major programs (e.g., education, health, welfare) would break the back of the Highway Commission's supporters.

Even more pressure to liberate the highway reserve funds occurred when the budgetary crisis led the state "College Board" to reluctantly propose closing two universities (Mississippi Valley State, the smallest of the historically black schools, and Mississippi University for Women) and two professional schools (the Ole Miss dental school and the Mississippi State veterinary school). This action mobilized the black community and women's groups as well as the two most powerful alumni associations—Ole Miss and Mississippi State. The governor's strategy of manipulating the intense debate over taxes versus spending appeared to work; he managed to pit boosters of the universities against highway supporters. Within the business community, this choice was especially difficult, because highways and universities were both perceived to be critical to attracting new industry.

The Highway Commission energized its well-placed allies on the House Transportation Committee and the Senate Appropriations Committee, including the two chairmen whose districts received large amounts of highway financing. Legislative supporters of highways attacked the reorganization plan by raising the specter of the loss of popular sovereignty over highways if the commission were to become an appointed body. The Highway Department also mobilized its more than 3,000 employees, who are spread across the state, to join in the lobbying fray. A proposal to shift highway financing from the traditional "pay as you go" basis to long-term bonds complicated the debates. After a series of emotional legislative battles that included overriding some gubernatorial vetoes, the legislature finally adjourned, unable to override Governor Allain's line-item veto of the Highway Department's $436 million fiscal year 1987 appropriation. With only ten weeks before the start of the next fiscal year, the more than 3,000 highway department employees faced loss of their jobs. Intense political pressure produced a special legislative session that eventually enacted a highway bill.

Highway politics coupled with a persistent budget crisis resulted in a policy "failure." Postmortems on the legislative session reached a consensus that a lack of leadership in making difficult decisions and an unwillingness to compromise had produced the stalemate. The governor rejected a compromise by the House Transportation Committee to begin the consolidation process. The house and the senate could not agree on the bond proposal or on using earmarked funds to save other programs. Despite the severe fiscal strain, the legislature declined to close any of the small universities, forcing higher education to make a new round of deep budget cuts across all the institutions. And the state's most powerful political figure, the Speaker of the house, failed to forge a coalition behind a plan to end the five-year-long budget crisis. Instead of breaking the "no more taxes" versus "no more cuts" impasse, the Speaker's team patched together a budget from one-time funds and then left town.

DIFFERENTIAL OUTCOMES IN THE POLICY PROCESS

The determinants of state variation in public policy help explain why education reform succeeded and highway reform failed. First, the larger societal context contributed to the source of both problems—inadequate schools and inadequate highways. Mississippi's poverty limits the actions of public officials. Nevertheless, variation in economic and social conditions around the state does exist and does affect policymakers. For example, legislative opponents of education reform represented particular types of districts: oil and gas production areas, counties with significant private school enrollments, and the more "underdeveloped" or "traditional" areas of the state.[43]

Second, both policy proposals encountered the rigidity of the traditional culture's "If it ain't broke, why try to fix it?" philosophy. Despite highly visible shortcomings and growing choruses of complaints, anti-change forces relied on the logic and symbols of the traditional culture to thwart reform for years. A large coalition of interest groups based in the modern sectors of the state's society finally pushed forward education reform by countering the old imagery with the argument that "a horse drawn wagon, even if working, just won't do in the space age." For example, pro-education forces ran television ads stressing the use of computers in traditional family farming. By linking educational progress with positive aspects of traditional Mississippi culture (e.g., self-reliant individuals taking care of themselves, civility, productivity), reformers put Old Guard opponents on the defensive.

However, the highway reorganization effort failed to attract a broad base of support even from groups that would probably benefit from a new approach to highway management. Highway reformers never could overcome the public's attachment to popularly elected highway officials. Rural dwellers, who depend on good highways, perceived reorganization as a threat to their traditional control of roads and highways. In a sense, highway reform was victimized by negative symbols in the state's culture (e.g., loss of popular sovereignty, centralization of power in the state capital, one-person control).

Third, institutional differences created varying opportunities or constraints that critically shaped the evolution and the success or failure of the two policy proposals. The Highway Commission operated from a position of institutional strength, being independent of formal gubernatorial control and having access to special earmarked funds. The commission decides the interdistrict division of highway dollars, and individual commissioners can assign projects around their districts to reward their friends and punish their enemies. The commissioners also exercise personal authority over Highway Department personnel in each district. On the other hand, the state superintendent of education is unable to exercise much influence over legislators, so educational reform was delayed for many years. Education money is distributed by a state-mandated, attendance-based formula, and the superintendent and the Department of Education can influence local school district personnel only indirectly through the regulatory process.

Fourth, policy success or failure clearly depended on leadership attributes and behavior. Governor Winter entered office on a wave of popularity and immediately used it to launch his education reform plan. Even though his proposals suffered defeat in two successive legislative sessions, he continued his campaign but switched from traditional closed-door bargaining with the legislature to a strategy of going public. Winter's statewide publicity campaign mobilized education boosters, energized legislative supporters, and threw the anti-reform factions on the defensive. When the oil and gas industry and its legislative allies threatened to undermine the governor's forty-six-point plan, his willingness to compromise on revenue sources kept the reform bill alive. Similarly, the willingness of black legislators to accept further sales tax increases as the price of kindergartens also made possible the reform's passage.

Governor Allain entered office burdened with serious allegations about his personal life. This campaign mud weighed down the first two years of his term and left him only a short time to gain his goals. Once Allain decided to act, he faced an independent state agency backed by a solid legislative coalition. Pressure by the commissioners on legislators who worked to correct abuse in highway policy ranged from speeches given by commissioners in a legislator's hometown to having highway employees work against a legislator's reelection and ultimately to halting projects in a legislator's district. Conversely, the commission rewarded its legislative friends by concentrating funds and projects in their electoral districts.[44] Understandably, few legislators openly challenged the commission's practices. Governor Allain's inability to attract citizen opinion to his side also made it difficult for legislative allies to frame an acceptable compromise.

To be successful in Mississippi's policy process, advocates of change must overcome the traditional resistance inherent in the state's political culture. Groups opposed to change defend their privileges not merely by typical legislative and interest group methods, but also by appealing to the philosophy and values of Mississippi's traditional life-style. Groups favoring progress should link their proposals to positive aspects of this traditional culture in order to legitimize their view of the state's future as well as to attract a sufficient base of leadership and public support. Before advocates of change can marshal enough votes to secure passage of their proposals, they need to demonstrate their allegiance to the state's traditions and their willingness to accommodate the competing interests within the larger economic and social context.

CHAPTER ELEVEN

The Dynamics of Mississippi Local Government

Gerald Gabris

County government in Mississippi, as in most states, has changed little during the past hundred years. . . . Movements for governmental reform in other jurisdictions have affected it but slightly; it is still the "dark continent" of the state's political system. The result of this neglect of a fundamental portion of the government is a system that is antiquated, inefficient, and devoid of the principles that make for responsible administration.

Robert B. Highsaw and Charles N. Fortenberry, 1954.[1]

INTRODUCTION

Several years ago, during a debate featuring Mississippi gubernatorial candidates, one candidate commented that local government in Mississippi means "small" government. When asked to clarify the term "small," the candidate responded: "I mean that once you drive into the community the only way to leave is to back out." While this may overstate the rural nature of Mississippi local government, many communities are indeed quite small. Of 292 municipalities in the state, only 104 have populations larger than 2,000, and only a handful have more than 20,000 people.[2] Mississippi local government, in addition to cities and counties, includes 484 special districts (including 152 school districts).[3]

Many political observers have viewed local government as being backward and unresponsive to socially disadvantaged citizens, reflecting its rural nature. Such unresponsiveness is rooted in a traditionalistic political culture entailing a government with few responsibilities and limited to preserving the status quo, which benefits the political and social elite. Government is also based on interpersonal relations and oriented toward a patron-client structure. In such a culture there has historically been great public tolerance of corruption that served the ruling political elite.

By the late 1980s this traditionalistic political culture was starting to be challenged, and considerable change and emerging progressivism began to characterize Mississippi local government. Many Mississippi cities and a growing number of counties are following the advice of former Vicksburg mayor Demery Grubbs: "If you are not the lead dog the view always remains the same." Mississippi cities, and to a lesser extent counties, are beginning to centralize administrative authority and are becoming more professionally managed. This trend is especially evident in larger cities and counties. Despite increased professionalism, most Mississippi communities refuse to adopt the classic model of municipal reform that strongly emphasizes professional council-manager government. Hence they are relatively unusual in reflecting the principles of Jacksonian democracy. Mississippi communities incorporate administrative professionals into structures that still place a heavy emphasis on the power and accountability of elected officials.

MUNICIPAL GOVERNMENT

The Mississippi State Code permits three classes of municipal incorporation based on the size of the local jurisdiction.[4] Any municipality with a population greater than 2,000 is classified as a "city" and can adopt any form of government permitted by state law. Municipalities with populations between 300 and 1,999 are classified as towns, and communities with fewer than 300 people are designated villages. Villages and towns must adopt the code charter (weak mayor, strong council) form of government. Mississippi has 104 cities and 188 towns and villages.

Most cities provide a full range of services, such as police and fire protection, public schools, garbage collection, streets, utilities, cemeteries, cultural and recreational facilities, and community development. The smallest towns and villages sometimes offer little more than basic services, such as police protection. Cities depend heavily on revenue from property taxes on land, homes, automobiles, and businesses and on charges for utilities and other services. They also receive income from the sales tax, equivalent to 1.2 cents for each dollar spent in the community.[5] An important trend is increasing state government funding support for public education, evident in legis-

lative passage in 1989 of an equity funding program. The program is designed to reduce the gap in spending between rich and poor school districts
by requiring an equal level of spending per student, with the state helping
fund those districts that are too poor to come up with enough money.[6]

The English poet Alexander Pope wrote, "For forms of government let
fools contest; Whatever is best administered is best." Nevertheless, in many
Mississippi communities, debate over the "best" form of government becomes heated. Community leaders are well aware that the form of government chosen exerts a major influence on who wields power, how decisions
are made, and how scarce resources are allocated. A brief description of the
four forms of city government is in order.

The Code Charter Form (Weak Mayor, Strong Council)

In Mississippi the code charter form, which is actually a weak mayor, strong
council type of government, is required of all cities unless they specifically
adopt another form. Cities may designate a different form of government in
their original charters or change to another through a referendum. Such
changes in form of government normally require a petition by 10 percent of
the registered voters and a simple majority vote in a public referendum.
(Changes to the mayor-council form in cities with populations under 40,000
require a petition of 20 percent of registered voters.)

The great majority of Mississippi cities (approximately 70 percent) employ the code charter form of government. With this form, cities may elect
either a five- or seven-person board of aldermen; four or six of these aldermen must be elected from geographic wards. In addition to the mayor, one
alderman may be elected at large. A key attribute of this government form is
that the aldermanic board is both a legislative (policy-making) and an executive (administrative) body. The board makes all policy decisions involving
the budget, purchasing, and organizational structure matters and approves
the hiring and firing of all government workers. The mayor is a weak executive (a mere figurehead) unless the board grants more authority. Even in code
charter government, however, a mayor with a dynamic personality and cha-
risma can acquire considerable power.

In the code charter form, power is usually fragmented among several
board members, and department heads have considerable autonomy from
any centralized source of administrative authority. Problems of governance
arise when a board is split (mayors in this form can break tie votes) or if
board members believe the mayor is trying to exert too much control over the

administration of city government. Cities operating under the code charter form are permitted by state law to employ a chief administrative officer (CAO), but the board decides how much power and authority the CAO may exercise.

The Mayor-Council or Strong Mayor Form

In 1976 the state legislature passed a law allowing cities to adopt the strong executive form of government—an important step toward centralizing administrative authority. The mayor, who is elected at large, serves as the chief executive officer and has the power to hire and fire city employees. The only limit on the mayor's authority is that when first appointed, department heads must be approved by a majority of council members. Hence the mayor can hire high-level administrators directly answerable to him (or her) and can fire them without cause. The strong mayor also enjoys a broad "item" veto power over any policy or appropriation ordinance passed by the city council. The council is prohibited by law from intervening in the affairs of city administration and must obtain the mayor's permission before talking to any city employee. Therefore the mayor in this form of government is a true executive who directs personnel, budget implementation, and details of organizational structure, and the council is a true policy-making branch. By the late 1980s, eight Mississippi cities had adopted this form, with more adoptions likely to come. These eight cities had the largest populations in the state.[7]

The Council-Manager Plan

Only four cities in Mississippi—Grenada, Pascagoula, Gautier, and Moorehead—currently employ the council-manager form of government. This form requires the city council to hire a professional city manager (having at minimum a four-year college degree) as the chief executive officer of the city. Though lacking a veto power over city council decisions, the city manager has complete authority over the day-to-day operations of city government, and city council members are legally prohibited from interfering with the manager's executive duties. The manager is responsible for hiring and firing all city workers, for preparing the budget, for purchasing, and for setting up an organizational structure that delivers public services. Few cities operate under the council-manager form, because most Mississippians do not wish to place this much authority into the hands of an appointed administrator, even though the manager serves at the pleasure of the city council and can be terminated at any time.

The Commission Form

Until the mid-1980s the commission form of government was widely used in the largest cities in Mississippi. In this form, three officials are elected at large, with one serving as mayor and the remaining two as department heads. None of the commissioners (not even the mayor) has more authority than the others, and all three have equal voting power on the commission. This form of government fragments executive and legislative authority, and most resources, manpower, and money are divided into three roughly equal portions. Because the commission form ran into so many legal challenges, fewer and fewer cities are using this option, and it may soon become extinct.

CURRENT TRENDS IN FORM OF GOVERNMENT

There were no strong mayor cities in Mississippi before 1980, but since then eight municipalities have switched to this form of government. These changes partly reflected a desire to create a more centralized leadership directly accountable to voters. Population is a key factor related to the form of government employed, since the smaller the city, the more likely it is to use the code charter form (table 13). Indeed, all cities with populations under 10,000 retain the code charter form of government. Yet many city leaders think this is not the most effective form of government; only 48 percent of the smallest cities perceive that this weak executive form is most effective.[8] Instead, most respondents (59 percent) believe that some type of strong executive system—either the mayor-council or council-manager plan—is preferable. (Very few officials continue to favor the commission plan.) Another indicator that Mississippi cities are recognizing the value of professional administrators is that 48 percent of respondents believe a professional administrator would increase the overall effectiveness of city government. Yet only 18 percent of all cities currently employ professional administrators.

In the 1990s more and more Mississippi cities will probably centralize their executive authority. Some will switch from the weak mayor form of government to a strong mayor system or hire a professional chief administrative officer. In this way Mississippi cities will retain a strong flavor of Jacksonian democracy yet centralize authority and introduce sophisticated administrative practices. Hence municipal reform in Mississippi should continue to be somewhat different from the classic reform pattern found in other states.

Table 13: Administrative Preferences of Chief Executives by Community Size

	Community Population					
	2,000 to 7,500	7,501 to 10,000	10,001 to 20,000	20,001 to 40,000	Over 40,000	All Communities Combined
Current form of Municipal Government						
Code Charter	100%	100%	56%	37%	0%	68%
Commission	0	0	11	13	40	9
Strong mayor	0	0	11	40	40	19
Council Manager	0	0	22	10	20	4
What is the most effective form of municipal government?						
Code charter	48	0	20	13	0	34
Commission	5	20	0	13	0	6
Strong mayor	26	20	20	63	60	32
Council manager	21	60	60	11	40	27
Does your city have a salaried professional administrator or CAO?						
Yes	4	40	56	38	60	18
No	96	60	44	62	40	82
Would (does) a professional administrator improve the effectiveness of your city government?						
Yes	42	60	44	63	80	48
No	58	40	56	37	20	52

Source: 1985 survey of Mississippi city chief executive officers conducted by the author at Mississippi State University. The number of people interviewed was eighty-four.

Note: Table entries are percentages, which total 100% in each column.

MUNICIPAL BUREAUCRATIC TRENDS

The term "bureaucratic" refers to the classic Weberian model that posits that organizations hire people based on merit, engage in considerable job specialization, rely heavily on written rules and objectives, and retain employees on a career basis. Bureaucratic organizations also employ the principle of hierarchy and engage in rational decision making (seeking the most appropriate means to achieve a desired goal) as part of their standard operating procedure.[9] This contrasts with the traditional authority model, which relies on a patrimonial organization and patronage politics.

Mississippi cities, particularly the larger ones, are exhibiting more and more bureaucratic traits and behavioral characteristics (table 14). In the largest cities, personnel management has become highly specialized, as shown by the existence of a separate personnel department and the employment of full-time personnel directors. More and more Mississippi cities rely on a "position classification" system that standardizes job descriptions and pay grades for employees performing comparable work and states in writing what is expected of employees. This departs from traditional systems, which assume that city employees have no specialized knowledge, skills, or abilities and that nearly anyone can adequately perform municipal work. Most cities rely on a written personnel manual. Most of the larger cities use a civil service method to hire employees instead of a system based on nepotism and patronage.

Another indicator of bureaucratization pertains to budgeting. Most cities (60 percent) have a professional budget or finance officer. The larger cities also have capital improvement budgets, and a great majority engage in systematic capital improvement planning. The purchasing function has also become specialized; 40 percent of all cities have a central purchasing officer, and 43 percent have computerized their budgets. Larger municipalities are more likely than smaller cities to employ a modified line-program budget format, which normally requires more technical proficiency to implement than does line-item budgeting. The largest cities are also more likely to engage in quantitative revenue forecasting exercises before preparing annual budgets.

COUNTY GOVERNMENT

A board of supervisors is empowered to serve as the general governing and policy-making authority for each county, administering the county budget and county departments. It has jurisdiction over the maintenance of roads,

Table 14: Administrative Trends Perceived by Chief Executives

	Community Population					
	2,000 to 7,500	7,501 to 10,000	10,001 to 20,000	20,001 to 40,000	Over 40,000	All Communities Combined
Does the city have a formal personnel department?						
Yes	4%	60%	44%	62%	80%	22%
Does the city have a personnel director or officer?						
Yes	9	60	33	75	100	27
Does the city use a civil service method of hiring employees in at least some departments?						
Yes	9	40	44	87	100	27
Does the city have a position/classification system?						
Yes	30	60	63	38	80	39
Does the city have a formal written employee handbook?						
Yes	58	60	89	88	100	67
Does the city use validated tests and performance instruments?						
Yes	0	0	20	50	80	12

Does the city have a capital improvements budget?

Yes	39	80	63	50	100	49

Is the city's budget now on computer?

Yes	28	40	88	75	80	43

Does the city have a central purchasing officer?

Yes	28	60	44	63	100	40

Is the budget

Line item	74	100	56	88	60	74
Program	2	0	0	0	0	2
Performance	7	0	0	0	0	5
Line program	4	0	33	12	40	11
Program performance	6	0	11	0	0	5
Other	7	0	0	0	0	3

Source: 1985 survey of Mississippi city chief executives conducted by the author at Mississippi State University. The number of people interviewed was eighty-four.

Note: Table entries are percentages.

bridges, courthouses and jails, hospitals, health departments, libraries, and garbage disposal. County supervisors serve as extensions of the state government at the local level. The major source of county revenue is the property tax.[10] Revenue is also received from state government and outside sources. Counties elect several positions at large, such as county clerk, sheriff, circuit clerk, and treasurer. Usually there is little cooperation between counties and cities, though sometimes a city will permit its police and fire services to assist county residents in an emergency. Some cities and counties, however, are beginning to consolidate their economic development activities.

The 1954 quotation beginning this chapter, which refers to county government as the "dark continent" of Mississippi's political system, may still be relatively accurate.[11] A university professor in the state, familiar with the politics of county government, recently referred to one county board of supervisors as a "banana republic." An explanation for why county government is so reluctant to change and become more efficient lies in the state's traditionalistic political culture, which stresses the importance of preserving traditional political practices and the status quo. We now turn to a description of the traditional "beat" system of county government, and the factors contributing to its resistance to change.

The Fragmented District Plan

As in most states, Mississippi counties use the commission or district form of government.[12] As required by the state constitution, each county is divided into five districts (of relatively equal populations) called "beats," and each beat elects a single representative called a supervisor. The five supervisors constitute the official board of supervisors for each county. The board elects one supervisor as "president," but with no more power than the other supervisors. With 82 counties, Mississippi has 410 county supervisors. (Until recently, each beat also elected two justices of the peace, creating 820 justices of the peace in the state.) Unlike cities, state law does not permit counties to alter their basic form (structure) of government. Their only options historically were to hire a county administrator (who is very similar to a municipal CAO and who serves at the pleasure of the board) or to adopt a centralized road administration system.

Under this traditional "beat" system, county supervisors serve as executives within their districts or beats. They primarily oversee the construction and maintenance of roads and bridges, a vital responsibility in rural Mississippi, where citizens often wish to improve the poor condition of the roads. Hence, many supervisors perceive their jobs primarily as being "road foremen." Indeed, many have been elected after campaigns that stress their road construction experience. One successful candidate, for example, ran on the platform that he could operate a trench digger more effectively and less expensively than if the county contracted out for the work.

One Person One Vote, Plus Equal Road Mileage

The road function is so important that the "road budget" is the principal source of funds for each supervisor. In the beat system, regardless of road mileage supervisors generally divide the budget into five equal parts. Rarely are countywide priorities established based on the general interest of the entire county. Instead, each supervisor remains fixed on his beat and his share of the budgetary pie.[13] This practice of dividing the budget equally among the supervisors reduces conflict among them.

Recent reapportionment deliberations in one Mississippi county illustrate this principle of equal division of the budget. Several plans developed by the local planning district would have met United States Justice Department requirements for equally populous beats that did not discriminate against blacks. The major delay was produced by the county supervisors, who sought to ensure that each beat had approximately the same road mileage. With equal road mileage, the road budget could justifiably be divided into five equal parts.

Desire to Avoid Controversy

In their classic book *Small Town in Mass Society,* Arthur Vidich and Joseph Bensman point out that politicians in small towns prefer the appearance of harmony and strive to avoid controversy.[14] This often makes them reluctant to become informed about politically sensitive problems, and they may fail to take action to solve them. Mississippi county supervisors share these characteristics of small town politicians in general. Some are very reluctant to publicly discuss potentially divisive issues, and they prefer to solve such problems behind closed doors.

One county's board of supervisors, for example, was faced with difficult decisions involving reapportionment and replacement of the board president. The supervisors preferred to decide these issues privately, even though they were subject to the open meeting requirements of state law. (Despite open meetings, very few citizens take the time to attend board meetings unless a controversial item is on the agenda.) To avoid discussing these controversial issues in front of the reporter who was assigned by her newspaper to cover board meetings, the board president recessed the meeting, and board members reconvened in the men's restroom of the courthouse. Though she was unable to attend this informal meeting, the reporter embarrassed the supervisors by publicly reporting their subterfuge, thereby bringing an end to these clandestine bathroom meetings.[15]

My Beat Is My Kingdom

The real power of a county supervisor resides in the beat and in a network of friends, neighbors, and relatives who continually reelect the supervisor. Traditionally, supervisors have rewarded supporters with jobs, lucrative contracts, and other perquisites of office. Because jobs are scarce in rural Mississippi, the prospect of working for county government is very appealing to poor whites and blacks. Other favors included burying deceased people on private property at no charge, graveling and grading private driveways, digging wells, and blacktopping county roads that lead to supporters' property. These activities are not as serious as the equally pervasive custom of kickbacks associated with county contracts. Recent FBI investigations have unveiled a large number of kickback schemes and practices.[16]

Under the beat system, supervisors have total control over personnel decisions, contracting, and equipment purchases within their beats and do not usually have to answer to the board as a whole. In most counties there is a gentlemen's agreement (also called logrolling) of not questioning or challenging the hiring, purchasing, and equipment decisions of another supervisor, even though such activities may appear suspect. As in other professions, supervisors are accused of hearing no evil, speaking no evil, and seeing no evil involving fellow supervisors. Supervisors frequently buy road machinery and equipment for their own beats, even if it duplicates equipment in a neighboring beat. Equipment and workers are strategically located in road barns throughout the supervisor's beat.

Extreme Fragmentation and Duplication

Supervisors seldom set priorities that reflect the general interests of the entire county. Because they have so much power within their own beats, supervisors tend to become autonomous of one another and reluctant to share resources or equipment with other districts. The resulting fragmentation is illustrated by an instance of inclement weather that severely damaged the roads in two beats of one county. Two supervisors were forced to spend most of their road repair allocation long before the end of the fiscal year. The other three beats did not suffer extensive damage and were flush with road funds, but initially they refused to help the less fortunate beats. Only after considerable bargaining did the affluent beats agree to lend money to the beats in need, and only after the latter had agreed to eventually pay back this "loan." Such bargaining is a common practice in reallocating money within Mississippi counties.

Potential for Corruption and the Myth of Accountability

County supervisors argue that their system is close to the people and therefore directly accountable and democratic. They contend that if professional administrators were hired and centralization took place, the "common folk" would lose access to county government and receive poorer services. Yet some political observers think sufficient accountability to the public is lacking. Supervisors are elected from very small districts where only a plurality vote is required for political victory. Once elected in the beat system, they serve in legislative, executive, and sometimes judicial capacities. Supervisors have almost total control within their beats, since there are no checks and balances on their decisions. Moreover, there are no provisions for a recall vote or for public referenda. The result is that some supervisors forget that they are agents of state government, implementing state (not local) programs and state law places limits on the practices that they can engage in.

THE COUNTY UNIT PLAN AS A STRUCTURAL SOLUTION

Pressure to reform county government in Mississippi is hardly new, but until the mid-1980s there was not enough political support to sustain reform. The Mississippi Economic Council (MEC) has consistently championed county administrative reform by conducting studies and developing a professional administrator model that it urges all counties to adopt. Many county supervisors have opposed the MEC's recommendations and refused to adopt them. For years the Mississippi Association of Supervisors (MAS) was successful in blocking efforts in the state legislature to reform county administrative practices. In 1983 the legislature did pass a bill requiring that all Mississippi counties adopt a "county unit road system" by July 1, 1984, unless the county board of supervisors voted to exempt their county from that provision. When the bill passed, the great majority of boards of supervisors voted against having their counties operate under the unit plan.

What Is the Unit Plan?

Before the latest wave of reform in 1988, it was not clear what constituted a county unit plan, based on a simple reading of the state code.[17] There was no common interpretation of the unit system's necessary components, so counties were given considerable latitude in interpreting the statute. Many supervisors preferred this vagueness, because it gave them the opportunity to implement something that they could call a unit plan, but that in reality had little effect on their power and decision-making practices. Provision for the county unit plan was not even in the section of the state code dealing with county government but was in that portion dealing with state-aid roads. The only requirement of the unit plan was that counties place the road and bridge function into a centralized department headed by a county engineer. This employee would be responsible for purchasing all equipment and coordinating all road and bridge maintenance for the entire county, rather than for specific beats. The intent was to eliminate extensive duplication of road equipment and to achieve greater cost effectiveness. Moreover, the plan allowed for setting priorities in county road needs.

By 1987, twenty-two counties claimed to have implemented a county unit plan, though no two plans were alike. Some counties felt that simply hiring a road foreman who was accountable to the county board (and whom the board could tightly control) rather than to individual supervisors was sufficient to meet the legal requirements of the unit plan. Oktibbeha County employed this approach. Other counties, such as Neshoba, hired full-time professional administrators and implemented a comprehensive reform. Yet even Neshoba County, with the election of a new group of supervisors in 1987, attempted to repeal the reforms of the previous board and return to a less sophisticated unit system. Other large counties, such as Hinds (where the capital of Jackson is situated) and Lauderdale (which includes Meridian), adopted moderately comprehensive plans. In any event, compared with most other counties, these twenty-two had taken the most dramatic steps in reforming how road work was conducted, how employees were hired, and how items were purchased.

In view of this situation, reformist governor Ray Mabus in 1988 actively campaigned for the legislature to mandate the county unit system across the state. The version of the unit system reported out of the legislature required a centralized equipment storage facility (barn) and the hiring (or designation) of a countywide administrator.[18] County supervisors were successful in watering down the legislation by requiring that referenda be held separately for each county on whether the unit system should be adopted and that each county board of supervisors report to the state auditor before the referendum their estimate of the additional expenditures required to implement the unit system. Supervisors in some counties were accused of inflating the estimates in an effort to scare voters with the threat of a tax increase. Many supervisors campaigned against the referendum by holding public meetings and running ads in the newspaper. Despite the controversy, voters in forty-seven counties (especially the more urban counties) voted for this county unit system.

Why Are Many County Supervisors Reluctant to Change?

Mississippi supervisors are paid over $20,000 annually for serving in their part-time official capacity. This is a large salary in a state with the lowest median family income in the nation. As a consequence, the job of supervisor is attractive for economic reasons. Supervisors realize this and feel that because they are so highly paid they must appear to earn their keep. Supervisors are candid and pragmatic about their reluctance to hire professional administrators, even though their county's operations would be run more efficiently through greater administrative centralization. A common concern is, "If we hire an administrator for $40,000 a year and let him run the county, soon my people will ask what am I [the supervisor] needed for?"

Most supervisors, who usually work part time, contend that they provide sufficient managerial leadership and direction to their road crews and employees. They justify their relatively high salaries by contending that they are "working" public officials and not just policymakers. In one instance the supervisors of a less affluent county became concerned when a more affluent neighboring county elected financially independent supervisors. These affluent supervisors proceeded to serve as policymakers and hired a professional administrator to oversee day-to-day county operations. The less affluent county supervisors feared the actions of their affluent colleagues would lead the public to conclude that there was little need for the continued existence of county supervisors. Indeed, if too many counties started to elect policy-oriented supervisors who employed professional administrators, the traditional role of the supervisor might become extinct!

Even in the face of the recent wave of unit system reform, some of the fundamental political realities of county government in Mississippi have not changed. Mississippi county supervisors are accountable to only a small block of voters, and they receive relatively high salaries in a poor state. Especially in counties employing the beat system, supervisors exert considerable clout within their own beats, having few checks and balances on their actions. The unit system has successfully removed supervisors from the day-to-day administration of the road function, but county administrators must be responsive to the wishes of supervisors or risk losing their jobs.

Some of the larger and more progressive counties will continue to implement more innovative and professional systems of management and public service delivery. Citizens in such counties are more sophisticated and are less likely to tolerate the inefficiency, corruption, and fragmentation of traditional county government. But in most counties, supervisors should continue to retain considerable autonomy, avoiding substantive management reforms that may imperil the status quo. In short, county supervisors represent a declining yet still powerful political force, reflecting the traditionalistic political culture of the state. Changes that substantially alter their power will continue to entail some hard-fought battles.

FORCES EFFECTING CHANGE IN MISSISSIPPI LOCAL GOVERNMENT

Mississippi municipalities and counties have experienced considerable change since 1980, as many have sought to professionalize their operations. The state's largest cities have adopted the strong mayor form of government, and many code charter cities have hired professional chief administrative officers. In 1985 the legislature granted cities limited home rule authority. The number of counties operating some type of county unit system has risen in recent years from twenty-two to forty-seven. Important social and political forces are impelling change in Mississippi local governments.

Race

The South's history of racial discrimination led to the 1965 Voting Rights Act, which required that the federal government approve any changes in voting procedures to ensure that they do not discriminate against blacks. Until recently, use of the "commission" form of government in larger cities had the effect of excluding blacks from serving on city councils. Even if blacks composed 40 percent of a city's population, the at-large election of all three commissioners from the geographic confines of the entire city would result in the election of all whites. Faced with court challenges by numerous black leaders and interest groups and a better than even chance of losing, many cities switched (or were ordered to switch) to a form of government that provided for ward elections. Such ward elections improved the electoral prospects of black candidates, especially in highly concentrated black wards.

Cities abandoning the fractionated commission form did not want to repeat the same management problems under a weak mayor, strong council system. Neither were they ready for the other extreme—strong appointive executives provided by the council-manager plan. Hence, beginning with Biloxi in 1980, cities abolishing the commission form have adopted the strong mayor option. An example of switching from a commission form of government to the strong mayor variety in order to avoid a court-ordered change is provided by Hattiesburg. Hattiesburg officials preferred more centralized leadership instead of fragmentation, and they streamlined city organization by reducing the number of municipal departments from forty-five to five. In view of the state's traditionalistic political history, it is somewhat ironic that many of Mississippi's larger cities took advantage of discrimination lawsuits, using them as a leveraging tool for transforming city governments into more centralized and efficient municipal organizations.

Some change is also evident at the county level. The effect of the 1965 Voting Rights Act in enfranchising more blacks has led to the election of a significant number of black county supervisors. As of 1989, 68 of the 410 county supervisors in Mississippi were black. Blacks therefore held 16.6 percent of these important county positions, a far cry from their history of virtual exclusion from political power. However, concern that the Mississippi Association of Supervisors had never elected a black as its presiding officer contributed to the formation of a parallel organization—the Mississippi Association of Black Supervisors.

Economic Development

Another force producing change in Mississippi cities is the belief that to attract opportunities for economic development, it is necessary to provide more effective, desirable, and dependable services at the local level. Mississippi local officials feel that improved schools, water services, and public health and safety programs help attract and retain blue chip industries and businesses. Local economic development has been linked to progressive political and community leadership. Cities such as Tupelo, Meridian, Starkville, and Biloxi have inaugurated special leadership programs, designed to promote economic development by improving local government and services.

The state Department of Economic Development (DED) and the research and development center also provide technical assistance to local governments to help them attract industry. Many communities proudly display road signs that designate them "key" communities, which means they have met standards deemed highly desirable by industry.[19] Cities under DED's stewardship have also implemented small business incubator programs to help fledgling businesses get off the ground. Many cities and counties have even established their own departments of economic development and have hired full-time professional economic development directors.

Less Tolerance of Incompetent and Corrupt Officials

A number of conditions have historically provided Mississippi local officials with considerable freedom of action, even in illegally enriching themselves at public expense. Local government tends to be extremely fragmented and decentralized, and officials are autonomous and face few checks and balances from other officials. Mississippi has a large number of local officials, who are directly accountable only to the small number of voters who elect them.

Citizens are becoming increasingly intolerant of official inefficiency and corruption. Auditor Ray Mabus in the mid-1980s started the crackdown on previously common but illegal practices of county supervisors. Supervisors could no longer gravel private driveways or bury people on private property free of charge. In the late 1980s an FBI sting operation led to the indictment of 57 county supervisors on corruption charges; it was estimated that the indictments could eventually reach 100 of the 410 supervisors.[20] Public pressure has led an increasing number of counties and cities to adopt more efficient government forms, such as the unit system and the strong mayor, as well as hiring more administrative professionals. Although Mississippi has a long way to go, there are far fewer courthouse gangs than twenty years ago.

CONSTRAINTS

Although local government in Mississippi is changing because of a concern for racial justice, economic development, and honesty and efficiency, powerful environmental forces temper the magnitude and rapidity of change. Many political observers feel that the foremost impediment to change is the state legislature.

The State Legislature

The Mississippi state legislature is very reluctant to delegate revenue-generating powers to local jurisdictions, so home rule in Mississippi does not grant any new taxing authority. The legislature has rejected county efforts to levy county sales taxes, for example. In addition to placing very strict limits on a municipality's taxing powers, the state code sets rather narrow boundaries regarding general responsibilities and powers. Although cities and counties have some freedom to set their own millage rates (a mill equals one dollar for every thousand dollars of assessed valuation) for property tax levels, the legislature has set a cap of 10 percent on annual increases in that rate. The state severely restricts the level of bonded indebtedness cities are allowed, and the state code is very specific on how municipal and county governments are to be structured and organized. In short, cities owe their origin to state law, so the state legislature retains ultimate authority over municipalities; indeed, it could even abolish local government if it wished to.[21]

Jacksonian Democracy

Jacksonian democracy dies hard. While increasingly centralizing power and employing more professional administrators, Mississippi local governments retain a large number of elected positions. Few Mississippians want to place substantial authority and power into the hands of nonelected officials, even though a number of elected officials are perceived as incompetent or opposed to needed changes. Democracy is a central value. In the early 1980s dissatisfaction with the city manager led Meridian to replace the council-manager plan (which had been in place for forty years) with the strong mayor option. Among cities changing their forms of government, only the newly incorporated city of Gautier (1986) has chosen a council-manager plan. A stress on "democracy" can also heighten political conflict. During a discussion one strong mayor had with his senior staff, it was suggested that he alter a policy to deal with the concerns of some members of the city council. The mayor retorted that in a democracy the majority rules, and that since he was elected by a majority he would rule—without interference from the council.

Fiscal Limitations

A final constraint on progress in local government is severe fiscal austerity. Mississippi is a very poor state, so the resource base that provides tax revenue to pay for government services is very limited. Furthermore, consistent with its traditionalistic culture, Mississippi government is dominated by a low tax, low expenditure philosophy, especially at the local level. Many citizens appear unwilling to pay for improving local services, even if they can afford to do so.

Public hostility to higher taxes is illustrated by recent reassessment efforts. In the late 1970s the Hinds County circuit court ruled that property tax assessments had to be equalized across the state and property appraisals had to reflect true market value. Before the decision, in many areas older property had not been reappraised for many years, despite an appreciation in value. Hence new property owners would pay higher taxes than older property owners even though their property was not significantly more valuable. Reappraisal was successful in equalizing tax payments for everyone whose property had the same market value, but some owners of older homes were enraged because their taxes had increased by 200 percent. Though such percentage increases may appear high, many older property owners had been paying only $200 or $300 a year in property taxes to begin with. The public outcry led the legislature to establish uniform assessment ratios so that the same amount of revenue would be collected as in the years before reassessment. Reassessment therefore did not increase city or county revenues, which might have been used to improve the quality of services being delivered.

THE RISE OF BLACK POLITICAL LEADERSHIP

An important source of change in Mississippi local government has been the increased numbers of black elected officials. After the 1965 federal Voting Rights Act outlawed various voting devices that white local officials used to prevent blacks from voting, the number of black voters and black elected officials soared. In Mississippi, the number of black elected city and county officials rose steadily from only 57 in 1970 to 359 in the late 1980s (fig. 8). These black leaders generally shared a progressive political philosophy that urged government to provide more social welfare opportunities to disad-

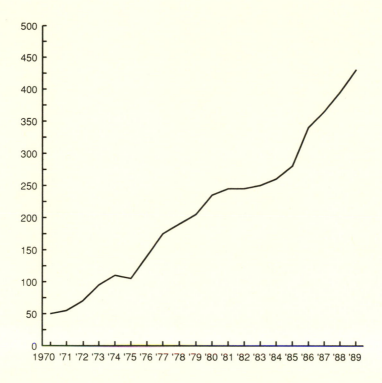

Figure 8. Rising number of black elected officials in Mississippi. These are the number of city and county offices in Mississippi held by blacks. (*Source*: U.S. Bureau of the Census, *Statistical Abstract of the United States, 1970–1990* [Washington, D.C.: U.S. Department of Commerce, 1970–90].)

vantaged citizens. They therefore posed a major challenge to the state's traditionalistic political culture and its conservative white leaders. Black leaders won political power by relying on the lessons they had learned from the harsh experience of being a minority in a segregated society. Yet even with federal protection, blacks encountered many obstacles in seeking the complete political and economic empowerment of the black community.

Black political empowerment began with the election of Charles Evers in 1969 as mayor of Fayette, a black majority town with a significant white minority (23 percent). The transfer of power was relatively smooth, since many blacks felt the defeated white incumbent had generally treated blacks fairly, and Evers repeatedly stressed cooperation between the races. Evers behaved pragmatically rather than ideologically, denouncing welfare as leading to dependency and endorsing some conservative candidates who promised to create jobs for the unemployed. Evers's election was credited with helping poor blacks by creating job opportunities, uniting the black community, and gaining blacks more respect from whites.[22]

On the other hand, Evers encountered white opposition to his effort to erect a memorial to his slain brother, civil rights worker Medgar Evers, in the town's Confederate Park. Some whites also opposed his hiring of blacks and his use of the police force to protect blacks from violence by whites. At least one black citizen felt that whites mistreated blacks in retaliation for Evers's election by refusing to extend them credit. Success itself can breed discontent by raising expectations. Many black constituents felt that fair treatment was no longer sufficient, but that the mayor should provide for the economic welfare of his constituents.[23]

At times Mississippi blacks had to overcome numerous obstacles to their taking office, as illustrated by the Bennie Thompson saga in the black majority town of Bolton. Thompson had acquired a confrontational image as a disciple of the Student Non-Violent Coordinating Committee's (SNCC) principles of "black power." In 1969 Thompson and two other blacks were able to take the aldermanic seats they had been elected to only after a federal court dismissed charges of election irregularities lodged by whites. In the process, a state law requiring elected election commissioners to be property owners was struck down as a device that often produced all-white commissions unsympathetic to blacks. The victory was nevertheless a hollow one, since the white minority on the city council upheld the white mayor's veto of progressive measures that served the needs of the black population.[24]

In 1973 Thompson was elected mayor of Bolton, and five blacks swept the aldermanic seats. A political conflict ensued as the former white mayor appointed a white majority election commission even though this appointment power reportedly was vested in the board of aldermen. In the absence of declared Republican and Independent candidates, whites filed as candidates with the white town clerk in secret, presumably to lull the black candidates into defeat in the general election. Thompson and his black colleagues took office only after a federal court rejected white election challenges, and a state law that had not been submitted for federal approval (preclearance) under the Voting Rights Act was struck down.[25]

Occasionally Mississippi's traditionalistic political culture has offered fierce resistance to black leaders after they have entered office. In 1977 Eddie Carthan was elected mayor of Tchula, a Delta town with an 80 percent black population. Carthan related how a representative of the white economic power structure had tried to bribe him with $10,000 to "run Tchula the way it has always been run," but Carthan refused to continue the practice of hiring the relatives of white planters and merchants and instead hired a number of blacks.[26] Meanwhile the lone white alderman, who owned 900 acres of cotton and 650 acres of soybeans, and two black aldermen formed an anti-Carthan coalition that began to wrest power from the mayor. These two black aldermen were raised in the plantation sector of the county, and one researcher concluded that they exhibited "vestiges of the 'plantation mentality' which regarded Afro-Americans as clients of a white 'boss.' "[27]

The political conflict in Tchula escalated, as the anti-Carthan coalition boarded up the town hall while Carthan was out of town and ordered the police chief to guard the door and shoot trespassers. The conflict culminated in a physical struggle between Carthan, his deputies, the police chief hired by the aldermanic board, and a black deputy of the police chief. Carthan was found guilty of assault on the black deputy and received a three-year prison sentence. Shortly after the trial, two jurors claimed they had been "tricked and misled" into the verdict, and the black deputy recanted his testimony and charged that the entire incident was a "set-up to get Carthan." Questions over whether Carthan had received justice became so great that he received support from Amnesty International, and Governor Winter suspended his assault sentences (the federal government also suspended a bank fraud sentence that Carthan had received).[28]

As the first black county tax assessor in Mississippi, Evan Doss took office in 1972 and was unable to find documentation supporting the property values listed on the tax rolls. He also encountered a practice of unequal and regressive tax assessments. The property of low- and average-income residents (mostly black) was assessed at 25 percent of true value, while the property of wealthier citizens (usually white) was assessed at rates as low as 10 percent. The Claiborne County Board of Supervisors opposed Doss's efforts to equalize taxes, even cutting his office's budget. Doss responded by going to the people to explain and defend his effort to eliminate tax inequities. He held public meetings at the courthouse, met regularly with community leaders, and even delivered a statewide press conference. Tax equalization was finally attained after a majority of blacks was elected to the county board of supervisors.[29]

Once attaining office, black mayors have actively pursued a "purposive welfare program . . . designed to satisfy the basic material needs and express wishes of their constituents."[30] Being elected in primarily black cities having weak local economies has meant very limited tax revenues, forcing mayors to aggressively seek federal funding. Black mayors initially sought federal funds that met the immediate basic needs of their constituents, such as housing, jobs, day care, and welfare. They then pursued capital improvements designed to provide permanent improvements in their communities. Yet problems remain in these impoverished localities. Federal aid declined in the 1980s, and many cities have been unable to build an independent economic base to sustain themselves.[31]

By the 1980s, growing public sensitivity to the tremendous poverty of Mississippi was leading to increased biracial cooperation in pursuing economic goals. In 1988 Robert M. Walker won a special election to become the first black elected as mayor of a majority white city (Vicksburg), and he went on to be reelected in 1989. His political success has been attributed to his backing of economic issues that benefit both races and to a low-key style that avoids confrontation. Walker's campaign platform pledged better housing, an improved business climate, new incentives for industry, and a campaign against drug use. He also allayed white fears by rejecting racial quotas and targets and pledging that no city workers would lose their jobs if he was elected. Walker first gained election after defeating a politically inexperienced candidate backed by the county sheriff's "courthouse gang." These "rural rednecks" apparently frightened the more genteel white elites as well as the "Yankee" outsiders (such as the non-Mississippi natives employed at the large Army Corps of Engineers installation) into supporting Walker.[32]

ULTIMATE CHANGE: THE POSSIBILITY OF METRO GOVERNMENT IN MISSISSIPPI

One of the most difficult things to obtain in local government is an agreement by two or more local governments to consolidate functions, services, and even political offices. To achieve an intergovernmental agreement and to move in the direction of government consolidation is the mark of an extremely mature and sophisticated local leadership. Several Mississippi local governments were exploring this possibility as the 1980s came to a close. Those considering a possible merger of city and county functions included Adams County and the city of Natchez, Jackson County on the Gulf Coast and several of its cities, and Harrison County and its cities.

The basic rationale for consolidation is that more efficient government services and better cost effectiveness will result. Under a consolidated government citizens would theoretically pay less tax money and receive better and more comprehensive services. People living in the county, for example, would receive police and fire protection and improved public works projects. Reducing the number of government officials that industry leaders have to deal with should make it easier to pursue a centralized and cohesive economic development policy. By consolidating populations, the cities and counties would increase the size of their jurisdictions, which might translate into greater political power when dealing with the state legislature and federal agencies. In these ways consolidation is a logical movement toward even greater centralization and bureaucratic specialization.

One barrier to consolidation of local government is that while one political leader may gain from such reform, several others could lose. Furthermore, some residents fear that those living in the other area being consolidated with theirs may gain more in improved services while they will simply be required to pay higher taxes. Urban residents sometimes fear that improving services in rural areas without requiring those areas to raise their taxes could lead to higher taxes or diminished services in urban areas. Some living in rural areas fear losing control of the local taxing power, which could lead to urban residents' voting to significantly increase the tax burden of rural residents. Furthermore, the cultural heritage of Jacksonian democracy in Mississippi preserves a large numbers of elected officials, hindering any reduction in their numbers. It is therefore improbable that trends toward greater centralization will lead to extensive municipal and county consolidation in the near future.

CONCLUDING OBSERVATION: BECOMING MODERN BY DOING IT TRADITIONALLY

Mississippi local government is definitely changing, but it is changing "Mississippi style," according to its own rules. Mississippi local governments are striving to hold on to Jacksonian democracy by giving substantial power to "elected" versus appointed officials. Although executive authority has been centralized in the largest cities, this has led to reorganization toward the strong mayor as opposed to the council-manager form of government. In smaller cities, citizens have retained a weak mayor, strong council form of government but have made it more efficient by hiring chief administrative officers. Since CAOs derive their authority solely from the elected board of aldermen and are directly accountable to the board, this practice permits Mississippi communities to acquire administrative professionalism within the context of political accountability. The power of tradition appears stronger in county government than in Mississippi cities. County governments are only slowly moving toward operational centralization, and only a groundswell of public support for reform could speed the process.

CHAPTER TWELVE

Mississippi in the Federal Union:
An "Approach-Avoidance" Dilemma

Dale Krane

After 1950 *they [that is, the civil rights measures] were blocked in the Civil Rights Committee. Do you know why? Because of seniority I was maneuvered into chairmanship of the Civil Rights Subcommittee. Yes. . . . Eastland of Mississippi [tapping his chest] . . . became boss of the committee that had all of the civil rights bills! And they said I broke the law and so I did! You know the laws says the committee has got to meet once a week. Why, for the three years I was chairman, that committee didn't hold a meeting. I didn't permit them to meet. I had to protect the interests of the people of Mississippi. I had special pockets put in my pants and for three years I carried those bills around in my pockets everywhere I went and every one of them was defeated!*

Former senator James O. Eastland[1]

Great numbers of Mississippians receive food stamps and other forms of federal food assistance. [United States senator] Cochran has resolved his doubts on the side of the program, fighting hard to defend them against severe cuts. . . . Mississippi's poverty and dependence on federal help shape Cochran's point of view on other issues as well. He has been a strong defender of the federal rural housing program. . . . Cochran also successfully sponsored an amendment to add $30 million to the "developing institutions" program, which gives money to traditionally black colleges concentrated in Mississippi and other Southern states.

Politics in America, 1987[2]

Perhaps no other state in the Union has experienced such a range of conflict and cooperation with the national government as Mississippi. In various periods of the state's history, Mississippians have viewed Washington, D.C., as the home of the devil incarnate, the primary cause of the state's shortcomings and woes. At other times Mississippians have looked to Washington as the fount of salvation, the source of aid necessary to the state's resurrection. Because the national government–Mississippi relationship has fluctuated dramatically between periods of "massive resistance" and "massive dependence," Mississippi has experienced an ambivalent, "approach-avoidance" dilemma with respect to the national government.

This extreme variation in Mississippi's federal relations is a direct function of the state's political culture. Daniel Elazar has pointed out that different states respond to national government action in different ways and that this variation in state response can be explained, at least in part, by the variation in political culture among the fifty states.[3] Likewise, the degree of cooperation or conflict in national-state relations, according to Elazar, is a function of "overall state deviation from national patterns and norms" as well as from "national policies and interests" and of "intrastate sharing of common patterns and norms" as well as "common policies and interests."[4] That is, the probability of state-national government conflict increases as national and state norms in culture and politics diverge. Consequently one would expect state-national conflict when national policy is perceived as a threat to the people and interests that dominate a state's political system, and conversely, one would expect state-national cooperation when national policy is perceived as benefiting the state's economic and political interests.

No matter what the policy preferences of a state's citizens happen to be, American state governments function as constituent units of a larger federal union. Federalism compounds the task of governance because policy must be formulated and implemented within a framework of multiple structures and interests. Since individuals within a federal country exercise citizenship simultaneously in national and state governments, each level possesses authority relatively autonomous of the other. Unlike the "top-down" relationships in unitary nations (e.g., Britain or France), interactions between the national government and the other constituent units in a federal union are characterized by *interdependence*. Although the national government is presumed to be supreme when conflicts over national versus state prerogatives arise, political realities usually temper the national government's use of its supremacy.

The interdependence of national and state governments in the American federal union is reinforced by nonconstitutional factors. First, the nation's extensive pluralism expresses itself in the diversity of preferences and goals found among the fifty states. Second, these diverse objectives receive representation within the national government, especially in the legislative branch. Third, the policy of the national government is not so much purely "national" in character on many issues as it is a bargain among the states or geographically dispersed interests. Fourth, because United States citizens prefer not to support a large national administrative structure, implementation of "national" policy depends heavily on the actions of the autonomous state governments. Consequently, national-state interactions often become working partnerships.

Despite the power asymmetry between the national government and an individual state, control within the federal arrangement is reciprocal. The national government, for example, relies on state governments to implement national programs, but national policy goals may be distorted or even ignored by state government action. If the national government raises the cost of compliance with national policies too high (or keeps the payment for compliance too low), then one or more states may not cooperate. But raising the cost of compliance threatens the working partnership, and increasing the payments to buy compliance can break the national budget. States face a similar dilemma. States depend on the national government for additional resources, but to cooperate fully with national policy may mean sacrificing state autonomy. To resist national policy risks the loss of desirable resources, but to set the price of cooperation too high also risks the loss of the new resources or, even worse, the imposition of penalties. Five important policy areas will illustrate the influence of Mississippi's political culture on the state's interactions with the national government. Insights drawn from these cases will help identify the factors that account for the state's decision to oppose or cooperate with national policy goals.

MISSISSIPPI VERSUS THE UNITED STATES

Mississippi's "closed society" was shattered by the nation's Second Reconstruction.[5] Among the various federal civil rights initiatives, the decisions to enfranchise black citizens and to desegregate public schools posed the most direct threat to traditional southern institutions and life-styles. These two policy struggles provide a wealth of information about the conditions that provoke state-national conflict and that lead to its resolution. Though both campaigns were part of the larger crusade to achieve equal rights for black citizens, each was a separate front, with different troops pursuing radically different strategies. The dynamics underlying these policy struggles illuminate the "approach-avoidance" problem in Mississippi's resistance to new national civil rights policy goals.

School desegregation was primarily a legal assault against the dual educational system. The "war of words" waged by the NAACP Legal Defense and Education Fund in the rarefied atmosphere of the federal courts contrasted sharply with the "war of bodies" fought on the streets and in the jails of Mississippi (and other southern states) by the Council of Federated Organizations (COFO). The key decision of *Brown v. Board of Education* was a precursor to the hostility that was unfortunately unavoidable in achieving school desegregation. In the case of voting rights, the inevitable conflict preceded the formulation of national government policy. Only after the atrocities of Philadelphia, Mississippi, and Selma, Alabama, where whites were killed, did Congress act to enforce the Fifteenth Amendment.

Voting Rights

The 1965 Voting Rights Act radically shifted the burden of proof from the victims of racially discriminatory voting practices to the perpetrators of these practices and brought the discussion of these issues to the Washington, D.C., environment rather than leaving these legal issues to be resolved in local, parochial federal district courts in the South.[6] Sections 2, 3, and 4 of the act were written "to overcome the immediate dilemma of vote denial"; that is, the Voting Rights Act suspended literacy tests, registration procedures, "good moral character" tests, and "understanding" tests from being used to prevent black voter registration. Section 5 "attempted to prevent the states from passing new legislation that would abridge or dilute the voting strength of the newly registered blacks in the covered jurisdictions."[7] Any changes in state or local voting procedures or regulations after November 1, 1964, had to be approved either by the attorney general in the United States Department of Justice (DOJ) or by the United States District Court in the District of Columbia.

Justice and COFO did not wait for a court test before implementing section 4. Three days after President Johnson signed the act (August 6, 1965), federal voting examiners began registering black citizens in Mississippi. By the end of 1967, only 60 of the 245 "covered" counties in the South had been visited by federal examiners, who helped register approximately 150,000 new voters. In Mississippi federal examiners judiciously avoided certain

counties. For example, federal voting examiners never entered Sunflower County, the home of United States senator James O. Eastland,
then chairman of the Senate Judiciary Committee; ironically, Sunflower
County is also the home of Fannie Lou Hamer, the noted civil rights activist who suffered serious beatings during her attempts to register to vote.
With the election of Richard Nixon, federal examining activity prac-
tically ceased.[8] In Mississippi, "Governor Johnson, anxious about the
state's image, after the 1966 shooting of James Meredith, reluctantly provided protection by the state police" for civil rights workers registering
black citizens.[9] From 1966 to 1971 voter registration drives conducted by
COFO's member organizations raised the percentage of black Mississippians
enfranchised from 6.7 percent to 62 percent.[10] The gap between black and
white registration rates quickly narrowed to about 10 percent. In a very real
sense, implementation of section 4 eliminated the most blatant and overt
techniques of minority vote denial.

Unlike the rapid results obtained under section 4, the implementation of
section 5 has been a tedious process slowed by a number of factors. First,
DOJ's Civil Rights Division (CRD) has never been given the personnel or the
resources to become the primary enforcer of the act. Second, "section 5 requirements must be enforced in a fiscally dry environment";[11] that is, CRD
does not control any federal assistance funds (such as those available in education or housing) by which it can "purchase" section 5 compliance. Third,
although the Voting Rights Act provides for legal sanctions against state and
local officials who fail to submit electoral changes for "preclearance," DOJ
has never applied the sanctions. Fourth, the act imposes on CRD a sixty-day
time limit for reviewing of proposed electoral changes submitted by covered
jurisdictions. If the sixty-day limit is passed, the proposed change in election
rules becomes official, even if the change is discriminatory. Because of this
lack of compliance-inducing tools, since 1969 CRD has adopted an implementation strategy that "shares the responsibility" for section 5 enforcement with the very state and local officials who are the targets of the act.[12]
This combination of factors has led to DOJ's policy of bargaining with covered jurisdictions over decisions, which are made case by case rather than
according to a general principle or rule.

Several important consequences for the political success of black candidates in Mississippi follow from DOJ's willingness to rely on negotiations
with local officials as its primary strategy of section 5 enforcement. First, as
part of bargaining with local jurisdictions, CRD staffers impart substantial
advice and counsel on what minimum actions are necessary to comply with

section 5. This posture of guidance makes the submission process almost painless and makes it very easy for local attorneys to obtain DOJ approval of electoral changes.[13] Second, because CRD bargains with local officials, the attorney general sometimes approves electoral changes that do not ensure full representation of minority voters.[14] Third, because CRD shares section 5 enforcement responsibility with state and local officials, some of whom still bitterly oppose the Voting Rights Act, a significant portion of local jurisdictions seek to avoid compliance, and many are successful. Estimates put the level of noncompliance (failure even to submit a proposed electoral change for federal approval) in Mississippi at approximately 30 percent.[15]

The success achieved by section 4 in ending the terror tactics and opening the ballot box to black citizens often blinds observers to the less than full compliance with section 5. Unfortunately, efforts to dilute the impact of black registration continue. Examples of subtle attempts by state and local officials to minimize black voter strength in Mississippi can be found in the efforts to "crack" or fragment black populations among several different electoral districts, thus preventing the election of a black representative.[16] Other forms of racial gerrymandering include "packing"—concentrating black citizens into a single district to minimize the number of elected black officials—and "stacking"—assigning majority black jurisdictions to larger electoral districts that include sufficient majority white jurisdictions to eliminate the possibility that minority votes will control the outcome.[17] In addition to gerrymandering, one finds examples of techniques aimed at making it difficult for black citizens to become candidates, examples of changes in polling place location (sometimes at the last minute) designed to impede minority access to the ballot, and occasional examples of vote fraud.[18]

The weakness of section 5 enforcement can be seen in the level of black officeholding in Mississippi. In absolute terms, there are more black elected officials in Mississippi than in any other state, but their proportion (10.4 percent) in relation to the proportion of black citizens in the state's population (35.2 percent) remains distant.[19] Although section 4 of the 1965 Voting Rights Act ended the highly visible and violent means of disfranchising blacks, the less than vigorous enforcement of section 5 by the national government has not guaranteed the full representation of Mississippi's registered black voters.

School Desegregation

Efforts to eliminate "separate but equal" schools moved with the slow pace of lawsuits. In 1969 the United States Supreme Court finally declared that the clock had run out on "all deliberate speed" (*Alexander v. Holmes County, Mississippi*) and that "freedom of choice" plans only continued segregation (*Green v. School Board of New Kent County, Virginia*). These two rulings gave DOJ, the United States Office of Education, and private plaintiffs the tools to end the delaying tactic of court appeals by recalcitrant school boards. At the same time, these two cases gave the green light to the Office of Civil Rights to enforce title VI of the 1964 Civil Rights Act, which permitted the denial of federal funds to segregated educational institutions. Congressional passage in 1965 of the Elementary and Secondary Education Act (ESEA), especially title I, with its funds for educationally disadvantaged children, "provided HEW with the leverage necessary to negotiate [desegregation] plans with most Southern school districts."[20] Because the national government could withhold title I funds, school board officials in the nation's poorest state were confronted with the unpalatable choice between continued segregation with its loss of federal dollars and integration with its attendant impact on traditional life-styles.

In general, the response of Mississippi school districts to this "approach-avoidance" dilemma was determined by the nature of the local political subculture. School district response varied from continued extreme resistance to complete cooperation. Although a few school boards chose to forfeit federal funds, white flight from public schools became the more common response to school desegregation. In some counties the number of pupils attending private schools more than doubled between 1968 and 1971. Similarly, about one thousand white teachers resigned from thirty school districts. Eventually, the erosion of white support for local school taxes became the ultimate form of defiance. Not all of the extreme resistance to school integration took place in the Delta counties with majority black populations. Serious resistance to integration also occurred in communities characterized by relatively equal proportions of blacks and whites. Among jurisdictions with black populations above 40 percent, poorer, more rural communities tended to defy integration orders whereas more urban and affluent communities tended to comply.[21]

A third response to school desegregation came with the actions of many school district officials who, though personally opposed to integration, moved to obey national policy because it was the "law of the land." Although a few overwhelmingly white school districts desegregated without a court order, most school boards preferred to wait for such an order, which allowed them to pass the onus of integration to the federal government. Unlike leadership in the defiant districts, leaders in the "cooperative" districts not only saw the handwriting on the wall but also believed it was crucial to control the process of change. Public meetings bringing black and white parents together to develop plans for the assignment of pupils did much to quell rumors and build support for the new arrangements. Details such as the transference of a star football player to a new school or the procedures for selecting the next year's cheerleaders were issues that could spark a violent reaction if not handled with care. Where communities engaged in an integrated planning process, cooperation was achieved relatively smoothly.

A final response to national desegregation policy can be termed "evasion," or minimal compliance. Dual school systems were ended, but the new unified system could hardly be considered integrated. Examples of efforts to minimize the impact of integration include assigning black teachers to classrooms with only black students; retaining a white superintendent and principals; eliminating many extracurricular activities such as school clubs, proms, and yearbooks (to avoid social mixing); "ability grouping" of youngsters to ensure that only blacks from "better homes" are assigned to classrooms populated with upper- and middle-class white students; and using funds differentially among schools within the same school district. In general, rural county schools are more likely to engage in some form of evasion than the county seat and municipal schools.

Overall, school desegregation has been a remarkable success story in Mississippi. Evasion continues today, and the NAACP still files lawsuits to combat the more subtle forms of segregation, but the change from a totally segregated school system to one of the nation's most integrated was astonishingly swift. In the 1965–66 school year, fewer than 1 percent of Mississippi black students attended school with whites; by the 1972–73 school year, 91.5 percent of black students in Mississippi did so.[22] Most private schools in Mississippi are primarily fundamentalist religious schools that struggle along with very small enrollments (e.g., four hundred to five hundred students in kindergarten to twelfth grade). Few national policies that have required the total abandonment of a social institution have been implemented so thoroughly as school desegregation in Mississippi. Clearly the national government's use of both "carrot" (ESEA funds) and "stick" (legal action) were factors necessary to the success of the desegregation campaign.

MISSISSIPPI AS PART OF THE UNITED STATES

Even though residents of some Mississippi towns such as Vicksburg refused until recently to celebrate July 4 (the date Vicksburg fell to Grant's siege) as a national holiday, the state has not been constantly at war with the national government on every issue. Historically, Mississippians sent their political leaders to Washington, D.C., with two instructions: preserve the state's traditional segregated life-style and obtain funds and projects that would help improve the state's economic conditions. Over the past half century, Mississippi has benefited immensely from the influence of the state's powerful United States senators and congressmen (table 15). In addition to these committee chairmen, the Mississippi delegation as a unit has been an integral component of the southern-conservative coalition since its formation in the 1930s.

All this congressional seniority with its concomitant clout, of course, was used for many years to stymie the campaign to end segregation. The record on this issue is indisputable. At the same time, Mississippi's congressional delegation used its power to procure for the state large sums of federal aid, especially economic development and national defense projects. The scale of some projects has been enormous; for example, the $2 billion, 234-mile Tennessee-Tombigbee Waterway required removing more material than was excavated for the Panama Canal![23] Mississippi's congressional influence has also yielded some notorious cases of pure pork barrel. Senator James Eastland and Congressman Jamie Whitten for years combined forces to boost subsidies to the state's small number of very large cotton plantations, including Eastland's own estate.[24] At one time the state's United States senators and congressmen could be counted on to steadfastly oppose federal "welfare" assistance such as food stamps, Medicare, and even aid to education. However, the post-1965 tide of black voters combined with the previously unregistered low-income white "redneck" voters created a new political reality in the state that makes opposing federal assistance programs risky. In addition, the new system of caucus control in the United States House has forced some of the state's congressional Democrats to move to more moderate positions as the price of retaining their seniority and chairmanships.

Another way to illustrate the relation between Mississippi and the national government is to examine the character of federal assistance sent to the state. In 1988 Mississippi received $1.324 billion in aid from the national government, of which the principal types were public welfare (44.6 percent), highways (10.0 percent), and economic development (6.9 percent).[25] These federal funds account for about one-quarter of the total revenues for the state and its local governments (1988: 23.6 percent, rank first) and about one-third of state and local government expenditures. In 1989 Mississippi, while ranked fifty-first in per capita income (of the fifty states and the Dis-

Table 15: Selected Members of Mississippi's Congressional Delegation

Name	Formal Positions Held	Dates
Sen. Pat Harrison	President pro tempore	1938–41
Sen. James Eastland	Chairman, Judiciary Committee	1956–78
	President pro tempore	1972–78
Sen. John Stennis	Chairman, Armed Services Committee	1969–81
	Chairman, Appropriations Committee	1987–88
	President pro tempore	1987–88
Rep. Jamie Whitten	Chairman, Agriculture Subcommittee	1949–52
	Member, Appropriations Committee	1956 to date
	Chairman, Appropriations Committee	1979–to date
Rep. William Colmer	Chairman, Rules Committee	1967–73
Rep. G. V. Meredith	Chairman, Veterans' Affairs Committee	1981 to date
Rep. Trent Lott	Minority whip	1981–88

Note: Selected list of formal legislative positions held as of November 1991.

trict of Columbia), ranked seventeenth in federal spending per person ($3,740).[26] Other evidence demonstrates the benefits Mississippi garners from Washington. The state's total federal tax burden, or "the balance of payments to the federal government versus the payments received from the federal government," is quite revealing of the state's fiscal condition in the Union and of the state's political clout in Congress. For fiscal year 1984 Mississippi paid seventy-one cents for each dollar received from Washington.[27] Simply put, Mississippians obtain the benefits of national government financed programs at a 30 percent discount.

Two other features of federal aid—the purpose of the aid and the type of recipient—reveal important policy outcomes of national government assistance to Mississippi. A standard classification of aid programs by purpose distinguishes between "developmental" aid, intended to foster economic growth, and "redistributive" aid, designed to transfer resources to make opportunities available to certain categories of persons (e.g., children, the elderly, the handicapped, the illiterate). Typically, both types of programs can be targeted either to individual recipients or to jurisdictions (e.g., social security is paid to individuals, but Community Development Block Grants are awarded to cities and counties). Since 1945 redistributive aid to Mississippi as a proportion of total federal assistance (69 percent) has exceeded developmental aid (31 percent) two to one. By contrast, there is an almost even split between individuals and jurisdictions as recipients.

Despite the political rhetoric in opposition to welfare programs often heard from Mississippi's congressional delegation, the state has benefited from federal funds for education, health, housing, and welfare. No doubt some of these funds flow to Mississippi because the formulas established by Congress to distribute federal aid take into account a state's level of poverty. But one must also realize that members of Congress need to be reelected, and consequently a number of aid programs are designed so that Congress can claim credit for them. It is usually easier to claim credit for a project granted to a local jurisdiction (e.g., title I money for educationally disadvantaged children goes to school districts) than to claim credit for payments made to a class of individuals (e.g., Aid to Families with Dependent Children [AFDC] goes to the parent/guardian), especially individuals who might not be held in the highest esteem by the influential contributors to congressional campaigns. As a result, a significant proportion of aid, even redistributive aid, comes to Mississippi via jurisdictions. This practice allows the state's congressional delegation to have the best of both worlds: conservative pronouncements against "welfare" and political credit for helping distressed communities gain federal dollars.

Governor's Office of Federal-State Programs

The principal liaison between Mississippi and Washington, D.C., is the Governor's Office of Federal-State programs (FSP). In 1968 Governor John Bell Williams, the last of the Old Guard, white supremacist governors, issued an executive order establishing the position of coordinator of federal-state programs. Surprisingly, Governor Williams appointed as coordinator David Bowen, a young, liberal (by Mississippi standards) former college professor who had experience in Washington with the United States Chamber of Commerce. The coordinator was responsible for supervising federal grants, which at that time were scattered among fifteen state agencies. In effect, the coordinator's office became the clearinghouse that gave the governor control over federal assistance funds. Governor Williams took little interest in the potential power available in the newly established office. However, Bowen understood the attraction federal grants had for economically depressed Mississippi communities, and he parlayed his position into a successful campaign for the United States House of Representatives in 1972.

Others were also quick to learn about the political utility of federal grants. Governor Cliff Finch (1976–80), the second governor following John Bell Williams, openly admitted his use of the governor's "sign off" authority to leverage votes in the state legislature.[28] By 1980, authority over the scattered federal grants was fully consolidated into an expanded governor's office, thus enhancing the political and managerial power of the state's chief executives.

Reorganization of the Governor's Office of Federal-State Programs during the tenure of Governor William Winter (1980–84) produced a major shift in the state's management of federal funds. Instead of fifteen agencies operating their own units for the planning, auditing, and administration of federal grants, these functions were concentrated in a single agency under a director who reported to the governor. FSP's structure included four program departments and three administrative support departments. Not only did the FSP's organization reduce duplication of grant-related activity, the new arrangement also created a centralized system of fiscal control that performed all accounting and reporting functions for federal grants. This increased administrative capacity was accompanied by the creation of a Governor's Policy Council, composed of state legislators, directors of selected state agencies, and citizens appointed by the governor.

The FSP's importance flows from its role as a clearinghouse for the acquisition and management of federal grants. Besides financial control over grants, FSP subunits, staffed by highly trained professionals, perform a variety of grant-related tasks such as data processing, legal counseling, policy analysis, program evaluation, and technical assistance to local jurisdictions and other grant recipients. These services not only fulfill the state's administrative obligations to the national government but also ensure that state agencies and local communities that have received grants will use the funds appropriately. In addition, FSP works directly with the state's ten planning and development districts to coordinate the distribution of federal funds in accord with the state's comprehensive plan for economic development.

The transformation of the coordinator's position into a full-fledged agency reflected Governor Winter's desire to improve the management capacity of state government. At the same time, the consolidation of federal grant administration into the governor's office yielded several political benefits for the incumbent. First, the 1980 statute, by centralizing grant management in an office directly under the governor, reduced the influence of individual state agencies and the state legislature over the operation of federal assistance programs in Mississippi. Second, the governor and not the legislature became the decision point for the statewide distribution of federal funds. As a result, federal grants serve as a source of discretionary dollars that the governor can allocate in ways beneficial to the governor's policy and political agendas. In recognition of the political dimensions of FSP, Governor Winter appointed the first woman to head the office and Governor Allain appointed the first black woman to serve as director.

The importance of the Governor's Office of Federal-State Programs was recognized by the 1989 Executive Reorganization Act, which moved FSP's functions into the new Department of Finance and Administration. The jobs usually performed by FSP will now be the responsibility of various divisions within this new department. The governor should retain much of his influence over federal grants, since the executive director heading the Finance and Administration Department is appointed by the governor (with senate consent) and serves at the governor's pleasure.

Community Development Block Grants

An important federal source of discretionary money for Mississippi localities is the Community Development Block Grant (CDBG) program. Congress established the CDBG program in 1974 to provide local jurisdictions more choice and flexibility in reversing the processes of neighborhood decay than was allowed by the old urban renewal program. Approximately 70 percent of CDBG funds are designated automatically for urban counties and metropolitan areas, which in Mississippi include Jackson, Biloxi, Gulfport, Moss Point, and Pascagoula.[29] The state's remaining cities and its eighty-two counties are required to file an application to compete for the remaining 30 percent of funds under the Small Cities component of the CDBG program.

From 1975 to 1981 the United States Department of Housing and Urban Development (HUD) administered this Small Cities component and used its discretionary authority to promote housing rehabilitation. HUD preferred to make a relatively small number of awards in large dollar amounts in order to force localities to continue the old urban renewal strategy of comprehensive neighborhood revitalization (table 16). One serious consequence of HUD's administration in Mississippi was that the smallest communities (under 5,000)—remember, in Mississippi this is the typical community size—where "need" is often the most acute, lost out in the award competition. The larger communities (above 5,000) often could afford to hire a grants administrator to write applications for CDBG funds or possessed the management capacity to operate the comprehensive slum removal projects favored by HUD.[30]

Table 16: Small Cities Community Development Block Grant Awards in Mississippi, 1975–1988

Year	Total Awarded[a]	Number of Awards[b]	Average Award
HUD administration			
1975	$ 9,758,968	33	$295,726
1976	12,670,075	33	383,942
1977	15,744,078	43	366,141
1978	20,310,078	38	534,476
1979	26,104,000	49	532,735
1980	30,875,000	47	656,915
1981	30,183,000	43	720,875
1975–81 average		41	498,687
State administration			
1982	33,204,641	97	342,316
1983	29,031,749	101	287,443
1984	30,218,520	114	265,075
1985	28,400,517	84	338,101
1986	23,824,992	74	321,959
1987	26,458,231	88	300,662
1988	26,141,315	66	396,081
1982–88 average		89	321,662

Sources: Edward T. Jennings, Jr., Dale Krane, Alex N. Pattakos, and B. J. Reed, eds., *From Nation to States: The Small Cities Community Development Block Grant Program*, "The Mississippi Experience," 113 (Albany, N.Y.: State University of New York Press, 1986); "*Publius, the Journal of Federalism* 17, no.4 (Fall 1987): 89; and the Governor's Office of Federal-State Programs, State of Mississippi.

[a]Dollars actually expended or encumbered during fiscal year.

[b]Number of awards made during fiscal year.

HUD's control over the Small Cities CDBG funds was transferred to state governments in 1982 as part of President Reagan's "New Federalism" initiatives. State officials, not federal personnel, were permitted to devise their own procedures for awarding federal dollars to community development projects in their respective states. This intergovernmental transfer of the Small Cities CDBG program was based on the belief that state governments understood and could better serve the needs of their local communities than could the national government.[31] Responsibility for administration of the

Small Cities program in Mississippi was assigned to the Governor's Office of Federal-State Programs by Governor Winter.

Mississippi officials avoided the problems experienced by other states. A Policy Advisory Committee, composed of representatives of local governments and groups benefiting directly from urban renewal programs, developed a set of program goals and specific policies for the program. This committee served to minimize misunderstandings between state and local officials over the nature of the new state-administered program. A Technical Advisory Committee, composed primarily of professional staff from the FSP, prepared a program design, an application procedure, and a process to determine which jurisdictions would receive CDBG grants.[32] Applications for funding are rated in terms of the quality of the proposed development activities (in accordance with national and state program goals) and the management capacity of the local jurisdiction.[33] This relatively objective and rational decision process was designed "to take the politics out of the award process." As Ann Cook, executive director of FSP, explained, "[because] our applicants want a fair shake, the perception of mistreatment needs to be eliminated."[34]

The most important feature of the state-administered program is the discretion state officials are allowed in making awards to local communities. Instead of continuing the federal practice of steering money toward housing rehabilitation, Mississippi officials permit local communities to apply for assistance in any of four categories: housing rehabilitation, economic development, public works, and urgent or emergency needs. Freed from HUD's preferences, local officials in Mississippi have overwhelmingly applied for Small Cities funds in support of public works or economic development projects. For the first four years of state administration, 60 percent of the awards were made for the improvement of public infrastructure facilities such as water and sewer systems, and only 5 percent were for housing projects. Economic development projects such as the construction or renovation of an industrial or commercial facility accounted for 15 percent of the 1982–85 awards, and almost 13 percent of the awards were in support of urgent needs or emergency relief projects such as cleanup after a tornado.[35]

The pattern of awards made by the governor's office is significantly different from the previous pattern of awards made by HUD (table 16). FSP officials more than doubled the number of annual awards, while at the same time reducing the dollar amount of each award. Second, approximately three-fifths of the awards have been made to the smallest communities (under 5,000). This strategy of more numerous but smaller grants permitted the governor's office to engage in a "share the wealth" philosophy that satisfies as large a number of jurisdictions as is feasible, given the state's allocation of national money. The strategy also enhances the governor's influence with localities and with the state legislature.[36]

The federal government has required that CDBG funds be used in projects that benefit "principally persons of low and moderate income" (LMI).[37] Under HUD administration of the program, no more than 25 percent of the total households in the community benefited by the grant could exceed the LMI threshold. When the Small Cities program was transferred to state governments in 1982, recipient groups feared that states like Mississippi with histories of neglect for low- and moderate-income persons would use their new discretionary authority to channel funds away from indigent populations and thus subvert national goals. However, Mississippi's pattern of CDBG awards compares favorably with that of other states. During the first four years of state control, the average proportion of LMI beneficiaries in Mississippi was 83 percent, which exceeds HUD's old "75–25" rule.[38] This outcome reflects the general poverty of Mississippi localities rather than a deliberate effort on the part of FSP officials to target CDBG money to particularly poverty-stricken jurisdictions. In such a poor state, almost any award system would likely distribute money so as to benefit a large percentage of low- and moderate-income persons, black and white.

The Small Cities CDBG program operated by the Governor's Office of Federal-State Programs reveals much about Mississippi's relationship with the national government. First, without the funds made available to the state, many Mississippi localities would have to forgo important physical infrastructure facilities, commercial and industrial projects, and housing renovation. That is, the quality of life would be lower, or local communities would have to raise even more revenue from their own sources. Second, even though modernization of state government has come late to Mississippi, state officials have demonstrated that they are capable of managing a major assistance program. As one of the professionals in FSP vehemently stated (a year after the Small Cities transfer was completed): "They [the HUD officials] didn't think we could do it [operate the CDBG program] and we did it!"[39] Finally, the new political realities of the state reinforce the national policy goal of assistance to low- and moderate-income persons. The electoral influence of blacks can be seen not just in Governor Allain's appointment of a black woman to direct FSP, but also in the significant increase in the number of CDBG awards to the smallest cities, many of which are majority black municipalities.[40]

Agricultural and Rural Development Pork Barrel

Using key committee assignments, members of Mississippi's congressional delegation have been very adroit at acquiring federal funds that benefit the state's agricultural industry and rural residents. In the 1980s their pragmatic concern with bringing home the federal bacon often took priority over a conservative philosophy of reducing the role of the federal government in society and even led to instances of friction with the Reagan administration. As chairman of the Agriculture Subcommittee of the House Appropriations Committee since 1949 and current chairman of the full committee, Congressman Jamie Whitten has earned the title "permanent secretary of agriculture." Examples of his delivery of federal pork barrel funds to Mississippi have included supplemental appropriations bills in 1983 for $100 million to bail out cotton farmers across the nation and $33 million to widen a highway in north Mississippi. In 1985 Whitten was successful in exempting flood control projects on the Mississippi River from new federal cost-sharing requirements (pushed by the Reagan administration) that demanded more local government support for such projects. He helped save Mississippi governments money by beating back an effort on the House floor by a Pennsylvania congressman to eliminate this exemption.[41]

Whitten has employed a number of techniques to protect federal programs that benefit rural Mississippi. During the budget-cutting years of the Reagan administration, his committee would typically exceed administration requests for programs benefiting rural communities, such as rural electrification, soil conservation, rural housing, and water purification, but then would appear to save money by funding popular crop price support programs and food stamps for only part of the year. Since the food stamp and price support programs had already been promised to beneficiaries and were authorized by law, Congress would feel compelled to pass supplemental appropriations later in the year. Whitten's committee therefore clashed with Reagan's budget director, David Stockman, who accused the committee of "budget-busting" and "scorekeeping gimmicks."[42]

The need to provide "emergency" supplemental appropriations for the federal crop price support system, administered by the Commodity Credit Corporation (CCC), gives Whitten "tremendous power." Not only is this program critically important to farm-state congressmen, but supplemental appropriation bills for the CCC have often served as vehicles for unrelated programs that "could not muster a majority of votes on their own." Such unrelated programs have included controversial measures and pet projects of urban as well as rural congressmen. Whitten has successfully fought efforts to provide the CCC "permanent, indefinite" appropriations, which would eliminate the need for these supplemental appropriation bills. Whitten was also successful in winning a provision that protected the CCC by specifically exempting it from automatic budget cuts triggered by the Gramm-Rudman Act. (Under Gramm-Rudman, across-the-board cuts in most federal programs are required when Congress and the president are unable to bring the budget deficit below a required level designed to provide a balanced budget by 1993.)[43]

Whitten also exercises influence as a frequent member of conference committees on agriculture appropriations bills, which iron out differences between the bills passed by the House and the Senate. In 1989 Whitten successfully stripped a senator's pet project from the conference committee agreement. The project, a $1.1 million grant for a private company in Arkansas to provide information to farmers about how to reduce their use of chemicals on crops, was backed by Senator Dale Bumpers of Arkansas. To mollify the senator, Senate Appropriations Committee chairman Robert Byrd promised to find the money in a different appropriations bill. This effort was also blocked, since another House appropriations subcommittee chairman refused to support it. The moral—it is important for members of Congress to gain the approval of the "permanent secretary of agriculture" for their proposals.[44]

The most visible symbol of federal pork barrel spending benefiting Mississippi is the $2 billion Tenn-Tom waterway. As a ranking Democrat and eventually chairman of the Senate Appropriations Committee, former Mississippi senator John Stennis had fought for this project for decades. It was publicly defended as a needed vehicle for barge traffic to transport coal to southern utilities and to foreign countries, and many Mississippians envisioned it as a boon to economic development in rural northeast Mississippi. In the 1980s Stennis led the project's southern supporters in turning back efforts by environmentalists, budget-conscious senators, and the railroad industry (who wanted to avoid competition in transporting bulk cargo) to kill the Tenn-Tom. In a critical appropriations battle in 1981, for example, Stennis patrolled the lobbies off the Senate floor and cornered undecided senators, seeking their support. He even reserved a room near the Senate floor to show senators a short film on the merits of the Tenn-Tom. Meanwhile, Tenn-Tom supporters such as Senator Howell Heflin of Alabama privately played on members' affection for Stennis, confiding that the project would help his reelection chances.[45]

The protection of federal programs oriented toward rural Mississippi has been a bipartisan effort. As chairman of a Senate agriculture subcommittee and of the appropriations subcommittee on agriculture, Republican Thad Cochran in 1982 successfully turned back Reagan administration efforts to slash funding for rural housing assistance. He argued that administration efforts to raise interest rates on rural housing loans to the market rate would make it more difficult for people to afford homes and could result in widespread defaults. He also helped kill the effort to lump rural housing aid into a block grant to be administered by the states however they wished, arguing that the existing system administered by the Farmers Home Administration was working well.[46]

In 1986 Cochran was instrumental in protecting large farmers in Mississippi. A growing number of fiscal conservatives and urban liberals were concerned about large landowning cotton and rice farmers who were individually receiving million-dollar price support payments. Efforts to cap payments to individual farmers at $250,000 narrowly failed in the Senate Agriculture subcommittee chaired by Cochran after the Mississippi senator produced seven proxy votes against the limitation. In a conference committee called after the House passed the payments cap, Cochran stalled the meeting, forcing cap supporters to seek another vote on this issue on the floor of each chamber. The measure finally passed the Senate as well as the House after Cochran admitted that the limits were ineffective because of various loopholes in the bill. In reference to the bill's opponents, cap proponent Congressman Silvio Conte from Massachusetts concluded, "I think they got off pretty damn easy."[47]

Successfully bringing home federal pork barrel funds has been instrumental in the 1988 reelection of the first black congressman from Mississippi since Reconstruction, Mike Espy, who represents the rural Delta district. Espy has promoted the Delta catfish-raising industry by establishing National Catfish Day and persuading the Defense Department to increase its purchase of catfish. He also helped establish the Lower Mississippi River Delta Development Commission, a committee to study the problems of the Mississippi River area, which could lead to federal support comparable to that provided by the Appalachian Regional Commission. Espy has also helped deliver a federal loan for an electronics company that brought new jobs to Yazoo City and federal funds for an extension of the Greenwood–Leflore County airport runway. By early 1988, 30 percent of Espy's campaign contributions were coming from white Delta farmers. On Labor Day the second cousin of one-time segregationist former senator James Eastland even hosted a gathering in honor of Espy at the Eastland family's plantation home.[48]

Because of their mutual dependence, both parties to the federal arrangement are trapped in an approach-avoidance dilemma. Consequently, ambivalence (the mixture of positive and negative feelings in approach-avoidance decision situations) is the central characteristic of many national-state government interactions. Variation in state political cultures creates this federalism quandary, but importantly, political culture also influences its resolution. As Jeffrey Pressman reminds us, "Policy outcomes [in the federal union] reflect both federal design and local political realities."[49]

When faced with multiple national policy demands, states must make choices between cooperation and opposition. The choices will be determined, according to Elazar, by the state's political culture. The reaction of a particular group (e.g., upper-class whites) to a national policy goal (e.g., school desegregation) will be a function of the group's interests. Recall that in Mississippi race and class operate as two distinct and powerful components of the state's political culture. One can deduce that the greater the perceived threat to class or race-based interests posed by national policy, the higher the probability of resistance.

Mississippi's white elites have cooperated with national policies such as farm supports and economic development programs because these types of subsidies pose little if any threat to traditional black-white race relations. Farm subsidies benefit the large producers, and development projects boost the local economy and provide employment, thus reducing the pressure for progressive state taxes to support the underclass. By contrast, school desegregation and the enfranchisement of black citizens provoked massive resistance by white elites (and nonelites) because the two national policy goals directly threatened the traditional social order. Unfortunately, violence was used to oppose both national policies. However, the degree of resistance varied in intensity and longevity for these policies. Schools were eventually desegregated with fewer violent incidents than were associated with voter registration.[50] In 1964 some Mississippi schools were desegregated peacefully, but in that year very few blacks were registered, and force against blacks who tried to register to vote was vicious and widespread. This difference in level of resistance can be attributed to the different impact the two national policies had on the state's upper class. Registration of blacks posed a direct threat to white political control of state and local government, whereas school desegregation did not pose a direct threat to affluent whites, since many had always sent their children to private schools.

The cost of compliance versus noncompliance with a national policy must also be considered in the relationship between Mississippians and the national government. Because agricultural subsidies are outright payments and the "matching" requirements associated with developmental aid allow economically strapped communities to achieve growth (e.g., a new industrial park) at a discount price, cooperation is in effect "purchased" by the national government. But notice that the implementation of school desegregation also included money by which the national government could "purchase" compliance. The "carrot" offered to local school districts was the title I ESEA money targeted to supplement local funds for the education of "educationally disadvantaged" children (many of whom were black). On the other hand, Congress did not include funds to "purchase" compliance with the Voting Rights Act. The results are clearly different. By 1973 approximately 93 percent of all Mississippi schoolchildren attended integrated public schools, but in 1985 almost 30 percent of the state's localities remained in violation of section 5 of the Voting Rights Act.

Interaction between the political cultures of Mississippi and of the nation determines to a great extent the degree of joint action or inaction in various policy areas. Without sensitivity to this clash of political cultures, one misses important dynamics that shape the traditionalism-modernity struggle in Mississippi politics as well as the state's willingness to cooperate in the pursuit of national policy goals.

CHAPTER THIRTEEN

Tradition versus Modernity in Mississippi Politics

Stephen D. Shaffer and Dale Krane

The catharsis Mississippi underwent in the 1960s released the state psychologically. After his election in 1971, Governor William Waller adopted as an almost formal state slogan the phrase, "Mississippi— the State of Change." The transformation in Mississippi in recent years has been more swift than in any other state.

Jack Bass and Walter DeVries, 1977[1]

I believe that despite the terrible racist image Mississippi has had in the past, despite her historic reputation for political demagoguery, despite racial violence and especially lynching, despite all the statistics about being on the bottom, Mississippi, and especially urban Mississippi, offers a better life for most black people than any other state in which I have lived or visited.

Margaret Walker, (1986)[2]

In the past few decades the pace of change in Mississippi has been exhilarating. The closed, traditionalistic society with its benighted past has given way, in many instances, to a more modern, open, and pluralistic society. Historically governed by a political elite that disfranchised most blacks and some whites, Mississippi today possesses an integrated political system with a level of public participation in politics that compares favorably with that in the rest of the nation. Similarly, the century-old domination by a lily-white Democratic party has been replaced by a more competitive two-party system with an integrated Democratic party led by the only black state party chairman in the nation. Mississippi Democrats increasingly face strong challenges by a well-funded Republican party that has captured both of the state's United States Senate seats and carried the state in the past three presidential elections. Traditionally reluctant to spend government money to solve social problems, Mississippi led the nation in 1982 with its Education Reform Act and continues to reform government and education. What makes these changes so remarkable are the obstacles that had to be overcome. Perhaps nowhere else in America did the forces for progress so directly confront the defenders of entrenched custom and history. Understanding how this transformation has proceeded reveals much about the political dynamics that have created a "New Mississippi."

ESCAPING THE POLITICS OF FRUSTRATION

> With its predominantly agricultural economy, tremendous distances separate the planter and the tenant to form the base for a lively political conflict. Mississippi politics in the end reduces itself to a politics of frustration. . . .
>
> Mississippi politics is a politics of frustration not only because of the race question; its politics distills down to oratory also because the state is miserably poor. The gap between the rich and the poor is wide, but as a whole the state is so poor that a welfare politics can only become a politics of fulmination and little more.[3]

When Key painted this classic picture of Mississippi politics, the traditional, closed society was at its zenith. For example, white ladies, even of modest means, could hire a black housemaid for a dollar a day and lunch. The civil rights movement of the 1950s and 1960s posed a major challenge to the state's traditionalistic society. Federal institutions seized the initiative in promoting racial equality through the 1964 Civil Rights Act, the 1965 Voting Rights Act, title I of the 1965 Elementary and Secondary Education Act, and the Supreme Court decisions of *Brown, Alexander,* and *Green.* Defenders of the old order organized themselves to battle changes in the state's segregated political and social systems. Some even resorted to violence against blacks who sought to exercise their civil rights. In the 1960s white Mississippians refused to support Democratic presidential candidates who were civil rights advocates, and they elected governors who promised to maintain the traditional social structure. The refusal of white Democrats to fully integrate their party led to the formation of a black-dominated Democratic party faction,

Table 17: Time Line of Political Events in Mississippi

Year	Traditionalistic Events	Modernization Events
1954	Brown decision resisted	
1955	Budget Commission formed	
1957		AFL–CIO formed
1960	Independent Presidential electors win	
1962	Ole Miss riot	
1963	Evers assassinated	MSU backs racial moderation
1964	Freedom Summer resisted Blacks terrorized Goldwater supported	Civil Rights Act Freedom Democrats formed
1965		Business urges race moderation Voting Rights Act
1967		First black legislator elected
1968	Segregationist Williams governor Loyalists resisted by regular Democrats Wallace carries state	First Federal-state programs coor- dinator appointed
1969		Immediate desegregation ordered ACLU organized
1972		Common Cause organized Republican president wins state Two Republican congressmen win
1975		Some judicial reforms
1976		MAE formed Democratic party unified Strong executive cities permitted
1978		Republican senator elected
1979	Tax cut	Judicial Performance Committee
1980		Winter becomes Governor
1981		Judicial fee system outlawed
1982		Teacher demonstration Mississippi First formed Lay board of education estab- lished Education Reform Act Income tax increases First woman supreme court judge

Table 17: Time Line of Political Events in Mississippi (continued)

Year	Traditionalistic Events	Modernization Events
1983		Separation of powers decision
1984		Legislators removed from executive bodies
		Fiscal Management Board established
1985		First black supreme court judge
1986	Spending cuts	Black congressman Espy elected
	Transportation department proposal	
	dies	Gubernatorial succession
		Special fund reform begins
1987		House reform, Speaker revolt
		Highway bill passes
		Black Democratic state party chairman
1988	Constitutional convention issue dies	
	in legislature	Mabus becomes governor
		Significant education spending increase
		Unit system referendum
1989		Judicial redistricting reform
		Attorney general ends state resistance to civil rights lawsuits
		Robert Walker elected mayor of Vicksburg
		Education Equity Funding Act
1990		Education Reform 2 enacted but unfunded
1991	Higher education funding cut	

which was recognized by national Democratic conventions and permitted to vote instead of the regular Democrats (table 17).

This accelerating series of events undercut the pillars of Mississippi's traditional life-style. An increasing number of Mississippians recognized the futility of continued resistance and counseled racial tolerance. A number of candidates attempted with some success to build "redneck-blackneck" coalitions by making economic appeals to working-class whites and blacks. By the 1970s governors were actively pursuing a united, biracial Democratic party. As desegregation efforts succeeded in encouraging blacks to become more politically active, blacks were increasingly elected to public office. The more liberal attitudes of blacks led most into the Democratic party, the more liberal party nationally, so the state Democratic party became a less conservative organization. Black influence in the state Democratic party grew in the 1980s through proportionate black representation in the party organization, the nomination and election of Mike Espy, the only black congressman in the nation from a rural district, and the selection of the only black state party chairman in the nation, Ed Cole.

The expanding pluralism of Mississippi's society, fueled by demographic and economic changes, began to emerge from the shadow of race conflict. Television transmitted national values and attitudes into homes across the state. Younger Mississippians, raised in an integrated society and less tied to tradition, became an important element of change. Political contests often became battles across generations. Many well-educated professionals employed in various industries moved to Mississippi and settled in urban areas. Many of them initiated or joined interest groups seeking to change the status quo, such as the AFL-CIO, the ACLU, Common Cause, and the Mississippi Association of Educators (MAE). Business and professional groups began to challenge the public philosophy of the Old Guard that opposed any change.

As the "Americanization" of the Magnolia State proceeded, many Mississippians became distressed because their state ranked last (or nearly last) on most indicators of a good quality of life, and they began to back pro-change candidates and propositions. The 1980s therefore saw a flurry of reforms in the state's institutions and public policies (table 17). Legislative power was weakened as legislators were removed from executive branch boards and commissions, and the governor's power was strengthened by measures such as gubernatorial succession. Progressive legislators curbed the power of the Speaker of the house and enacted democratic reforms that gave more power to the entire membership. Voters elected modernizing governors (e.g., Winter and Mabus) who promoted political reforms such as the unit system and increased funding for educational improvements. By the late 1980s, the forces of traditionalism found themselves on the defensive on more and more issues. Although they suffered defeats on a number of fronts, the Old Guard continued to oppose the passage of other progressive measures.

But do all these events and changes mean that Mississippi has "escaped" from its previous "politics of frustration"? Key tied Mississippi's political features to the state's agricultural system, its race relations, its poverty, and its rurality. The time line of history has created new conditions that have undermined the traditionalistic society. Certainly a new economy and a new pattern of race relations have emerged since Key wrote his classic book. But, poverty and rurality have not disappeared in Mississippi. Recent reforms in government and politics lead many observers to conclude with some justification that Mississippi has shed its old ways, while others are not so optimistic. Measuring the degree of change is important, yet understanding the dynamics driving change is even more important. That is, if a process has been set in motion that permits Mississippi to "escape" from the "frustrating" elements of its past that have shackled the state's progress, then it becomes crucial to describe how this process of change functions. By gaining a deeper understanding of the state's transformation, we can more accurately determine the possibilities for leaving behind the "frustrations" of the traditionalistic society.

THE SEQUENCE OF CHANGE

Politics, we must always remember, is a supremely human activity. Changes in a state's culture, demography, economy, and society affect politics only as these changes alter the political behavior of citizens. The human element is therefore the primary factor in understanding the emergence of a "new Mississippi." Average citizens in Mississippi have often been ahead of their public officials in supporting progressive policies. For example, opinion polls in 1981 demonstrated strong public support for educational reforms, which were finally enacted in a 1982 special legislative session. Citizens also supported gubernatorial succession before the legislature finally permitted a public referendum on this issue. Figure 9 identifies the critical factors fostering modernization in Mississippi and shows how they have operated to shape political change in the state.

Until the Great Depression, the state's elites had adhered to a firm stance against any alterations in their plantation economy and agrarian traditions.[4] The Depression's devastation of the state's agricultural economy initiated the modern era of change in Mississippi, as Delta planters were forced to "balance agriculture with industry" (BAWI). This policy innovation set in motion a series of events that contributed to more change, some of it unforeseen and unintended. The growth of manufacturing led to the rise of commercial and industrial leaders whose interests competed with those of the planters. The new industrial sector also gave birth to organized labor in the state. Likewise, BAWI attracted newcomers to the state. After World War II, the mechanization of cotton farming ended sharecropping and accelerated

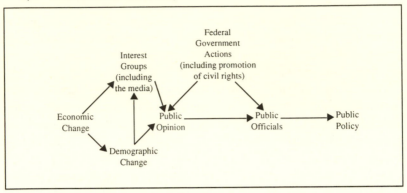

Figure 9. Sequence of change in Mississippi.

the movement of blacks into the state's urban areas (or out of the state). The Sunbelt diversification of Mississippi's economy eventually produced a highly pluralized set of pressure groups that greatly expanded the different interests and opinions expressed within the political arena.

In the 1950s some argued that the human heart—people's attitudes, beliefs, and perceptions—could not be moved by governmental decree, and that racial "brotherhood by bayonet" was therefore unwise. But in reality federal initiatives such as school desegregation and the protection of civil rights and voting rights led to a near revolutionary transformation of public opinion in southern society. Before the Voting Rights Act, public officials and political commentators ignored the attitudes of blacks when discussing public opinion in the South, since the electorate was overwhelmingly white and frequently supported segregationist candidates. The enfranchisement of blacks produced a tidal wave of voters who possessed relatively liberal views and changed the currents of public opinion within the state's electorate. This flood of new voters resulted in the election of more black public officials in Mississippi than in any other state. Indeed, a black candidate, Jesse Jackson, carried Mississippi's 1988 Democratic presidential primary.

The increased number of legislators sympathetic to progressive ideas—blacks, progressive whites, and white legislators from districts with a large number of blacks—has led to the adoption of more progressive public policies. Demographic changes have also converted public opinion in the state from a homogeneous mind-set on segregation to a heterogenous and competitive marketplace of ideas. Young people, who have been raised in an integrated, more tolerant society and who have been bombarded by the cacophony of values and voices transmitted by television, function as powerful agents of change. Young adults are much more supportive of equal rights for historically disadvantaged groups than the older generation. College-educated professionals often take the lead in pushing for reforms that end traditional practices.

The emergence of progressive interest groups constitutes another important step in the development of a more pluralistic and modern society. The NAACP has worked to elect more blacks to office by challenging racial gerrymandering and other legal barriers to the full participation of black voters. The MAE has been very successful at supporting pro-education legislative and gubernatorial candidates such as Governor Mabus and has defied the traditionalistic culture entailing deference to legislators by staging public demonstrations. A victory by the "old guard" in the 1982 legislative session when education reform suffered a temporary setback led to the formation of Mississippi First, which helped to pass the Education Reform Act and defeat some legislative opponents at the polls. Although traditional forces remain strong in the state, Mississippi today more closely parallels the national norm, in which a multitude of groups and organizations mobilize members and money to influence elections and legislative outcomes.

Many of the state's interest groups use sophisticated methods for communicating their message via newspapers, radio, and television. The media in Mississippi play at least four important roles in the process of change. First, they serve as channels by which public officials, candidates for office, and various interest groups communicate with each other and with the larger public. Second, the media, especially the larger newspapers, educate the public about conditions within the state. Perhaps the best example can be found in the Jackson *Clarion-Ledger*'s series of articles on Mississippi public schools that won the 1983 Pulitzer Prize for Distinguished Public Service.[5] Third, editorialists in the press and on the air act as referees of the electoral process when they evaluate and judge the quality of a candidate and the ethics of a candidate's actions. Fourth, members of the press often become participants in the political process when they act as consultants to public officials or as managers of candidates.[6] Taken together, these four roles provide the media with enormous power to shape the course of politics. It is no coincidence that a change in ownership of the state capital's two newspapers is associated with the growing clout of progressive political forces.[7]

Public opinion drives public policy because the prolonged struggle between the emerging progressive forces and the entrenched traditionalistic political culture turns on winning the minds and hearts of the state's citizens. As the electorate's political attitudes became more progressive in the 1970s, voters began to elect pro-change candidates to public office. Governors Winter and Mabus, for example, were leaders in the education and political reform movements, and an increasing number of legislators and judges share these reformist values. Since public policy is made by elected officials in our democracy, the influx of more progressive public officials has led to more progressive public policies and institutional reforms.

Policy change comes about because of the interrelationships among a number of forces—the economy, demographic changes, national government actions, interest groups, the media, public opinion, and public officials. It is also important to observe that changes occurring in various sectors of the economy and in social relationships affect public policy through the actions of individuals, especially as public opinion changes over time. The central role that public officials play in shaping public policy leads us to trace the evolution of the selection of elected officials in Mississippi.

THE SHIFTING POLITICAL COALITIONS IN MISSISSIPPI

Electoral competition in the early decades of this century was characterized by battles between affluent white planters in the Delta and poor "peckerwoods" farmers in the Hills. These feuds did not undercut the *traditionalistic political culture,* because both sides concurred in the exclusion of blacks from the political process, and this class-based competition occurred within only one political party—the Democratic party—which in the South was the defender of the old social order. The Delta aristocrats adhered to a conservative stance in defense of their economic and social privileges, while the lower income Hill whites were neopopulist and more liberal in seeking to raise the quality of their life through government action (fig. 10). There were also differences in style, as Delta aristocrats were more paternalistic toward blacks and unwilling to resort to the racist rhetoric that neopopulist candidates from the Hills often employed.

The conversion of black political aspirations into action marked the beginning of the end for the old Hills versus Delta distinction that characterized the state's traditionalistic society. During the height of the civil rights struggles, the Democratic party was split into two factions: the "regulars," traditional white conservatives opposed to integration; and the "loyalists," blacks and pro-integration whites such as organized labor and some religious groups. With the passage of the 1965 Voting Rights Act, not only did blacks register to vote, but so did many less affluent, "redneck" whites (who were prodded to register by conservative whites as a means of maintaining a white

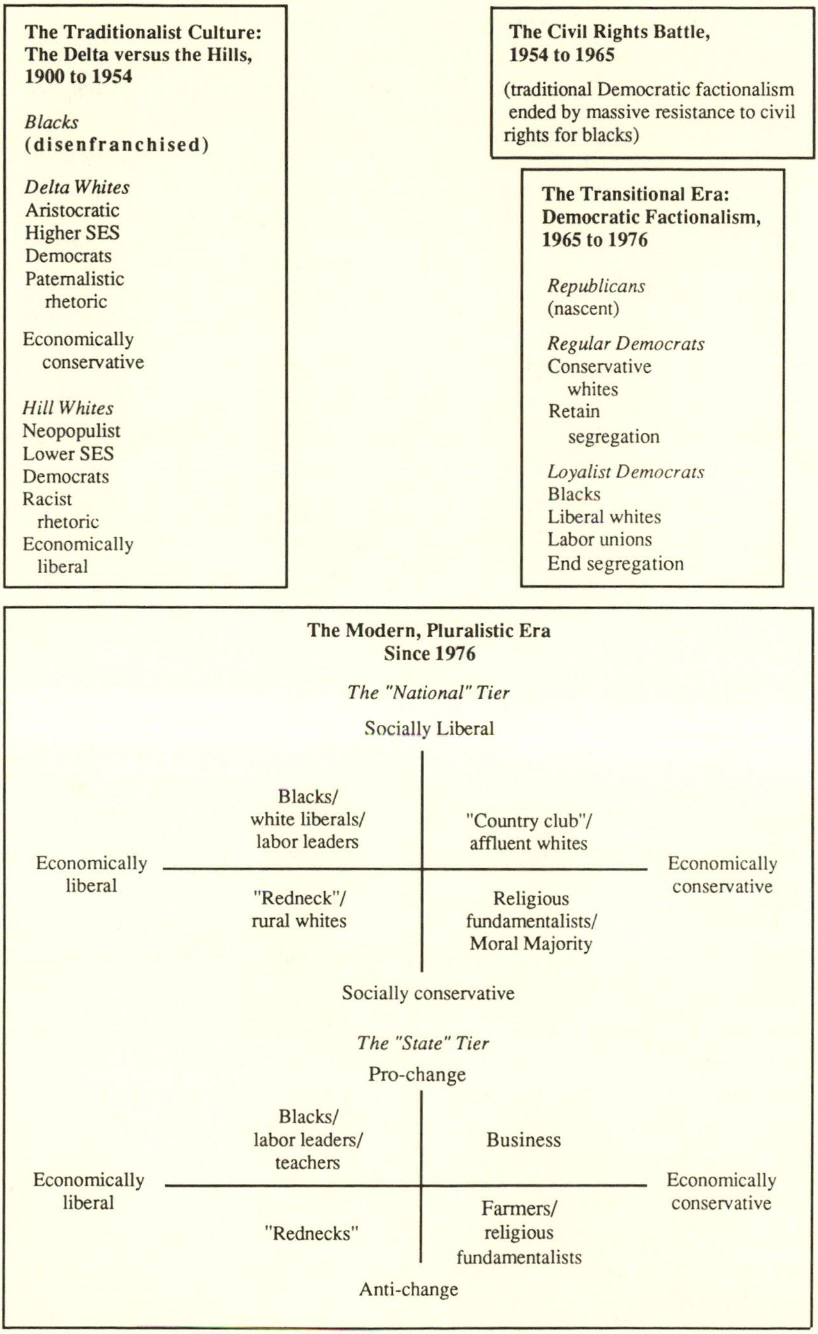

The Traditionalist Culture: The Delta versus the Hills, 1900 to 1954	The Civil Rights Battle, 1954 to 1965

The Traditionalist Culture:
The Delta versus the Hills,
1900 to 1954

Blacks
(**disenfranchised**)

Delta Whites
Aristocratic
Higher SES
Democrats
Paternalistic
  rhetoric

Economically
  conservative

Hill Whites
Neopopulist
Lower SES
Democrats
Racist
  rhetoric
Economically
  liberal

The Civil Rights Battle,
1954 to 1965

(traditional Democratic factionalism
ended by massive resistance to civil
rights for blacks)

The Transitional Era:
Democratic Factionalism,
1965 to 1976

Republicans
(nascent)

Regular Democrats
Conservative
  whites
Retain
  segregation

Loyalist Democrats
Blacks
Liberal whites
Labor unions
End segregation

The Modern, Pluralistic Era
Since 1976

The "National" Tier

Socially Liberal

	Socially Liberal	
Economically liberal	Blacks/ white liberals/ labor leaders	"Country club"/ affluent whites
	"Redneck"/ rural whites	Religious fundamentalists/ Moral Majority

Economically liberal — Economically conservative

Socially conservative

The "State" Tier

Pro-change

Economically liberal	Blacks/ labor leaders/ teachers	Business
	"Rednecks"	Farmers/ religious fundamentalists

Economically liberal — Economically conservative

Anti-change

Figure 10. Shifting political coalitions in Mississippi.

majority in many jurisdictions). This burst of new voters produced a three-cornered electoral system that pitted three groups against each other—(1) economically conservative, wealthier whites, (2) poorer, neopopulist "rednecks," and (3) the newly mobilized and liberal blacks. Candidates during the 1970s struggled to construct winning coalitions out of these unstable elements. Governor Finch, for example, succeeded in building a "blackneck-redneck" coalition in his gubernatorial race but failed in his run for the United States Senate.

One of the most interesting features of this *transitional era* was the pivotal power of black voters. Ironically, immediately after their enfranchisement blacks in Mississippi, because they formed a large, solid bloc of voters, could make or break candidates by their support or lack of support. Thad Cochran became the first Mississippi Republican in the United States Senate since Reconstruction when a significant proportion of black voters cast their ballots for Charles Evers, a black candidate, abandoning the white Democratic candidate. Ticket splitting was another important feature of this transition era. Conservative whites increasingly cast their votes for Republican presidential candidates in response to the Democratic party's push for racial equality, but these same conservative whites continued their traditional support for Democratic candidates for state and local offices. These "Republicrats" tried to maximize their political influence and advance their economic interests by claiming to be "independent" while selectively supporting particular candidates of either party. William Alexander, for example, used the Democratic label to win a seat to the state senate, where he became president pro tempore. At the same time, Senator Alexander also served as a prominent member of the statewide committee to elect a Republican candidate to the White House in 1980. This "independence" became so rampant that a number of Democrats sought to penalize party members who publicly supported any Republican candidate.

Not only did internal factionalism and splinter groups challenge the Democrats, but the state Republican party increasingly appealed to many Mississippians. The civil rights revolution ended the political monopoly enjoyed by the old whites-only Democratic party and made it socially acceptable to become a Republican. With the advent of the Nixon administration's Southern Strategy, many conservative whites could pursue their economic and social interests by joining the GOP. As the Republican party grew in strength, the two Democratic factions finally united in the mid-1970s into a broad biracial coalition.

Political competition today mirrors the increased diversity of the state. In this *modern, pluralistic era* urban-rural divisions have replaced the old Delta-Hills split, and the lines of electoral cleavage have multiplied. As more and more groups and organizations with distinctive orientations on national and state issues, partisanship, and socioeconomic status (SES) mobilize and project their interests into the political arena, electoral coalitions have become more pluralistic and more volatile. Blacks, who generally have a lower SES and a Democratic partisan orientation, tend to be liberal on national and state issues. Urban whites tend to be in higher SES levels, have more conservative views on many national economic issues, and are more Republican in orientation. Yet the more professional and higher educational backgrounds of many urban whites leads them to be more tolerant on social issues and to lack sympathy for the old traditionalistic political culture. Many rural whites have lower SES, and therefore support economically progressive policies. An attachment to tradition leads to rural white support for conservative social policies and for the state's traditionalistic institutions and practices. Rural whites are also more likely to vote Democratic out of habit.

A two-tier political alignment has emerged within Mississippi elections in this modern, pluralistic era. For contests over "national" offices (president, United States Senate, United States House), a coalition built from the economically conservative "country-club" whites, socially conservative religious fundamentalists, and the "pickup truck" whites faces a coalition composed of economically and socially liberal blacks and whites (fig. 10). To some extent political battles at this "national" level continue to exhibit the old race divisions, but that interpretation ignores the more complex alignments along economic and social issues that have evolved in Mississippi. The modest proportion of Republican identifiers swells into a majority in national elections as various groups with "Democratic" leanings follow their traditional values.

At the "state" level, Mississippi elections display an alignment of groups and interests different from that on the "national" tier. The state's poverty makes not so strange political bedfellows out of the black community, the modern business sector, the professions, and many poorer whites. These groups all depend on progressive state government policies to achieve their economic goals. Surprisingly, many individuals with "Republican" leanings among the business groups often sacrifice their "national" political views in order to work together with economically liberal Democrats at the state level. Die-hard defenders of the traditionalistic order, now primarily associated with agrarian interests or conservative religious groups, still cling to the "no change" position.

A key problem for the state's Democratic party in contemporary presidential and United States Senate elections is that national issues and ideological terms such as "liberalism" and "conservatism" are often salient to voters. Thus many conservative urban and rural whites will join together to help elect Republican candidates such as Presidents Reagan and Bush, and blacks will constitute the core of support for the losing Democratic candidate. A winning strategy for Democrats running for these offices is to de-emphasize ideology, as Carter did in 1976, and seek to unite blacks and rural whites who share the same Democratic partisanship and lower SES. One way of accomplishing this is to emphasize economic issues on which the two groups have similar views, such as the need for more jobs and benefits such as social security and medical care that help both races. This is difficult to accomplish when the national Democratic party nominates candidates like Mondale and Dukakis, who also tend to be fairly liberal on noneconomic issues such as national defense, crime, and life-style concerns.

The Democratic party remains dominant in state elections because of its ability to avoid national ideological labels and to maintain a broad coalition uniting blacks and whites who share similar partisan identifications and economic interests. Republican gubernatorial candidates therefore often find their support concentrated in urban areas with more professional, more highly educated, and higher-income populations. The 1987 gubernatorial contest between Reed and Mabus demonstrates that these coalitions are capable of shifting. A greater Republican effort at injecting national issues into state politics may attract more Republican support among rural whites, while a more progressive orientation among Democratic candidates on state issues may help the Democrats make gains among urban whites. On the other hand, the lower visibility of many state and local offices leads many voters who are less informed about the candidates to simply vote their partisan identifications. This continues to help the Democratic party, since it receives the support of blacks and many rural whites, while Republican support remains concentrated in the larger cities.

THE PERSISTENT STRUGGLE FOR REFORM

Welcome to Jackson—The White Shoe Capital of the World.
    You'll probably find more people wearing white shoes here than anywhere else in the country.
They're the establishment. They run Mississippi. . . .

THE WHITE SHOES have made some changes, but we're still
rolling along behind every other state in almost every category. . . .

The white shoes have made some changes, but the things wrong
with the state are not much different from the faults of 20 years ago
and 20 years before that.[8]

The "white shoe crowd" that James Young wrote about in 1973 still
wields powerful influence within the policy process at the state level and remains especially entrenched in Mississippi's small towns and villages. Nevertheless, the state has made significant progress toward a more modern,
pluralistic society with greater representation of and concern for the disadvantaged in society. Readers may be impressed with the progressive reforms
of the 1970s and 1980s, in view of Mississippi's long history of racism, poverty, and backwardness. Yet the progressive changes of the past two decades
should not blind us to critical features of the old traditionalistic culture that
persist even today.

Despite increased funding for educational improvements, Mississippi remains a low tax–low spending state. In keeping with the conservative philosophy that stresses self-reliance and a respect for private property and
wealth, taxes are kept as low as possible. Hence many public services remain limited in quality and availability, and raising taxes to improve public
services is a difficult task because of the state's traditional institutions and
culture. The constitution of 1890 requires an overwhelming 60 percent vote
margin in the state legislature in order to raise taxes. Similarly, school bond
referenda need a 60 percent vote to pass. Furthermore, the dominant government institution, the legislature, is a fragmented and slow-moving body
where efforts to institute policy changes such as tax increases can be stalled
at several different stages of the legislative process.

This reluctance to use the public sector for the common good is reinforced
by the small-town culture and life-style. The emphasis on self-reliance in the
state's close-knit communities produces a paradoxical form of "private regardingness" that opposes action in the larger public interest.[9] This "private
regarding" philosophy manifests itself, for example, in the denominational
divisions of Mississippi towns; some churches espouse theologies that often
reinforce the antigovernment, low tax attitudes. As one visits these small
towns, one commonly finds individual churches with modest congregations
owning facilities (e.g., classrooms, day-care center, gymnasium, social
hall) that exceed any public structure in cost and luxury. Members of these
local churches often prefer to promote the "public good" through private re-

ligious activities rather than achieving the same ends through "public" government activities necessitating higher taxes.[10] Similar attitudes and behavior can be found at the local country club.[11] If it were not for federal grants, many Mississippi localities would not have "public" facilities.

Another obstacle to the use of public policy for the common good derives from continuing traces of racism. Especially in communities where the proportion of blacks and whites is relatively equal, an uneasy truce exists. Bond issues to improve public schools or parks often meet defeat because the money would build facilities that would be used primarily, if not exclusively, by blacks. The white mayor in one such town admitted that if it were not for a federal grant, the black children would not have a swimming pool.[12] Rear-guard defenders of the old order can throw large obstacles in the path of "public regarding" behavior.

Despite rising turnout among blacks and the growing number of black elected officials in Mississippi, problems involving race and class persist. Perceptions held by many blacks of white insensitivity to black concerns spark periodic lawsuits, boycotts, and demonstrations. Public officials remain disproportionately white, male, and from higher SES levels, contributing to insufficient government concern for the problems of the disadvantaged in society.[13] Although this is the case in many parts of the nation, higher SES political domination in a tradition-bound society like Mississippi may be especially effective in slowing the state's evolution to a modern, progressive society.

The regressive tax system that depends heavily on sales and gasoline taxes, with their disproportionate burden on the poor, stands as a fortress of "private regardingness." One reform strategy would increase progressive income tax rates for wealthier citizens. But the prospects for significant changes in Mississippi's tax system appear poor, since major reform would have to muster the required 60 percent vote margin in the legislature—an institution dominated by the economically advantaged. Furthermore, business and other interest groups would likely oppose tax reform that, because of the linkage in tax rates between individual and corporate income taxes, would increase the tax burden on business. Even some lower-income citizens who lack an understanding of complex political issues would oppose tax reform because they fail to recognize that taxes would rise only for higher-income people.

Perhaps the greatest barrier to building a progressive, enlightened society with a high quality of life continues to be the widespread poverty in the state. Public services are limited not only by past practices, but also by the absence of wealth and by the limited tax base. Progressive groups at the local level can often marshal resources for facilities and projects designed or justified as "economic development" (e.g., an industrial park), but many of these same persons turn around and oppose public projects that appear to be "redistributive" (e.g., air-conditioning in schools, public housing). The incantation that "a limited amount of money is available" is used to rationalize the expenditure of funds for one type of project versus another. Ideological and philosophical differences over the "proper" strategy to foster growth pit the "white shoe crowd" against the modernizers.

The civil rights movement brought significant reform to Mississippi by promoting legal integration and protecting voting rights, but blacks have made less progress economically. Even though the Delta accounts for almost half of the state's farm income, the semifeudal conditions leave these majority black population counties in desperate poverty. Job opportunities are scarce, and the pay for many available jobs is fixed below the minimum wage.[14] Urban areas provide more opportunities for poor blacks, yet the affluent suburbs in Mississippi, as in other states, are overwhelmingly white. The legal right to buy a house wherever desired is of limited help if one lacks the money to buy a home. The right to attend the public university of one's choice is important but is reserved for those who can afford to pay the tuition (which remains among the highest in the region).

The not-so-dead hand of history remains alive in Mississippi's traditional political structures. Jacksonian democracy continues to prevail in the form of a multitude of elected public offices. Progressive governors (indeed, all governors) have limited authority over the executive branch itself, because several top state executive officers are elected independently of the governor and may harbor higher political ambitions that lead to conflict with the governor. The desire to elect numerous public servants at the county and local levels hinders administrative reform, professionalism, and the efficient use of tax dollars. Hence the principles of Jacksonian democracy are quite compatible with Mississippi's traditionalistic political culture. And one must remember that Jacksonian democracy in the 1830s was a "white man's democracy" that excluded blacks and women from political power. Therefore these change-oriented groups were unable to challenge the state's political culture for many years—until they were politically mobilized in the latter part of the twentieth-century after being legally enfranchised.

The constitution of 1890, written in a repressive era that sought to promote white supremacy, preserves Jacksonian democracy and important remnants of a traditionalistic society. The constitution provides for the election of key state executive officials, prohibiting the governor from having an appointive cabinet such as Presidents have. It also establishes the unwieldy "beat" system for county government, requiring that each county be subdivided into five districts with a supervisor selected from each district. And the 1890 constitution requires the extraordinary margin of 60 percent in order to raise taxes, creating situations where the majority will may be thwarted in order to preserve the antitax philosophy of the state's traditionalistic order.

The sources and features of Mississippi's traditionalistic culture are reviewed in figure 11. The Delta planters helped establish traditional political forms, which were then preserved by the rural nature of the state, Jacksonian democracy, and the constitution of 1890. Institutional arrangements also preserve important aspects of the traditionalistic culture. Governors have limited power to implement progressive programs, since the legislature is the dominant institution. But the legislature is a fragmented and slow-moving body where numerous hurdles in the bill-passage process must be overcome, hindering the enactment of modern public policies. Hence problems associated with the state's traditionalistic culture, such as poverty, remnants of racism, corruption, class divisions, and regressive taxes, persist.

A final barrier to reformers who seek to change the state's traditionalistic political order consists of public apathy and limited public understanding of complex political issues. Even in the 1980s, the political awareness of average Mississippians was so low that in one poll fewer than half of the respondents could recall the names of their United States congressmen.[15] Semiliterate voters can be swayed by straightforward but overly simple arguments reflecting the tradition of Jacksonian democracy. Two such arguments are that "democracy" is best served by direct popular election of as many public officials as possible, and that the policy-making process should be dominated by state legislators and county supervisors who are "close to the people." Yet because of public apathy and unawareness of many political matters, "Jacksonian democracy" often translates into increased influence in state elections and policy-making for powerful and active pressure groups, many of them devoted to preserving the traditional status quo. Public understanding of the complexities of such issues is hindered by the deemphasis on the study of government and civics in the elementary and secondary schools.[16] And as in many states, even university students can graduate without completing a required class in government or politics.[17]

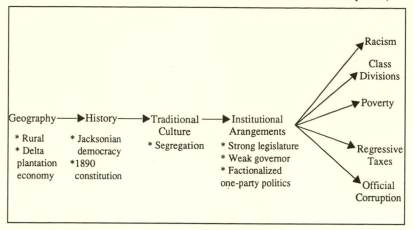

Figure 11. Remnants of a traditionalistic society.

TOWARD A BETTER SOCIETY

Everybody seems so full of hope and dreams, and it's not just rhetoric. . . . There's a real spirit of change this time.[18]

This quotation by Mississippi-born Pulitzer Prize winning playwright Beth
Henley reflected many Mississippians' hopes for the future as the decade of
the 1980s came to a close. Yet because "the past is not dead" in the state's
small towns, their special sense of "place" creates an atmosphere where
"there's no halfway measures in . . . [Mississippi]."[19] Modernizers and
traditionalists contest with passion and vigor for the destiny of their locality
and that of the state. At the same time that biracial coalitions succeed in electing blacks and progressive whites to important public office in some communities, other localities are convulsed by the pain of race polarization when
efforts are mounted to improve schools or public facilities. But "beneath its
older layers of xenophobia and violence lies an honor and civility" not found
in many other places in America.[20] It is this "honor and civility" in Mississippi that has permitted "the one state least equipped financially and emo-
tionally, to deal with all the implications of . . . finally havin' to do it [inte-
grate] first."[21]

   As Mississippians struggle over the goal of "progress," one must not
lose sight of the many important strengths of the state. Even in its larger
cities, Mississippi retains a small-town atmosphere where the individual is

important and people care about other people. One reason for the low level of spending on public safety is the relatively low crime rate in the state. Hence most residents do not fear taking a walk in their neighborhood at night.

An important source of this concern for other people is the central importance of the family and religion in Mississippi. In the rural and small-town culture of the state, such social institutions provide the entertainment and diversions that cultural opportunities (including nightclubs and expensive restaurants) often provide in more urban and cosmopolitan states. The advantage of social institutions such as the family and religion is that they can impart a moral code of behavior that stresses a concern for the well-being of other human beings. Interactions with one's family, church members, and neighbors are psychologically beneficial diversions compared with the numerous frustrations of modern urban life found in other states.

Traditional small-town values of dignity, loyalty, patriotism, and piety can provide a very sturdy foundation for a political, economic, and social order that will promote the well-being of all citizens. A fundamental requirement for such a society of abundant opportunities is an increase in "brain power" rather than in "muscle power" jobs that can provide an adequate standard of living to replace the widespread economic poverty. Because an important prerequisite for attracting better jobs is an educated and highly skilled work force, it is essential to improve education at all levels in the state. Perhaps the winds of progress that have swept Mississippi in the past few decades really will become a hurricane that will provide economic, political, and social opportunities to all Mississippians and thus allow them to leave behind the "frustrations" of the past.

CHAPTER FOURTEEN

Sources for Research on Mississippi Politics

Stephen D. Shaffer and Dale Krane

Mississippi has produced some of the finest writers and artists in America, so the state's contribution to the humanities and fine arts is significant. Mississippi's influence in other fields, such as the study of political science, has been less noticeable. In a resource-poor environment, funding available for applied research has tended to focus on the natural sciences, engineering, agriculture, and related fields. The arts and humanities have benefited from state commissions associated with agencies of the federal government. The discipline of political science in Mississippi lacks comparable funding opportunities, limiting research on government and politics in the state.

GENERAL SOURCES OF INFORMATION

Citizens wishing to learn about government and politics in Mississippi may want to attend the Mississippi Political Science Association meeting, held each year in the winter or spring. Most of the sessions are roundtables, and in recent years very few convention papers have been available for distribution. The proceedings of the association are not recorded in any manner, such as on microfilm, so personal attendance at the conventions is required. Mississippi also lacks a state journal on political science, thereby limiting research on government and politics in the state.

Some general political science and public administration journals publish articles on Mississippi government and politics from time to time. Such articles have regularly appeared in *Publius: The Journal of Federalism,* for example. Articles about Mississippi have occasionally appeared in the *Journal of Politics,* the journal of the Southern Political Science Association, *Southeastern Political Review,* and *Polity.* The newspaper that provides the most extensive coverage of state government and politics is the Pulitzer Prize winning Jackson *Clarion-Ledger*. Other thorough newspapers include its major competitor, the Memphis *Commercial Appeal*, as well as the *Northeast Mississippi Daily Journal*, based in Tupelo.

Valuable information about Mississippi's political history is provided by the *Journal of Mississippi History*, published quarterly by the Mississippi Department of Archives and History in cooperation with the Mississippi Historical Society. It has printed a number of articles on politically relevant subjects, such as the settlement of the state, the reestablishment of conservative white political power after Reconstruction, the disfranchisement of blacks, the 1890 constitution, and prominent governors of the twentieth century. The Mississippi Department of Archives and History houses the personal and public papers of a number of Mississippi political leaders, as do many of the libraries of state universities.

Some interesting arts and humanities journals are published in Mississippi. *Mississippi Quarterly: The Journal of Southern Culture*, is published quarterly by the College of Arts and Sciences at Mississippi State University and includes humanities and occasional social science articles on the past and present of the South. *Mississippi Review*, which includes fiction and poetry, is published twice a year by the Center for Writers at Southern Station, University of Southern Mississippi. The *Southern Quarterly: A Journal of the Arts in the South*, also published by the University of Southern Mississippi, has included a number of issues on special topics, such as small towns, the South and films, art and feminism in the South, and Elvis Presley.

Several particularly useful collections of cultural essays are noteworthy. James H. Street's *Look Away: A Dixie Notebook* (New York: Viking Press, 1936) combines autobiography and journalism to produce a series of stories that reveal the reality of pre–World War II Mississippi, including some startling reports about lynchings. A more recent collection of essays on the influence of Mississippi's culture on its politics can be found in Fred Powledge, *Journey through the South: A Rediscovery* (New York: Vanguard Press, 1979). In a four-chapter section titled "Mississippi Shadows and Light," Powledge investigates the traditional attitudes and institutions that opposed change in Mississippi and recounts the factors that led to the "springtime" in Mississippi's race relations. An intimate collection of personal narratives about life in Mississippi is provided by the essayist Willie Morris in *Terrains of the Heart and Other Essays on Home* (Oxford: Yoknapatawpha Press, 1981). In writing about his life in Mississippi and other states, Morris talks about the state's civility, coming home to the University

of Mississippi, a presidential visit to Mississippi, and reflections on politicians such as Bilbo. An informative study of the productivity of Mississippi
workers is provided in *Mississippi Workers: Where They Come from and
How They Perform, a Study of Working Forces in Selected Mississippi Industrial Plants,* by B. M. Wofford and T. A. Kelly (University: University of
Alabama Press, 1955).

THE UNIVERSITY PRESS OF MISSISSIPPI

The University Press of Mississippi in Jackson publishes some thought-provoking books, primarily in the humanities, that help provide an inter-
disciplinary understanding of politics in the state. Peggy W. Prenshaw and
Jesse O. McKee's *Sense of Place: Mississippi* (1979) is based on a symposium held at the University of Southern Mississippi, attended by native Mississippians working in the arts, humanities, and social sciences. The symposium sought to identify the distinctiveness of Mississippi, its land, people,
and culture, and to show how residents' strong "sense of place" affects their
values and the values of their community. It also examined how government
agencies, the media, and businesses affected people's bond with their environment.

Another book that illuminates Mississippi's special culture is *Mississippi
Writers: Reflections of Childhood and Youth,* volume 2, *Nonfiction,* edited
by Dorothy Abbott (1986), part of the Center for the Study of Southern Culture series at the University of Mississippi. Memorable stories by Mississippi writers pertain to growing up in Mississippi, the Delta Blues, and living through the civil rights struggle. Another interesting book is *Mississippi
Heroes,* edited by Dean Faulkner Wells and Hunter Cole (1980), which examines such figures as William Faulkner, Medgar Evers, William Percy, Jeff
Davis, and Governor Conner. An especially noteworthy reference volume
on prominent black Mississippians is George A. Sewell and Margaret L.
Dwight's *Mississippi Black History Makers* (1984), which serves as a thorough biography on prominent native blacks in the fields of politics, civil
rights, business, education, literature, journalism, the arts, religion, science, sports, and the military.

An indispensable history book published by the University Press of Mississippi is Richard McLemore's edited *A History of Mississippi* (1973). This
two-volume collection contains informative essays on the settlement of Mississippi, public education, Reconstruction and redemption, the 1890 constitution, the Progressive Era, the effects of World War II, and the civil rights

era. It also has excellent essays on twentieth-century developments in agriculture, industrialization efforts, the labor movement, urbanization, and higher education. Written by Mississippians from different professional realms (academia, business, politics) and edited by Walter M. Mathews, *Mississippi 1990* (1981) gives voice to the aspirations and hopes of the state's leaders. This volume's importance derives from its scenarios of the future as projected by many of the very individuals who were in leadership positions that enabled them to act on their visions.

Books that focus even more directly on political matters include Thomas E. Kynerd's *Administrative Reorganization of Mississippi Government: A Study in Politics* (1978), which examines three major twentieth-century campaigns to reform and restructure Mississippi's executive branch. In this rare analysis of state government reorganization, Kynerd not only describes the details of each proposed reorganization but also explains why each reform proposal failed. Michael De L. Landon's *The Honor and Dignity of the Profession: A History of the Mississippi State Bar,* 1906–1976 (1979) provides a comprehensive review of the issues that have historically faced the state bar, such as judicial reform, race relations, Prohibition, and women's rights. Martha H. Swain's *Pat Harrison: The New Deal Years* (1978) chronicles the political career of an influential Mississippi congressman who initially supported Franklin Roosevelt's liberal agenda but eventually joined the conservative coalition in opposition to his later proposals.

AN INTRODUCTION TO THE POLITICAL HISTORY OF MISSISSIPPI

Several books provide an informative introduction to the history and politics of Mississippi, describing the state's traditionalistic political culture and analyzing the rise and effects of the civil rights movement. In addition to the more standard cultural histories, the autobiographies of Mississippi's celebrated authors constitute a vast lode that can be mined for insights into the state's culture. For those who believe that humor reveals much about culture, one should not fail to listen to the stories told (on records and audiocassettes) by Jerry Clower, the famous "Mouth of Mississippi."

John K. Bettersworth wrote a number of history books for use in the state's high schools and colleges. One of the best is *Mississippi: A History* (Austin, Tex.: Steck, 1959). It provides an excellent account of the settlement of the state, the Civil War, and the era of Reconstruction, and it also examines the constitution of 1890, the politics of the early 1900s, and economic developments in the twentieth-century. The book provides a broad review of the accomplishments of twentieth-century governors, and the state's cultural contributions in literature and the arts.

John Ray Skates's *Mississippi: A Bicentennial History* (New York: W. W. Norton, 1979) is another excellent monograph on the history and culture of the state. Skates not only concisely chronicles the major events in Mississippi history but also conveys in an entertaining style the unique features of the state's folkways and traditions. An indispensable source for information about Mississippi's traditional culture is the volume produced by the Federal Writers' Project of the Works Progress Administration. *Mississippi: The WPA Guide to the Magnolia State* (New York: Viking Press, 1938; reprinted 1988 by the University Press of Mississippi) contains several chapters that portray important elements of pre–World War II life-styles such as political rallies, the influence of country churches, white and black folkways, and an assessment of the quality of life in the state.

An informative volume that emphasizes the political history of the state is *Mississippi: Conflict and Change,* edited by James W. Loewen and Charles Sallis (New York: Pantheon, 1974). Its publication generated considerable controversy, because unlike the writers of many textbooks on Mississippi history that glorified the past, the authors refrained from de-emphasizing the state's history of racial discrimination. Consequently this textbook provides an excellent account of the salience of race to Mississippi politics throughout the state's history. Another helpful volume on the state's history is *Mississippi: A History,* edited by George H. Ethridge (Jackson, Miss.: Historical Record Association, n.d.). It reviews each gubernatorial administration and its accomplishments and includes the text of the governor's inaugural address as well as a listing of all members of the legislature. It also provides a historical biography of prominent persons in the state.

A fascinating account of the historical struggle between the Delta and the Hills is provided by Albert D. Kirwan's *Revolt of the Rednecks—Mississippi Politics:* 1876–1925 (Lexington: University of Kentucky Press, 1964). It examines how the constitutional convention of 1890 and the populist movement combined to disfranchise Mississippi blacks, and how Hill candidates like Bilbo and Vardaman gained political support by raising the race issue. An authoritative examination of an important religious group in the state is Richard A. McLemore's *A History of Mississippi Baptists,* 1780–1970 (Jackson: Mississippi Baptist Convention Board, 1971).

Some interesting biographies, autobiographies, and organizational histories that have political relevance have been written. *Congressman from Mississippi,* an autobiography by Frank E. Smith (New York: Pantheon, 1964) details his political career as a moderate on the explosive issue of race relations and his defeat in 1962 after being criticized as a friend of President Kennedy and a supporter of New Frontier programs. *The Percys of Mississippi: Politics and Literature in the New South,* by Lewis Baker (Baton Rouge: Louisiana State University Press, 1983), discusses Percy's Senate days as well as such historical developments in Mississippi as the activities of the Klan. *Coming of Age in Mississippi* was written by a young black woman, Anne Moody (New York: Dial Press, 1968). *The Delta Council: Fifty Years of Service to the Mississippi Delta,* by William M. Cash and R. Daryl Lewis (Stoneville, Miss.: Delta Council, 1986), describes an important organization in the Delta region.

An important and informative book on the state's political system is *Mississippi Government and Politics in Transition,* edited by David M. Landry and Joseph B. Parker (Dubuque, Iowa: Kendall/Hunt, 1976). It provides basic information about the three branches of government and state political parties, as well as original research on elections and voting behavior. Robert B. Highsaw and Charles N. Fortenberry's *The Government and Administration of Mississippi* (New York: Thomas Y. Crowell, 1954) is a classic volume on government in the Magnolia State. In addition to a thorough discussion of the structure of government, it provides a detailed examination of important public policies. Researchers can gain insight into continuity and change in Mississippi government and politics during the past few decades by comparing the current book with the Landry and Parker and the Highsaw and Fortenberry predecessors.

Books reflecting professional research into specific aspects of politics and government in Mississippi offer valuable information. An extensive analysis of the state legislature is provided in David B. Ogle's *Strengthening the Mississippi Legislature* (New Brunswick, N.J.: Rutgers University Press, 1971). It is based on a study by the Eagleton Institute of Politics assessing Mississippi's legislative organization, operations, procedures, and facilities and makes recommendations for improvements. Minion K. C. Morrison's *Black Political Mobilization: Leadership, Power, and Mass Behavior* (Albany: State University of New York Press, 1987) provides a comparative analysis of the problems facing contemporary black political leaders by conducting an in-depth study of three Mississippi towns that elected black mayors. Three books are invaluable to any understanding of the struggle over black political empowerment. Howard Ball, Dale Krane, and Thomas P. Lauth, Jr.'s *Compromised Compliance: Implementation of the 1965 Voting Rights Act* (Westport, Conn.: Greenwood Press, 1982) provides the seminal analysis of the federal Justice Department's enforcement of this act and documents how local public officials resisted one of its key sections. In a chapter in Chandler Davidson's edited volume *Minority Vote Dilution* (Washington, D.C.: Howard University Press, 1984), the same authors compare the actions and perceptions of city and county attorneys in Mississippi and Georgia who were involved in enforcement of the Voting Rights Act. Frank R. Parker's *Black Votes Count: Political Empowerment in Mississippi after 1965* (Chapel Hill: University of North Carolina Press, 1990) provides detailed evidence (including maps and charts) demonstrating a variety of legal techniques used by public officials to minimize black electoral power.

THE CIVIL RIGHTS MOVEMENT IN MISSISSIPPI

Some fascinating books on the civil rights movement in Mississippi are available. These books are not just poignant reminders of past conditions and struggles; they also reveal much about the behavior of the Old Guard and the distinctive features of Mississippi's traditionalistic political culture. James W. Silver's *Mississippi: The Closed Society* (New York: Harcourt, Brace, and World, 1966) exposes the individuals, institutions, and practices that maintained the state's segregated society and fueled the fierce and massive resistance to desegregation. Russel H. Barrett's *Integration at Ole Miss* (Chicago: Quadrangle Books, 1965) is a detailed account of how James Meredith integrated the University of Mississippi and of the violence and political manipulations that resulted. Both authors were faculty members at the University of Mississippi at the time. *Letters from Mississippi,* edited by Elizabeth Sutherland (New York: McGraw Hill, 1965), is a product of the Mississippi Project Parents' Committee. *For Us the Living* is Mrs. Medgar Evers's autobiographical homage to her slain husband (New York: Doubleday, 1967) and James Farmer's *Lay Bare the Heart: An Autobiography of the Civil Rights Movement* (New York: Arbor House, 1985) takes the reader into the minds and hearts of the civil rights leaders. Jason Berry's reporting in *Amazing Grace: With Charles Evers in Mississippi* (New York: Saturday Review Press, 1973) covers the years immediately after the passage of the 1965 Voting Rights Act, including Evers's 1971 gubernatorial race.

The events of the pivotal summer of 1964 are captured in a number of chilling chronicles and cooler analyses. Seth Cagin and Philip Dray's *We Are Not Afraid: The Story of Goodman, Schwerner, and Chaney and the Civil Rights Campaign for Mississippi* (New York: Macmillan, 1988) examines the murder of three civil rights workers in Mississippi. Florence Mars, a native of Noxubee County, probes the tragedy with great sensitivity in *Witness in Philadelphia* (Baton Rouge: Louisiana State University Press, 1977). Mars's volume goes beyond a simple reporting of the murders to describe the local culture and politics that sustained the atmosphere of fear and violence in Philadelphia and in the state at this time. Len Holt, in *The Summer That Didn't End* (New York: William Morrow 1965), offers a highly detailed description of the 1964 events that utilizes the multiple viewpoints of COFO, the federal troops, the courts, the "white folks" project, the Mississippi Freedom Democratic party, and the Democratic National Convention.

Other informative books on civil rights in Mississippi include: *The Delta Ministry,* by Bruce Hilton (London: Macmillan, 1969), which examined how this civil rights group supported by the National Council of Churches helped bring social change to blacks in the poor Mississippi Delta region; *Attack on Terror: The FBI against the Ku Klux Klan in Mississippi,* by Don Whitehead (New York: Funk and Wagnalls, 1970), which recounts the FBI's use of klansman-informants in their fight against the Mississippi Ku Klux Klan in the 1960s; and *Blood Justice: The Lynching of Mack Charles Parker,* by Howard Smead (New York: Oxford University Press, 1986), which provides a case study of a drastic method of ensuring white supremacy in the old South.

Two additional and highly useful sources about the civil rights struggle in Mississippi are worthy of mention. *My Soul Is Rested* (New York: G. P. Putnam's Sons, 1977) is a collection of in-depth interviews conducted by Howell Raines of participants in the civil rights movement. Mississippi's chapter, subtitled "SNCC and the Home-Grown Heroes," includes interviews with such prominent native Mississippians as Amzie Moore, Fannie Lou Hamer, Julian Bond, and Marion Barry. The collection also contains an interview with Robert Patterson, a leader of the Citizens' Council in Mississippi. Taylor Branch's *Parting the Waters: America in the King Years,* 1954–1963 (New York: Simon and Schuster, 1988) describes the events in Mississippi from the broader vantage point of historical changes in the United States during the lifetime of Martin Luther King, Jr. Especially useful are Branch's chapters "The Summer of the Freedom Rides, "Moses in McComb, King in Kansas City," "The Fall of Ole Miss," "Greenwood and Birmingham Jail," and "Firestorm."

BASIC REFERENCE MATERIALS

An indispensable reference tool is the state's "blue book," the *Mississippi Official and Statistical Register,* produced by the secretary of state's office every four years. Among other items, it provides extensive information about state agencies and their staff members, a short biography of state legislators that includes their committee assignments, a listing of all county officers, and recent election results for statewide offices by county. Another useful reference book is the *Mississippi Statistical Abstract,* produced annually by the Mississippi State University Division of Research, College of Business and Industry. It provides a wealth of statistical information on health issues, education, welfare, labor, industry, agriculture, geography, and juvenile crime.

Essential reference material on the state's congressional delegation is provided by publication nationally every two years of Congressional Quarterly's *Politics in America* and the National Journal's *The Almanac of American Politics.* Both provide a narrative discussion of each congressional district and its demographic composition as well as a description of the Congressman's behavior and committee assignments. Items of information include a summary of their votes on key roll-call issues, how they are rated by interest groups, and recent election returns. The annual *Congressional Quarterly Almanac* provides a thorough discussion of the content of many legislative bills, their history in the legislative process, and how the state's congressmen and senators voted on roll-call votes.

Invaluable reference books pertaining to the legislative branch include *Mississippi Laws,* published by the secretary of state's office after each legislative session, which includes the text of all laws passed; the *Journal of the House of Representatives of the State of Mississippi,* an annual publication of all house floor proceedings and roll calls; and the *Journal of the Senate of the State of Mississippi,* an annual publication of all senate floor proceedings and roll calls.

A number of useful reference works pertain to the state judicial branch. A good introduction to the state's highest court is provided by John Ray Skates Jr.'s *A History of the Mississippi Supreme Court, 1817–1948* funded by the Mississippi Bar Foundation, Jackson, in 1973. In addition to a narrative on the history of the court under each of the state's constitutions, a biographical sketch of all supreme court judges up to 1948 is provided. Skates concludes that the court historically has practiced judicial restraint, being reluctant to declare state laws unconstitutional. The entire text of published state supreme court decisions, including author, vote margin, written dissents, and the names of lawyers of both parties is found in *Southern Reporter* (West Publishing Company). Useful current reference material is provided by the following state government documents—the *Mississippi Judicial Directory and Court Calendar* (published by the secretary of state), the *Mississippi Supreme Court Annual Report,* and the *Mississippi Commission on Judicial Performance Annual Report.*

Associations of local officials publish various magazines of interest to their members. The Mississippi Municipal Association publishes monthly *Mississippi Municipalities,* which discusses issues of interest to local public servants as well as anyone concerned with local government. The Mississippi Association of Supervisors with three other associations of county officials, publishes monthly *Mississippi Supervisor,* and *Chancery Clerk, Circuit Clerk, Tax Assessor and Collector,* which discusses issues of interest to county public servants and anyone concerned with county government. Both publications can be obtained from the associations' headquarters in Jackson.

Quite often, valuable information about existing and proposed laws can be obtained from the publications of interest groups or professional associations, which can be obtained by calling the associations' headquarters in Jackson. Some relevant publications include *Mississippi Business,* produced by the Mississippi Economic Council; *the MMA Legislative Bulletin,* produced by the Mississippi Manufacturers Association; *Farm Flashes,* produced by the Mississippi Farm Bureau Federation; the *Mississippi State Medical Legislative Report,* produced by the Mississippi State Medical Association; and *The Mississippi Lawyer,* published by the Mississippi State Bar Association.

Other useful reference sources about state government are produced by various organizations. The state auditor's office and the state Fiscal Management Board produce informative annual reports on the sources of state revenue and the amounts appropriated for state programs. Information about changes in the state's economic life can be obtained from the Research and Development Center in Jackson. Commentary on federal and state court decisions is often provided in the *Mississippi Law Journal,* published three times a year by the University of Mississippi law school students; issues of the journal are sometimes devoted to prominent public policies, such as the fall 1988 issue on education reform in Mississippi.

INSTITUTES STUDYING MISSISSIPPI GOVERNMENT AND POLITICS

The Public Policy Research Center (formerly the Bureau of Government Research, and before that the Bureau of Public Administration) at the University of Mississippi has been active over the years in publishing material on Mississippi government and politics. Current reference material includes:

the *Manual of Mississippi Municipal Government,* periodically updated, which provides helpful information about form of government, election requirements, personnel and financial administration, planning and development, and intergovernmental relations; and the *Handbook for Mississippi Legislators,* published every four years, which discusses legislative officers, committees, and the stages a bill must go through. Interested persons may wish to receive the Center's quarterly newsletter, *Public Administration Survey.*

The Center has published various reference sources on state election returns. *Mississippi Election Statistics,* 1900–1967 by F. Glenn Abney (1968), provides county-level election returns for president, United States Senate, all state offices, and selected referenda. *Mississippi Election Statistics for State Offices,* 1971–1979 (1982) provides county returns for all primaries and general elections for all state offices in the elections of 1971, 1975, and 1979.

Research on the state's constitution has especially interested the Center. *The Constitution of Mississippi as Originally Adopted* (1982) provides the original text of each of Mississippi's four constitutions. It must be relied on for the unamended, original state constitutions, since the secretary of state's office publishes the latest amended version of the state's constitution. The proceedings of a recent symposium on the state's constitution involving academics, public officials, and knowledgeable political observers has been published in *A Contemporary Analysis of Mississippi's Constitutional Government* (1986).

The Center's earlier research on Mississippi's constitution is provided in two publications. *Modernizing Mississippi's Constitution,* by William N. Ethridge, Jr. (1950), examines the three branches of government, has valuable reference material on when each government bureau was created and the legal justification for its existence, and includes statistical information on circuit and chancery court cases disposed of and the number of days the courts have been in session. *Yesterday's Constitution Today: An Analysis of the Mississippi Constitution of* 1890, edited by Edward H. Hobbs (1960), contains analyses of the constitution and recommendations for changes by nine academics, legislators, and lawyers. Subjects examined include the three branches of government, the bill of rights, corporations, elections, and apportionment.

The John C. Stennis Institute of Government at Mississippi State University engages in applied research on Mississippi state and local government. Recent projects have included: four mayor-alderman-councilmen information seminars held throughout the state; various studies to evaluate the form of government for cities and counties in Mississippi; and in cooperation with the John C. Stennis Center for Public Service Training, establishment of a state executive development institute.

Personnel connected with the John C. Stennis Institute have been especially active in research on the organizational structure of county government. A valuable report on county government reform that received much statewide visibility is *The County Government Reorganization Act of* 1988: *An Information Report* (1988), by William M. Wiseman, Katri Welford, and Charles W. Washington. An earlier report on the benefits of the unit system reform was *Converting to the Unit System: The Neshoba County Experience,* by William M. Wiseman (1987), published by the Department of Political Science at Mississippi State University and the Governmental Services Division of the Research and Development Center.

The Social Science Research Center (SSRC) at Mississippi State University focuses primarily on applied sociological research, which is published in the Sociology Research Report series. The series examines such diverse issues relevant to public policy analysis as drunken driving, the elderly, education reform, infant mortality, criminal justice, and agricultural concerns. An upcoming volume on the problems of the Mississippi Delta should provide an especially original and invaluable study of that region's social life.

The SSRC has sometimes published material that is directly relevant to the study of Mississippi government and politics. *Mississippi Votes: The Presidential and Gubernatorial Elections,* 1947–1964, by Tip H. Allen, Jr. (1967), provides county election returns. Especially valuable are some excellent maps that illustrate voting patterns by racial composition of the counties and by the Delta versus Hills geographic division.

The SSRC sponsors yearly statewide public opinion polls measuring Mississippians' attitudes on important political and social concerns. *The* 1981 *Annual Mississippi Poll: A Study of Mississippians' Political Attitudes,* by Stephen D. Shaffer (1982), provides a nice comparison of Mississippi attitudes with national views. *The* 1984 *Annual Mississippi Poll: A Study of Mississippians' Political and Social Attitudes,* by Stephen D. Shaffer and Wolfgang Frese (1984), includes a study of changing attitudes over time as well as a comparison with the nation.

BOOK CHAPTERS ON MISSISSIPPI POLITICS

Much of the scholarly literature on the politics of Mississippi that has achieved national recognition in the field of political science is found in isolated chapters of books on southern politics. The classic example is V. O. Key, Jr., *Southern Politics* (New York: Vintage, 1949), which in a chapter titled "Mississippi: The Delta and the Hills" provides some entertaining accounts of political campaigns in the 1920s, 1930s, and 1940s, as well as some informative maps of regional splits in election results.

William C. Havard updated Key's portraits of politics in southern states in a collection of essays written by researchers specializing on each state titled *The Changing Politics of the South* (Baton Rouge: Louisiana State University Press, 1972). Charles Fortenberry and F. Glenn Abney, "Mississippi: Unreconstructed and Unredeemed," combined election return maps, interviews, opinion polls, and statistical analyses from the period 1950 to 1971. While identifying many of the changes that occurred during this time, they pessimistically warned readers against concluding that a "new Mississippi" was about to emerge.

Neal R. Peirce's *The Deep South States of America* (New York: W. W. Norton, 1974) contains an optimistic chapter titled "Hope at Last," which outlines the important social and economic changes that swept the state in the 1960s and 1970s and tells how they shaped the state's political agenda. Essentially journalistic in approach, Peirce weaves together a large number of interviews with the state's economic and political leaders into what may be the single best essay on this revolutionary period (1950–72) in Mississippi politics. Jack Bass and Walter DeVries's *The Transformation of Southern Politics* (New York: New American Library, 1977) establishes the historical salience of race in state politics and details how the civil rights movement transformed Mississippi and brought it "Out of the Past." The political career of United States Senator James Eastland serves as a vehicle to depict white resistance to black civil rights demands in Robert Sherrill's "Jim Eastland, Child of Scorn," found in Sherrill's collection of essays on southern political leaders titled *Gothic Politics in the Deep South: Stars of the New Confederacy* (New York: Grossman, 1968).

The 1980s have seen a proliferation of contemporary social science research on Mississippi politics published as book chapters. Dale Krane and Tip H. Allen, Jr., trace the evolution, fragmentation, and recombination of factions within the Mississippi Democratic party in "Factional Durability in Mississippi's Gubernatorial Elections, 1927–1975," published in Robert P. Steed, Laurence Moreland, and Tod Baker's edited volume *Party Politics in the South* (New York: Praeger, 1980). Alexander P. Lamis' *The Two-Party South* (New York: Oxford University Press, 1984) provides a revealing account of recent electoral politics and concludes that in Mississippi "It's All

Black and White." Stephen Shaffer's "Changing Party Politics in Mississippi," in Robert H. Swansbrough and David M. Brodsky's edited book *The
South's New Politics: Realignment and Dealignment* (Columbia: University
of South Carolina, 1988), analyzes how the parties' fortunes in the state
changed in the 1980s and which demographic groups were most responsible
for partisan changes. Well-documented accounts of the 1984 national election campaigns in Mississippi written by Lamis, and the 1988 national elections written by Shaffer, as well as analyses of state public opinion polls, are
included in two volumes edited by Steed, Moreland, and Baker, *The 1984
Presidential Election in the South* (New York: Praeger, 1985) and *The 1988
Presidential Election in the South* (New York: Praeger, 1991).

COMPARING MISSISSIPPI WITH OTHER STATES

An indispensable volume that provides basic institutional and policy information about Mississippi and other states is *The Book of the States,* produced
annually by the Council of State Governments in Lexington, Kentucky. It
contains a wealth of comparative information on state governors' powers
and terms of office, legislative membership turnover, bills introduced and
passed, and judicial selection methods. Valuable electoral information includes registration procedures, campaign finance laws, and election returns
across the states. State financial data include revenue by type of tax, expenditure by program, and state income and corporate tax rates. Other valuable
information pertains to compensation of public officials, number of state
government employees, types of public programs, and intergovernmental
relations.

Another valuable reference source that permits comparisons between
Mississippi and other states is the *Statistical Abstract of the United States,*
published annually by the Bureau of the Census of the United States Department of Commerce. The *Statistical Abstract* provides information about
population, income, labor, and commerce. It also details state rankings on
issues like health care, education, welfare, and crime. Each state's turnout
rate and partisan orientations in federal elections are also provided.

The Advisory Commission on Intergovernmental Relations in Washington, D.C., produces a number of informative publications dealing with the
functional and policy relationships among federal, state, and local governments, as well as various issues of government finance. Invaluable publications include the annual *Significant Features of Fiscal Federalism,* which
compares the states in taxes and spending on public programs, and the peri-

odic *Measuring State Fiscal Capacity,* which compares states in their tax capacity (a measure of the state's tax base or potential, which is related to the wealth of the state) and tax effort (the tax burden in terms of taxes actually levied). The most comprehensive comparison of the structure and administrative operation of the fifty states can be found in *The Question of State Government Capability* (January 1985). A wealth of information on state political parties and campaign finance is provided in *The Transformation in American Politics: Implications for Federalism* (August 1986). National opinion polling data are available in the annual *Changing Public Attitudes on Government and Taxes*.

An indispensable academic publication that provides a comparative analysis of state institutions and public policies is Virginia Gray, Herbert Jacob, and Robert B. Albritton's *Politics in the American States,* 5th ed. (Glenview, Ill.: Scott, Foresman, 1990). This book (and its previous editions) permits a comparison between Mississippi and other states in regard to such issues as partisan competition, voter turnout, pressure group activities, gubernatorial power, judicial selection, and state spending on various public programs. Its theoretical discussion is especially informative in shedding light on why Mississippi is different from the rest of the nation.

Other academic sources also permit readers to compare Mississippi political patterns with those found in other states. Daniel J. Elazar's *American Federalism: A View from the States,* 3d ed. (New York: Harper and Row, 1984) sets forth his seminal framework for the study of each state's political culture and also maps the migration patterns that have shaped each state's population and culture. The text also contains valuable comparative state rankings on program innovation, the salience of variables that affect state-local political conflict, and the forces of localism versus centralism in each state. Comparative information on intergovernmental relations includes how much discretionary authority local governments exercise and education centralization within each state.

Alan Rosenthal's *Legislative Life: People, Process, and Performance in the States* (New York: Harper and Row, 1981) provides a comparative analysis of legislatures across the fifty states. Mississippi and other state legislatures can be compared on legislative compensation, session length, and size of legislature, among other issues. Malcolm E. Jewell and David M. Olson's *Political Parties and Elections in American States,* 3d ed. (Chicago: Dorsey, 1988) permits numerous party and electoral comparisons across the states, including party identification and registration data, strength of state and local party organizations, type of open or closed primary system, gubernatorial general election turnout, and patterns of party control of state government.

Other informative publications that permit comparisons between Mississippi and other states on various issues include *State Government Finances,* published by the United States Census Bureau, which provides estimates of state sales and income taxes burdens in each state; Lucinda Simon's *A Legislator's Guide to Staffing Patterns* (Denver, Colo.: National Conference of State Legislatures, 1979), which provides comparative information on state legislative staffing support; the National Center for State Courts' *Publications,* which contains listings for major topics in the judicial field, such as technology, court administration, and trial and appellate processes; and the American Bar Association's *A Handbook on State Judicial Salaries,* which includes useful salary data.

DISSERTATIONS AND THESES

A final source of information about Mississippi government and politics is doctoral dissertations and master's theses, produced by universities both in and outside Mississippi. Some examples follow.

Some interesting research has been completed on the state's labor force and the rise of labor unions. A 1965 dissertation at the University of Alabama written by Donald Crumpton Mosley was titled "History of Labor Unions in Mississippi." It includes the 1911 strike, a chronology of AFL and CIO organizing activity, and organized labor's stance on civil rights. Especially interesting is employer resistance to labor unions in the form of the MEC and Manufacturers Association, as well as the geographic source of antiunionism in North Mississippi. A 1962 dissertation at the University of Pittsburgh by Frank Ethridge Cotton, Jr., "Major Changes in the Mississippi Labor Force, Their Causes and Effects," examines migration into and out of Mississippi from 1870 to 1950, occupational changes, and the decline of agriculture and the rise of manufacturing.

A diversity of subjects have been addressed by dissertations. A 1983 Cornell University dissertation by Melvin Philip Lucas, "The Development of the Second Party System in Mississippi, 1817–1846," details the early political culture of Mississippi, the different interests of the two parties, and how the parties developed from 1832 to 1839. A 1985 Mississippi State University dissertation by Kenneth H. Williams, "Mississippi and Civil Rights, 1945–1954," argues that the early civil rights movement paved the way for the more prominent movement of the late 1950s and 1960s. A 1976 Mississippi State University dissertation by Sandra Stringer Vance, "The Congressional Career of John Bell Williams," tells how William's vocal defense of segregation, membership in the conservative coalition, and frequent opposition to the national Democratic party led to a loss of congressional seniority after the 1964 presidential election.

State representative Eric Charles Clark has thoroughly examined important aspects of the political history of Mississippi—the role of the 1890 constitutional convention and the evolution of economic development policy. His master's thesis, "The Mississippi Constitutional Convention of 1890: A Political Analysis" (University of Mississippi, 1975), analyzes the events and issues leading up to the convention, as well as the convention's deliberations and decisions regarding legislative malapportionment and restricting of the franchise. Clark's doctoral dissertation, "Industrial Development and State Government Policy in Mississippi, 1890–1980" (Mississippi State University, 1989), examines state leaders' historical hostility toward industry, analyzes twentieth-century efforts to promote industrialization, and details each governor's policy initiatives designed to attract industry.

Epilogue

As Mississippi approaches the year 2000, the winds of change continue to transform the political landscape. In the November 1991 state elections, voters narrowly elected the first Republican governor and lieutenant governor since Reconstruction, Kirk Fordice and Eddie Briggs. At the start of a new legislative session in 1992, veteran black legislator Robert Clark was elected to the number-two leadership position in the state house, Speaker pro tempore. An increasing number of political leaders joined the bandwagon of such reform proposals as initiative and referendum, first pushed by Secretary of State Dick Molpus, which would permit voters to enact laws even in the face of legislative opposition. These dramatic developments illustrated how many Mississippians were struggling to transcend their state's traditionalistic political environment.

Reformist governor Ray Mabus, who had had significant legislative accomplishments in his first two years of office, faced a national recession and a tight state budget in his last two years. Lieutenant Governor Brad Dye, a fellow Democrat, was unable to persuade enough legislators in the state senate to support a referendum that would permit voters to decide whether or not to legalize a state lottery which would help pay for Mabus's BEST education reform program. Legislators also rejected other Mabus proposals to pay for BEST, such as legalizing video poker and raising various user fees. As Dye, House Speaker Tim Ford, and other legislative leaders pleaded with Mabus to consider a tax increase, Mabus refused to budge. A political drama of incessant bickering between the governor and legislative leaders continued to unfold. As polls showed most Mississippians favoring improved public education and a state lottery, voters watched the lottery languish in the legislature, BEST go unfunded, and a tight budget victimize even current spending on elementary, secondary, and higher education. Many people were fed up and eager for a change.

Mabus and Dye narrowly survived the Democratic primary over tough opponents who stressed an anti-incumbency message—"populist" gubernatorial candidate Wayne Dowdy and "reformist" lieutenant governor hopeful Ken Harper. Despite a 3 to 1 spending advantage, Mabus then fell victim to Vicksburg construction executive Kirk Fordice, a long-time conservative Republican-party activist who had upset education advocate and state auditor Pete Johnson in the Republican runoff, while three-term incumbent Dye was unseated by senate critic Eddie Briggs. Voters also rejected several key legislators who had opposed a public referendum on the lottery, as well as two of Dye's chief lieutenants. In January 1992, Tim Ford turned back a challenge to his Speakership by veteran legislator Ed Perry. While some political observers had accused Ford of trying to repeal some of the 1987 house reforms and of allying himself with "old-guard" supporters of former Speaker Buddie Newman, Ford nevertheless found himself pushing veteran black legislator Robert Clark for the number-two position. Not only did this move split the Black Caucus and help re-elect Ford as Speaker, but it contributed to the defeat of the progressive Speaker pro tempore and Ford critic Cecil Simmons.

The election of conservative Republican Kirk Fordice, a supporter of Barry Goldwater and Ronald Reagan, as governor prompted some journalists and editors to attack him even before he had taken the oath of office. Many progressives feared that his campaign pledges of smaller government, budget cuts, and a possible tax cut would further hamper the effort of public leaders to improve the quality of life in the state. Speculation arose that a conservative wave was sweeping the state, which might reinforce the traditionalistic political culture, historically dedicated to limited government and elite rule. However, while conservative, many of Fordice's initial actions were inconsistent with such a closed political system. Supporting initiative, referendum, and even term limitation, Fordice sought to deliver on his campaign promise to take government away from the "professional politicians" and give it back to the people. Seeking out good advice wherever he could obtain it, Fordice appointed numerous task forces that included such prominent citizens as university presidents and superintendents of education. Meanwhile, Lieutenant Governor Eddie Briggs reflected public discontent with the ways things were going by unseating most committee chairs, especially those associated with his predecessor, and appointing many freshmen as vice-chairs. Five of the chamber's nine Republicans received committee chairmanships, including a pro-lottery senator named to head the key Constitution Committee.

And so the struggle between the forces of modernization and traditionalism continues. Traditionalists take heart in the renewed strength of conservatism among political leaders, reflected in a likely commitment to limited government and low taxes. Modernizers point to growing political support for measures that would further open the political system to the people, such as initiative, referendum, lobby-law reform, and term limitation. In the final analysis, the increasing number of electoral victories by Republicans provides an additional important avenue for the public to shape the political agenda. Public officials are on notice that Mississippians want a government that will improve the quality of life for themselves and their children. Whereas historically voters could pursue this agenda only within the framework of one political party, today Mississippians can seek desirable political leaders within either of the two parties. Such intense political competition between as well as within political parties may lead to a more open political system that generates more innovative, efficient, or effective programs.

Thus, as Mississippi approaches the twenty-first century, the battle between traditionalists and modernizers continues, but on a rapidly changing battlefield. And while the pace of change over the past few decades has been great, developments in the early 1990s suggest that Mississippians will face even faster and more dramatic transformations in state politics and government in the years ahead.

Notes

CHAPTER I

1 "Educational Consultant: State's Reforms Must Be Bigger and Better," *Jackson Clarion-Ledger,* July 31, 1989, p. 1A.

2 James W. Silver, *Mississippi: The Closed Society* (New York: Harcourt, Brace, and World, 1963).

3 Willie Morris, *Terrains of the Heart and Other Essays on Home* (Oxford, Miss.: Yoknapatawpha Press, 1981), p. 75.

4 Jason Berry, "Amazing Grace," in *Mississippi Writers: Reflections of Childhood and Youth,* ed. Dorothy Abbot, Vol. 2, *Nonfiction* (Jackson: University Press of Mississippi, 1986), p. 14.

5 John Kincaid, "Introduction," in *Political Culture, Public Policy and the American States,* ed. John Kincaid (Philadelphia: Institute for the Study of Human Issues, 1982), p. 6.

6 Gabriel A. Almond and Sidney Verba, *The Civic Culture: Political Attitudes and Democracy in Five Nations* (Boston: Little, Brown, 1965), p. 14.

7 Daniel J. Elazar, *American Federalism: A View from the States,* 3d ed. (New York: Harper and Row, 1984), p. 112.

8 Kincaid, "Introduction," p. 9.

9 Elazar, *American Federalism,* pp. 112–14.

10 Kincaid, "Introduction," p. 9.

11 The previous three paragraphs are drawn from Elazar, *American Federalism.* Previous research in political science has found much support for Elazar's theory of political culture. Ira Sharkansky, "The Utility of Elazar's Political Culture," *Polity* 2 (1969): 66–83, confirms that states with traditionalistic cultures tend to have suffrage restrictions, low turnout, and limited services in the fields of education, welfare, and highways. Charles A. Johnson, "Political Culture in American

States: Elazar's Formulation Examined," *American Journal of Political Science* 20 (1976): 491–509, also finds limited popular participation in politics and governmental decision making and limited support for social welfare programs in traditionalistic cultures, as well as little governmental innovation and limited interparty competition. Susan Welch and John G. Peters, "State Political Culture and the Attitudes of State Senators toward Social, Economic Welfare, and Corruption Issues," *Publius: The Journal of Federalism* 10 (Spring 1980): 59–67, found that state senators were most conservative on economic welfare and "social" (civil liberty) issues in states with traditionalistic cultures. John Kincaid, "Dimensions and Effects of America's Political Cultures," *Journal of American Culture* 5 (1982): 84–92, found that states with traditionalistic cultures had the lowest objective quality of life (reflecting limited government services) and the lowest turnout in presidential elections and were least likely to have ratified the United States Equal Rights Amendment. Readers wishing additional insight into Elazar's theory of political culture should consult Kincaid, *Political Culture*.

12 Russell L. Hanson, "The Intergovernmental Setting of State Politics," in *Politics in the American States: A Comparative Analysis,* 4th ed., ed. Virginia Gray, Herbert Jacob, and Kenneth N. Vines (Boston: Little, Brown, 1983), p. 31. See Welch and Peters, "State Political Culture," and Kincaid, "Dimensions and Effects."

13 Hanson, "Intergovernmental Setting," p. 31.

14 Ibid., p. 33.

15 V. O. Key, Jr., *Southern Politics in State and Nation* (New York: Vintage, 1949), p. 229.

16 Morris, *Terrains,* p. 237.

17 John Shelton Reed, *One South: An Ethnic Approach to Regional Culture* (Baton Rouge: Louisiana State University Press, 1982), p. 170.

18 The 1990 population figures are from the final census count released in January 1991, which was not adjusted for suspected undercounting of minorities and other groups. Statistical adjustments for census inaccuracies yield a state population that ranges from a low estimate of 2,561,000 to a high estimate of 2,658,000. See "Census Confirms Undercount," *USA Today*, April 19, 1991, p. 3A. Census data were obtained from the Center for Population Studies at the University of Mississippi and from "Mississippi by the Numbers," *Jackson Clarion-Ledger,* January 27, 1991, p. 13A. The term SMSA is a statistical standard used by federal agencies. Each SMSA includes one or more central counties that contain an urbanized area having at least 50,000 inhabitants. An SMSA may also include other counties that have a close social and economic relationship with these central counties.

19 John Ray Skates, *Mississippi: A Bicentennial History* (New York: W. W. Norton, 1979), p. 4.

20 James W. Loewen and Charles Sallis, eds., *Mississippi: Conflict and Change* (New York: Pantheon Books, 1974), p. 17.

21 James H. Street, *Look Away! A Dixie Notebook* (Westport, Conn.: Greenwood Press, 1977; originally published 1936), p. 40.

22 Ibid., p. 53.

23 Ibid., pp. 54–55.

24 Harvey Johnson, Interview, as quoted in Dale Krane, "The 'New Federalism'—A Practitioner's Perspective," *Intergovernmental News* (Section for Intergovernmental Administration and Management, American Society for Public Administration), vol. 5 (1981).

25 Morris, *Terrains*, p. 10.

26 Southern Growth Policies Board, *Halfway Home and a Long Way to Go: The Report of the Commission on the Future of the South* (Research Triangle Park, N.C.: Southern Growth Policies Board, 1986), p. 7.

27 Morris, *Terrains*, p. 199.

28 Florence Mars, "Witness in Philadelphia," in Abbot, *Mississippi Writers*, pp. 420–21.

29 Street, *Look Away*, p. 75.

30 With the attachment of antidiscrimination regulations to federal grants for public works and community development, black sections of Mississippi towns have experienced a face-lift that has provided a full range of amenities.

31 Thomas D. Clark, "Recollections of a Mississippi Boyhood," in Abbott, *Mississippi Writers*, p. 122.

32 Ibid.

33 Key, *Southern Politics*, p. 229.

CHAPTER 2

1 The quotation is found in John Dittmer, "The Politics of the Mississippi Movement, 1954–1964," in *The Civil Rights Movement in America*, ed. Charles W. Eagles (Jackson: University Press of Mississippi, 1986), pp. 65–96. Professor Tip H. Allen, Jr., provided helpful suggestions for this chapter, such as on the Ole Miss crisis. The research assistance provided by undergraduate student Charles J. Anderson is also appreciated.

2 *Jackson Clarion-Ledger*, June 22, 1989, p. 1A.

3 Charles D. Lowery, "The Great Migration to the Mississippi Territory, 1798–1819," in *A Mississippi Reader: Selected Articles from the Journal of Mississippi History*, ed. Edmond Gonzales (Jackson: Mississippi Department of Archives and History, 1980), p. 80.

4 W. B. Hamilton, "Mississippi 1817: A Sociological and Economic Analysis,"

Journal of Mississippi History 29 (1967): 270–92; Aubrey Keith Lucas, "Education in Mississippi from Statehood to Civil War," in *A History of Mississippi,* 2 vols., ed. Richard McLemore (Hattiesburg: University and College Press of Mississippi, 1973), 1:352–73; George Duke Humphrey, "Public Education for Whites in Mississippi," *Journal of Mississippi History* 3 (1941): 26–36; William D. McCain, "Education in Mississippi," *Journal of Mississippi History* 22 (1960): 153–66.

5 Christopher S. Johnson, "Poor Relief in Antebellum Mississippi," *Journal of Mississippi History* 49 (1987): 2–3.

6 William K. Scarborough, "Heartland of the Cotton Kingdom," in McLemore, *History,* 1:310–331.

7 James W. Loewen and Charles Sallis, eds., *Mississippi: Conflict and Change* (New York: Pantheon, 1974), p. 67.

8 M. Philip Lucas, "Beyond McCormick and Miles: The Pre-partisan Political Culture of Mississippi," *Journal of Mississippi History,* 44 (1982): 329–48.

9 Everett Carll Ladd, Jr., *American Political Parties: Social Change and Political Response* (New York: W. W. Norton, 1970).

10 Glover Moore, "Separation from the Union," in McLemore, *History,* 1:423–26.

11 John K. Bettersworth, *Mississippi: A History* (Austin, Tex.: Steck, 1959), pp. 170–231; John Edmond Gonzales, "Flush Times, Depression, War, and Compromise," in McLemore, *History,* 1:295.

12 John Ray Skates, *Mississippi: A Bicentennial History* (New York: W. W. Norton, 1979), pp. 99–100.

13 George D. Humphrey, "The Failure of the Mississippi Freedmen's Bureau in Black Labor Relations, 1865–1867," *Journal of Mississippi History* 45 (1983): 23–38; William Harris, "The Reconstruction of the Commonwealth, 1865–1870," in McLemore, *History* 1: pp. 548–51; Donald G. Nieman, "The Freedmen's Bureau and the Mississippi Black Code," *Journal of Mississippi History* 40 (1978): 91–118; Skates, *Mississippi,* pp. 112–14.

14 Loewen and Sallis, *Mississippi,* pp. 152–55.

15 David G. Sansing, "Congressional Reconstruction," in McLemore, *History,* 1:578–79.

16 Ibid., pp. 586–89.

17 James G. Revels, "Redeemers, Rednecks, and Racial Integrity," in McLemore, *History,* 1:594–95; Bettersworth, *Mississippi,* 334–35.

18 Revels, "Redeemers," pp. 601–2; Clyde J. Faries, "Redneck Rhetoric and the Last of the Redeemers: The 1899 McLaurin-Allen Campaign," *Journal of Mississippi History* 33 (1971): 283–98.

19 Bettersworth, *Mississippi,* pp. 191, 192, 307.

20 Ibid., pp. 323, 324, 333.

21 Loewen and Sallis, *Mississippi,* pp. 178–81; Revels, "Redeemers," pp. 613–19.

22 James P. Coleman, "The Mississippi Constitution of 1890 and the Final Decade of the Nineteenth Century," in McLemore, *History,* 2:8–13.

23 Jack Bass and Walter DeVries, *The Transformation of Southern Politics* (New York: Basic Books, 1976), p. 192.

24 Coleman, "Mississippi Constitution," pp. 8–13; Loewen and Sallis, *Mississippi,* pp. 185–86.

25 Loewen and Sallis, *Mississippi,* p. 188.

26 V. O. Key, *Southern Politics in State and Nation* (New York: Vintage, 1949), pp. 229–53.

27 Tip H. Allen, Jr., and Dale Krane, "Class Replaces Race: The Reemergence of Neopopulism in Mississippi Gubernatorial Politics," *Southern Studies* 19 (1980): 183.

28 Key, *Southern Politics,* pp. 229–53.

29 Albert D. Kirwan, *Revolt of the Rednecks—Mississippi Politics: 1876–1925* (Lexington: University of Kentucky Press, 1964), pp. 146–80; William F. Holmes, "James K. Vardaman: From Bourbon to Agrarian Reformer," *Journal of Mississippi History* 31 (1969): 97–115. One biography on Vardaman is George Coleman Osborn, *James Kimble Vardaman: Southern Commoner* (Jackson, Miss.: Hederman Brothers, 1981).

30 Vincent A. Giroux, Jr., "The Rise of Theodore G. Bilbo, 1908–1932," *Journal of Mississippi History* 43 (1981): 180–209; William Saunders Rutledge, "The John J. Henry-Theodore G. Bilbo Encounter, 1911," *Journal of Mississippi History* 34 (1972): 357; Key, *Southern Politics,* pp. 229–53.

31 Key, *Southern Politics,* p. 240.

32 Nannie Pitts McLemore, "James K. Vardaman, a Mississippi Progressive," *Journal of Mississippi History* 29 (1967): 1–11; Loewen and Sallis, *Mississippi,* pp. 194, 238, 239.

33 Allen and Krane, "Class Replaces Race," p. 183.

34 Charles Granville Hamilton, *Progressive Mississippi* (Aberdeen, Miss.: Gregg-Hamilton, 1978), pp. 184–85; Martha Bigelow, "Mississippi Progressivism," *Journal of Mississippi History* 29 (1967): 202–9.

35 Eric Clark, "Regulation of Corporations in the Mississippi Constitutional Convention of 1890," *Journal of Mississippi History* 48 (1986): 31–42.

36 Richard A. McLemore, "Higher Education in the 20th Century," in McLemore, *History,* 2:430–33; Giroux, "Rise," pp. 206–7. Also, see Aubrey Keith Lucas, "The Mississippi Legislature and Mississippi Higher Education, 1890–1960" (Ph.D. diss., Florida State University, 1966).

37 Neal R. Peirce and Jerry Hagstrom, *The Book of America: Inside Fifty States Today* (New York: W. W. Norton, 1983), p. 467.

38 Ibid., pp. 467–68.

39 Skates, *Mississippi,* p. 135.

40 William Winter, "Governor Mike Conner and the Sales Tax, 1932," *Journal of Mississippi History* 41 (1979): 224–25; J. Oliver Emmerich, "Collapse and Recovery," in McLemore, *History,* 2:102–3; Loewen and Sallis, *Mississippi,* p. 240.

41 Bettersworth, "Mississippi," pp. 425, 446–47; Clark, "Regulation," p. 37.

42 Ibid.

43 Donald C. Mosley, "The Labor Union Movement," in McLemore, *History,* 2:254–73.

44 Nancy Weaver and Paul Beaver, "Mississippi Delta: Empty Hands in a Fertile Land," *Jackson Clarion-Ledger,* December 17, 1980, special supplement. U.S. Department of Commerce, Bureau of the Census, *Historical Statistics of the United States: Colonial Times to* 1970 (White Plains, N.Y.: Kraus International Publications, 1989), p. 30.

45 "State's History Helped Stop Growth," *Jackson Daily News,* August 28, 1980, sec. B, p. 10.

46 Bettersworth, *Mississippi,* pp. 422–31; Emmerich, "Collapse and Recovery," pp. 115–17; Bass and DeVries, *Transformation,* pp. 188–89.

47 *Memphis Commercial Appeal,* January 20, 1948. Also see Walter Lord, *The Past That Would Not Die* (New York: Harper and Row, 1965), pp. 5–38, 60–77.

48 Loewen and Sallis, *Mississippi,* pp. 247–51; Bass and DeVries, *Transformation,* pp. 194–96.

49 Howell Raines, *My Soul Is Rested: Movement Days in the Deep South Remembered* (New York: Bantam Books, 1978), p. 127.

50 Loewen and Sallis, *Mississippi,* pp. 253–55. Bass and DeVries, *Transformation,* p. 195.

51 Rhoda Lois Blumberg, *Civil Rights: The 1960s Freedom Struggle* (Boston: Twayne, 1984), p. 55.

52 James W. Silver, *Mississippi: The Closed Society* (New York: Harcourt, Brace, and World, 1963), pp. 35–42.

53 Loewen and Sallis, *Mississippi,* p. 257.

54 As quoted in Silver, *Mississippi,* pp. 41–42.

55 Taylor Branch, *Parting the Waters: America in the King Years,* 1954–63 (New York: Simon and Schuster, 1988), esp. chaps. 13, 17, 19, and 21.

56 Bass and DeVries, *Transformation*, pp. 199–201. The conversations between Governor Barnett and President Kennedy are played publicly as part of the exhibit in the Kennedy Presidential Library.

57 Russel H. Barrett, *Integration at Ole Miss* (Chicago: Quadrangle Books, 1965), pp. 115–16; Lord, *Past*, pp. 169–71, 188–89, 195–96; Silver, *Mississippi*, pp. 6, 41.

58 Loewen and Sallis, *Mississippi*, pp. 264–65. For a definitive account of the Ole Miss riot and its importance to the civil rights struggle in Mississippi, see Tip H. Allen, Jr., "Mississippi Nationalism in the Desegregation Crisis of September 1962," *Canadian Review of Studies in Nationalism* 14 (1987): 49–63.

59 Loewen and Sallis, *Mississippi*, pp. 266–75; Shirley Tucker, *Mississippi from Within* (New York: Arco, 1965); Seth Cagin and Philip Dray, *We Are Not Afraid: The Story of Goodman, Schwerner, and Chaney and the Civil Rights Campaign for Mississippi* (New York: Macmillan, 1988); Blumberg, *Civil Rights*, pp. 83–97.

60 Don Whitehead, *Attack on Terror: The FBI against the Ku Klux Klan in Mississippi* (New York: Funk and Wagnalls, 1970), pp. 177, 189, 233, 313.

61 William Simpson, "The Birth of the Mississippi 'Loyalist Democrats,' 1965–1968," *Journal of Mississippi History* 44 (1982): 27–46; Loewen and Sallis, *Mississippi*, pp. 277–78; Bass and DeVries, *Transformation*, pp. 203–10.

62 Mississippi State basketball teams had won the conference title for three years in a row. The school obeyed the "unwritten law," and the basketball team stayed out of the NCAA tournament to prevent its white players from possibly playing a team with black athletes. But in 1963 newly inaugurated university president D. W. Colvard publicly faced the wrath of the radical white supremacists when it was discovered that the basketball team had secretly left the state to play in the NCAA tournament.

63 Loewen and Sallis, *Mississippi*, pp. 273, 278–79; Terry Alford, "'Attention White People!' The Underground Press in Mississippi: 1962–1968," *Journal of Mississippi History* 49 (1987): 146.

64 Neil R. McMillen, "Development of Civil Rights, 1956–1970," in McLemore, *History*, 2:164–65; Loewen and Sallis, *Mississippi*, p. 279.

65 *USA Today*, July 28, 1987, p. 13A.

66 Wanda Cantrell, "South Must Change Economic Focus," *Jackson Clarion-Ledger*, May 16, 1986, pp. 1A, 16A.

67 Ibid.

68 Lewis H. Smith and Robert S. Herren, "Mississippi," in *Reagan and the States*, ed. Richard P. Nathan, Fred C. Doolittle, and associates (Princeton: Princeton

University Press, 1987), pp. 208–30. Also see Beverly W. Hogan, "It's Time for State, Local Leaders to Set Budget Priorities," *Jackson Clarion-Ledger,* March 2, 1986, sect. 1, pp. 1–2.

CHAPTER 3

1 Eric C. Clark, "Regulation of Corporations in the Mississippi Constitutional Convention of 1890," *Journal of Mississippi History* 48 (1986): 41.

2 Benjamin F. Wright, *The Growth of American Constitutional Law* (New York: Regnal and Hitchcock, 1942), p. 10.

3 Robert V. Haynes, "The Road to Statehood," in *A History of Mississippi,* 2 vols., ed. Richard A. McLemore (Hattiesburg: University and College Press of Mississippi, 1973), 1:245–47.

4 For the original texts of Mississippi's four constitutions, see *The Constitutions of Mississippi as Originally Adopted* (University, Miss.: Bureau of Governmental Research, 1982).

5 Wilbourne M. Drake, "The Framing of Mississippi's First Constitution," *Journal of Mississippi History* 29 (1967): 327.

6 See Mississippi Constitution (1817), arts. 3, 4, 5, 6.

7 *Memphis Commercial Appeal,* February 3, 1924.

8 Porter L. Fortune, Jr., "The Formative Period," in McLemore, *History,* 1:278–82.

9 Mississippi Constitution (1832), arts. 3, 5, 7; Robert Lowery and William H. McCardle, *A History of Mississippi* (Jackson, Miss.: R. H. Henry, 1891), pp. 272–73; Fortune, "Formative Period," pp. 282–83.

10 William C. Harris, "The Reconstruction of the Commonwealth," in McLemore, *History,* 1:556–57, 560–61.

11 Robert B. Highsaw and Charles N. Fortenberry, *The Government and Administration of Mississippi* (New York: Thomas Y. Crowell, 1954), pp. 17–18; Harris, "Reconstruction," pp. 566–70.

12 *Journal of the Proceedings of the Constitutional Convention of the State of Mississippi* (1868), pp. 295–96, 519, 543; Mississippi Constitution (1869), arts. 4, 5, 6, 8, 10.

13 John R. Skates, *Mississippi: A Bicentennial History* (Dubuque, Iowa: W. W. Norton, 1979), pp. 122–23; James P. Coleman "The Mississippi Constitution of 1890 and the Final Decade of the Nineteenth Century," in McLemore, *History,* 2:5–12.

14 Skates, *Mississippi,* p. 124; Coleman, "Mississippi Constitution of 1890," p. 3. See also Mississippi Constitution (1890), art. 12, sec. 244.

15 Dunbar Rowland, *History of Mississippi: The Heart of the South* (Chicago: S. J. Clark, 1925), 2:252.

16 *Williams v. Mississippi,* 170 U.S. 213 (1898); Mississippi Constitution (1890), art. 5, sec. 140; art. 13, sec. 256; Coleman, "Mississippi Constitution of 1890," p. 17.

17 Coleman, "Mississippi Constitution of 1890," p. 15.

18 Mississippi Constitution (1890), arts. 4, 5, 7, 8, 15.

19 *Journal of the Proceedings of the Constitutional Convention of the State of Mississippi* (1890), pp. 549–50, 697. In *Sproul v. Fredericks,* 69 Miss. 898 (1892), the state supreme court ruled that since the act calling the convention had not specified submission, the convention was sovereign.

20 The criticisms are taken from a compilation of deficiencies derived from the following: interview with Morris W. H. Collins, Jr., chairman of Committee on Executive Article, Mississippi Constitutional Study Commission, February 23, 1987; interview with Brad Pigott, president of Mississippi First, March 2, 1987; David M. Landry and Joseph B. Parker, eds., *Mississippi Government and Politics in Transition* (Dubuque, Iowa: Kendall/Hunt, 1976); Edward H. Hobbes, ed., *Yesterday's Constitution Today: An Analysis of the Mississippi Constitution of 1890* (University, Miss.: Bureau of Public Administration, University of Mississippi, 1960); addresses by William F. Winter, former governor, and Gil Carmichael, Republican party figure, to the political leadership class, Mississippi State University, November 26 and December 5, 1986, respectively; and *Wall Street Journal,* August 19, 1986.

21 For additional details on revision methods, see Tip H. Allen, Jr., and Coleman B. Ransone, Jr., *Constitutional Revision in Theory and Practice* (University, Ala.: Bureau of Public Administration, University of Alabama, 1962), pp. 3–16.

22 Daniel C. Vogt, "Government Reform, the 1890 Constitution, and Mike Conner," *Journal of Mississippi History* 48 (1986): 43–56.

23 See Constitutional Study Commission, *A Draft of a New Constitution for the State of Mississippi,* December 1986.

24 Interviews with Collins and with Tom Sawyer, members of Constitutional Study Commission, March 28, 1987.

25 For a discussion of the Speaker's powers, see Sid Salter, "Newman Not a Devil, but an Infighter," *Starkville Daily News,* April 1, 1987.

26 *Clarion-Ledger/Jackson Daily News,* January 11, 1987.

27 *Meridian Star,* February 7, March 12, 1987.

28 *Jackson Daily News,* February 25, 1987, and interview with Tyrone Ellis, state representative and chairman of Legislative Black Caucus, May 27, 1987.

29 Memorandum to members of the House Constitution Committee from Hugh

Ketchum, president of Mississippi Manufacturers Association, January 19, 1987; and Mississippi Farm Bureau Federation, *Farm Flashes,* February 13, March 13, 1987.

30 *Meridian Star,* January 10, March 14, 1987; *Clarion-Ledger/Jackson Daily News,* March 15, 1987.

31 Mississippi House of Representatives, roll call, amendment to 1984–88 rules, January 9, 1987; *Mississippi Official and Statistical Register,* 1984–88 (Jackson: Mississippi Secretary of State, 1985) p. 156; "How the House Voted," *Clarion-Ledger/Jackson Daily News,* April 12, 1987.

32 *Clarion-Ledger/Jackson Daily News,* February 17, 1985; *Jackson Daily News,* March 11, 12, 1987.

33 *Jackson Clarion-Ledger,* May 2, 1988, p. 1A; May 4, 1988, p. 1A; May 5, 1988, p. 1A.

34 Mississippi, Legislative Reference Bureau, Constitutional Amendments, *Mississippi Constitution of* 1890 (Jackson, Miss., 1985).

35 Numan V. Bartley and Hugh D. Graham, *Southern Politics and the Second Reconstruction* (Baltimore: Johns Hopkins University, 1975).

CHAPTER 4

1 David Bodenhamer, "Images and Impressions of Mississippi and the Sense of Place: Native View/Outside View," in *Sense of Place: Mississippi,* ed. Peggy Prenshaw and Jesse McKee (Jackson: University Press of Mississippi, 1979), p. 58.

2 Statement made after a series of house rules reforms making the chamber's procedures more democratic were enacted despite Newman's opposition. Dan Davis, "House Strips Newman's Powers, 75–45," *Clarion-Ledger/Jackson Daily News,* January 10, 1987, p. 1A.

3 Kay Lehman Schlozman and John T. Tierney, *Organized Interests and American Democracy* (New York: Harper and Row, 1986), p. 201, indicates that the conventional wisdom is that states having strong parties tend to have weak interest groups, and vice versa. L. Harmon Ziegler classifies Mississippi as a state having strong pressure groups; see his "Interest Groups in the States," in *Politics in the American States: A Comparative Analysis,* 4th ed. ed. Virginia Gray, Herbert Jacob, and Kenneth N. Vines (Boston: Little, Brown, 1983), p. 100.

4 Peggy W. Prenshaw and Jesse O. McKee, *Sense of Place: Mississippi* (Jackson: University Press of Mississippi, 1979), pp. 48–49.

5 Jack Bass and Walter DeVries, *The Transformation of Southern Politics: Social*

Change and Political Consequence since 1945 (New York: New American Library, 1977), p. 200.

6 The Moral Majority favors conservative positions on a range of public policies. Nationally, it is led by the Reverend Jerry Falwell. Its supporters often cite religious values to defend their positions. Detractors argue that the group encourages government intrusion into the private lives of citizens, such as by opposing abortion and wanting to require religious practices in the public schools. Some political observers feel that the group has been hurt nationally by an image of intolerance and self-righteousness.

7 Stephen D. Shaffer, *The* 1981 *Annual Mississippi Poll: A Study of Mississippians' Political Attitudes* (Mississippi State: Social Science Research Center, Mississippi State University, 1982), pp. 17, 39.

8 Stephen D. Shaffer and Wolfgang Frese, *The* 1984 *Annual Mississippi Poll: A Study of Mississippians' Political and Social Attitudes* (Mississippi State: Social Science Research Center, Mississippi State University, 1984), p. 9.

9 Stephen D. Shaffer, "Changing Political Patterns in a-Deep South State," paper presented at the Citadel Symposium on Southern Politics, the Citadel, Charleston, South Carolina, March 25–27, 1982.

10 Prenshaw and McKee, *Sense of Place*, pp. 112–17.

11 Shaffer and Frese, 1984 *Annual Mississippi Poll*, p. 7.

12 Shaffer, 1981 *Annual Mississippi Poll*, pp. 38–42.

13 Public opinion data of the Mississippi Delta are drawn from "Perceptions and Attitudes of Mississippi Delta Residents," by Stephen D. Shaffer, appearing in "Portrait of the Delta," a manuscript edited by David Mason and available from the Social Science Research Center at Mississippi State University. These data are drawn from a statewide telephone poll that interviewed 348 Delta residents and 517 non-Delta residents from April 11 to April 24, 1988.

14 V. O. Key, *Southern Politics in State and Nation* (New York: Vintage, 1949), pp. 230–46.

15 Bass and Devries, *Transformation*, pp. 194–202.

16 Neil R. McMillen, "Development of Civil Rights, 1956–1970," in *A History of Mississippi*, 2 vols., ed. Richard A. McLemore (Hattiesburg, Miss.: University and College Press of Mississippi, 1973), 2:154–76.

17 Shaffer, 1981 *Annual Mississippi Poll*, pp. 76–79.

18 Ibid., pp. 85–97.

19 Norman Nie, Sidney Verba, and John Petrocik, *The Changing American Voter*, enl. ed. (Cambridge: Harvard University Press, 1979), p. 254.

20 Shaffer, 1981 *Annual Mississippi Poll*.

21 Shaffer and Frese, 1984 *Annual Mississippi Poll*, p. 31.

22 Stephen D. Shaffer, series of press releases from the 1986 Mississippi Poll, MSU University Relations.

23 Shaffer and Frese, 1984 *Annual Mississippi Poll,* p. 30. Pertinent results from a number of statewide public opinion polls are available from the Social Science Research Center at Mississippi State University.

24 Shaffer, 1986 press releases, MSU University Relations.

25 Polls by other organizations have yielded similar results. A University of Southern Mississippi poll found support for a lottery, mandatory seat-belt law, and increased funding for education (*Jackson Clarion-Ledger,* April 14, 1987, p. B1). A *Clarion-Ledger/Jackson Daily News* poll found support for raising teacher salaries to the Southeast average, greater equalization of public school funding across poor and rich districts, the unit system, and a new state constitution (*Clarion-Ledger/Jackson Daily News,* December 27, 1987, p. H1, and January 3, 1988, p. H1).

26 Nie, Verba, and Petrocik, *Changing American Voter,* pp. 253–56.

27 David Knoke, "Stratification and the Dimensions of American Political Orientations," *American Journal of Political Science* 23 (1979): 772–91; Everett C. Ladd and Charles D. Hadley, *Transformations of the American Party System,* 2d ed. (New York: W. W. Norton, 1978).

28 Keith Poole and L. Harmon Zeigler, *Women, Public Opinion, and Politics* (New York: Longman, 1985).

29 Neal Peirce, *The Deep South States of America* (Cambridge: Harvard University Press, 1974).

30 Shaffer, "Changing Political Patterns."

31 See Stephen D. Shaffer, "Perceptions and Attitudes."

32 Ziegler, "Interest Groups," pp. 99–103.

33 Interview with Hugh Ketchum, president, Mississippi Manufacturers Association, February 12, 1987; "Manufacturers Say State Could Lure Firms Better," *Jackson Clarion-Ledger,* January 3, 1987, p. B7; *MMA Legislative Bulletin,* January 29, 1987.

34 Interview with Edward Blake, public affairs director, Mississippi Farm Bureau Federation, February 23, 1987; Legislative newsletter, *Farm Flashes,* February 13, 1987; "Convention Fears Come to Forefront," *Starkville Daily News,* February 1, 1988, pp. 1, 14.

35 Interview with Bob Pittman, president, Mississippi Economic Council, February 17, 1987. Also see newspaper *Mississippi Business,* February 9, 1987.

36 Interview with Benjamin Woods, executive director, Mississippi Bankers Association, February 16, 1987.

37 Interview with Spence Dye, president, Retail Association of Mississippi, February 16, 1987.

38 "House Panel Kills Bills Limiting Liability Claims," *Jackson Clarion-Ledger*, March 4, 1987, p. 8B.

39 Interview with Bucky Murphy, lobbyist, Mississippi State Medical Association, February 19, 1987. Also see *Mississippi State Medical Legislative Report*, January 16, 1987.

40 See magazine *Mississippi Supervisor*, February 1987.

41 Interview with Charles Williams, former president and lobbyist for sixteen years for the Mid-Continent Oil and Gas Association, Mississippi/Alabama Division, February 26, 1987.

42 Much of the information on Mississippi interest groups was drawn from telephone interviews with group representatives. Each group representative was administered the same survey, which was a condensed version of the questionnaire employed by Schlozman and Tierney in *Organized Interests and American Democracy.*

43 Interview with William Conlee, president of Mississippi Right to Life, February 27, 1987; also see "Jackson Clinic Seeks Limit on Anti-Abortion Protests," *Jackson Clarion-Ledger*, March 3, 1987, p. 4B.

44 "Religion Affects Outcome of Lawmaker's Decisions," *Clarion-Ledger/Jackson Daily News*, April 19, 1986, p. C1.

45 Interview with Thomas Knight, president, Mississippi AFL-CIO, February 18, 1987.

46 Interview with David Bongiolatti, executive director, Mississippi Association of Educators, February 18, 1987.

47 "State NAACP Renews Fight against Racism," *Jackson Clarion-Ledger*, March 2, 1987, p. 1; "Canton Aldermen Appoint Black to School Board," *Jackson Clarion-Ledger*, March 4, 1987, p. B1.

48 Interview with Hilary Chiz, executive director, state American Civil Liberties Union, February 16–17, 1987; "ACLU Fights for 'Rights' Staff," *Clarion-Ledger/Jackson Daily News*, March 15, 1987, p. H1.

49 Interview with Paul Neville, president, Mississippi chapter of Common Cause, February 12, 1987.

50 Interview with Brad Pigott, chairman, Mississippi First, February 17, 1987.

51 Jay Eubank, "New Education Group Expects to Have Clout," *Jackson Clarion-Ledger,* August 3, 1989, p. B1.

52 Interview with Mississippi Federation of Business and Professional Women spokespersons included Frances Coleman, legislative action chair, February 12 and 19, 1987, and Janet Harris, president, February 26, 1987.

CHAPTER 5

1 F. John Wade, "The Development of Mississippi's Economy since 1950," in *Sense of Place: Mississippi*, ed. Peggy W. Prenshaw and Jesse O. McKee (Jackson: University Press of Mississippi, 1979), pp. 179–88.

Funding support for the research in this chapter was provided by the Social Science Research Center and John C. Stennis Institute of Government at Mississippi State University. The helpful comments of Douglas Feig and assistance provided by Jeong-sook Kim and Sheila Pickett Putnam are also appreciated.

2 Raymond Tatalovich, "The Role of the Mississippi Electorate in a Changing Political System," in *Mississippi Government and Politics in Transition*, ed. David M. Landry and Joseph B. Parker (Dubuque, Iowa: Kendall/Hunt, 1976).

3 Wade, "Development," pp. 183–84.

4 William F. Winter, "New Directions in Politics, 1948–1956," in *A History of Mississippi*, 2 vols., ed. Richard A. McLemore (Hattiesburg: University and College Press of Mississippi, 1973), 2:146.

5 Sidney Verba and Norman Nie, *Participation in America* (New York: Harper and Row, 1972).

6 V. O. Key, Jr., *Southern Politics* (New York: Vintage, 1949).

7 Ibid., p. 286; James Loewen and Charles Sallis, *Mississippi: Conflict and Change* (New York: Pantheon, 1974), p. 237; David J. Ginzl, "Lily-White versus Black and Tans: Mississippi Republicans during the Hoover Administration," *Journal of Mississippi History* 42 (1980): 194–211.

8 Norman H. Nie, Sidney Verba, and John R. Petrocik, *The Changing American Voter*, enl. ed. (Cambridge: Harvard University Press, 1979), p. 268.

9 Jack Bass and Walter DeVries, *The Transformation of Southern Politics* (New York: New American Library, 1977), pp. 194–202; Alexander P. Lamis, *The Two-Party South* (New York: Oxford University Press, 1984), pp. 44–49; Billy Burton Hathorn, "Challenging the Status Quo: Rubel Lex Phillips and the Mississippi Republican Party, 1963–1967," *Journal of Mississippi History* 47 (1985): 240–65.

10 John K. Bettersworth, *Mississippi: The Land and the People* (Austin, Tex.: Steck-Vaughn, 1981), p. 328.

11 Bass and DeVries, *Transformation*, pp. 213–16.

12 Lamis, *Two-Party South*, pp. 52–55.

13 Polls conducted by the Republican party in the 1970s suggest that some of the partisan change occurred between 1978 and 1981. A 1975 poll indicated that only 6 percent of voters called themselves Republicans, and 51 percent were Democrats, with the rest being Independent and don't knows. A 1978 poll of all eligible voters

found that 12 percent were Republicans, 57 percent Democrats, and 31 percent Independents (Bass and DeVries, *Transformation*, 1977, p. 216; *Eagle,* Mississippi Republican party newsletter, December 1986, p. 7).

14 The survey data I rely on in this chapter are from statewide telephone polls of adult Mississippi residents using random digit dialing and having approximately 75 percent response rates, conducted by the Mississippi State University Social Science Research Center. The dates and numbers of completed interviews are: October–November 1981 = 616; September 1982 = 894; April 1984 = 610; February 1986 = 611; April 1988 = 632; April 1990 = 601. The 1982 survey was sponsored by the *Clarion-Ledger/Jackson Daily News*. All data are weighted by the relevant demographic characteristics based on the 1980 census and more recent population projections.

15 Lamis, *Two-Party South,* pp. 56–57.

16 "Charges Tie Allain to Male Prostitutes," *Jackson Clarion-Ledger,* October 26, 1983, pp. 1A, 12A.

17 Stephen D. Shaffer, "Voting in Four Elective Offices: A Comparative Analysis," *American Politics Quarterly* 10 (1982): 5–30.

18 James Sundquist, *Dynamics of the Party System* (Washington, D.C.: Brookings Institution, 1973), p. 199.

19 Both liberal and conservative blacks are heavily Democratic, though liberal blacks became even more Democratic and conservative blacks slightly less Democratic after 1981: 89 percent of liberal blacks were Democrats in 1986, compared with 68 percent in 1981; 61 percent of conservative blacks were Democrats in 1986, compared with 72 percent in 1981. Republicans made no gains among conservative blacks but lost among liberals, since only 2 percent of liberal blacks were Republicans in 1986 compared with 5 percent in 1981.

20 Key, *Southern Politics*; Ladd and Hadley, *Transformations*.

21 Nie, Verba, and Petrocik, *Changing American Voter,* p. 228. For instance, between 1981 and 1986, among college-educated blacks 80 percent were Democrats and 1 percent were Republicans, while among black high-school dropouts 73 percent were Democrats and 10 percent were Republicans. On the average, 77 percent of high-income blacks were Democrats and 4 percent were Republicans, while 71 percent of low-income blacks were Democrats and 8 percent were Republicans.

22 A lesson from history is instructive. Kristi Andersen, for example, found that new voters helped the Democratic party become the majority party in America during the 1930s. See Kristi Anderson, "Generation, Partisan Shift, and Realignment: A Glance Back to the New Deal," in Nie, Verba, and Petrocik, *Changing American Voter*.

23 In the 1980s, on the average 86 percent of blacks over sixty were Democrats and 5 percent were Republicans, while 67 percent of blacks under thirty were Democrats and 9 percent were Republicans.

24 In the early 1960s, Philip Converse argued that migrants to the South were more Republican than were native southerners. See Phillip Converse, "On the Possibility of Major Political Realignment in the South," in *Change in the Contemporary South*, ed. A. P. Sindler (Durham, N.C.: Duke University Press, 1963), pp. 195–222. The Mississippi poll's indicator of number of years lived in the state is not identical to that in Converse's study, which looked at region of childhood. Our indicator nevertheless measures the length of exposure to the traditionally solid Democratic political environment of Mississippi.

25 Keith T. Poole and L. Harmon Zeigler, *Women, Public Opinion and Politics* (New York: Longman, 1985).

26 A more detailed analysis of partisan changes in Mississippi and the South as a whole is provided in Robert Swansbrough and David M. Brodsky, *The South's New Politics: Realignment and Dealignment* (Columbia: University of South Carolina Press, 1988). Particularly relevant is the chapter by Stephen D. Shaffer, "Changing Party Politics in Mississippi," pp. 189–203.

27 Key, *Southern Politics*; Dale Krane and Tip H. Allen, Jr., "Factional Durability in Mississippi's Gubernatorial Elections, 1927–75," in *Party Politics in the South*, ed. Robert P. Steed, Laurence W. Moreland, and Tod A. Baker (New York: Praeger, 1980).

28 William Crotty, *American Parties in Decline,* 2d ed. (Boston: Little, Brown, 1984).

29 Harold Stanley, "Southern Partisan Changes: Dealignment, Realignment, or Both?" *Journal of Politics* 50 (1988): 64–88. Consistent with Mississippi electoral patterns, Stanley documents how both realignment and dealignment are shaping southern party politics in general. An increasing number of southerners are thinking of themselves as Republicans but, like others, often voting in an independent fashion for the more attractive candidate.

30 Alan Ehrenhalt, *Politics in America,* 1986 (Washington, D.C.: Congressional Quarterly, 1985).

31 Stephen D. Shaffer and Douglas Feig, *The* 1982 *Annual Mississippi Poll: A Survey of Political Attitudes* (Mississippi State: Social Science Research Center, Mississippi State University, 1983), p. 44.

32 Ehrenhalt, *Politics,* pp. 840–41.

33 Stephen D. Shaffer and Wolfgang Frese, *The* 1984 *Annual Mississippi Poll: A Study of Mississippians' Political and Social Attitudes* (Mississippi State: Social Science Research Center, Mississippi State University 1984), p. 42.

34 *Clarion-Ledger/Jackson Daily News,* October 9, 1988, p. 31.

35 *Clarion-Ledger/Jackson Daily News,* October 9, 1988, p. 3I; December 13, 1988, page 1A; *Starkville Daily News,* May 25, 1988, page 4A.

36 *Jackson Clarion-Ledger,* October 22, 1988, p. 1A; September 25, 1988, p. 3B; July 24, 1988, p. 3B; October 12, 1988, p. 3B; August 5, 1988, p. 1B; September 11, 1988, pp. 1B, 6B; *Starkville Daily News,* August 3, 1988, p. 5.

37 A detailed account of the 1988 presidential and Senate campaigns in Mississippi and an extensive analysis of the election results are provided in Stephen D. Shaffer's "Mississippi" chapter in *The 1988 Presidential Election in the South,* ed. Laurence W. Moreland, Robert P. Steed, and Tod A. Baker, eds. (New York: Praeger, 1991).

38 Jules Witcover, *Marathon: The Pursuit of the Presidency, 1972–1976* (New York: Viking, 1977), p. 198.

39 "Governor," *Jackson Daily News,* August 5, 1987, p. 14A.

40 The 1980 television ad appears in the HBO program "And If I'm Elected," (narrated by the Smothers Brothers).

41 Jeff Copeskey, "Selling the Candidates, 1987," *Clarion-Ledger/Jackson Daily News,* July 12, 1987, p. 1H.

42 A 1988 statewide poll conducted by Mississippi State University illustrated Mabus's strength among higher SES residents: 67 percent of those with some college and 63 percent of the over $20,000 income group rated Mabus's performance as excellent or good. A somewhat lower 59 percent of high-school dropouts and 54 percent of the under $10,000 income group rated him favorably.

43 James Gibson, Cornelius Cotter, John Bibby, and Robert Huckshorn, "Assessing Party Organizational Strength," *American Journal of Political Science* 27 (1983): 193–222.

44 Much information in this section of the chapter was derived from interviews with Ebbie Spivey, Republican state party chairman, March 5, 1987; Evelyn McPhail, Republican state party chairman, January 25, 1988; Brian Martin, executive director, state Democratic party, March 3, 1987, January 19, 1988; Lisa Walker, executive director, state Democratic party, October 12, 1990; and Michael Harrell, communication director, state Republican party, October 15, 1990.

45 "Local Republicans Take Stance," *Starkville Daily News,* February 25, 1987, p. 5.

46 "New Executive Director Hired for Democrats," *Jackson Clarion-Ledger,* July 9, 1989, p. B1; "GOP Criticizes Democratic Executive Director Selection," *Starkville Daily News,* July 17, 1989, p. 1.

47 Written questionnaires were distributed to the delegates at the state party conventions. The Republican convention was held on April 14, 1984, and 203 delegates

completed the surveys, for a response rate of 44 percent. The Democratic convention was held on May 5, 1984, and 514 delegates completed surveys, for a response rate of 30 percent. The demographic and candidate preference makeup of those returning surveys was very similar to all delegates. For comparison, on the ideological self-identification questionnaire item the results for the general public were Democrats: 18 percent liberal, 60 percent moderate, and 22 percent conservative; Republicans: 7 percent liberal, 50 percent moderate, and 43 percent conservative.

CHAPTER 6

1 John Quincy Adams, "The Mississippi Legislature," in *Mississippi Government and Politics in Transition*, ed. David M. Landry and Joseph B. Parker (Dubuque, Iowa: Kendall/Hunt, 1976), p. 58.

2 William J. Keefe and Morris S. Ogul, *The American Legislative Process: Congress and the States,* 4th ed. (Englewood Cliffs, N.J.: Prentice-Hall, 1977), pp. 7–8.

3 Ibid., pp. 8–9.

4 Ibid., p. 6.

5 In the course of preparing this chapter, I conducted many interviews, most by telephone, ranging in length from fifteen minutes to one hour. I would like to thank the following people for their cooperation and assistance in providing basic information, though I accept responsibility for the conclusions drawn in this chapter:

> Joseph Baddley, administrative assistant to the lieutenant governor of the state of Mississippi, now semiretired
>
> Gary Chittom, assistant to the president and director of member relations of The Mississippi Farm Bureau Federation
>
> Edward Custer, executive director of the Mississippi Dairy Products Association
>
> Spence Dye, president of the Retail Association of Mississippi
>
> Billy Gore, assistant attorney general of the state of Mississippi
>
> Charles J. Jackson, Jr., clerk of the Mississippi house of representatives
>
> John Pennebaker, member of the Mississippi house of representatives
>
> Edward Peters, district attorney, Hinds and Yazoo counties, seventh circuit court district
>
> H. Scott Ross, member of the Mississippi house of representatives
>
> A. D. Seale, Jr., associate director of the Mississippi Experiment Station, retired
>
> Kim Sutherland, public affairs manager, Mississippi Highway Commission

6 Mississippi is one of only five states that hold gubernatorial or legislative elections in odd-numbered years (the others are Kentucky, Louisiana, New Jersey, and Virginia). The years in which elections are held are specified in the state constitution of 1890. This practice provides the greatest possible insulation of these state elections from national forces; hence state election results are unaffected by the outcomes of presidential and congressional races.

7 William Pound, "Reinventing the Legislature," *State Legislatures*, 1986, 16–20.

8 Some supporters of Jesse Jackson have argued that runoff primaries discriminate against black candidates, since it may be easier for a black candidate to receive a plurality of the vote in the first primary than to receive a majority of the vote in the runoff Democratic primary. The runoff theoretically provides an opportunity for supporters of the white Democratic candidates to combine and throw their support to the strongest white candidate. On the other hand, runoff primaries put a premium on successful coalition building, strengthening the Democratic party. If runoff primaries were eliminated and a black candidate received the Democratic party nomination with less than a majority of the primary vote, supporters of the losing white candidates might throw their support to the Republican candidate. Such a situation could encourage the Republican party to contest more legislative seats and contribute to the growth of the Republican party and to Republican electoral victories.

9 See 377 U.S. 533 (1964); Adams, "Mississippi Legislature," pp. 57–88.

10 Ibid., p. 60.

11 James W. Loewen and Charles Sallis, *Mississippi: Conflict and Change* (New York: Pantheon, 1974).

12 Andrea Paterson, "Is the Citizen Legislator Becoming Extinct?" *State Legislatures*, 1986, 22.

13 Ibid., p. 22.

14 States have interpreted such conflict-of-interest provisions differently. For example, the Nebraska state courts recently ruled that it did not violate the state constitution for public educators to serve in the state legislature.

15 *Mississippi Official and Statistical Register,* 1984–1988 (Jackson: Mississippi Secretary of State, 1985), pp. 129, 161.

16 Ibid., pp. 125–28, 157–60.

17 Fred R. Harris and Paul L. Hain, *America's Legislative Processes: Congress and the States* (Glenview, Ill.: Scott, Foresman, 1983), p. 271.

18 *The Book of the States,* 1986–1987 (Lexington, Ky.: Council of State Governments, 1987), p. 123.

19 Ibid., p. 121.

20 Ibid., p. 122.

21 Lucinda Simon, *A Legislator's Guide to Staffing Patterns* (Denver: National Conference of State Legislatures, 1979).

22 In both chambers there are methods whereby standing committees can be circumvented, but they are not often used successfully.

23 Woodrow Wilson, *Congressional Government* (New York: Meridian Books, 1956), p. 62; first published in 1885.

24 In the wake of the house revolt, a group of seven dissident state senators unsuccessfully sought to transfer the powers of the lieutenant governor over committee assignments, chairmanships, and referral of bills to committees to the senate pro tempore. See Joe O'Keefe, "Group Opens Fire on Dye's Senate Power," *Jackson Clarion-Ledger,* May 7, 1988, p. 1A.

25 Walter J. Oleszek, *Congressional Procedures and the Policy Process,* 2d ed. (Washington, D.C.: CQ Press, 1984), p. 115.

26 *Book of the States,* pp. 91–94.

27 Ibid.

28 Much of the factual information for this section on the struggle to reform the house rules is derived from a lecture delivered by Speaker Pro Tempore Cecil Simmons at the Taft Seminar for Teachers. The seminar, cosponsored annually by the John C. Stennis Institute of Government at Mississippi State University, was held in Jackson in summer 1988.

29 H.B. 522, 1984.

30 H.B. 536, 1986.

CHAPTER 7

1 William N. Ethridge, Jr., *Modernizing Mississippi's Constitution* (University, Miss.: Bureau of Public Administration, 1950), p. 48.

2 Joseph A. Schlesinger, "The Politics of the Executive," in *Politics in the American States: A Comparative Analysis*, ed. Herbert Jacob and Kenneth N. Vines (Boston: Little, Brown, 1965), p. 229; and Thad L. Beyle, "Governors," in *Politics in the American States: A Comparative Analysis,* 4th ed., ed. Virginia Gray, Herbert Jacob, and Kenneth N. Vines (Boston: Little, Brown, 1983), p. 202.

3 So far all Mississippi governors have been men.

4 John Ray Skates, *Mississippi: A Bicentennial History* (New York: W. W. Norton, 1979), p. 173.

5 They are regarded as a "Yuppie youth brigade" because they were elected before age forty. See Peter J. Boyer, "The Yuppies of Mississippi: How They Took over the Statehouse," *New York Times Magazine,* February 28, 1988, pp. 24–26.

6 For fiscal year 1990, the largest budget items in the general fund were the Minimum Foundation Program in the Department of Education, constituting 41.28

percent of the general fund; the Institutions of Higher Learning (10.06 percent); Medicaid program in the newly created Department of Human Services (6.43 percent); mental health in the Department of Human Services (4.48 percent); and the junior colleges (3.81 percent). Spending on these programs within these agencies constituted 66.07 percent of a total state general fund budget of $1,906,859,390. Chapter 9 provides a detailed analysis of the various components of the state's budget, and chapter 10 examines the public policies administered by state agencies.

7 John W. Turcotte to Thomas H. Handy, 14 April 1987. Mr. Turcotte is director of the legislature's Performance Evaluation and Expenditure Review committee (PEER).

8 Thirty-three staff positions are provided by legislation, but there are always other personnel on "temporary" assignment to the governor's staff from some state agency or agencies. These temporary staff members, as many as six or eight, are professionals usually assigned to work on reports.

9 Maurice Dantin, personal interview with the governor's staff member in his capitol office in Jackson, Mississippi, April 17, 1986. At the time of the interview, Dantin had been a legislator, a candidate for governor, and a member of the staffs of two governors. Afterward he was again an unsuccessful gubernatorial candidate.

10 Thad L. Beyle and Robert Dalton, "Appointment Power: Does It Belong to the Governor?" in *Being Governor: The View from the Office*, ed. Thad L. Beyle and Lynn R. Muchmore (Durham, N.C.: Duke University Press, 1983), table 10.3, pp. 109–10.

11 Mississippi joins twenty-two states that also allow their governors two consecutive four-year terms. Governors in nineteen states are in a stronger position, since there is no constitutional limit on the number of terms they may serve. Eight governors have more limited terms than Mississippi's. See *Book of the States,* 1986–1987 (Lexington, Ky.: Council of State Governments, 1986), table 2.9. pp. 51–52.

12 Beyle, "Governors," p. 181.

13 John J. Harrigan, *Politics and Policy in States and Communities,* 2d ed. (Boston: Little, Brown, 1984), p. 235.

14 Thomas E. Kynerd, *Administrative Reorganization of Mississippi Government: A Study in Politics* (Jackson: University Press of Mississippi, 1978), p. 3.

15 Mississippi did not obtain one hundred or more boards and agencies until about midcentury. In his 1950 call to the legislature to reorganize the state's administrative structure, Governor Wright stated, "We now have 103 agencies carrying on our governmental functions." As quoted in ibid., p. 63.

16 Albert D. Kirwan, *Revolt of the Rednecks: Mississippi Politics,* 1876–1925 (Lexington: University of Kentucky Press, 1951; reprinted Gloucester, Mass.: Pete Smith, 1964), pp. 127–32; Allen R. Richards, "The Traditions of Government in the States," in *The Forty-eight States,* ed. American Assembly (New York: Columbia University Press, 1953), p. 53.

17 The foregoing synopsis was derived from the excellent account of state politics of the era given in Kirwan, *Revolt,* chaps. 9–13.

18 Kynerd, *Administrative Reorganization,* pp. 11–13, 16–17.

19 Mississippi, *Mississippi Laws,* 1918, chap. 225.

20 Robert G. Highsaw and Charles N. Fortenberry, *The Government and Administration of Mississippi* (New York: Thomas Y. Crowell, 1954), p. 93.

21 John Quincy Adams, "The Mississippi Legislature," in *Mississippi Government and Politics in Transition,* ed. David M. Landry and Joseph B. Parker (Dubuque, Iowa: Kendall/Hunt, 1976), p. 66.

22 See, for example, Beyle, "Governors," p. 180.

23 Mississippi Constitution (1890), art. 5, sec. 125.

24 James C. Cobb, *The Selling of the South: the Southern Crusade for Industrial Development,* 1936–1980 (Baton Rouge: Louisiana State University Press, 1982), p. 5.

25 United States Social Security Administration, *Social Security Bulletin* 34 (September 1971): 16; Elmer B. Staats, "Intergovernmental Relations: A Fiscal Perspective," *Annals of the American Academy of Political and Social Sciences* 416 (November 1974): 33.

26 Thad L. Beyle, "The Executive Branch: Organization and Issues, 1984–1985," in *Book of the States,* 1986–1987, p. 45.

27 Nicholas Henry, *Governing at the Grassroots,* 3d ed. (Englewood Cliffs, N.J.: Prentice-Hall, 1987), p. 177.

28 Larry Sabato, *Goodbye to Good-time Charlie: The American Governorship Transformed,* 2d ed. (Washington, D.C.: Congressional Quarterly Press, 1983), pp. 9–11.

29 In thirty states the governor shares this power with the legislature, see *Book of the States,* 1986–1987, table 3.2, pp. 83–85.

30 *Jackson Clarion-Ledger,* December 10, 14, and 16, 1982, p. 1 all dates: an excellent series of articles tracing the political moves of the whole session, December 6–21, 1982.

31 *Book of the States,* 1986–1987, table 3.14, pp. 111–12.

32 James P. Coleman, personal interview with the former governor in his law office in Ackerman, Mississippi, June 18, 1981.

33 Dantin interview.

34 *Jackson Clarion-Ledger,* February 27, 1987, p. 1; also March 1, 1987, p. 1.

35 The story was related to an editor of this book by a state agency head.

36 Brad Dye, personal interview with the lieutenant governor in a committee room of the capitol in Jackson, Mississippi, November 1, 1982.

37 Jay Eubank, "Do You Know Who Your Lawmakers Are? Most People in State Can't Name Theirs," *Jackson Clarion-Ledger,* January 7, 1990, p. 14A. Such polls understate citizens' awareness of their legislators, however. Citizens are better able to identify the names of their elected officials when they are listed on a ballot or read to them. Such basic "name recognition" ability may signify little knowledge about their performance in office, however.

38 Jay Eubank and Andy Kanengiser, "Public Gives Poor Marks to Legislature," *Jackson Clarion-Ledger,* January 14, 1990, p. 1A.

39 *Jackson Clarion-Ledger,* January 18, 1990, p. 1A; also, January 23, p. 5A.

40 Beyle, "Governors," pp. 202, 458–59.

CHAPTER 8

1 Ronald G. Marquardt, "The Judiciary: Traditional and Complex," in *Mississippi Government and Politics in Transition,* ed. David M. Landry and Joseph B. Parker (Dubuque, Iowa: Kendall/Hunt, 1976), p. 104.

2 Henry Robert Glick and Kenneth N. Vines, *State Court Systems,* Foundations of State and Local Government Series (Englewood Cliffs, N.J.: Prentice-Hall, 1973), p. 12.

3 Larry Houchins, executive director of the Mississippi State Bar Association, interview by author, Jackson, Mississippi, May 12, 1987.

4 Neville Patterson, retired chief justice of Mississippi Supreme Court, interview by author, Jackson, Mississippi, May 20, 1987.

5 Daniel Elazar, *American Federalism: A View from the States* (New York: Thomas Y. Crowell, 1966), p. 97.

6 Glick and Vines, *State Court,* p. 12.

7 Patterson interview.

8 Ronald G. Marquardt, "Incremental Change in a Changing Society: Evolution of a State Legal System," paper delivered at annual meeting of Southwestern Political Science Association, Houston, Texas, March 20–23, 1985.

9 Harold J. Spaeth, *Supreme Court Policy Making: Explanation and Prediction* (San Francisco: W. H. Freeman, 1979), pp. 1–8.

10 Robert Church, Mississippi Judicial College, telephone interview by the author, May 16, 1989.

11 Lists of the circuit court and chancery court districts and maps are available in the *Mississippi Official and Statistical Register* and the *Mississippi Judiciary Directory and Court Calendar* (Jackson: Mississippi Secretary of State).

12 National Center for State Courts, interview by author, February 16, 1990.

13 Mississippi Supreme Court, *Mississippi Supreme Court Annual Report,* 1988, p. 4.

14 Diane E. Wall, "Judicial Incumbency: The Case of Mississippi Supreme Court, 1932–1985," *Southeastern Political Review* 15 (1987): 112.

15 *Russell v. State,* 312 So. 2d 422 (Miss. 1975).

16 David W. Allen and Diane E. Wall, "The Behavior of Women State Supreme Court Justices: Are They Tokens or Outsiders?" *Justice System Journal* 12 (1987): 232–45.

17 Patterson interview.

18 308 So. 2d 71 (Miss. 1975).

19 *Hall v. State,* 539 So. 2d 1338 (Miss. 1989). Jack Elliott, "Legislature, High Court's Relationship Getting Cooler," *Starkville Daily News,* March 7, 1989, p. 4.

20 441 So. 2d 1329 (Miss. 1983).

21 *Dye v. State ex rel Hale,* 507 So. 2d 332 (Miss. 1987).

22 Diane E. Wall, "A Woman of Many Firsts: The Honorable Lenore Prather," *Journal of Mississippi History*, forthcoming.

23 Herbert Jacob, "Courts," in *Politics in the American States: A Comparative Analysis,* 4th ed., ed. Virginia Gray, Herbert Jacob, and Kenneth N. Vines (Boston: Little, Brown, 1983), p. 226.

24 Houchins interview, May 10, 1989.

25 *Jackson Clarion-Ledger,* May 4, 1986, p. 1H.

26 Reuben Anderson, justice of Mississippi Supreme Court, interview by author, Jackson, Mississippi, December 15, 1987.

27 *Mississippi Code Ann.,* 9–17–1, 1986 Supp.

28 *Mississippi Commission on Judicial Performance Annual Report* (Jackson: Mississippi Commission on Judicial Performance, 1988), p. 28.

29 The Jackson School of Law was an approximately sixty-year-old unaccredited proprietary law school that was purchased by Mississippi College as the beginning of Mississippi College School of Law. Unknown to most Mississippians today, a private black law school existed from 1878 to 1880 at Rust College. Willie Rose, "Historical Notes on Black Lawyers in Mississippi," *Mississippi Lawyer* 33 (March–April 1987): 38. Also, before World War I Millsaps College had a law school, but it closed during the war owing to a lack of students. Frank E. Everett,

"Lawyers, Courts, and Judges," in *A History of Mississippi*, 2 vols., ed. Richard McLemore (Hattiesburg: University and College Press of Mississippi, 1973), 2:377.

30 Ellie Fortner, Mississippi Judicial College, telephone interview by author, March 2, 1990.

31 The first bar association existed from 1821 to 1825, and the second was active from 1886 to 1894. Michael de L. Landon, *The Honor and Dignity of the Profession: A History of the Mississippi State Bar*, 1906–1976 (Jackson: University Press of Mississippi, 1979), pp. 3–4, 92.

32 *Mississippi Code Ann.*, 73–3–143 and 145.

33 Anderson interview. He commented that the Magnolia Bar Association was started in Mississippi in the 1950s when blacks could not be members of the American Bar Association. It currently provides a forum for blacks to communicate about common issues, which are different from other lawyers' legal practice.

34 Marquart, "Incremental Change," p. 5.

35 *Brown v. Vance*, 637 F. 2d 272 (5th Cir. 1981).

36 *Judicial Performance Annual Report*, 1986, p. 10.

37 *Judicial Performance Annual Report*, 1987, p. 10, and *Judicial Performance Annual Report*, 1988, p. 11.

38 Anderson interview.

39 Lenore Prather, justice of Mississippi Supreme Court, interview by author, Jackson, Mississippi, May 20, 1987. *Albright v. Albright*, 437 So. 2d 1003 (Miss. 1983).

40 Roy Noble Lee, chief justice of Mississippi Supreme Court, interview by author, Jackson, Mississippi, December 15, 1987.

41 Patterson interview.

42 *Kirksey v. Allain*, 635 F. Supp. 347 (S.D. Miss. 1986).

43 Sid Salter, "Why Isn't State Government Serious Business?" *Starkville Daily News*, June 4, 1986, p. 6.

44 *Martin v. Mabus*, 700 F. Supp. 327 (S.D. Miss. 1988). *Kirksey v. Allain* was consolidated with *Martin v. Allain*, 658 F. Supp. 1183 (S.D. Miss. 1987) and later renamed *Martin v. Mabus* for the new governor.

45 Robert Naylor, Jr., "Moore Won't Be Waging Losing Battles," *Jackson Clarion-Ledger*, February 26, 1989, p. 1B. Even with the settlement, a federal judge ordered the state to pay $425,000 for the plaintiffs' legal fees. Jack Elliott, Jr., "Payments Delayed over Legal Fees Dispute," *Starkville Daily News*, March 9, 1990, p. 4.

46 Carroll Rhodes, Hazelhurst attorney, telephone interview by author, May 11, 1989.

47 Diane E. Wall and Mary Geter, "Unanticipated Outcomes of Voting Rights Litigation in Mississippi: Women and Minorities in a Judicial Election," paper presented at the 1989 meeting of the American Political Science Association, Atlanta.

48 Patterson interview.

49 Ibid.

50 Prather interview.

51 Tom Brennan, "Chief Justice Hopes to Streamline Court Proceedings," *Jackson Clarion-Ledger,* September 21, 1986, p. 1B.

52 Lee interview.

53 Marquardt, "Incremental Change," p. 6.

54 Patterson interview.

55 Susan Gordon, Mississippi Supreme Court clerk, interview by author, May 20, 1987.

56 Houchins interview, May 12, 1987.

57 Carl Baar, *Separate but Subservient: Court Budgeting in the American States* (Lexington, Mass.: Lexington Books, 1975), p. 83.

58 American Bar Association, *A Handbook on State Judicial Salaries* (Chicago: American Bar Association, 1986).

59 Patterson interview.

60 *Jackson Clarion-Ledger,* April 22, 1984, p. 1C.

61 "Rankin Clerk Has Top Salary," *Starkville Daily News,* April 23, 1989, p. 3A.

62 Judiciary Committee of Young Lawyers Section of Mississippi State Bar and the Court Liaison and Judicial Administration Committee of Mississippi State Bar, "Position Paper Supporting an Increase in Mississippi Judicial Salaries" (n.d.), p. 9.

63 Wall, "Judicial Incumbency," p. 123.

64 Prather interview.

65 Patterson interview.

66 Ibid.

67 *Jackson Clarion-Ledger,* April 26, 1987, p. 1.

68 Anderson interview.

69 "Jurors Hear Opening Arguments in Pruett Trial," *Starkville Daily News,* February 13, 1988, p. 7A.

70 Lee interview.

71 Patterson interview.

72 A computer program for legal materials, such as LEXIS, enables the researcher to obtain a printout of both federal and state court case citations for specific issues or of all the decisions by a specific justice. Naturally computer time is rather expensive. Currently, data on Mississippi's state supreme court may be obtained by a computer program for legal sources.

73 Mississippi Judicial Council, *First Annual Report of the Mississippi Judicial Council,* 1979.

74 Patterson interview.

75 Ibid.

76 Charles J. Younger, former Lowndes County justice court judge and current Lowndes County chancery court clerk, interview by author, February 3, 1988.

77 Brantley, telephone interview by author, February 3, 1988.

78 Prather interview. She was the first supreme court justice to be appointed through a new nominating commission process.

79 Marquardt, "Judiciary," p. 108.

80 Wall, "Judicial Incumbency."

81 Ibid., p. 129.

82 Patterson interview.

83 Lee interview.

84 Prather interview.

85 Glick and Vines, *State Court,* p. 6.

86 *Mississippi Code Ann.,* 89–19–1, 1986 Supp.

87 *Rules of the Mississippi Commission on Judicial Performance, Including Amendments through May,* 1984" (Jackson: Mississippi Commission on Judicial Performance, 1980), pp. 7–8.

88 *Judicial Performance Annual Report,* 1988, p. 14.

89 *Judicial Performance Annual Report,* 1986, p. 20.

90 Ibid., pp. 20–22.

91 *Judicial Performance Annual Report,* 1988, pp. 24–27.

92 Glick and Vines, *State Court,* pp. 67–68.

93 "Group Says Judges 'Fix' Many DUI," *Starkville Daily News,* April 9, 1987, p. 2.

94 "Former Judge Pleads Guilty," *Jackson Clarion-Ledger,* April 19, 1987, p. 7B.

95 "Group Says Judges 'Fix' Many DUI," *Starkville Daily News,* April 9, 1987, p. 2.

96 *Starkville Daily News,* May 5, 1989, p. 2.

97 Glick and Vines, *State Court,* p. 11.

98 Anderson interview.

99 *Jackson Clarion-Ledger,* January 17, 1988, p. 1H.

CHAPTER 9

1 Donald S. Vaughn, "Budgeting in Mississippi State Government," *Public Administration Survey* 4, no. 2 (1956): 3.

2 Paul D. Warner, "Mississippi Economic Review and Outlook," Mississippi Research and Development Center, March 1987, p. 1.

3 U.S. Bureau of the Census, *Statistical Abstract of the United States*, 1980, 100th ed. (Washington, D.C.: U.S. Department of Commerce, 1980).

4 Warner, "Mississippi Economic Review," p. 1.

5 Ibid.

6 *Survey of Current Business* (U.S. Department of Commerce, Bureau of Economic Analysis), August 1989, p. 34.

7 U.S. Bureau of the Census, *Statistical Abstract of the United States*, 1989, 109th ed. (Washington, D.C.: U.S. Department of Commerce, 1989).

8 *Alexander et al. v. State of Mississippi By and Through Allain*, 441 So. 2d 1329 (Miss. 1983).

9 Much of the discussion of Mississippi's budget system before 1956 is based on the article by Vaughn, "Budgeting in Mississippi."

10 The members of the expanded Budget Commission included the lieutenant governor, the Speaker of the house, the president pro tempore of the senate, the chairs of the Senate and House Appropriations Committees, the chairs of the Senate Finance Committee and House Ways and Means Committee, two other senators appointed by the lieutenant governor, and two other representatives appointed by the Speaker of the house.

11 David B. Ogle, *Strengthening the Mississippi Legislature* (New Brunswick, N.J.: Rutgers University Press, 1968), pp. 103–19. Because of his long standing acquaintance with legislative members and his willingness to be assertive, former governor William Winter was able to influence the commission to a greater extent than other governors. Unlike other governors, Winter actually ran the meetings and was able to have his preferred candidate, Jim Cofer, selected as staff director. Cofer, who was publicly criticized by legislative members once Winter left office, resigned as the staff director of the newly organized Fiscal Management Board a few months later.

12 Edward J. Clynch, "Budgeting in Mississippi: Are Two Budgets Better Than One?" *State and Local Government Review* 18 (1986): 49–50. The Clynch piece describes the Mississippi budget process in place since 1984.

13 James E. Anderson, Richard W. Murray, and Edward L. Farley, *Texas Politics: An Introduction* (New York: Harper and Row, 1979), pp. 265–76.

14 This story was related to me by a member of Governor Allain's staff.

15 Mississippi Fiscal Management Board, *Comprehensive Annual Financial Report for Fiscal 1988*, January 1989, p. 36.

16 "College Board Committees Act on Financial Matters," *Starkville Daily News*, December 19, 1985, p. 1.

17 Richard A. Musgrave and Peggy B. Musgrave, *Public Finance in Theory and Practice,* 3d ed. (New York: McGraw-Hill, 1983), pp. 242–54; Robert D.

Lee and Ronald W. Johnson, *Public Budgeting Systems*, 3d ed. (Baltimore: University Park Press, 1983), pp. 38–45.

18 Mississippi first reported the corporate income tax separately from the personal income tax in fiscal year 1976.

19 Kathie Gilbert, *A Brief Introduction to the Mississippi Tax System* (Jackson: Mississippi Research and Development Center, 1984), pp. 10–13. The 1979 tax law increased standard deductions for single persons and married persons filing jointly from $1,500 to $2,300 and from $1,500 to $3,400. The personal exemption for a married couple increased from $6,500 to $9,500, and the exemption for dependents from $750 to $1,500. The exemption for a single taxpayer increased from $4,500 to $6,000. See David Bates, "Legislature's Tax Break Increases Deductions, Exemptions," *Jackson Clarion-Ledger,* February 4, 1979, p. 3A.

20 Mississippi was still able to expand its revenues between 1970 and 1985 even though individuals in given income brackets did not pay higher taxes. One source of additional state money appears to have been an increase in the number of taxpayers in higher tax brackets, owing both to inflation and to real economic growth. Also, increases in business taxes and nontax items paid by businesses and individuals fueled the expansion of state revenues. Businesses have paid higher taxes since 1982, when the rate on income above $10,000 was raised from 4 to 5 percent.

21 Donald Phares, "State and Local Tax Burden across the Fifty States," *Growth and Change* 16, no. 2 (April 1985): 34–42.

22 Ibid.

23 Mississippi Economic Council Taxation Committee, *Taxes on Business,* (Jackson: Mississippi Economic Council, 1982), p. 31.

24 Bill Allain, state of the state address, delivered on January 14, 1986, and reprinted January 15 by *Jackson Clarion-Ledger*.

25 Dan Davis, "Allain Has Fiscal Stand Set in Stone," *Jackson Clarion-Ledger,* February 4, 1986, p. 1A.

26 Bill Minor, "Mississippi Is a Leader in One Category: Sales Tax Burden," *Jackson Clarion-Ledger,* March 6, 1983, p. 3J.

27 Susan Hansen, "Extraction: The Politics of State Taxation," in *Politics in the American States*, ed. Virginia Gray, Herbert Jacob, and Kenneth N. Vines (Boston: Little, Brown, 1983), pp. 440–49.

28 U.S. Bureau of the Census, 1980 *Census of Population: Detailed Population Characteristics, Part 26 (Mississippi)* (Washington, D.C.: U.S. Department of Commerce, 1980), pp. 484, 536–41.

29 Rose Ragsdale, "Sales Tax up to Six Percent Today," *Jackson Clarion-Ledger,* December 1, 1983, p. 12B.

30 Minor, "Mississippi Is a Leader."

31 Keep in mind that all functional areas received substantially more money in 1988 than in 1964. The question being addressed concerns changes in the percentage of money allocated to major functions.

32 Public opinion regarding spending programs, measured in 1981 and 1984, is provided in Stephen D. Shaffer and Wolfgang Frese, *The 1984 Annual Mississippi Poll: A Study of Mississippians' Political and Social Attitudes* (Mississippi State: Social Science Research Center, Mississippi State University, 1984), p. 30.

33 This information was provided by the Mississippi Department of Education.

CHAPTER 10

1 As quoted in Barbara A. Bardes, Mack C. Shelley II, and Steffen W. Schmidt, *American Government and Politics Today: The Essentials,* 2d ed. (St. Paul, Minn.: West, 1988), p. 7.

2 The figures and rankings mentioned in this section are drawn from the following sources: *Statistical Abstract of the United States,* selected years; *Mississippi Statistical Abstract,* selected years; and *Significant Features of Fiscal Federalism,* selected years.

3 Advisory Commission on Intergovernmental Relations (ACIR), *Significant Features of Fiscal Federalism, Revenues and Expenditures,* 1990, vol. 2 (Washington, D.C.: ACIR, 1990), p. 179.

4 See Andy Kanengiser, "Layoff Threat Tempers Cheer of State Pay Raises," *Jackson Clarion-Ledger,* October 1, 1990, p. B1.

5 John Saunders and Jiafang Chen, *Agriculture in Mississippi: 1945–1987* (Mississippi State: Social Science Research Center, Mississippi State University, 1989), pp. 1–6. Dick Molpus, *Mississippi Official and Statistical Register, 1988–1992* (Jackson: Mississippi Secretary of State, 1989), pp. 117, 309–12.

6 Alexander P. Lamis, "Mississippi," in *The 1984 Presidential Election in the South,* ed. Robert P. Steed, Laurence W. Moreland, and Tod A. Baker (New York: Praeger, 1985), p. 56.

7 Mississippi State Highway Department, 1986 *Annual Report.*

8 U.S. Department of Transportation, Federal Highway Administration, *Highway Statistics,* 1985.

9 Molpus, *Mississippi Official and Statistical Register,* pp. 118, 365, 443, 503.

10 Molpus, *Mississippi Official and Statistical Register,* p. 122–24. "Controversial Measures Could Return Next Year," *Jackson Clarion-Ledger,* February 28, 1990, p. 1A.

11 Molpus, *Mississippi Official and Statistical Register*, p. 366–67. Bruce A. Williams, "Bounding Behavior: Economic Regulation in the American States," in *Politics in the American States: A Comparative Analysis*, 4th ed., ed. Virginia Gray, Herbert Jacob, and Kenneth N. Vines (Boston: Little, Brown, 1983), pp. 355–62.

12 Basic factual information was provided by a staff member of the Workers' Compensation Commission, February 28, 1990.

13 Lea Anne Brandon and Reagan Walker, "Residency Rules Boost Enrollment at All-White Academies," *Jackson Clarion-Ledger*, August 12, 1990, pp. 1A, 15A.

14 Andy Kanengiser, "Outdated Textbooks Give State's Schools Bad Image," *Jackson Clarion-Ledger*, November 23, 1986, p. 3J. Dennis Kelly, "How States Measure up on Federal 'Wall Chart,'" *USA Today*, May 3, 1990, p. 4D. Also see charts on states' listings on per pupil spending and teacher pay in *Memphis Commercial Appeal*, September 26, 1990, p. B2.

15 1988 *Annual Report of the State Superintendent of Public Education to the Legislature of Mississippi*. Also see Andy Kanengiser, "State Gets Good, Bad Marks in Education Report," *Jackson Clarion-Ledger*, May 4, 1989, pp. 1A, 20A, and Pat Ordovensky, "States Are at a Standstill in Educational Progress," *USA Today*, May 4, 1989, p. 6D. Also review Kelly, "How States Measure Up," and Lea Anne Brandon, "Report: State Near bottom in Student Achievement," *Jackson Clarion-Ledger*, May 3, 1990, p. B1. A comprehensive source of information on education in each state is provided in *Digest of Education Statistics*, published yearly by the National Center for Education Statistics, U.S. Department of Education.

16 The system also maintains five degree-granting centers and four other resident centers that offer coursework at locations away from the eight senior campuses.

17 See three articles by Lea Anne Brandon in the *Jackson Clarion-Ledger*: "State Losing Teachers to Greener Paychecks," July 29, 1990, p. 1A, 13A; "Swelling Student Tide Filling State's Colleges, September 2, 1990, p. B1; and "College Study: Funding below Region Average," September 17, 1990, pp. 1A, 7A.

18 Only Mississippi State, Southern Mississippi, and Ole Miss are larger.

19 According to Department of Health, State of Mississippi, 1985 *Annual Report*, the state ranked third in syphilis cases ($57.5/100,000$), was eleventh in gonorrhea cases ($591.4/100,000$), and ranked in the top ten in tuberculosis.

20 The 1971–73 infant mortality rate was 26.3 per 1,000 live births. In 1987 Mississippi's infant mortality rate had dropped to 14.4. To compare Mississippi with other states, refer to U.S. Department of Health and Human Services, Public Health Service, *Health United States 1990*, DHHS Publication 91-1232 (Hyatts-

ville, Md.: U.S. Department of Health and Human Services, 1991), p. 69.

21 Edith R. Hornor, *Almanac of the Fifty States* (Palo Alto, Calif.: Information Publications, 1991), p. 435.

22 Only Alabama paid less, at $118 per month.

23 A frequently used estimate of the "adequacy" of AFDC payments is the ratio of AFDC assistance grants per family to state median family income. Robert B. Albritton, "Subsidies: Welfare and Transportation," in Gray, Jacob, and Vines, *Politics in the American States,* pp. 394–95.

24 Albritton, "Subsidies," p. 395.

25 The arrival of nationally based firms in Mississippi's small towns raised wage rates so much that most middle-class families who had maids in the 1950s and 1960s could no longer attract or afford domestic help. This demise of home domestic employment significantly changed the life-style of white middle-class women and encouraged many of them to enter the salaried work-force. This transition fueled the women's movement in the state.

26 See Richard H. Kraemer and Charldean Newell, *Texas Politics,* 3d ed. (St. Paul, Minn.: West, 1987), especially chaps. 6, 7, 8, and 9.

27 Jack L. Walker, "Innovation in State Politics," in *Politics in the American States,* ed. Herbert Jacob and Kenneth N. Vines (Boston: Little, Brown, 1971), p. 358.

28 V. O. Key, *Southern Politics in State and Nation* (New York: Vintage, 1949) p. 241.

29 Peter J. Boyer, "The Yuppies of Mississippi: How They Took over the Statehouse," *New York Times Magazine,* February 28, 1988, pp. 24–76.

30 J. W. Loewen and Charles Sallis, *Mississippi: Conflict and Change* (New York: Pantheon, 1974), p. 247.

31 See Fred Anklam, Jr., "Education Financing Not Equal," *Jackson Clarion-Ledger,* December 2, 1982, p. 1.

32 See Nancy Weaver, "Economy Depends on Education," *Jackson Clarion-Ledger,* November 30, 1982, p. 1.

33 Governor Winter's financial proposal was simple: raise the state's severance tax on oil and gas from 6 percent to 9 percent and place this new money in a trust fund generating interest that would be earmarked for education.

34 The forty-six-point plan contained provisions for compulsory attendance, kindergartens, professional development programs for teachers and administrators, performance-based accreditation standards for school districts, random audits of school districts' finances and quality, establishment of a state school management institute, incentive scholarships for math and science teachers, a reading improvement program for the first three grades, and set of tax changes (income,

sales, and severance taxes) to cover the cost of the reforms. If passed, the complete package would have put Mississippi in the forefront of education renewal in the nation.

35 Legislators expressed very little serious opposition to the administrative aspects of the governor's plan (e.g., teacher and principal standards and professional development programs for both, performance-based school accreditation, random surveys of schools to check on compliance with accreditation standards). Rather, the opposition centered on the options in the areas of early childhood education (kindergartens versus reading assistants for teachers in the first three grades), teachers' pay, and tax increases (sales versus personal income versus severance taxes).

36 The house, sensitive to its 14 (out of 122) black members (especially the chairman of the Education Committee), rejected any increase in the already high sales tax and devised a plan to spread the cost over all aspects of the economy, personal income, oil and gas severance taxes, insurance premiums, tobacco and alcohol and video game machines. The senate, more rural (and with only 2 black members out of 52), defended a sales tax hike and opposed any other type of tax increase.

37 On December 8, Governor Winter modified his original position on the severance tax increase to exempt all new wells for the first three years, wells that produced less than ten barrels a day, and persons whose royalty payments were less than $24,000 a year (it was estimated these exemptions would cover about 90 to 95 percent of all royalty recipients).

38 Robert S. Friedman, "State Politics and Highways," in Jacob and Vines, *Politics in the American States,* p. 487.

39 Albritton, "Subsidies: Welfare and Transportation," pp. 401–10. Compared with near-to-last rankings in the nation in education and social welfare spending, Mississippi ranked twentieth in highway expenditures per capita, twenty-second in highway spending as a percentage of total state spending, and thirty-first in highway density. Part of the explanation for this relatively high priority for highways lies in the geographically large, sparsely populated nature of the state.

40 *Jackson Daily News,* February 12, 1986, p. 10A.

41 Ibid.

42 The Fiscal Management Board in the governor's office estimated the highway fund had $23 million unencumbered.

43 Douglas Feig, Dale Krane, and Stephen Shaffer, "Escaping the 'Politics of Frustration': An Analysis of the 1982 Education Reform Act," revised version of a paper delivered at the 1983 annual meeting of Southern Political Science Association.

44 Joe Atkins and Sidney Cearnal, "Bucking the Highway Dept. Can Be Costly," *Jackson Daily News,* February 12, 1986, p. 1A.

CHAPTER 11

1 Robert B. Highsaw and Charles N. Fortenberry, *The Government and Administration of Mississippi* (New York: Thomas Y. Crowell, 1954), p. 356. This chapter has benefited from the helpful assistance of William "Marty" Wiseman, assistant professor of political science at Mississippi State University. Statements regarding local governments and their officials are based on several sources, including newspaper articles and academic research projects with a number of cities.

2 U.S. Bureau of the Census, 1982 *Census of Governments,* vol. 1, *Government Organization* (Washington, D.C.: U.S. Department of Commerce, 1982).

3 This chapter focuses on cities and counties rather than on special districts. A good introduction to local government is provided by George S. Blair, *Government at the Grass Roots* (Pacific Palisades, Calif.: Palisades, 1986), p. 12.

4 Title 21, *Mississippi Code 1972, Annotated.*

5 David M. Landry and Joseph B. Parker, *Mississippi Government and Politics in Transition* (Dubuque, Iowa: Kendall/Hunt, 1976), pp. 136–40.

6 Andy Kanengiser, "House OKs Equal Money for Schools," *Jackson Clarion-Ledger,* February 23, 1990, p. 1.

7 Strong mayor cities included the only metro areas in the state, with Jackson and Hinds County and Biloxi and Gulfport on the coast; all three switched from the commission form of government. Other strong mayor cities were Bay St. Louis, Greenwood, Hattiesburg, Laurel, and Meridian.

8 In 1985 I implemented a statewide survey of municipal executive officials, including mayors, city managers, and chief administrative officers. Surveys were sent to 104 municipalities, and 84 responses (from different cities) were returned, for a response rate of about 80 percent.

9 A. M. Henderson and Talcott Parsons, eds., *Max Weber: The Theory of Social and Economic Organization* (New York: Free Press, 1964), pp. 329–41.

10 Landry and Parker, *Mississippi Government,* pp. 128–34.

11 See note 1 above.

12 The commission form is used in over 2,500 counties of a total of 3,041 county governments. See Blair, *Government,* p. 105.

13 Gerald T. Gabris, William A. Giles, and Dale A. Krane, "Dynamics in Rural Policy Development: The Uniqueness of County Government," *Public Administration Review* 40 (January–February 1980): 24–29.

14 Arthur Vidich and Joseph Bensman, *Small Town in Mass Society* (Princeton, N.J.: Princeton University Press, 1968), pp. 110–13.

15 By 1989 the state courts had begun to crack down on violations of the open meetings law. One court ruled that supervisors must personally pay for any expenditures authorized behind closed doors.

16 "Mississippi: Stinging the Good Ole Boys," *Newsweek,* August 10, 1987, p. 21.

17 Title 65, *Mississippi Code 1972 Annotated.*

18 Rather than pay for a separate countywide administrator, the bill permits counties to designate the chancery clerk as county administrator. Many counties have followed this route, especially less populous and poorer counties.

19 So many cities in Mississippi have become "key communities" that the designation has become less meaningful as an indicator of their potential for economic development.

20 "Mississippi," *Newsweek*, p. 21.

21 This principle of state sovereignty over cities was upheld in the famous court decision in *City of Clinton v. Cedar Rapids and Missouri Railroad Company,* 24 Iowa 455 (1868).

22 K. C. Morrison and Joe C. Huang, "The Transfer of Power in a Mississippi Town," *Growth and Change* 4 (April 1973): 25–29. George Alexander Sewell and Margaret L. Dwight, *Mississippi Black History Makers,* rev. and enl. ed. (Jackson: University Press of Mississippi, 1984), pp. 59–66.

23 Ibid.

24 Minion K. C. Morrison, *Black Political Mobilization: Leadership, Power, and Mass Behavior* (Albany: State University of New York Press, 1987), pp. 84–92.

25 Ibid.

26 John Kincaid, "Beyond the Voting Rights Act: White Responses to Black Political Power in Tchula, Mississippi," *Publius: The Journal of Federalism* 16 (Fall 1986): 155–72.

27 Minion K. C. Morrison, "Preconditions for Afro-American Leadership: Three Mississippi Towns," *Polity* 17 (Spring 1985): 504–29. Another perspective on this conflict is offered by a longtime observer of Mississippi politics, Marty Wiseman, who argues that the Carthan case was primarily a "black-on-black" power struggle. Though whites took sides, he believes that the internal power struggle among blacks would have occurred in any case.

28 Kincaid, "Beyond the Voting Rights Act."

29 Sewell and Dwight, *Mississippi Black History Makers,* pp. 73–75.

30 Minion K. C. Morrison, "Federal Aid and Afro-American Political Power in Three Mississippi Towns," *Publius: The Journal of Federalism* 17 (Fall 1987): 100.

31 Ibid., pp. 97–111.

32 Alan Ehrenhalt, "For the Black Mayor of Vicksburg, Political Success Means Staying Calm," *Governing,* April 1989, pp. 36–40.

CHAPTER 12

1 Robert Sherrill, *Gothic Politics in the Deep South* (New York: Grossman, 1968), p. 210.

2 Alan Ehrenhalt, ed., *Politics in America: The 100th Congress* (Washington, D.C.: Congressional Quarterly, 1987), p. 818.

3 Daniel J. Elazar, *American Federalism: A View from the States,* 3d ed. (New York: Harper and Row, 1984), p. 14.

4 Elazar, *American Federalism,* pp. 16–18.

5 Numan V. Bartley and Hugh D. Graham, *Southern Politics and the Second Reconstruction* (Baltimore: Johns Hopkins University Press, 1975).

6 Howard Ball, Dale Krane, and Thomas P. Lauth, Jr., *Compromised Compliance: Implementation of the 1965 Voting Rights Act* (Westport, Conn.: Greenwood Press, 1982), pp. 49–50.

7 Ball, Krane, and Lauth, *Compromised Compliance,* p. 48.

8 Mack H. Jones, "The Voting Rights Act as an Intervention Strategy for Social Change: Symbolism or Substance?," in *The Voting Rights Act: Consequences and Implications,* ed. Lorn S. Foster (New York: Praeger, 1985), pp. 63–84.

9 Neal R. Peirce, "Mississippi: Hope at Last," in *The Deep South States of America: People, Politics, and Power in Seven Deep South States,* ed. Neal R. Peirce (New York: W. W. Norton, 1974), p. 185.

10 Richard Scher and James Button, "Voting Rights Act: Implementation and Impact," in *Implementation of Civil Rights Policy,* ed. Charles S. Bullock III and Charles M. Lamb (Monterey, Calif.: Brooks/Cole, 1984), p. 42. Civil rights groups were especially active in counties with large numbers of unregistered blacks. High levels of civil rights activity then led to federal intervention. See David C. Colby, "The Voting Rights Act and Black Registration in Mississippi," *Publius: The Journal of Federalism* 16 (Fall 1986): 123–37.

11 Dale Krane, "Implementation of the Voting Rights Act: Enforcement by the Department of Justice," in Foster *Voting Rights Act,* pp. 123–26.

12 Howard Ball, Dale Krane, and Thomas P. Lauth, Jr., "The View from Georgia and Mississippi," in *Minority Vote Dilution,* ed. Chandler Davidson (Washington, D.C.: Howard University Press, 1984), pp. 183–86.

13 Krane, "Implementation of the Voting Rights Act," p. 151.

14 Frank R. Parker, "Racial Gerrymandering and Legislative Reapportionment," in Davidson, *Minority Vote Dilution*, pp. 85–117.

15 Krane, "Implementation of the Voting Rights Act," p. 151.

16 A proposal adopted in 1973 to redistrict Hinds County supervisors' districts by splitting the black population concentrated in the city of Jackson among all five districts and combining it with rural areas that were more heavily white led to such strangely shaped districts that two were termed a "turkey" and a "baby elephant." An excellent documentation of these and other discriminatory tactics is provided in Frank R. Parker, *Black Votes Count: Political Empowerment in Mississippi after* 1965 (Chapel Hill: University of North Carolina Press, 1990); pp. 153–57 recount the saga of the Jackson redistricting proposal.

17 Parker, "Racial Gerrymandering."

18 Ball, Krane, and Lauth, *Compromised Compliance*, p. 160.

19 1987 *Roster of Black Elected Officials* (Washington, D.C.: Joint Center for Political Studies, 1988).

20 Charles S. Bullock III, "Equal Educational Opportunity," in Bullock and Lamb, *Implementation of Civil Rights Policy*, p. 67.

21 See the Pulitzer Prize winning series of articles on public schools in Mississippi published in 1982 by the *Jackson Clarion-Ledger*.

22 Bullock, "Equal Educational Opportunity," p. 65.

23 Joseph Weiler, Lewis Nolan, and Shirley Downing, "A New Lifestyle in the Red Clay Hills, *Memphis Commercial-Appeal*, April 21, 1974, sec. 6, pp. 1 and 3.

24 Peirce, *Deep South States*, p. 202.

25 1990 *Statistical Abstract of the United States*. Programs included as part of Public Welfare are Compensatory Education, Medicaid, Lower Income Housing Assistance, and Family Support Administration. Economic Development included Wastewater Treatment, Community Development, and Employment Training.

26 *Governing* 3 (June 1990): 61. Edith R. Hornor, ed., *Almanac of the Fifty States* (Palo Alto, Calif.: Information Publications, 1990).

27 U.S. Department of the Treasury, *Federal-State-Local Fiscal Relations: Report to the President and the Congress* (Washington, D.C.: Office of State and Local Finance, 1985), p. 145.

28 The national government requires that the executive officer of a recipient jurisdiction agree to the regulations applicable to the use of federal funds. That is, when the governor signs the necessary documents, that commits the state to abide by federal regulations, such as affirmative-action hiring in programs funded, even partially, with federal dollars. Failure of the state to meet its obligations once the governor has "signed off" on the grant can result in legal action against the executive. Because grant applications will not be accepted by federal agencies without

appropriate documents, this "sign off" authority, in effect, gives the governor a de facto veto over all grant applications from the state. Note that this same "sign off" authority also strengthens the position of mayors vis-à-vis city councils in the development of local grant proposals.

29 For a complete description of the Small Cities CDBG program, see Edward T. Jennings, Jr., Dale Krane, Alex N. Pattakos, and B. J. Reed, eds., *From Nation to States: The Small Cities Community Development Block Grant Program* (Albany, N.Y.: State University of New York Press, 1986).

30 For more detail about Mississippi's CDBG award procedures, see Dale Krane, "The Mississippi Experience," in Jennings et al., *From Nation to States*, pp. 99–126.

31 Edward T. Jennings, Jr., and Dale Krane, "A New Initiative for an Established Program," in Jennings et al., *From Nation to States*, pp. 1–21.

32 Krane, "Mississippi Experience."

33 Ibid.

34 Ann H. Cook, executive director, Governor's Office of Federal-State Programs, State of Mississippi. Interview with author, Jackson, Miss., November 1983.

35 Detailed tables of the various aspects of Small Cities CDBG awards made in Mississippi from 1975 to 1985 can be found in Dale Krane, "Devolution of the Small Cities CDBG Program in Mississippi, *Publius: The Journal of Federalism* 17 (Fall 1987): 81–96.

36 Ibid.

37 Michael Reagan and John Sanzone, *The New Federalism*, 2d ed. (New York: Oxford University Press, 1981), p. 141.

38 See U.S. General Accounting Office, *States Are Making Good Progress in Implementing the Small Cities Community/Development Block Grant Program*, GAO/RCED-83-186, September 8 (Washington, D.C.: GAO 1983), p. 16.

39 Krane, "Mississippi Experience," p. 122.

40 One recent assessment of the Small Cities program in Mississippi written by the director of the Mississippi Institute for Small Towns, which represents the black municipalities, observed, "That change has taken place is not surprising. . . . What is surprising is the degree to which these changes ameliorated social equity concerns. Obviously, the State of Mississippi has performed much better than most had expected in this regard." See Harvey Johnson, Jr., "The Mississippi Small Cities CDBG Program: Devolution and Evolution," paper presented to the eighteenth annual Southeastern Conference of the American Society for Public Administration, Pensacola, Fla., October 9, 1986, p. 33.

41 Phil Duncan, ed., *Politics in America*, 1990 (Washington, D.C.: Congressional

Quarterly, 1989), pp. 823–26; *Congressional Quarterly Almanac, 1985*, pp. 198–200.

42 *Congressional Quarterly Almanac, 1983*, pp. 517–18.

43 *Congressional Quarterly Almanac, 1987*, pp. 391–94.

44 *Congressional Quarterly Almanac, 1989*, p. 3150.

45 *Congressional Quarterly Weekly Report*, September 13, 1980, p. 2722; November 7, 1981, pp. 2199–2200.

46 *Congressional Quarterly Almanac, 1982*, pp. 68–72.

47 *Congressional Quarterly Almanac, 1986*, pp. 308–10.

48 *Jackson Clarion-Ledger*, February 14, 1988, p. 1B; February 21, 1988, p. 5B; August 13, 1988, p. 8B; September 6, 1988, p. 1A; October 24, 1988, p. 1A; November 3, 1988, p. 3B.

49 Jeffrey L. Pressman, *Federal Programs and City Politics* (Berkeley: University of California Press, 1975), p. 83.

50 James W. Loewen and Charles Sallis, *Mississippi: Conflict and Change* (New York: Random House, 1974), pp. 268–82.

CHAPTER 13

1 Jack Bass and Walter DeVries, *The Transformation of Southern Politics* (New York: New American Library, 1977), p. 187.

2 Margaret Walker, "Mississippi and the Nation in the 1980s," in *Mississippi Writers: Reflections of Childhood and Youth*, vol. 2. *Nonfiction*, ed. Dorothy Abbott (Jackson: University Press of Mississippi, 1986), p. 612.

3 V. O. Key, *Southern Politics in State and Nation* (New York: Vintage, 1949), p. 230.

4 For example, see Stark Young, "Not in Memoriam, but in Defense," in *I'll Take My Stand: The South and the Agrarian Tradition*, by Twelve Southerners (New York: Harper and Row, 1962), pp. 328–59.

5 Bill Minor, the dean of political reporters in Mississippi, has publicly acknowledged that he and some of his colleagues kept the issue of gubernatorial succession alive. Mr. Minor, in fact, appears to claim some of the credit for the eventual passage of this reform.

6 This approach to the functions of media in the political arena is based on the model found in Stephen Hess, *The Presidential Campaign*, rev. ed. (Washington, D.C.: Brookings Institution, 1978).

7 The two main newspapers in Jackson, the *Clarion-Ledger* and the *Daily News*, were owned by the Hederman family. The family was socially prominent, and members were ardent, even rabid, defenders of the traditional order in Missis-

sippi. In the late 1970s the papers were sold to the Gannett chain. Not only did the editorial tone change, but the paper's technical quality also improved.

8 James Young, "The White Shoe Crowd Keeps on Shufflin' Along," *Memphis Commercial-Appeal,* September 16, 1973, sec. 6, p. 2.

9 Private regardingness and public regardingness are two philosophies that some observers of city politics claim describe the political behavior of different parts of the local electorate. "Private regarding" persons are depicted as individualistic and selfish; thus they pursue only their own personal or group interests at the expense of others. By contrast, "public regarding" persons are depicted as generous and goodhearted; thus they are willing to pay taxes that confer benefits on persons other than themselves. To some extent, "private regarding" persons see government and politics as a zero-sum marketplace where what they gain, others lose. "Public regarding" persons, on the other hand, view government and politics in terms of a commonwealth where everyone's interests are interdependent. See James Q. Wilson and Edward C. Banfield, "Public Regardingness as a Value Premise in Voting Behavior," *American Political Science Review* 58 (1964): 876–87.

10 The power of theology to guide personal actions influences Mississippi local politics in not so subtle ways. Churches that advocate a "social gospel" will encourage their members to aid the poor and the needy. Churches that preach the millennial view that Armageddon is imminent encourage their followers to ignore the conditions of this world and prepare for the coming Judgment Day.

11 The hometown of two recent governors closed its public swimming pool during the era of civil rights battles, and it has not reopened. Whites go to private pools.

12 This admission was made to one of the authors of this chapter.

13 Sidney Verba and Norman Nie, *Participation in America: Political Democracy and Social Equality* (New York: Harper and Row, 1972), argues that this situation poses a problem nationally.

14 For example, see Nancy Weaver and Paul Beaver, "Mississippi Delta: Empty Hands in a Fertile Land," *Jackson Clarion-Ledger,* December 17, 1980, special supplement.

15 For example, in a 1981 poll only 33 percent could recall the names of their congressmen. See Stephen D. Shaffer's *The* 1981 *Annual Mississippi Poll: A Study of Mississippians' Political Attitudes* (Mississippi State: Social Science Research Center, Mississippi State University, 1982).

16 Many of the civics and government teachers in Mississippi are primarily athletic coaches or physical education teachers, often lacking a sophisticated understanding of state and national government and politics.

17 Most students voluntarily select one government class as a social science–human-

ities elective, and usually that is a class in American national government. Very
few university students ever complete a class in Mississippi government and politics.

18 Quoted in Peter J. Boyer, "The Yuppies of Mississippi: How They Took over the
Statehouse," *New York Times Magazine,* February 28, 1988, p. 40.

19 Hodding Carter as quoted in "Loving and Hating It," in Willie Morris, *Terrains
of the Heart and Other Essays on Home* (Oxford, Miss.: Yoknapatawpha Press,
1981), p. 74.

20 Willie Morris, "Different Terrains," in Morris, *Terrains of the Heart,*
p. 197.

21 Hodding Carter, quoted in Morris, *Terrains of the Heart,* p. 74.

The Contributors

TIP H. ALLEN, JR. Professor of political science at Mississippi State University and coauthor of *Constitutional Revision in Theory and Practice* and *Mississippi Votes,* Dr. Allen has studied the Mississippi political scene for over four decades.

EDWARD J. CLYNCH. Professor and head of the Political Science Department at Mississippi State University and coauthor of *Governors, Legislators, and Budgets: Diversity across the American States,* Dr. Clynch is a leading analyst of state budgetary politics and the author of numerous articles in public administration journals.

DOUGLAS G. FEIG. Professor of political science and associate dean of the College of Arts and Sciences at Mississippi State University, Dr. Feig is coauthor of *Research Methods and Statistics* and of scholarly works on Mississippi and southern politics.

GERALD GABRIS. Associate professor of public administration at Northern Illinois University (formerly at Mississippi State University), Dr. Gabris has written numerous articles in public administration journals and analyzed local government in Mississippi.

THOMAS H. HANDY. Associate professor emeritus of political science at Mississippi State University, Dr. Handy has written scholarly works on Mississippi state government and studied the state political scene for over five decades.

DALE KRANE. Associate professor of public administration at the University of Nebraska, Omaha (formerly at Mississippi State University), coauthor of *Compromised Compliance: Implementation of the* 1965 *Voting Rights Act* and coeditor of *From Nation to States: The Small Cities Commu-*

nity Development Block Grant Program, Dr. Krane has written scholarly works on public policy in Mississippi.

STEPHEN D. SHAFFER. Professor of political science at Mississippi State University and director of the Mississippi Poll telephone survey, Dr. Shaffer has written scholarly works on Mississippi and national electoral politics and serves as a commentator on the political scene.

DIANE E. WALL. Assistant professor of political science at Mississippi State University, Dr. Wall has written scholarly works on the judicial system in Mississippi and nationally.

Index